CliffsNotes®

Math Review
for
Standardized Tests

2ND EDITION

CliffsNotes®

Math Review
for
Standardized Tests

2ND EDITION

by
Jerry Bobrow, Ph.D.
revised by
Ed Kohn, M.S.

Contributing Authors
Peter Z. Orton, Ph.D.
Ray Shiflett, Ph.D.
Michael Clapp, Ph.D.

Consultants
Dave Arnold, M.A.
Dale Johnson, M.A.
Pam Mason, M.A.

WILEY
Wiley Publishing, Inc.

Editorial	*Composition*
Acquisitions Editor: Greg Tubach	**Proofreader:**
Project Editor: Elizabeth Kuball	Wiley Publishing, Inc. Composition Services
Technical Editors: Mary Jane Sterling, Abraham Mantell	

CliffsNotes® Math Review for Standardized Tests, 2nd Edition

Published by:
Wiley Publishing, Inc.
111 River Street
Hoboken, NJ 07030-5774
www.wiley.com

Published by Wiley, Hoboken, NJ
Published simultaneously in Canada

Library of Congress Cataloging-in-Publication data is available from the publisher upon request.

ISBN: 978-0-470-50077-4

Printed in the United States of America
10 9 8 7 6 5 4 3

About the Author

Jerry Bobrow, Ph.D., was a national authority in the field of test preparation. As founder of Bobrow Test Preparation Services, he administered test-preparation programs at over 25 California institutions for over 30 years. Dr.Bobrow authored over 30 national best-selling test preparation books, and his books and programs have assisted over 2 million test takers. Each year, the faculty at Bobrow Test Preparation Services lectures to thousands of students on preparing for graduate, college, and teacher credentialing exams.

Table of Contents

Introduction 1
Why You Need This Guide. 1
What This Guide Contains 1
Range of Difficulty and Scope. 2
A General Guideline 3
How to Use This Guide. 3

PART I: BASIC SKILLS REVIEW

Arithmetic and Data Analysis. 6
Diagnostic Test. 6
Questions 6
Arithmetic. 6
Data Analysis 7
Answers. 8
Arithmetic. 8
Data Analysis 9
Arithmetic Review 10
Preliminaries 10
Groups of Numbers. 10
Ways to Show Multiplication. 11
Common Math Symbols. 11
Properties of Basic Mathematical Operations. 11
Some Properties (Axioms) of Addition 11
Some Properties (Axioms) of Multiplication 12
A Property of Two Operations 13
Place Value 13
Expanded Notation. 14
Grouping Symbols: Parentheses,
Brackets, Braces 15
Parentheses ( ) 15
Brackets [ ] and Braces { } 15
Order of Operations 16
Rounding Off 18
Signed Numbers: Positive Numbers and Negative Numbers 19
Number Lines 19
Addition of Signed Numbers 20
Subtraction of Signed Numbers 21

Minus Preceding Parenthesis 23
Multiplying and Dividing Signed Numbers 24
Multiplying and Dividing Using Zero 24
Divisibility Rules. 25
Examples: Divisibility Rules 25
Common Fractions 27
Numerator and Denominator 27
Negative Fractions 27
Proper Fractions and Improper Fractions 27
Mixed Numbers. 28
Equivalent Fractions. 29
Reducing Fractions. 29
Enlarging Denominators 30
Factors 31
Common Factors 32
Greatest Common Factor 32
Multiples. 33
Common Multiples 34
Least Common Multiple 34
Adding and Subtracting Fractions 35
Adding Fractions 35
Adding Positive and Negative Fractions .37
Subtracting Fractions 38
Subtracting Positive and Negative Fractions. 39
Adding and Subtracting Mixed Numbers .40
Adding Mixed Numbers. 40
Subtracting Mixed Numbers. 42
Multiplying Fractions and Mixed Numbers. 43
Multiplying Fractions 43
Multiplying Mixed Numbers. 45
Dividing Fractions and Mixed Numbers .46
Dividing Fractions. 46
Dividing Complex Fractions 46
Dividing Mixed Numbers. 47
Simplifying Fractions and Complex Fractions 48
Decimals 50
Changing Decimals to Fractions 50
Adding and Subtracting Decimals. 51
Multiplying Decimals. 52
Dividing Decimals 53
Changing Fractions to Decimals 53

Percentage. 54
  Changing Decimals to Percents 54
  Changing Percents to Decimals 55
  Changing Fractions to Percents. 56
  Changing Percents to Fractions. 57
  Important Equivalents That Can Save You Time 58
  Finding Percent of a Number 58
  Other Applications of Percent. 59
  Percent—Proportion Method. 60
  Finding Percent Increase or Percent Decrease 63
Powers and Exponents 64
  Operations with Powers and Exponents. 65
  Scientific Notation 66
  Multiplication in Scientific Notation. 68
  Division in Scientific Notation 69
  Squares and Cubes 70
Square Roots and Cube Roots 72
  Square Roots 72
  Simplifying Square Roots. 75
Data Analysis Review. 77
  Probability 77
  Combinations and Permutations 80
  Statistics. 83
    Some Basics: Measures of Central Tendencies. 83
    Mean 83
    Weighted Mean. 84
    Median. 85
    Mode 86
    Range 87
  Standard Deviation 88
  Number Sequences 90
  Measures. 92
    Measurement Systems 92
    Converting Units of Measure 94
Arithmetic and Data Analysis Review Test 97
  Questions 97
    Arithmetic. 97
    Data Analysis 102
  Answers. 103
    Arithmetic. 103
    Data Analysis 107
Arithmetic Glossary of Terms 108

Algebra 113
Diagnostic Test. 113
Questions 113
Answers. 115
Algebra Review 118
Some Basic Language. 118
Understood Multiplication. 118
Letters to Be Aware of. 118
Basic Terms in Set Theory 118
Special Sets. 118
Describing Sets. 119
Types of Sets 119
Operations with Sets 119
Variables and Algebraic Expressions 120
Key Words Denoting Addition 121
Key Words Denoting Subtraction 121
Key Words Denoting Multiplication 121
Key Words Denoting Division. 121
Evaluating Expressions 122
Equations. 125
Solving Equations. 125
Literal Equations. 130
Ratios and Proportions 132
Ratios 132
Solving Proportions for Value 134
Solving for Two Unknowns Systems of Equations 136
Monomials and Polynomials. 142
Adding and Subtracting Monomials. 143
Multiplying Monomials 144
Dividing Monomials. 145
Adding and Subtracting Polynomials 147
Multiplying Polynomials. 148
Dividing Polynomials by Monomials. 151
Dividing Polynomials by Polynomials 152
Factoring 156
Factoring out a Common Factor 156
Factoring the Difference between Two Squares. 157
Factoring Polynomials Having Three
Terms of the Form $Ax^2 + Bx + C$ 158
Solving Quadratic Equations. 163
Algebraic Fractions 168

Operations with Algebraic Fractions. 169
   Multiplying Algebraic Fractions. 170
   Dividing Algebraic Fractions 171
   Adding or Subtracting Algebraic Fractions 172
Inequalities. 176
   Solving Inequalities 176
   Graphing on a Number Line 178
   Graphing Inequalities. 178
   Intervals 179
Absolute Value 180
Analytic Geometry 182
   Coordinate Graphs 182
   Graphing Equations on the Coordinate Plane 185
   Slope and Intercept of Linear Equations. 193
   Graphing Linear Equations Using Slope and Intercept 196
   Graphing Linear Equations Using the x-intercept and
     y-intercept. 198
   Finding an Equation of a Line 199
Roots and Radicals 200
   Simplifying Square Roots. 200
   Operations with Square Roots. 202
   Addition and Subtraction of Square Roots after Simplifying 204
   Products of Nonnegative Roots. 205
"False" Operations. 206
Algebra Review Test 210
   Questions 210
   Answers. 218
Algebra Glossary of Terms 225

Geometry **229**
Geometry Diagnostic Test. 229
   Questions 229
   Answers. 234
Geometry Review 238
   Angles 238
   Types of Angles. 239
     Right Angle 239
     Acute Angle 239
     Obtuse Angle. 239
     Straight Angle 240
   Pairs of Angles. 241
     Adjacent Angles. 241
     Vertical Angles. 241

Complementary Angles. 242
Supplementary Angles. 242
Angle Bisector 243
Lines. 245
Straight Lines 245
Line Segments 245
Rays 245
Types of Lines 246
Intersecting Lines 246
Perpendicular Lines 246
Parallel Lines. 247
Parallel Lines Cut by Transversal. 247
Polygons 250
Regular Polygons. 250
Diagonals of Polygons 251
Convex Polygons. 251
Concave Polygons 251
Triangles 251
Types of Triangles by Sides 252
Equilateral Triangles. 252
Isosceles Triangles 252
Scalene Triangles 253
Types of Triangles by Angles 253
Right Triangles. 253
Obtuse Triangles 253
Acute Triangles 254
Facts about Triangles. 255
Base and Height. 255
Median. 255
Angle Bisectors. 256
Angles Opposite Equal Sides. 257
Angles of an Isosceles Triangle 257
Angles of an Equilateral Triangle. 258
Unequal Angles 258
Adding Sides of a Triangle 258
Exterior Angles. 259
Pythagorean Theorem 262
Special Triangles 265
Isosceles Right Triangles (45°-45°-90° Right Triangles). 265
30°-60°-90° Right Triangles 267
Quadrilaterals 270
Types of Quadrilaterals. 270
Square 270

Rectangle 270
Parallelogram 271
Rhombus 271
Trapezoid 272
Comparing Quadrilaterals 272
Practice: Polygon Problems 275
Sum of the Interior Angles of a Polygon 276
Perimeter and Area of Polygons 277
Perimeter of Polygons 277
Area of Polygons 278
Circles 281
Parts of a Circle 281
Radius 281
Diameter 282
Chord 283
Arc 283
Circumference and Area of a Circle 284
Circumference 284
Area 285
Angles in a Circle 286
Central Angles 286
Inscribed Angles 287
Concentric Circles 288
Tangents to a Circle 289
Congruence and Similarity 289
Volumes of Solid Figures 290
Volume of a Cube 290
Volume of a Rectangular Solid 290
Volume of a Right Circular Cylinder (Circular Bases) 291
Surface Areas of Solid Figures 292
Surface Area of a Rectangular Solid 292
Surface Area of a Right Circular Cylinder 293
Right Triangle 298
Geometry Review Test 299
Questions 299
Answers 307
Geometry Glossary of Terms 311

Word Problems 316
Diagnostic Test 316
Questions 316
Answers 317

Word Problems Review 318
  Solving Technique. 318
  Key Words and Phrases 319
    Add. 319
    Subtract 319
    Multiply 319
    Divide 320
  Simple Interest. 320
  Compound Interest. 323
  Ratio and Proportion. 326
  Motion. 329
  Percent. 332
  Percent Change. 336
  Number. 339
  Age 343
  Geometry 347
  Work 351
  Mixture 355
Word Problems Review Test 360
  Questions 360
  Answers. 362
Word Problems Glossary of Terms 363

PART II: STRATEGIES AND PRACTICE

Answer Sheet for Practice Sections 367
  Mathematical Ability 367
  Quantitative Comparison 368
  Data Sufficiency. 368

Mathematical Ability. 369
  Mathematical Ability Strategies 369
  Information Provided in the Test Booklet. .369
    Data That May Be Used as Reference for the Test. 369
  Suggested Approach with Examples 370
    Mark Key Words 370
    Pull Out Information 372
    Plug in Numbers 374
    Work from the Answers 376
    Approximate 380
    Make Comparisons 381
    Mark Diagrams 382
    Draw Diagrams 386

Procedure Problems. 388
Multiple-Multiple-Choice. 390
A Patterned Plan of Attack. 392
Mathematical Ability Practice. 393
Arithmetic 393
Questions 393
Algebra 400
Questions 400
Geometry 407
Questions 407
Procedure Problems 417
Answer Key for Mathematical Ability Practice 420
Arithmetic. 420
Algebra. 421
Geometry 422
Procedure Problems. 422
Mathematical Ability Answers and Explanations 423
Arithmetic 423
Algebra 429
Geometry 434
Procedure Problems 440

Quantitative Comparison 442
Quantitative Comparison Strategies 442
Directions. 442
Analysis 442
Suggested Approach with Examples 443
Cancel Out Equal Amounts. 443
Make Partial Comparisons. 443
Keep Perspective 444
Plug In 0, 1, −1 444
Simplify. 445
Look for a Simple Way 446
Mark Diagrams 446
Use Easier Numbers 447
A Patterned Plan of Attack. 448
Quantitative Comparison Practice. 449
Directions. 449
Arithmetic and Data Analysis 449
Questions. 449
Algebra 451
Questions. 451

Geometry 453
   Questions 453
  Answer Key for Quantitative Comparison Practice 456
   Arithmetic and Data Analysis 457
   Algebra 457
   Geometry 457
Quantitative Comparison Answers and Explanations 458
  Arithmetic and Data Analysis 458
  Algebra 460
  Geometry 463

Data Sufficiency 467
Data Sufficiency Strategies 467
  Directions 467
  Analysis 467
  Suggested Approach with Examples 468
   Determine Necessary Information 468
   Don't Solve Unless Necessary 468
   Use a Simple Marking System 469
   Use Only Common Knowledge 469
   Mark Diagrams 470
   Draw Diagrams 471
Â Patterned Plan of Attack 472
Data Sufficiency Practice 473
  Directions 473
  Arithmetic 473
   Questions 473
  Algebra 475
   Questions 475
  Geometry 478
   Questions 478
  Answer Key for Data Sufficiency Practice 482
   Arithmetic 482
   Algebra 482
   Geometry 483
Data Sufficiency Answers and Explanations 483
  Arithmetic 483
  Algebra 485
  Geometry 488

Final Suggestions 491

Why You Need This Guide

Are you planning to take the . . .

GRE   SAT

GMAT   PRAXIS

CSET   CBEST

PSAT   ACT

PPST

or any other standardized test with a math section?

During the author's 30 years of offering test preparation programs at over 30 universities, the most requested supplementary aid has been a text, guide, or wonder drug to help give candidates a "fighting chance" on the math questions encountered on standardized tests. *CliffsNotes Math Review for Standardized Tests,* 2nd Edition, is designed specifically to review, refresh, reintroduce, diagnose, and, in effect, give you that "fighting chance" by focusing squarely on a test-oriented review.

This is the most unique math guide available today. Not only is it clear, concise, and easy to use, but its focus by test-preparation experts on standardized tests gives insight on problem types. Our unique approach will bring back memories of mathematical rules and concepts once learned but since forgotten through lack of use or understanding. Throughout this guide, language is nontechnical but consistent with the terminology used on most standardized tests.

What This Guide Contains

CliffsNotes Math Review for Standardized Tests, 2nd Edition, provides an excellent and extensive overview of the areas of concern for most test takers:

- Arithmetic and data analysis
- Algebra
- Geometry
- Word problems
- Strategies for common problem types

- Unique test-type problems
  - Math ability
  - Quantitative comparison
  - Data sufficiency

Each review section includes a diagnostic test, explanations of rules and concepts with examples, practice problems with complete explanations, a review test, and a glossary.

If you're taking the GRE, GMAT, SAT, PSAT, ACT, CSET, CBEST, PRAXIS, PPST, or any other exam with a math section, this book was designed for you.

Range of Difficulty and Scope

The range of difficulty and scope of problem types on standardized tests vary significantly, depending upon which exam is taken. For example,

- The ACT includes math problems drawing from arithmetic, algebra I, geometry, and algebra II.

- The GMAT includes math problems from only arithmetic, algebra I, and geometry, but it is heavily laden with word problems. It also includes a section or two of data sufficiency, a unique problem type.

- The SAT, PSAT, and GRE include math problems from arithmetic, algebra I, and geometry. They also include a problem type called quantitative comparison, unfamiliar to many test takers.

- The PRAXIS, CBEST, and PPST include problems from basic arithmetic to simple algebra I concepts and basic geometry. The CBEST has many word-type problems and some basic statistics problems. Although these tests draw upon the more basic mathematical concepts, procedure problems are quite common. (Procedure problems do not ask for a final numerical answer, but rather "how" a problem should be worked to be solved.)

- The CSET is similar in nature to the tests given for the PRAXIS, CBEST, and PPST, except that it has two components. One part is the standard multiple-choice format. The other part requires constructed responses to a specific prompt. Problems come from basic arithmetic, algebra I, geometry, and data analysis, including probability and statistics.

A General Guideline

From a strictly mathematical perspective, the ACT requires the greatest range and highest level of math skills of the exams mentioned. Although the GMAT does not require algebra II, its problems tend to be more complex, more rigorous, and more demanding of insights and techniques than, say, the PRAXIS, CBEST, CSET, or PPST. The SAT, PSAT, and GRE would probably fall in the middle category of difficulty, because their questions tend to be less difficult than the ACT and GMAT, but more difficult than the PRAXIS, CBEST, CSET, and PPST.

As you work through this book, keep in mind which questions will be appropriate for you. The practice problems in each area are generally arranged so that the first few are easiest and the last few are most difficult. Therefore, an ACT or GMAT candidate should work all the practice problems, whereas a PRAXIS candidate will probably not have to be concerned with the most difficult in each set. Be sure to check the CliffsNotes book for the specific exam you'll take to determine the level of difficulty for your math questions. Make use of the informational bulletins and the online information from the test makers. *Review the appropriate level of math. Use your time effectively!*

How to Use This Guide

1. Review the materials concerning your test provided by the testing company. This information is usually available at no charge and will detail the areas and question types for your particular exam.
2. Take the diagnostic test in arithmetic.
3. Check your answers on the diagnostic arithmetic test. If your results warrant extensive arithmetic study, then . . .
4. Work through the arithmetic and data analysis review and practice problems.
5. If your results on the arithmetic and data analysis diagnostic test do not warrant extensive arithmetic review, but you still have some weakness in that area, *skip Step 4* but concentrate on the review sections pertinent to your weaknesses. (The diagnostic test answers are keyed to appropriate review pages.)
6. Take the arithmetic review test.

7. Based on your results on the review test, review any sections still requiring improvement.

8. Follow the same procedure (steps 2 through 7) for each review section (algebra, geometry, word problems).

9. Notice that the final section of this guide includes chapters on test strategies and special problem types appearing on some exams—math ability, quantitative comparison, and data sufficiency. The particular exam you're taking will determine which of these areas are important to you. These questions will help "fine tune" your general math review and improve your problem-solving skills for your test.

10. Even if a unique problem type (say, quantitative comparison or data sufficiency) will not appear on your exam, you should also work these practice problems in the final section of this guide. These will help broaden your understanding of the particular math skill and give insight that may help solve the question types found on the test you'll take.

PART I

BASIC SKILLS REVIEW

Each review section includes

- A diagnostic test to assess your strengths and weaknesses
- Explanations of rules and concepts to demonstrate important mathematical processes
- Practice problems with complete explanations to enable you to apply the rules and concepts
- A review test to help you focus on areas still needing improvement
- A glossary to assist in your understanding of mathematical terms used in problems and explanations

Areas covered include

- Arithmetic and data analysis
- Algebra
- Geometry
- Word problems

Arithmetic and Data Analysis

Diagnostic Test

Questions

Arithmetic

1. Which of the following are integers? $\frac{1}{2}$, –2, 0, 4, 3.2

2. Which of the following are rational numbers? 5.8, 6, $\frac{1}{4}$, $\sqrt{4}$, $\sqrt{7}$, π

3. Is 37 prime?

4. Which of the following are perfect cubes? 1, 6, 8, 9, 27

5. The commutative property of addition is represented by

   (A) $2 + (3 + 4) = (2 + 3) + 4$
   (B) $2 + (-2) = 0$
   (C) $(3 + 5) = (5 + 3)$

6. $(6 \times 10^4) + (3 \times 10^2) + (4 \times 10^{-1}) =$

7. Simplify $3[3^2 + 2(4 + 1)]$.

8. Round 4.4584 to the nearest thousandth.

9. $-4 + 8 =$

10. $-12 - 6 =$

11. $(-6)(-8) =$

12. 2,730 is divisible by which of the following? 3, 4, 8

13. Change $5\frac{3}{4}$ to an improper fraction.

14. Change $\frac{32}{6}$ to a mixed number in lowest terms.

15. $\frac{2}{7} + \frac{3}{5} =$

16. $1\frac{3}{8} + 2\frac{5}{6} =$

17. $11 - \frac{2}{3} =$

18. $6\frac{1}{8} - 3\frac{3}{4} =$

19. $-\frac{7}{8} - \frac{5}{9} =$

20. $-\frac{1}{6} \times \frac{1}{3} =$

21. $2\frac{3}{8} \times 1\frac{5}{6} =$

22. $-\frac{1}{4} \div \frac{9}{14} =$

23. $2\frac{3}{7} \div 1\frac{1}{4} =$

24. $\dfrac{1}{3 + \dfrac{2}{1 + \dfrac{1}{3}}} =$

25. $0.08 + 1.3 + 0.562 =$

26. $0.45 - 0.003 =$

27. $8.001 \times 2.4 =$

28. $0.147 \div 0.7 =$

29. Change $\frac{3}{20}$ to a decimal.

30. Change 7% to a decimal.

31. 79% of 64 =

32. 40% of what is 20?

33. Change $\frac{1}{8}$ to a percent.

34. What is the percent increase of a rise in temperature from 80° to 100°?

35. If 1 kilometer equals 0.6 mile, then 25 kilometers equal how many miles?

36. Express 0.00000023 in scientific notation.

37. $(3.2 \times 10^3)(2.4 \times 10^8) =$

38. $(5.1 \times 10^6) \div (1.7 \times 10^2) =$

39. $8^3 \times 8^7 =$

40. $9^5 \div 9^2 =$

41. $(5^3)^2 =$

42. Approximate $\sqrt{30}$ to the nearest tenth.

43. Simplify $\sqrt{80}$.

44. $-\sqrt{9} =$

45. $\sqrt[3]{64} =$

Data Analysis

1. What is the probability of rolling two dice so they total 9?

2. In how many ways can the letters in the word *team* be arranged?

3. A scientist is trying to select three members for her research team from six possible applicants. How many possible combinations are there, assuming all applicants are qualified?

4. Find the arithmetic mean, mode, median, and range of the following group of numbers: 6, 4, 4, 2, 5, 9

5. Find the next number in the sequence: 2, 5, 11, 23, 47, ___

6. Find the standard deviation for the set of data given in the frequency table below.

x	f
0	2
1	3
2	2
3	1
4	1

Answers

Page numbers following each answer refer to the review section applicable to this problem type.

Arithmetic

1. $-2, 0, 4$ (p. 10)

2. $5.8, 6, \frac{1}{4}, \sqrt{4} \left(\sqrt{4} = 2 \right)$, (p. 10)

3. Yes (p. 10)

4. $1, 8, 27$ (p. 10)

5. C (p. 11)

6. $60,300.4$ (p. 14)

7. 57 (p. 15)

8. 4.458 (p. 18)

9. 4 (p. 20)

10. -18 (p. 21)

11. 48 (p. 23)

12. 3 (p. 25)

13. $\frac{23}{4}$ (p. 28)

14. $5\frac{2}{6} = 5\frac{1}{3}$ (p. 28)

15. $\frac{31}{35}$ (p. 35)

16. $4\frac{5}{24}$ (p. 40)

17. $10\frac{1}{3}$ (p. 42)

18. $2\frac{3}{8}$ (p. 42)

19. $-\frac{103}{72} = -1\frac{31}{72}$ (p. 39)

20. $-\frac{1}{18}$ (p. 43)

21. $\frac{209}{48} = 4\frac{17}{48}$ (p. 45)

22. $-\frac{7}{18}$ (p. 46)

23. $\frac{68}{35} = 1\frac{33}{35}$ (p. 47)

24. $\frac{2}{9}$ (p. 48)

25. 1.942 (p. 51)

26. 0.447 (p. 51)

27. 19.2024 (p. 52)

28. 0.21 (p. 53)

29. 0.15 (p. 53)

30. 0.07 (p. 55)

31. 50.56 (p. 58)

32. 50 (p. 59)

33. $12\frac{1}{2}\%$ or 12.5% (p. 56)

34. 25% (p. 63)

35. 15 miles (p. 94)

36. 2.3×10^{-7} (p. 66)

37. 7.68×10^{11} (p. 68)

38. 3×10^{4} (p. 69)

39. 8^{10} (p. 65)

40. 9^{3} (p. 65)

41. 5^{6} (p. 65)

42. 5.5 (p. 73)

43. $4\sqrt{5}$ (p. 75)

44. -3 (p. 72)

45. 4 (p. 73)

Data Analysis

1. $\frac{4}{36} = \frac{1}{9}$ (p. 77)

2. 24 (p. 80)

3. 20 (p. 80)

4. mean = 5 (p. 83), mode = 4
   (p. 86), median = $4\frac{1}{2}$ or 4.5
   (p. 85), range = 7 (p. 86)

5. 95 (p. 90)

6. 1.257 (p. 88)

Arithmetic Review

You should already be familiar with the fundamentals of addition, subtraction, multiplication, and division of whole numbers (0, 1, 2 , 3, . . .). The following is a review of signed numbers, fractions, decimals, and important additional topics from arithmetic and data analysis.

Preliminaries

Groups of Numbers

In doing arithmetic and algebra, we work with several groups of numbers.

- **Natural or counting numbers:** The numbers 1, 2, 3, 4, . . . are called natural or counting numbers.

- **Whole numbers:** The numbers 0, 1, 2, 3, . . . are called whole numbers.

- **Integers:** The numbers . . . –2, –1, 0, 1, 2, . . . are called integers.

- **Negative integers:** The numbers . . . –3, –2, –1 are called negative integers.

- **Positive integers:** The natural numbers are sometimes called the positive integers.

- **Rational numbers:** The numbers that can be expressed as fractions using integers are called rational numbers. Values such as $1\frac{1}{2} = \frac{3}{2}$ or $0.875 = \frac{7}{8}$ are called rational numbers. Since every integer can be expressed as that integer over 1, all *integers* are *rational numbers*.

- **Irrational numbers:** The numbers whose exact values cannot be expressed as fractions are called irrational numbers. Two examples of irrational numbers are $\sqrt{3}$ and π.

- **Real numbers:** Real numbers consist of all *rational* and *irrational numbers*. Typically, most standardized exams use only real numbers, which are the numbers you're used to using.

- **Prime numbers:** A prime number is a natural number greater than 1 that can be evenly divided only by itself and 1. For example, 19 is a prime number because it can be evenly divided only by 19 and 1, but 21 is not a prime number because 21 can be evenly divided by other numbers (3 and 7). The only even prime number is 2; thereafter, any even number may be divided evenly by 2. Zero and 1 are *not* prime numbers. The first ten prime numbers are 2, 3, 5, 7, 11, 13, 17, 19, 23, and 29.

- **Composite numbers:** A composite number is a natural number divisible by more than just 1 and itself: 4, 6, 8, 9, 10, 12, 14, 15, . . .

- **Odd numbers:** Odd numbers are integers not divisible by 2: ±1, ±3, ±5, ±7, . . .
- **Even numbers:** Even numbers are integers divisible by 2: 0, ±2, ±4, ±6, . . .
- **Squares:** Squares are the result when numbers are raised to the second power: ($2^2 = 2 \times 2 = 4$), ($3^2 = 3 \times 3 = 9$); 1, 4, 9, 16, 25, 36 . . .
- **Cubes:** Cubes are the result when numbers are raised to the third power: ($2^3 = 2 \times 2 \times 2 = 8$), ($3^3 = 3 \times 3 \times 3 = 27$); 1, 8, 27, 64, 125, 216 . . .

Ways to Show Multiplication

There are several ways to show multiplication. They are

- $4 \times 3 = 12$
- $4 \cdot 3 = 12$
- $(4)(3) = 12$
- $4(3) = 12$
- $(4)3 = 12$

Common Math Symbols

Symbol references:

- $=$ is equal to
- $\neq$ is not equal to
- $\approx$ is approximately equal to
- $>$ is greater than
- $<$ is less than
- $\geq$ is greater than or equal to
- $\leq$ is less than or equal to
- $\parallel$ is parallel to
- $\perp$ is perpendicular to
- $\cong$ is congruent to

Properties of Basic Mathematical Operations

Some Properties (Axioms) of Addition

Closure is when all answers fall into the original set. If you add two even numbers, the answer is still an even number; therefore, the set of even numbers *is closed* (has closure) under addition ($2 + 4 = 6$). If you add two odd numbers, the answer is not an odd number; therefore, the set of odd numbers is *not closed* (does not have closure) under addition ($3 + 5 = 8$).

Commutative means that the *order* does not make any difference:

$$2 + 3 = 3 + 2 \qquad\qquad a + b = b + a$$

Note: Commutative does *not* hold for subtraction:

$$3 - 1 \neq 1 - 3 \qquad\qquad a - b \neq b - a$$

Associative means that the *grouping* does not make any difference:

$$(2 + 3) + 4 = 2 + (3 + 4) \qquad (a + b) + c = a + (b + c)$$

The grouping has changed (parentheses moved), but the sides are still equal.

Note: Associative does *not* hold for subtraction:

$$4 - (3 - 1) \neq (4 - 3) - 1 \qquad a - (b - c) \neq (a - b) - c$$

The *identity element* for addition is 0. Any number added to 0 gives the original number:

$$3 + 0 = 3 \qquad\qquad a + 0 = a$$

The *additive inverse* is the opposite (negative) of the number. Any number plus its additive inverse equals 0 (the identity):

$3 + (-3) = 0$; therefore, 3 and -3 are additive inverses.

$-2 + 2 = 0$; therefore, -2 and 2 are additive inverses.

$a + (-a) = 0$; therefore, a and $-a$ are additive inverses.

Some Properties (Axioms) of Multiplication

Closure is when all answers fall into the original set. If you multiply two even numbers, the answer is still an even number; therefore, the set of even numbers *is closed* (has closure) under multiplication ($2 \times 4 = 8$). If you multiply two odd numbers, the answer is an odd number; therefore, the set of odd numbers *is closed* (has closure) under multiplication ($3 \times 5 = 15$).

Commutative means that the *order* does not make any difference:

$$2 \times 3 = 3 \times 2 \qquad\qquad a \times b = b \times a$$

Note: Commutative does *not* hold for division:

$$2 \div 4 \neq 4 \div 2$$

Associative means that the *grouping* does not make any difference:

$$(2 \times 3) \times 4 = 2 \times (3 \times 4) \qquad (a \times b) \times c = a \times (b \times c)$$

The grouping has changed (parentheses moved), but the sides are still equal.

Note: Associative does *not* hold for division:

$$(8 \div 4) \div 2 \neq 8 \div (4 \div 2)$$

The *identity element* for multiplication is 1. Any number multiplied by 1 gives the original number:

$$3 \times 1 = 3 \qquad\qquad a \times 1 = a$$

The *multiplicative inverse* is the reciprocal of the number. Any number multiplied by its reciprocal equals 1:

$2 \times \frac{1}{2} = 1$; therefore, 2 and $\frac{1}{2}$ are multiplicative inverses.

$a \times \frac{1}{a} = 1$; therefore, a and $\frac{1}{a}$ are multiplicative inverses.

Since 0 multiplied by any value can never equal 1, the number 0 has no multiplicative inverse.

A Property of Two Operations

The *distributive property* is the process of distributing the number on the outside of the parentheses to each term on the inside:

$$2(3 + 4) = 2(3) + 2(4) \qquad 2(3 - 4) = 2(3) - 2(4)$$
$$a(b + c) = a(b) + a(c) \qquad a(b + c) = a(b) - a(c)$$

Note: You cannot use the distributive property with the same operation:

$$3(4 \times 5 \times 6) \neq 3(4) \times 3(5) \times 3(6)$$
$$a(bcd) \neq a(b) \times a(c) \times a(d) \text{ or } (ab)(ac)(ad)$$
$$2 + (3 + 4) \neq (2 + 3) + (2 + 4)$$

Place Value

Each position in any number has *place value.* For instance, in the number 485, the 4 is in the hundreds place, the 8 is in the tens place, and the 5 is in the ones place. Thus, place value is as follows:

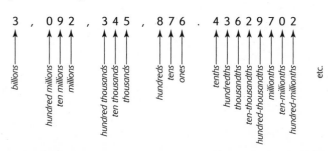

Practice: Place Value

1. Which digit is in the tens place in 483?

2. In 36,548, which digit is in the thousands place?

3. The digit 7 is in which place in 45,328.769?

4. Which digit is in the hundredths place in 25.0671?

5. Which digit is in the ten millions place in 867,451,023.79?

Answers: Place Value

1. 8

2. 6

3. tenths

4. 6

5. 6

Expanded Notation

Sometimes numbers are written in expanded notation to point out the place value of each digit. For example, 345 can be written

$$300 + 40 + 5$$
$$(3 \times 100) + (4 \times 10) + (5 \times 1)$$
$$(3 \times 10^2) + (4 \times 10^1) + (5 \times 10^0)$$

These last two are the more common forms of expanded notation—one with exponents, one without exponents. Notice that, in these, the digit is multiplied times its place value—1's, 10's, 100's, and so on.

Another example: 43.25 can be written

$$40 + 3 + 0.2 + 0.05$$
$$(4 \times 10) + (3 \times 1) + \left(2 \times \frac{1}{10}\right) + \left(5 \times \frac{1}{100}\right)$$
$$(4 \times 10^1) + (3 \times 10^0) + (2 \times 10^{-1}) + (5 \times 10^{-2})$$

Notice that the tenths place is 10^{-1} and the hundredths place is 10^{-2}, and so on.

Practice: Expanded Notation

Write in expanded notation using exponents.

1. 576

2. 1,489

3. 3.581

4. 302,400

Answers: Expanded Notation

1. $(5 \times 10^2) + (7 \times 10^1) + (6 \times 10^0)$

2. $(1 \times 10^3) + (4 \times 10^2) + (8 \times 10^1) + (9 \times 10^0)$

3. $(3 \times 10^0) + (5 \times 10^{-1}) + (8 \times 10^{-2}) + (1 \times 10^{-3})$

4. $(3 \times 10^5)+(0 \times 10^4)+(2 \times 10^3) + (4 \times 10^2) + (0 \times 10^1) + (0 \times 10^0)$
   or $(3 \times 10^5) + (2 \times 10^3) + (4 \times 10^2)$

Grouping Symbols: Parentheses, Brackets, Braces

Parentheses ( )

Parentheses are used to group numbers or variables. Everything inside parentheses must be done before any other operations. *For example:*

$$50(2 + 6) = 50(8) = 400$$

When a parenthesis is preceded by a minus sign, to remove the parentheses, change the sign of each term within the parentheses. *For example:*

$$6 - (-3 + a - 2b + c) = 6 + 3 - a + 2b - c = 9 - a + 2b - c$$

Brackets [ ] and Braces { }

Brackets and *braces* are also used to group numbers or variables. Technically, they're used after parentheses. Parentheses are to be used first, then brackets, then braces: {[( )]} Sometimes, instead of brackets or braces, you'll see the use of larger parentheses:

$$((3+4) \cdot 5) + 2$$

A number using all three grouping symbols would look like this

$2\{1 + [4(2 + 1) + 3]\}$

and would be simplified as follows (notice that you work from the inside out):

$2\{1 + [4(2 + 1) + 3]\} =$

$2\{1 + [4(3) + 3]\} =$

$2\{1 + [12 + 3]\} =$

$2\{1 + [15]\} =$

$2\{16\} =$

32

Order of Operations

If multiplication, division, exponents, addition, parentheses, and so on, are all contained in one problem, the *order of operations* is as follows:

1. Parentheses
2. Exponents and square roots
3. Multiplication and division (start with whichever comes first, left to right)
4. Addition and subtraction (start with whichever comes first, left to right)

For example:

1. $6 + 4 \times 3 =$

   $6 + 12 =$ (multiplication)

   18 (then addition)

2. $10 - 3 \times 6 + 10^2 + (6 + 1) \times 4 =$

   $10 - 3 \times 6 + 10^2 + (7) \times 4 =$ (parentheses first)

   $10 - 3 \times 6 + 100 + (7) \times 4 =$ (exponents next)

   $10 - 18 + 100 + 28 =$ (multiplication)

   $-8 + 100 + 28 =$ (addition/subtraction left to right)

   $92 + 28 = 120$

An easy way to remember the order of operations is: **P**lease **E**xcuse **M**y **D**ear **A**unt **S**ally (**P**arentheses, **E**xponents, **M**ultiplication or **D**ivision, **A**ddition or **S**ubtraction).

Practice: Order of Operations

Simplify:

1. $6 + 4 \times 3^2$

2. $3^2 + 6(4 + 1)$

3. $12 - 2(8 + 2) + 5$

4. $8[3(3^2 - 8) + 1]$

5. $6\{4[2(3 + 2) - 8] - 8\}$

6. $6(12 + 8) \div 2 + 1$

Answers: Order of Operations

1. $6 + 4 \times 3^2 =$

    $6 + 4 \times 9 =$

    $6 + 36 =$

    42

2. $3^2 + 6(4 + 1) =$

    $9 + 6(5) =$

    $9 + 30 =$

    39

3. $12 - 2(8 + 2) + 5 =$

    $12 - 2(10) + 5 =$

    $12 - 20 + 5 =$

    $-8 + 5 =$

    -3

4. $8[3(3^2 - 8) + 1] =$

$8[3(9 - 8) + 1] =$

$8[3(1) + 1] =$

$8[3 + 1] =$

$8[4] =$

32

5. $6\{4[2(3 + 2) - 8] - 8\} =$

$6\{4[2(5) - 8] - 8\} =$

$6\{4[10 - 8] - 8\} =$

$6\{4[2] - 8\} =$

$6\{8 - 8\} =$

$6\{0\} =$

0

6. $6(12 + 8) \div 2 + 1$

$6(20) \div 2 + 1 =$

$120 \div 2 + 1 =$

$60 + 1 =$

61

Rounding Off

To *round off* any number:

1. Underline the place value to which you're rounding off.
2. Look to the immediate right (one place) of your underlined place value.
3. Identify the number (the one to the right). If it's 5 or higher, round your underlined place value up 1. If the number (the one to the right) is 4 or less, leave your underlined place value as it is and change all the other numbers to its right to zeros.

For example: Round to the nearest thousand:

34<u>5</u>,678 becomes 346,000

92<u>8</u>,499 becomes 928,000

This works with decimals as well. Round to the nearest hundredth:

3.4678 becomes 3.47

298,435.083 becomes 298,435.08

Notice that the numbers to the right of the rounded digit are dropped when working with decimals.

Practice: Rounding Off

1. Round off 137 to the nearest ten.

2. Round off 4,549 to the nearest hundred.

3. Round off 0.4758 to the nearest hundredth.

4. Round off 99.483 to the nearest one.

5. Round off 6,278.38512 to the nearest thousandth.

Answers: Rounding Off

1. 140

2. 4,500

3. 0.48

4. 99

5. 6,278.385

Signed Numbers: Positive Numbers and Negative Numbers

Number Lines

On a *number line,* numbers to the right of 0 are positive. Numbers to the left of 0 are negative, as follows:

Given any two numbers on a number line, the one on the right is always larger, regardless of its sign (positive or negative). Note that fractions may also be placed on a number line. *For example:*

Practice: Number Line

Complete the number line below, and then locate which letters correspond with the following numbers:

1. +2

2. −3

3. $+1\frac{1}{2}$

4. $-\frac{1}{2}$

5. $+3\frac{1}{4}$

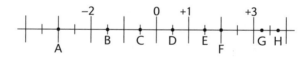

Answers: Number Line

1. F

2. A

3. E

4. C

5. G

Addition of Signed Numbers

When *adding two numbers with the same sign* (either both positive or both negative), add the numbers and keep the same sign. *For example:*

$$\begin{array}{r} +5 \\ \underline{+\ +7} \\ +12 \end{array} \qquad \begin{array}{r} -8 \\ \underline{+\ -3} \\ -11 \end{array}$$

When *adding two numbers with different signs* (one positive and one negative), subtract the numbers and keep the sign one of the number farthest from zero on the number line. *For example:*

$$+5 \qquad\qquad -59$$
$$\underline{+-7} \qquad \underline{++72}$$
$$-2 \qquad\qquad +13$$

Signed numbers may also be added "horizontally." *For example:*

$$+9 + 6 = +15$$
$$-12 + 9 = -3$$
$$8 + (-5) = 3$$

Practice: Addition of Signed Numbers

1. $+25 + 8 =$

2. $-10 + 15 =$

3. $\begin{array}{r} -7 \\ \underline{+-3} \end{array}$

4. $\begin{array}{r} -82 \\ \underline{++60} \end{array}$

5. $-18 + (+5) =$

Answers: Addition of Signed Numbers

1. $+33$
2. $+5$
3. -10
4. -22
5. -13

Subtraction of Signed Numbers

To *subtract positive and/or negative numbers,* just change the sign of the number being subtracted and then add. *For example:*

$$\begin{array}{cccc} +12 & -14 & -19 & +20 \\ \underline{-+4} & \underline{--4} & \underline{-+6} & \underline{--3} \end{array}$$

$$\begin{array}{cccc} +12 & -14 & -19 & +20 \\ \underline{+-4} & \underline{++4} & \underline{+-6} & \underline{++3} \\ +8 & -10 & -25 & +23 \end{array}$$

This may also be done "horizontally." *For example:*

$+12 - (+4) = +12 + (-4) = 8$
$+16 - (-6) = +16 + (+6) = 22$
$-20 - (+3) = -20 + (-3) = -23$
$-5 - (-2) = -5 + (+2) = -3$

Practice: Subtraction of Signed Numbers

1. $\begin{array}{r} +9 \\ \underline{-+3} \end{array}$

2. $\begin{array}{r} +25 \\ \underline{--9} \end{array}$

3. $+36 - (-5) =$

4. $-27 - (+4) =$

5. $-30 - (-2) =$

Answers: Subtraction of Signed Numbers

1. $+6$

2. $+34$

3. $+41$

4. -31

5. -28

Minus Preceding Parenthesis

If a *minus precedes a parenthesis,* it means everything within the parentheses is to be subtracted. Therefore, using the same rule as in subtraction of signed numbers, simply change every sign within the parentheses to its opposite, and then add. *For example:*

1. $9 - (+3 - 5 + 7 - 6) =$

   $9 + (-3 + 5 - 7 + 6) =$

   $9 + (+1) =$

   10

2. $20 - (+35 - 50 + 100) =$

   $20 + (-35 + 50 - 100) =$

   $20 + (-85) =$

   -65

Practice: Minus Preceding Parenthesis

1. $2 - (+5 - 3) =$

2. $6 - (+8 - 5 + 10) =$

3. $10 - (-12 - 5 + 3) =$

4. $25 - (-4 + 7 - 8 - 5 + 6) =$

Answers: Minus Preceding Parenthesis

1. $2 - (+2) = 2 + (-2) = 0$
2. $6 - (+13) = 6 + (-13) = -7$
3. $10 - (-14) = 10 + (+14) = 24$
4. $25 - (-4) = 25 + (+4) = 29$

Multiplying and Dividing Signed Numbers

To *multiply or divide* signed numbers, treat them just like regular numbers but remember this rule: An odd number of negative signs will produce a negative answer. An even number of negative signs will produce a positive answer. *For example:*

$$(-3)(+8)(-5)(-1)(-2) = +240$$
$$(-3)(+8)(-1)(-2) = -48$$
$$\frac{-64}{-2} = +32$$
$$\frac{-64}{+2} = -32$$

Practice: Multiplying and Dividing Signed Numbers

1. $(-3)(+9) =$

2. $-8 \div -2 =$

3. $(-8)(+3)(-2) =$

4. $\frac{-10}{+5} =$

5. $\frac{(-4)(+2)(-6)}{-12} =$

Answers: Multiplying and Dividing Signed Numbers

1. -27

2. $+4$

3. $+48$

4. -2

5. -4

Multiplying and Dividing Using Zero

Zero times any number equals zero. *For example:*

$$0 \times 5 = 0$$
$$0 \times (-3) = 0$$
$$8 \times 9 \times 3 \times (-4) \times 0 = 0$$

Likewise, zero divided by any nonzero number is zero. *For example:*

$$0 \div 5 = 0$$
$$\frac{0}{3} = 0$$
$$0 \div (-6) = 0$$

Important note: Dividing by zero is "undefined" and is not permitted. *For example:* $\frac{6}{0}$ and $\frac{0}{0}$ are not permitted because there is no such answer. The answer is *not* zero.

Divisibility Rules

The following set of rules can help you save time in trying to check the divisibility of numbers:

A number is divisible by	If
2	It ends in 0, 2, 4, 6, or 8
3	The sum of its digits is divisible by 3
4	The number formed by the last two digits is divisible by 4
5	It ends in 0 or 5
6	It is divisible by 2 and 3 (use the rules for both)
7	N/A (no simple rule)
8	The number formed by the last three digits is divisible by 8
9	The sum of its digits is divisible by 9

Examples: Divisibility Rules

1. Is 126 divisible by 3? The sum of the digits $1 + 2 + 6 = 9$. Because 9 is divisible by 3, 126 is divisible by 3.

2. Is 1,648 divisible by 4? Because 48 is divisible by 4, you know that 1,648 is divisible by 4.

3. Is 186 divisible by 6? Because 186 ends in 6, it is divisible by 2. The sum of digits $1 + 8 + 6 = 15$. Because 15 is divisible by 3, 186 is divisible by 3. 186 is divisible by 2 and 3; therefore it is divisible by 6.

4. Is 2,488 divisible by 8? Because 488 is divisible by 8, you know that 2,488 is divisible by 8.

5. Is 2,853 divisible by 9? The sum of the digits $2 + 8 + 5 + 3 = 18$. Because 18 is divisible by 9, you know that 2,853 is divisible by 9.

Practice: Divisibility

1. 4,620 is divisible by which of the following numbers?

    2, 3, 4, 5, 6, 7, 8, 9

2. 13,131 is divisible by which of the following numbers?

    2, 3, 4, 5, 6, 7, 8, 9

Answers: Divisibility

1. 2, 3, 4, 5, 6, 7

    2: The number is even.

    3: The sum of the digits $4 + 6 + 2 + 0 = 12$, which is divisible by 3.

    4: The number formed by the last two digits, 20, is divisible by 4.

    5: The number ends in 0.

    6: The number is divisible by 2 and 3.

    7: Divide 4,620 by 7 and you get 660.

    $\not{8}$: The number formed by the last three digits, 620, is not divisible by 8.

    $\not{9}$: The sum of the digits $4 + 6 + 2 + 0 = 12$, which is not divisible by 9.

2. 3, 9

    $\not{2}$: The number is not even.

    3: The sum of the digits $1 + 3 + 1 + 3 + 1 = 9$, which is divisible by 3.

    $\not{4}$: The number formed by the last two digits, 31, is not divisible by 4.

    $\not{5}$: The number does not end in 0 or 5.

    $\not{6}$: The number is not even.

    $\not{7}$: Divide and you'll see that there is a remainder.

    $\not{8}$: The number formed by the last three digits, 131, is not divisible by 8.

    9: The sum of the digits $1 + 3 + 1 + 3 + 1 = 9$, which is divisible by 9.

Common Fractions

Numerator and Denominator

Fractions consist of two numbers: a *numerator* (which is above the line) and a *denominator* (which is below the line).

$$\frac{1}{2} \begin{array}{l} numerator \\ denominator \end{array} \quad \text{or} \quad numerator \; 1/2 \; denominator$$

The denominator lets you know the number of equal parts into which something is divided. The numerator tells you how many of these equal parts are being considered. Thus, if the fraction is $\frac{3}{5}$ of a pie, then the denominator, 5, tells you that the pie has been divided into 5 equal parts, of which 3 (the numerator) are in the fraction. Sometimes it helps to think of the dividing line (in the middle of a fraction) as meaning "out of." In other words, $\frac{3}{5}$ would also mean 3 "out of" 5 equal pieces from the whole pie. All rules for signed numbers also apply to fractions.

Negative Fractions

Fractions may be *negative* as well as positive (see the number line on p. 19). However, negative fractions are typically written $-\frac{3}{4}$ not $\frac{-3}{4}$ or $\frac{3}{-4}$ (although they are all equal):

$$-\frac{3}{4} = \frac{-3}{4} = \frac{3}{-4}$$

Proper Fractions and Improper Fractions

A fraction like $\frac{3}{5}$, where the numerator is smaller than the denominator, is less than one. This kind of fraction is called a *proper fraction*. But sometimes a fraction may be more than or equal to one. This is when the numerator is larger than or equal to the denominator.

Thus, $\frac{12}{7}$ is more than one. This is called an *improper fraction*.

Here are some examples of proper fractions: $\frac{4}{7}, \frac{2}{5}, \frac{1}{9}, \frac{10}{12}$

Here are some examples of improper fractions: $\frac{7}{4}, \frac{3}{2}, \frac{10}{3}, \frac{16}{15}, \frac{8}{8}$

Mixed Numbers

When a term contains both a whole number and a fraction, it is called *a mixed number.* For instance, $5\frac{1}{4}$ and $290\frac{3}{4}$, are both mixed numbers. To change an improper fraction to a mixed number, you divide the denominator into the numerator. *For example:*

$$\frac{18}{5} = 3\frac{3}{5}$$

$$5\overline{)18}$$
$$\underline{15}$$
$$3$$

To change a mixed number to an improper fraction, you multiply the denominator times the whole number, add in the numerator, and put the total over the original denominator. *For example:*

$$4\frac{1}{2} = \frac{9}{2}$$

$$(2 \times 4) + 1 = 9$$

Practice: Mixed Numbers

Change the following improper fractions to mixed numbers:

1. $\frac{3}{2}$

2. $\frac{7}{4}$

3. $\frac{10}{3}$

4. $\frac{16}{5}$

5. $\frac{23}{4}$

Change the following mixed numbers to improper fractions:

6. $1\frac{3}{4}$

7. $4\frac{1}{2}$

8. $5\frac{3}{4}$

9. $21\frac{3}{4}$

10. $8\frac{4}{5}$

Answers: Mixed Numbers

1. $1\frac{1}{2}$

2. $1\frac{3}{4}$

3. $3\frac{1}{3}$

4. $3\frac{1}{5}$

5. $5\frac{3}{4}$

6. $\frac{7}{4}$

7. $\frac{9}{2}$

8. $\frac{23}{4}$

9. $\frac{87}{4}$

10. $\frac{44}{5}$

Equivalent Fractions

Reducing Fractions

A fraction must be *reduced to lowest terms.* This is done by dividing both the numerator and denominator by the largest number that will divide evenly into both. For example, $\frac{10}{25}$ is reduced to $\frac{2}{5}$ by dividing both numerator and denominator by 5.

Other examples:

$$\frac{30}{50} = \frac{30 \div 10}{50 \div 10} = \frac{3}{5} \quad \frac{8}{40} = \frac{8 \div 8}{40 \div 8} = \frac{1}{5} \quad \frac{9}{15} = \frac{9 \div 3}{15 \div 3} = \frac{3}{5}$$

Practice: Reducing Fractions

Reduce the following fractions:

1. $\frac{6}{8}$

2. $\frac{15}{20}$

3. $\frac{18}{36}$

4. $\frac{40}{90}$

5. $\frac{75}{30}$

Answers: Reducing Fractions

1. $\frac{3}{4}$

2. $\frac{3}{4}$

3. $\frac{1}{2}$

4. $\frac{4}{9}$

5. $\frac{5}{2}$

Enlarging Denominators

The *denominator* of a fraction may be *enlarged* by multiplying both the numerator and the denominator by the same number. *For example:*

$$\frac{1}{2} = \frac{1 \times 5}{2 \times 5} = \frac{5}{10} \qquad \frac{3}{4} = \frac{3 \times 10}{4 \times 10} = \frac{30}{40}$$

Practice: Enlarging Denominators

1. Change $\frac{3}{5}$ to tenths.

2. Express $\frac{3}{4}$ as eighths.

3. $\frac{5}{7} = \frac{?}{21}$

4. $\frac{2}{15} = \frac{?}{45}$

5. Change the fraction $\frac{3}{8}$ to an equivalent fraction with a denominator of 24.

Answers: Enlarging Denominators

1. $\dfrac{6}{10}$

2. $\dfrac{6}{8}$

3. $\dfrac{15}{21}$

4. $\dfrac{6}{45}$

5. $\dfrac{9}{24}$

Factors

Factors of a number are those whole numbers that, when multiplied together, yield the number. *For example:* What are the factors of 8?

$$8 = 2 \times 4 \quad 8 = 1 \times 8$$

Therefore, the factors of 8 are 1, 2, 4, and 8, because $4 \times 2 = 8$ and $1 \times 8 = 8$.

What are the factors of 24?

$$24 = 1 \times 24 \quad 24 = 2 \times 12 \quad 24 = 3 \times 8 \quad 24 = 4 \times 6$$

Therefore, the factors of 24 are 1, 2, 3, 4, 6, 8, 12, and 24.

Practice: Factors

Find the factors of the following:

1. 6

2. 9

3. 12

4. 48

Answers: Factors

1. 1, 2, 3, and 6

2. 1, 3, and 9

3. 1, 2, 3, 4, 6, and 12

4. 1, 2, 3, 4, 6, 8, 12, 16, 24, and 48

Common Factors

Common factors are those factors that are the same for two or more numbers. *For example:* What are the common factors of 6 and 8?

$$6: \boxed{1, 2,} \ 3, 6$$
$$8: \boxed{1, 2,} \ 4, 8$$

1 and 2 are common factors of 6 and 8. ***Note:*** Some numbers may have many common factors. *For example:* What are the common factors of 24 and 36?

$$24: \boxed{1, 2, 3, 4, 6,} \ 8, \boxed{12,} \ 24$$
$$36: \boxed{1, 2, 3, 4, 6,} \ 9, \boxed{12,} \ 18, 36$$

Thus the common factors of 24 and 36 are 1, 2, 3, 4, 6, and 12.

Practice: Common Factors

Find the common factors of the following:

1. 10 and 30

2. 12 and 18

3. 6 and 15

4. 70 and 80

Answers: Common Factors

1. 1, 2, 5, and 10
2. 1, 2, 3, and 6
3. 1 and 3
4. 1, 2, 5, and 10

Greatest Common Factor

The greatest common factor is the largest factor common to two or more numbers. *For example:* What is the greatest common factor of 12 and 30?

$$12: \boxed{1, 2, 3} \ 4, \boxed{6} \ 12$$
$$30: \boxed{1, 2, 3} \ 5, \boxed{6} \ 10, 15, 30$$

Notice that while, 1, 2, 3, and 6 are all common factors of 12 and 30, only 6 is the greatest common factor.

Practice: Greatest Common Factor

Find the greatest common factor of the following:

1. 6 and 12

2. 24 and 40

3. 24 and 60

4. 40 and 100

Answers: Greatest Common Factor

1. 6
2. 8
3. 12
4. 20

Multiples

Multiples of a number are found by multiplying that number by 1, by 2, by 3, by 4, by 5, and so on. *For example:*

- Multiples of 3 are: 3, 6, 9, 12, 15, 18, 21, and so on.
- Multiples of 4 are: 4, 8, 12, 16, 20, 24, 28, 32, and so on.
- Multiples of 7 are: 7, 14, 21, 28, 35, 42, 49, 56, and so on.

Practice: Multiples

Name the first seven multiples of the following:

1. 2

2. 5

3. 6

4. 8

5. 10

Answers: Multiples

1. 2, 4, 6, 8, 10, 12, 14

2. 5, 10, 15, 20, 25, 30, 35

3. 6, 12, 18, 24, 30, 36, 42

4. 8, 16, 24, 32, 40, 48, 56

5. 10, 20, 30, 40, 50, 60, 70

Common Multiples

Common multiples are those multiples that are the same for two or more numbers. *For example:* What are the common multiples of 2 and 3?

$$2 \longrightarrow 2 \; 4 \; \boxed{6} \; 8 \; 10 \; \boxed{12} \; 14 \; 16 \; \boxed{18} \; \text{etc.}$$
$$3 \longrightarrow \quad 3 \; \boxed{6} \quad 9 \quad \boxed{12} \quad 15 \quad \boxed{18} \; \text{etc.}$$

Notice that common multiples may go on indefinitely.

Practice: Common Multiples

Find the first three common multiples of the following:

1. 2 and 6

2. 3 and 4

3. 4 and 6

Answers: Common Multiples

1. 6, 12, 18

2. 12, 24, 36

3. 12, 24, 36

Least Common Multiple

The *least common multiple is* the smallest multiple that is common to, two or more numbers. *For example:* What is the least common multiple of 2 and 3?

$$2 \longrightarrow 2 \; 4 \; \boxed{6} \; 8 \; 10 \; \boxed{12} \; \text{etc.}$$
$$3 \longrightarrow \quad 3 \; \boxed{6} \quad 9 \quad \boxed{12} \; \text{etc.}$$

6 is the smallest multiple common to both 2 and 3. *Another example:*
What is the least common multiple of 2, 3, and 4?

$$2 \longrightarrow 2 \ 4 \ 6 \ 8 \ 10 \ \boxed{12} \ \text{etc.}$$
$$3 \longrightarrow \ \ 3 \ 6 \ 9 \ \ \ \ 12 \ \text{etc.}$$
$$4 \longrightarrow \ \ \ 4 \ \ \ 8 \ \ \ \ \ 12 \ \text{etc.}$$

12 is the least common multiple of 2, 3, and 4.

Practice: Least Common Multiple

Find the least common multiple of the following:

1. 3 and 4

2. 4 and 6

3. 3, 4, and 5

Answers: Least Common Multiple

1. 12

2. 12

3. 60

Adding and Subtracting Fractions

Adding Fractions

To add fractions, you must first change all denominators to their *lowest common denominator* (LCD), the lowest number that can be divided evenly by all the denominators in the problem. When you have all the denominators the same, you may add fractions by simply adding the numerators (the denominator remains the same). *For example:*

$$\begin{array}{c} \frac{3}{8} = \frac{3}{8} \\ +\frac{1}{2} = \frac{4}{8} \\ \hline \frac{7}{8} \end{array} \quad \left\{ \begin{array}{l} \text{one-half is} \\ \text{changed to} \\ \text{four-eighths} \end{array} \right. \qquad \begin{array}{c} \frac{1}{4} = \frac{3}{12} \\ +\frac{1}{3} = \frac{4}{12} \\ \hline \frac{7}{12} \end{array} \quad \left\{ \begin{array}{l} \text{change both} \\ \text{fractions to} \\ \text{LCD of 12} \end{array} \right.$$

In the first example, we changed the $\frac{1}{2}$ to $\frac{4}{8}$ because 8 is the lowest common denominator, and then we added the numerators 3 and 4 to get $\frac{7}{8}$. In the second example, we had to change both fractions to get the lowest common denominator of 12, and then we added the numerators to get $\frac{7}{12}$. Of course, if the denominators are already the same, just add the numerators. *For example:*

$$\begin{array}{r} \frac{6}{11} \\ +\frac{3}{11} \\ \hline \frac{9}{11} \end{array}$$

Note that fractions may be added across, as well. *For example:*

$$\frac{1}{2}+\frac{1}{3}=\frac{3}{6}+\frac{2}{6}=\frac{5}{6}$$

Practice: Adding Fractions

1. $\frac{1}{4}+\frac{3}{8}=$

2. $$\begin{array}{r} \frac{1}{2} \\ +\frac{3}{10} \\ \hline \end{array}$$

3. $\frac{7}{8}+\frac{3}{10}=$

4. $$\begin{array}{r} \frac{4}{15} \\ +\frac{2}{5} \\ \hline \end{array}$$

Answers: Adding Fractions

1. $\frac{1}{4}+\frac{3}{8}=\frac{2}{8}+\frac{3}{8}=\frac{5}{8}$

2. $\frac{1}{2}+\frac{3}{10}=\frac{5}{10}+\frac{3}{10}=\frac{8}{10}=\frac{4}{5}$

3. $\frac{7}{8}+\frac{3}{10}=\frac{35}{40}+\frac{12}{40}=\frac{47}{40}$ or $1\frac{7}{40}$

4. $\frac{4}{15}+\frac{2}{5}=\frac{4}{15}+\frac{6}{15}=\frac{10}{15}=\frac{2}{3}$

Adding Positive and Negative Fractions

The rules for signed numbers (p. 19) apply to fractions as well. *For example:*

1. $-\dfrac{1}{2} + \dfrac{1}{3} = -\dfrac{3}{6} + \dfrac{2}{6} = -\dfrac{1}{6}$

2. $\begin{aligned} +\dfrac{3}{4} &= +\dfrac{9}{12} \\ +-\dfrac{1}{3} &= -\dfrac{4}{12} \\ \hline +\dfrac{5}{12} \end{aligned}$

Practice: Adding Positive and Negative Fractions

1. $\begin{aligned} +\dfrac{4}{5} \\ -\dfrac{1}{10} \end{aligned}$

2. $\begin{aligned} -\dfrac{9}{10} \\ +\dfrac{4}{15} \end{aligned}$

3. $\left(+\dfrac{3}{4}\right) + \left(-\dfrac{1}{2}\right) =$

4. $\left(-\dfrac{3}{4}\right) + \dfrac{1}{3} + \left(-\dfrac{1}{6}\right) =$

Answers: Adding Positive and Negative Fractions

1. $\begin{aligned} \left(+\dfrac{4}{5}\right) &= \left(+\dfrac{8}{10}\right) \\ -\dfrac{1}{10} &= \quad -\dfrac{1}{10} \\ \hline &\qquad +\dfrac{7}{10} \end{aligned}$

2. $\begin{aligned} \left(-\dfrac{9}{10}\right) &= \left(-\dfrac{27}{30}\right) \\ \left(+\dfrac{4}{15}\right) &= \left(+\dfrac{8}{30}\right) \\ \hline &\qquad -\dfrac{19}{30} \end{aligned}$

3. $+\frac{3}{4}+\left(-\frac{1}{2}\right)=+\frac{3}{4}+\left(-\frac{2}{4}\right)=\frac{1}{4}$

4. $\left(-\frac{3}{4}\right)+\left(\frac{1}{3}\right)+\left(-\frac{1}{6}\right)=$

$\left(-\frac{9}{12}\right)+\left(\frac{4}{12}\right)+\left(-\frac{2}{12}\right)=-\frac{7}{12}$

Subtracting Fractions

To subtract fractions, the same rule (find the LCD) given on p. 35 applies, except that you subtract the numerators. *For example:*

$$\begin{array}{rl} \frac{7}{8}= & \frac{7}{8} \\ -\frac{1}{4}= & -\frac{2}{8} \\ \hline & \frac{5}{8} \end{array} \qquad \begin{array}{rl} \frac{3}{4}= & \frac{9}{12} \\ -\frac{1}{3}= & -\frac{4}{12} \\ \hline & \frac{5}{12} \end{array}$$

Again, a subtraction problem may be done across, as well as down:

$$+\frac{5}{8}-\left(+\frac{3}{8}\right)=+\frac{2}{8}=+\frac{1}{4}$$

Practice: Subtracting Fractions

1. $\begin{array}{r} \frac{3}{4} \\ -\frac{1}{2} \\ \hline \end{array}$

2. $\begin{array}{r} \frac{5}{6} \\ -\frac{1}{3} \\ \hline \end{array}$

3. $\begin{array}{r} \frac{3}{8} \\ -\frac{1}{9} \\ \hline \end{array}$

4. $\frac{5}{12}-\frac{2}{5}=$

Answers: Subtracting Fractions

1.
$$\frac{3}{4} = \frac{3}{4}$$
$$-\frac{1}{2} = -\frac{2}{4}$$
$$\frac{1}{4}$$

2.
$$\frac{5}{6} = \frac{5}{6}$$
$$-\frac{1}{3} = -\frac{2}{6}$$
$$\frac{3}{6} = \frac{1}{2}$$

3.
$$\frac{3}{8} = \frac{27}{72}$$
$$-\frac{1}{9} = -\frac{8}{72}$$
$$\frac{19}{72}$$

4. $\frac{5}{12} - \frac{2}{5} = \frac{25}{60} - \frac{24}{60} = \frac{1}{60}$

Subtracting Positive and Negative Fractions

The rule for subtracting signed numbers (p. 21) applies to fractions as well. *For example:*

1.
$$+\frac{9}{10} = +\frac{9}{10} = +\frac{9}{10}$$
$$--\frac{1}{5} = ++\frac{1}{5} = +\frac{2}{10}$$
$$+\frac{11}{10} = 1\frac{1}{10}$$

2. $+\frac{2}{3} - \left(-\frac{1}{5}\right) = \frac{10}{15} - \left(-\frac{3}{15}\right) = \frac{10}{15} + \frac{3}{15} = \frac{13}{15}$

3. $+\frac{1}{3} - \frac{3}{4} = +\frac{4}{12} - \frac{9}{12} = +\frac{4}{12} + \left(-\frac{9}{12}\right) = -\frac{5}{12}$

Practice: Subtracting Positive and Negative Fractions

1.
$$+\frac{3}{4}$$
$$-\frac{1}{3}$$

2. $+\dfrac{1}{6}-\left(-\dfrac{1}{3}\right)=$

3. $-\dfrac{1}{4}-\left(+\dfrac{2}{3}\right)=$

4. $-\dfrac{7}{12}-\left(+\dfrac{5}{6}\right)=$

Answers: Subtracting Positive and Negative Fractions

1. $+\dfrac{3}{4}=+\dfrac{9}{12}$

   $\underline{-\dfrac{1}{3}=-\dfrac{4}{12}}$

   $\quad\;\;+\dfrac{5}{12}$

2. $+\dfrac{1}{6}-\left(-\dfrac{1}{3}\right)=+\dfrac{1}{6}-\left(-\dfrac{2}{6}\right)=+\dfrac{1}{6}+\dfrac{2}{6}=\dfrac{3}{6}=\dfrac{1}{2}$

3. $-\dfrac{1}{4}-\left(+\dfrac{2}{3}\right)=-\dfrac{3}{12}-\left(+\dfrac{8}{12}\right)=-\dfrac{3}{12}+\left(-\dfrac{8}{12}\right)=-\dfrac{11}{12}$

4. $-\dfrac{7}{12}-\left(+\dfrac{5}{6}\right)=-\dfrac{7}{12}-\left(+\dfrac{10}{12}\right)=-\dfrac{7}{12}+\left(-\dfrac{10}{12}\right)=-\dfrac{17}{12}$ or $-1\dfrac{5}{12}$

Adding and Subtracting Mixed Numbers

Adding Mixed Numbers

To *add mixed numbers,* the same rule (find the LCD) shown on p. 35 applies, but make sure that you always add the whole numbers to get your final answer. *For example:*

$$2\dfrac{1}{2}=2\dfrac{2}{4} \leftarrow \begin{cases} \text{one-half is changed} \\ \text{to two fourths} \end{cases}$$

$$\dfrac{+\,3\dfrac{1}{4}=3\dfrac{1}{4}}{5\dfrac{3}{4}} \begin{cases} \text{remember to add the} \\ \text{whole numbers} \end{cases}$$

Sometimes you may end up with a mixed number that includes an improper fraction. In that case, you must change the improper fraction to a mixed number and combine it with the sum of the integers. *For example:*

$$2\frac{1}{2} = 2\frac{2}{4}$$
$$+5\frac{3}{4} = 5\frac{3}{4}$$
$$7\frac{5}{4}$$

And since $\frac{5}{4} = 1\frac{1}{4}$,

$$7\frac{5}{4} = 7 + 1\frac{1}{4} = 8\frac{1}{4}$$

Remember: The rules for adding signed numbers (p. 20) apply for mixed numbers as well.

Practice: Adding Mixed Numbers

1. $3\frac{1}{2}$
   $+1\frac{2}{6}$

2. $4\frac{3}{5}$
   $+2\frac{1}{10}$

3. $+4\frac{5}{6} + \left(-2\frac{1}{3}\right) =$

4. $-14\frac{3}{4}$
   $+21\frac{7}{8}$

Answers Adding Mixed Numbers Problems

1. $3\frac{1}{2} = 3\frac{3}{6}$
   $+1\frac{2}{6} = +1\frac{2}{6}$
   $4\frac{5}{6}$

2. $4\frac{3}{5} = 4\frac{6}{10}$
   $+2\frac{1}{10} = +2\frac{1}{10}$
   $6\frac{7}{10}$

3. $+4\frac{5}{6}+\left(-2\frac{1}{3}\right)=+4\frac{5}{6}+\left(-2\frac{2}{6}\right)=+4\frac{5}{6}-2\frac{2}{6}=2\frac{1}{2}$

4. $-14\frac{3}{4}=-14\frac{6}{8}$

$+21\frac{7}{8}=+21\frac{7}{8}$

$\phantom{4.\ +21\frac{7}{8}=}7\frac{1}{8}$

Subtracting Mixed Numbers

When you subtract mixed numbers, sometimes you may have to "borrow" from the whole number, just as you sometimes borrow from the next column when subtracting ordinary numbers. *For example:*

$$\begin{array}{r} 6\overset{4}{\cancel{5}}\overset{11}{1} \\ -129 \\ \hline 522 \end{array} \qquad \begin{array}{r} \overset{7}{\overset{6}{\cancel{4}}}\overset{3}{\cancel{1}}\frac{\cancel{1}}{6} \\ -2\frac{5}{6} \\ \hline 1\frac{2}{6}=1\frac{1}{3} \end{array}$$

you borrowed 1 from the 10's column

you borrowed one in the form $\frac{6}{6}$ from the 1's column, and added it to the $\frac{1}{6}$ to get $\frac{7}{6}$

To subtract a mixed number from a whole number, you have to "borrow" from the whole number. *For example:*

$$\begin{array}{r} 6=5\frac{5}{5} \\ -3\frac{1}{5}=3\frac{1}{5} \\ \hline 2\frac{4}{5} \end{array}$$

$\left\{\begin{array}{l}\text{borrow one in the form of}\\ \frac{5}{5} \text{ from the 6}\end{array}\right.$

$\left\{\begin{array}{l}\text{remember to subtract the}\\ \text{remaining whole numbers}\end{array}\right.$

Remember that the rules for signed numbers (p. 21) apply here also and that subtracting can be done across as well as down.

Practice: Subtracting Mixed Numbers

1. $3\frac{7}{8}$

$-1\frac{2}{8}$

2. $4\frac{3}{4}-1\frac{1}{2}=$

3. $15\frac{1}{4}$

  $-6\frac{1}{2}$

4. $24\frac{1}{8} - 16\frac{3}{4} =$

5. $\quad 102\frac{3}{6}$

  $- -53\frac{1}{2}$

Answers: Subtracting Mixed Numbers

1. $3\frac{7}{8}$

  $-1\frac{2}{8}$

  $2\frac{5}{8}$

2. $4\frac{3}{4} - 1\frac{1}{2} = 4\frac{3}{4} - 1\frac{2}{4} = 3\frac{1}{4}$

3. $15\frac{1}{4} = 15\frac{1}{4} = 1\overset{4}{\cancel{5}} \overset{\frac{5}{4}}{\cancel{\frac{1}{4}}}$

  $-6\frac{1}{2} = -6\frac{2}{4} = -6\frac{2}{4}$

  $\qquad\qquad\qquad\quad 8\frac{3}{4}$

4. $24\frac{1}{8} - 16\frac{3}{4} = 24\frac{1}{8} - 16\frac{6}{8} = 2\overset{3}{\cancel{4}}\overset{\frac{9}{8}}{\cancel{\frac{1}{8}}} - 16\frac{6}{8} = 7\frac{3}{8}$

5. $\quad 102\frac{3}{6} = \quad 102\frac{3}{6} = 102\frac{3}{6}$

  $- -53\frac{1}{2} = - -53\frac{3}{6} = +53\frac{3}{6}$

  $\qquad\qquad\qquad\qquad\qquad 155\frac{6}{6} = 156$

Multiplying Fractions and Mixed Numbers

Multiplying Fractions

To multiply fractions, simply multiply the numerators, and then multiply the denominators. Reduce to the lowest terms if necessary. *For example:*

$$\frac{2}{3} \times \frac{5}{12} = \frac{10}{36}$$

Reduce $\frac{10}{36}$ to $\frac{5}{18}$.

This answer had to be reduced because it wasn't in lowest terms. Because whole numbers can also be written as fractions ($3 = \frac{3}{1}$, $4 = \frac{4}{1}$, and so on), the problem $3 \times \frac{3}{8}$ would be worked by changing 3 to $\frac{3}{1}$.

Canceling when multiplying fractions: You could first have "canceled." That would've eliminated the need to reduce your answer. To cancel, find a number that divides evenly into one numerator and one denominator. In this case, 2 will divide evenly into 2 in the numerator (it goes in one time) and 12 in the denominator (it goes in 6 times). *Thus:*

$$\frac{\overset{1}{\cancel{2}}}{3} \times \frac{5}{\underset{6}{\cancel{12}}} = \frac{5}{18}$$

Remember: You may cancel only when *multiplying* fractions. The rules for multiplying signed numbers hold here, too (p. 24). *For example:*

$$\frac{1}{4} \times \frac{2}{7} = \frac{1}{\underset{2}{\cancel{4}}} \times \frac{\overset{1}{\cancel{2}}}{7} = \frac{1}{14} \quad \text{and} \quad \left(-\frac{\overset{1}{\cancel{3}}}{\cancel{8}_2} \right) \times \left(-\frac{\cancel{4}}{\cancel{9}_3} \right) = +\frac{1}{6}$$

Practice: Multiplying Fractions Problems

1. $\frac{3}{5} \times \frac{1}{2} =$

2. $\frac{7}{8} \times \frac{2}{3} =$

3. $-\frac{4}{7} \times \frac{14}{3} =$

4. $\frac{7}{10} \times \frac{5}{6} \times \frac{1}{3} =$

5. $7 \times \frac{2}{14} =$

Answers: Multiplying Fractions Problems

1. $\frac{3}{5} \times \frac{1}{2} = \frac{3}{10}$

2. $\frac{7}{8} \times \frac{2}{3} = \frac{7}{\underset{4}{\cancel{8}}} \times \frac{\overset{1}{\cancel{2}}}{3} = \frac{7}{12}$

3. $-\frac{4}{7} \times \frac{14}{3} = -\frac{4}{\underset{1}{\cancel{7}}} \times \frac{\overset{2}{\cancel{14}}}{3} = -\frac{8}{3} = -2\frac{2}{3}$

4. $\dfrac{7}{10} \times \dfrac{5}{6} \times \dfrac{1}{3} = \dfrac{7}{\overset{}{\underset{2}{\cancel{10}}}} \times \dfrac{\overset{1}{\cancel{5}}}{6} \times \dfrac{1}{3} = \dfrac{7}{36}$

5. $7 \times \dfrac{2}{14} = \dfrac{\overset{1}{\cancel{7}}}{1} \times \dfrac{2}{\underset{2}{\cancel{14}}} = \dfrac{2}{2} = 1$

Multiplying Mixed Numbers

To multiply mixed numbers, first change any mixed number to an improper fraction. Then multiply as previously shown (p. 44).

$$3\dfrac{1}{3} \times 2\dfrac{1}{4} = \dfrac{10}{3} \times \dfrac{9}{4} = \dfrac{90}{12} = 7\dfrac{6}{12} = 7\dfrac{1}{2}$$

or

$$\dfrac{\overset{5}{\cancel{10}}}{\underset{1}{\cancel{3}}} \times \dfrac{\overset{3}{\cancel{9}}}{\underset{2}{\cancel{4}}} = \dfrac{15}{2} = 7\dfrac{1}{2}$$

Change the answer, if in improper fraction form, back to a mixed number and reduce if necessary. *Remember:* The rules for multiplication of signed numbers apply here as well (p. 24).

Practice: Multiplying Mixed Numbers

1. $2\dfrac{1}{2} \times 3\dfrac{1}{4} =$

2. $3\dfrac{1}{5} \times 6\dfrac{1}{2} =$

3. $-5\dfrac{1}{4} \times 3\dfrac{3}{7} =$

4. $\left(-4\dfrac{9}{10}\right) \times \left(-3\dfrac{3}{7}\right) =$

Answers: Multiplying Mixed Numbers

1. $2\dfrac{1}{2} \times 3\dfrac{1}{4} = \dfrac{5}{2} \times \dfrac{13}{4} = \dfrac{65}{8} = 8\dfrac{1}{8}$

2. $3\dfrac{1}{5} \times 6\dfrac{1}{2} = \dfrac{16}{5} \times \dfrac{13}{2} = \dfrac{\overset{8}{\cancel{16}}}{5} \times \dfrac{13}{\underset{1}{\cancel{2}}} = \dfrac{104}{5} = 20\dfrac{4}{5}$

3. $-5\dfrac{1}{4} \times 3\dfrac{3}{7} = -\dfrac{21}{4} \times \dfrac{24}{7} = -\dfrac{\overset{3}{\cancel{21}}}{\underset{1}{\cancel{4}}} \times \dfrac{\overset{6}{\cancel{24}}}{\underset{1}{\cancel{7}}} = -18$

4. $\left(-4\dfrac{9}{10}\right) \times \left(-3\dfrac{3}{7}\right) = \left(-\dfrac{49}{10}\right) \times \left(-\dfrac{24}{7}\right) = \left(-\dfrac{\overset{7}{\cancel{49}}}{\underset{5}{\cancel{10}}}\right) \times \left(-\dfrac{\overset{12}{\cancel{24}}}{\underset{1}{\cancel{7}}}\right) = \dfrac{84}{5} = 16\dfrac{4}{5}$

Dividing Fractions and Mixed Numbers

Dividing Fractions

To *divide fractions,* invert (turn upside down) the second fraction (the one "divided by") and multiply. Then reduce, if necessary. *For example:*

$$\frac{1}{6} \div \frac{1}{5} = \frac{1}{6} \times \frac{5}{1} = \frac{5}{6} \qquad \frac{1}{6} \div \frac{1}{3} = \frac{1}{\underset{2}{6}} \times \frac{\overset{1}{3}}{1} = \frac{1}{2}$$

Here, too, the rules for division of signed numbers apply (p. 24).

Practice: Dividing Fractions

1. $\frac{1}{2} \div \frac{1}{3} =$

2. $\frac{3}{4} \div \frac{1}{2} =$

3. $\frac{3}{7} \div \frac{3}{14} =$

4. $\frac{3}{4} \div \left(-\frac{5}{8}\right) =$

Answers: Dividing Fractions

1. $\frac{1}{2} \div \frac{1}{3} = \frac{1}{2} \times \frac{3}{1} = \frac{3}{2} = 1\frac{1}{2}$

2. $\frac{3}{4} \div \frac{1}{2} = \frac{3}{\underset{2}{4}} \times \frac{\overset{1}{2}}{1} = \frac{3}{2} = 1\frac{1}{2}$

3. $\frac{3}{7} \div \frac{3}{14} = \frac{\overset{1}{3}}{\underset{1}{7}} \times \frac{\overset{2}{14}}{\underset{1}{3}} = \frac{2}{1} = 2$

4. $\frac{3}{4} \div \left(-\frac{5}{8}\right) = \frac{3}{4} \times \left(-\frac{8}{5}\right) = \frac{3}{\underset{1}{4}} \times \left(-\frac{\overset{2}{8}}{5}\right) = -\frac{6}{5} = -1\frac{1}{5}$

Dividing Complex Fractions

Sometimes a division-of-fractions problem may appear in this form; these are called *complex fractions.*

$$\frac{\dfrac{3}{4}}{\dfrac{7}{8}}$$

If so, consider the line separating the two fractions to mean "divided by." Therefore, this problem may be rewritten as

$$\frac{3}{4} \div \frac{7}{8} =$$

Now, follow the same procedure as shown on p. 46.

$$\frac{3}{4} \div \frac{7}{8} = \frac{3}{\overset{}{\underset{1}{4}}} \times \frac{\overset{2}{8}}{7} = \frac{6}{7}$$

Practice: Dividing Complex Fractions

1. $\dfrac{\dfrac{3}{4}}{\dfrac{1}{2}}$

2. $\dfrac{\dfrac{5}{6}}{\dfrac{1}{3}}$

3. $\dfrac{\dfrac{1}{2}}{\dfrac{3}{8}}$

4. $\dfrac{\dfrac{7}{8}}{\dfrac{1}{2}}$

Answers: Dividing Complex Fractions

1. $\dfrac{\dfrac{3}{4}}{\dfrac{1}{2}} = \dfrac{3}{4} \div \dfrac{1}{2} = \dfrac{3}{\overset{}{\underset{2}{4}}} \times \dfrac{\overset{1}{2}}{1} = \dfrac{3}{2} = 1\dfrac{1}{2}$

2. $\dfrac{\dfrac{5}{6}}{\dfrac{1}{3}} = \dfrac{5}{6} \div \dfrac{1}{3} = \dfrac{5}{\overset{}{\underset{2}{6}}} \times \dfrac{\overset{1}{3}}{1} = \dfrac{5}{2} = 2\dfrac{1}{2}$

3. $\dfrac{\dfrac{1}{2}}{\dfrac{3}{8}} = \dfrac{1}{2} \div \dfrac{3}{8} = \dfrac{1}{\overset{}{\underset{1}{2}}} \times \dfrac{\overset{4}{8}}{3} = \dfrac{4}{3} = 1\dfrac{1}{3}$

4. $\dfrac{\dfrac{7}{8}}{\dfrac{1}{2}} = \dfrac{7}{8} \div \dfrac{1}{2} = \dfrac{7}{\overset{}{\underset{4}{8}}} \times \dfrac{\overset{1}{2}}{1} = \dfrac{7}{4} = 1\dfrac{3}{4}$

Dividing Mixed Numbers

To *divide mixed numbers,* first change them to improper fractions (p. 28). Then follow the rule for dividing fractions (p. 46). *For example:*

1. $3\dfrac{3}{5} \div 2\dfrac{2}{3} = \dfrac{18}{5} \div \dfrac{8}{3} = \dfrac{\overset{9}{\cancel{18}}}{5} \times \dfrac{3}{\underset{4}{\cancel{8}}} = \dfrac{27}{20} = 1\dfrac{7}{20}$

2. $2\dfrac{1}{5} \div 3\dfrac{1}{10} = \dfrac{11}{5} \div \dfrac{31}{10} = \dfrac{11}{\underset{1}{\cancel{5}}} \times \dfrac{\overset{2}{\cancel{10}}}{31} = \dfrac{22}{31}$

Notice that after you invert and have a multiplication-of-fractions problem, you may then cancel tops with bottoms when appropriate.

Practice: Dividing Mixed Numbers

1. $3\dfrac{1}{2} \div \dfrac{3}{4} =$

2. $1\dfrac{1}{6} \div 4\dfrac{1}{2} =$

3. $\left(-5\dfrac{4}{5}\right) \div \left(2\dfrac{1}{2}\right) =$

4. $\left(-3\dfrac{1}{5}\right) \div \left(3\dfrac{1}{3}\right) =$

Answers: Dividing Mixed Numbers

1. $3\dfrac{1}{2} \div \dfrac{3}{4} = \dfrac{7}{2} \div \dfrac{3}{4} = \dfrac{7}{\underset{1}{\cancel{2}}} \times \dfrac{\overset{2}{\cancel{4}}}{3} = \dfrac{14}{3} = 4\dfrac{2}{3}$

2. $1\dfrac{1}{6} \div 4\dfrac{1}{2} = \dfrac{7}{6} \div \dfrac{9}{2} = \dfrac{7}{\underset{3}{\cancel{6}}} \times \dfrac{\overset{1}{\cancel{2}}}{9} = \dfrac{7}{27}$

3. $\left(-5\dfrac{4}{5}\right) \div \left(2\dfrac{1}{2}\right) = \left(-\dfrac{29}{5}\right) \div \dfrac{5}{2} = \left(-\dfrac{29}{5}\right) \times \left(\dfrac{2}{5}\right) = -\dfrac{58}{25} = -2\dfrac{8}{25}$

4. $\left(-3\dfrac{1}{5}\right) \div \left(-3\dfrac{1}{3}\right) = \left(-\dfrac{16}{5}\right) \div \left(-\dfrac{10}{3}\right) = \left(-\dfrac{\overset{8}{\cancel{16}}}{5}\right) \times \left(-\dfrac{3}{\underset{5}{\cancel{10}}}\right) = \dfrac{24}{25}$

Simplifying Fractions and Complex Fractions

If either numerator or denominator consists of several numbers, these numbers must be combined into one number. Then reduce if necessary. *For example:*

1. $\dfrac{28+14}{26+17} = \dfrac{42}{43}$

2. $\dfrac{\dfrac{1}{4}+\dfrac{1}{2}}{\dfrac{1}{3}+\dfrac{1}{4}} = \dfrac{\dfrac{1}{4}+\dfrac{2}{4}}{\dfrac{4}{12}+\dfrac{3}{12}} = \dfrac{\dfrac{3}{4}}{\dfrac{7}{12}} = \dfrac{3}{4} \div \dfrac{7}{12} = \dfrac{3}{\underset{1}{\cancel{4}}} \times \dfrac{\overset{3}{\cancel{12}}}{7} = \dfrac{9}{7} = 1\dfrac{2}{7}$

3. $\dfrac{2+\dfrac{1}{2}}{3+\dfrac{1}{4}} = \dfrac{2\dfrac{1}{2}}{3\dfrac{1}{4}} = \dfrac{\dfrac{5}{2}}{\dfrac{13}{4}} = \dfrac{5}{2} \div \dfrac{13}{4} = \dfrac{5}{\overset{}{\underset{1}{2}}} \times \dfrac{\overset{2}{\cancel{4}}}{13} = \dfrac{10}{13}$

4. $\dfrac{3-\dfrac{3}{4}}{-4+\dfrac{1}{2}} = \dfrac{2\dfrac{1}{4}}{-3\dfrac{1}{2}} = \dfrac{\dfrac{9}{4}}{-\dfrac{7}{2}} = \dfrac{9}{4} \div -\dfrac{7}{2} = \dfrac{9}{\overset{}{\underset{2}{4}}} \times -\dfrac{\overset{1}{\cancel{2}}}{7} = -\dfrac{9}{14}$

5. $\dfrac{1}{1+\dfrac{1}{1+\dfrac{1}{4}}} = \dfrac{1}{1+\dfrac{1}{\dfrac{5}{4}}} = \dfrac{1}{1+\left(1 \div \dfrac{5}{4}\right)} = \dfrac{1}{1+\left(1 \times \dfrac{4}{5}\right)} = \dfrac{1}{1+\dfrac{4}{5}} =$

$\dfrac{1}{1\dfrac{4}{5}} = \dfrac{1}{\dfrac{9}{5}} = 1 \div \dfrac{9}{5} = 1 \times \dfrac{5}{9} = \dfrac{5}{9}$

Practice: Simplifying Fractions and Complex Fractions

1. $\dfrac{-3-2}{-6+5} =$

2. $\dfrac{3+\dfrac{1}{2}}{5+\dfrac{5}{6}} =$

3. $\dfrac{2-\dfrac{7}{8}}{1+\dfrac{3}{4}} =$

4. $\dfrac{1+\dfrac{1}{2+\dfrac{1}{2}}}{3} =$

Answers: Simplifying Fractions and Complex Fractions

1. $\dfrac{-3-2}{-6+5} = \dfrac{-5}{-1} = 5$

2. $\dfrac{3+\dfrac{1}{2}}{5+\dfrac{5}{6}} = \dfrac{3\dfrac{1}{2}}{5\dfrac{5}{6}} = \dfrac{7}{2} \div \dfrac{35}{6} = \dfrac{\overset{1}{\cancel{7}}}{\underset{1}{2}} \times \dfrac{\overset{3}{\cancel{6}}}{\underset{5}{\cancel{35}}} = \dfrac{3}{5}$

3. $\dfrac{2-\dfrac{7}{8}}{1+\dfrac{3}{4}} = \dfrac{1\dfrac{1}{8}}{1\dfrac{3}{4}} = \dfrac{9}{8} \div \dfrac{7}{4} = \dfrac{9}{\overset{}{\underset{2}{8}}} \times \dfrac{\overset{1}{\cancel{4}}}{7} = \dfrac{9}{14}$

4. $\dfrac{1+\dfrac{1}{2+\dfrac{1}{2}}}{3} = \dfrac{1+\dfrac{1}{\dfrac{5}{2}}}{3} = \dfrac{1+\left(1 \div \dfrac{5}{2}\right)}{3} = \dfrac{1+\left(1 \times \dfrac{2}{5}\right)}{3} = \dfrac{1+\left(\dfrac{2}{5}\right)}{3} =$

$\dfrac{1\dfrac{2}{5}}{3} = \dfrac{\dfrac{7}{5}}{3} = \dfrac{7}{5} \div \dfrac{3}{1} = \dfrac{7}{5} \times \dfrac{1}{3} = \dfrac{7}{15}$

Decimals

Changing Decimals to Fractions

Fractions may also be written in *decimal* form (decimal fractions) by using a symbol called a *decimal point*. All numbers to the left of the decimal point are whole numbers. *All* numbers to the right of the decimal point are fractions with denominators of only 10, 100, 1,000, 10,000, and so on. *For example:*

$$0.6 = \frac{6}{10} = \frac{3}{5} \qquad 0.7 = \frac{7}{10} \qquad 0.07 = \frac{7}{100} \qquad 0.007 = \frac{7}{1,000}$$

$$0.0007 = \frac{7}{10,000} \qquad 0.00007 = \frac{7}{100,000} \qquad 0.25 = \frac{25}{100} = \frac{1}{4}$$

Read it: 0.8 (eight-tenths)

Write it: $\frac{8}{10}$

Reduce it: $\frac{4}{5}$

All rules for signed numbers also apply to decimals.

Practice: Changing Decimals to Fractions

Change the following decimals to fractions. Reduce if necessary.

1. 0.4

2. 0.09

3. 0.75

4. 0.062

Answers: Changing Decimals to Fractions

1. $0.4 = 4$ tenths $= \frac{4}{10} = \frac{2}{5}$

2. $0.09 = 9$ hundredths $= \frac{9}{100}$

3. $0.75 = 75$ hundredths $= \frac{75}{100} = \frac{3}{4}$

4. $0.062 = 62$ thousandths $= \frac{62}{1,000} = \frac{31}{500}$

Adding and Subtracting Decimals

To *add or subtract decimals,* just line up the decimal points and then add or subtract in the same manner you would add or subtract regular numbers. *For example:*

$$23.6 + 1.75 + 300.002 =$$

$$\begin{array}{r} 23.6 \\ 1.75 \\ +300.002 \\ \hline 325.352 \end{array}$$

Adding in zeros can make the problem easier to work:

$$\begin{array}{r} 23.600 \\ 1.750 \\ +300.002 \\ \hline 325.352 \end{array}$$

and

$$54.26 - 1.1 =$$

$$\begin{array}{r} 54.26 \\ -1.10 \\ \hline 53.16 \end{array}$$

and

$$78.9 - 37.43 =$$

$$\begin{array}{r} 78.\overset{8}{\cancel{9}}{}^{1}0 \\ -37.4\ 3 \\ \hline 41.4\ 7 \end{array}$$

A whole number has an understood decimal point to its right. *For example:*

$$17 - 8.43 =$$

$$\begin{array}{r} 1\overset{6}{\cancel{7}}.\overset{9}{\cancel{0}}{}^{1}0 \\ -8.4\ 3 \\ \hline 8.5\ 7 \end{array}$$

Practice: Adding and Subtracting Decimals

1. $19.6 + 5.02 =$

2. $108 + 71.04 =$

51

3. $0.16 - 0.043 =$

4. $12 - 0.061 =$

Answers: Adding and Subtracting Decimals

1. 24.62

2. 179.04

3. 0.117

4. 11.939

Multiplying Decimals

To *multiply decimals*, just multiply as usual. Then count the total number of digits above the line which are to the right of all decimal points. Place your decimal point in your answer so the same number of digits are to the right of the decimal point as there are above the line. *For example:*

$$
\begin{array}{r}
40.012 \leftarrow 3\ \text{digits} \\
\times \quad\ 3.1 \leftarrow 1\ \text{digit} \\
\hline
40012 \\
120036 \\
\hline
124.0372 \leftarrow 4\ \text{digits}
\end{array}
$$

$\left\{ \begin{array}{l} \text{total of 4 digits above the line} \\ \text{that are to the right of the decimal point} \end{array} \right.$

$\left\{ \begin{array}{l} \text{decimal point placed so there is} \\ \text{same number of digits to the right} \\ \text{of the decimal point} \end{array} \right.$

Practice: Multiplying Decimals

1. $\begin{array}{r} 30.1 \\ \times 2.65 \\ \hline \end{array}$

2. $30 \times 9.061 =$

3. $(0.906) \times (-0.1) =$

4. $(-0.012) \times (-0.003) =$

Answers: Multiplying Decimals

1. 79.765

2. 271.83

3. −0.0906

4. 0.000036

Dividing Decimals

Dividing decimals is the same as dividing other numbers, except that if the *divisor* (the number you're dividing by) has a decimal, move it to the right as many places as necessary until it's a whole number. Then move the decimal point in the *dividend* (the number being divided into) the same number of places. Sometimes you may have to add zeros to the *dividend* (the number inside the division sign). *For example:*

$$1.25\overline{)5.} = 125\overline{)500.}^{\,4.}$$

or

$$0.002\overline{)26.} = 2\overline{)26000.}^{\,13000.}$$

Practice: Dividing Decimals

1. Divide 8 by 0.4.

2. $0.2\overline{)6.84}$

3. Divide 30.6 by 0.05.

4. $90.804\overline{)181.608}$

Answers: Dividing Decimals

1. 20
2. 34.2
3. 612
4. 2

Changing Fractions to Decimals

To *change a fraction to a decimal,* simply do what the operation says. In other words, $\frac{13}{20}$ means 13 divided by 20. So do just that (insert decimal points and zeros accordingly). *For example:*

$$\frac{13}{20} = 20\overline{)13.00}^{\,0.65} = 0.65 \qquad \frac{5}{8} = 8\overline{)5.000}^{\,0.625} = 0.625$$

Practice: Changing Fractions to Decimals

Change each fraction to a decimal:

1. $\frac{1}{4}$

2. $\frac{3}{10}$

3. $\frac{3}{8}$

4. $\frac{7}{11}$

Answers: Changing Fractions to Decimals

1. 0.25

2. 0.3

3. 0.375

4. 0.6363 . . . (sometimes written $0.\overline{63}$)

Percentage

A fraction whose denominator is 100 is called a *percent*. The word *percent* means hundredths (per hundred). *For example:*

$$37\% = \frac{37}{100}$$

Changing Decimals to Percents

To change decimals to percents:

1. Move the decimal point two places to the right.

2. Insert a percent sign.

For example:

$$0.75 = 75\%$$
$$0.05 = 5\%$$
$$1.85 = 185\%$$
$$20.3 = 2,030\%$$
$$0.003 = 0.3\%$$

Practice: Changing Decimals to Percents

Change each decimal to percent.

1. 0.32

2. 0.8

3. 0.006

4. 1.75

Answers: Changing Decimals to Percents

1. 32%

2. 80%

3. 0.6%

4. 175%

Changing Percents to Decimals

To change percents to decimals:

1. Eliminate the percent sign.
2. Move the decimal point two places to the left (sometimes adding zeros will be necessary).

For example:

$$75\% = 0.75$$
$$23\% = 0.23$$
$$5\% = 0.05$$
$$0.2\% = 0.002$$

Practice: Changing Percents to Decimals

Change each percent to a decimal:

1. 25%

2. 80%

3. 2%

4. 0.4%

5. 300%

Answers: Changing Percents to Decimals

1. 0.25

2. 0.80 or 0.8

3. 0.02

4. 0.004

5. 3.00 or 3

Changing Fractions to Percents

To change a fraction to a percent:

1. Change to a decimal.
2. Change the decimal to a percent.

For example:

$$\frac{1}{2} = 0.5 = 50\%$$

$$\frac{2}{5} = 0.4 = 40\%$$

$$\frac{5}{2} = 2.5 = 250\%$$

$$\frac{1}{20} = 0.05 = 5\%$$

Practice: Changing Fractions to Percents

Change each fraction to a percent:

1. $\frac{1}{4}$

2. $\frac{3}{8}$

3. $\frac{7}{20}$

4. $\frac{7}{2}$

Answers: Changing Fractions to Percents

1. 25%
2. $37\frac{1}{2}$% or 37.5%
3. 35%
4. 350%

Changing Percents to Fractions

To *change percents to fractions:*

1. Drop the percent sign.
2. Write over 100.
3. Reduce if necessary.

For example:

$$60\% = \frac{60}{100} = \frac{3}{5}$$
$$230\% = \frac{230}{100} = \frac{23}{10}$$
$$13\% = \frac{13}{100}$$

Practice: Changing Percents to Fractions

Change each percent to a fraction:

1. 30%

2. 5%

3. 125%

4. 19%

Answers: Changing Percents to Fractions

1. $30\% = \frac{30}{100} = \frac{3}{10}$
2. $5\% = \frac{5}{100} = \frac{1}{20}$
3. $125\% = \frac{125}{100} = \frac{5}{4}$
4. $19\% = \frac{19}{100}$

Important Equivalents That Can Save You Time

Memorizing the following can eliminate unnecessary computations:

$$\frac{1}{100} = 0.01 = 1\%$$

$$\frac{1}{10} = 0.1 = 10\%$$

$$\frac{1}{5} = \frac{2}{10} = 0.2 = 0.20 = 20\%$$

$$\frac{3}{10} = 0.3 = 0.30 = 30\%$$

$$\frac{2}{5} = \frac{4}{10} = 0.4 = 0.40 = 40\%$$

$$\frac{1}{2} = \frac{5}{10} = 0.5 = 0.50 = 50\%$$

$$\frac{3}{5} = \frac{6}{10} = 0.6 = 0.60 = 60\%$$

$$\frac{7}{10} = 0.7 = 0.70 = 70\%$$

$$\frac{4}{5} = \frac{8}{10} = 0.8 = 0.80 = 80\%$$

$$\frac{9}{10} = 0.9 = 0.90 = 90\%$$

$$\frac{1}{4} = \frac{25}{100} = 0.25 = 25\%$$

$$\frac{3}{4} = \frac{75}{100} = 0.75 = 75\%$$

$$\frac{1}{3} = 0.33\frac{1}{3} = 33\frac{1}{3}\%$$

$$\frac{2}{3} = 0.66\frac{2}{3} = 66\frac{2}{3}\%$$

$$\frac{1}{8} = 0.125 = 0.12\frac{1}{2} = 12\frac{1}{2}\%$$

$$\frac{3}{8} = 0.375 = 0.37\frac{1}{2} = 37\frac{1}{2}\%$$

$$\frac{5}{8} = 0.625 = 0.62\frac{1}{2} = 62\frac{1}{2}\%$$

$$\frac{7}{8} = 0.875 = 0.87\frac{1}{2} = 87\frac{1}{2}\%$$

$$\frac{1}{6} = 0.16\frac{2}{3} = 16\frac{2}{3}\%$$

$$\frac{5}{6} = 0.83\frac{1}{3} = 83\frac{1}{3}\%$$

$$1 = 1.00 = 100\%$$

$$2 = 2.00 = 200\%$$

$$3\frac{1}{2} = 3.5 = 3.50 = 350\%$$

Finding Percent of a Number

To *determine percent of a number,* change the percent to a fraction or decimal (whichever is easier for you) and multiply. Remember, the word *of* means multiply. *For example:*

What is 20% of 80?

$$\frac{20}{100} \times 80 = \frac{1,600}{100} = 16 \text{ or } 0.20 \times 80 = 16.00 = 16$$

What is 12% of 50?

$$\frac{12}{100} \times 50 = \frac{600}{100} = 6 \text{ or } 0.12 \times 50 = 6.00 = 6$$

What is $\frac{1}{2}\%$ of 18?

$$\frac{\frac{1}{2}}{100} \times 18 = \frac{1}{200} \times 18 = \frac{18}{200} = \frac{9}{100} \text{ or } 0.005 \times 18 = 0.09$$

Practice: Finding Percent of a Number

1. What is 10% of 30?

2. What is 70% of 20?

3. What is $\frac{1}{4}$% of 1,000?

4. What is 250% of 12?

Answers: Finding Percent of a Number

1. $x = (0.10)(30) = 3$

2. $x = (0.70)(20) = 14$

3. $x = (0.0025)(1,000) = 2.5$

4. $x = (2.50)(12) = 30$

Other Applications of Percent

Turn the question word-for-word into an equation. For *what,* substitute the letter x; for *is,* substitute an *equal sign;* for *of* substitute a *multiplication sign.* Change percents to decimals or fractions, whichever you find easier. Then solve the equation. *For example:*

1. 18 is what percent of 90?

   $$18 = x(90)$$

   $$\frac{18}{90} = x$$

   $$\frac{1}{5} = x$$

   $$20\% = x$$

2. 10 is 50% of what number?

   $$10 = 0.50(x)$$

   $$\frac{10}{0.50} = x$$

   $$20 = x$$

3. What is 15% of 60?

   $$x = \frac{15}{100} \times 60 = \frac{90}{10} = 9$$

   or

   $$0.15(60) = 9$$

59

Practice: Other Applications of Percent

1. 20 is what percent of 80?

2. 15 is 20% of what number?

3. 18 is what percent of 45?

4. What is 65% of 20?

Answers: Other Applications of Percent

1. $20 = x(80)$

$$\frac{20}{80} = x$$

$$\frac{1}{4} = x$$

$$x = 25\%$$

2. $15 = (0.20)x$

$$\frac{15}{0.20} = x$$

$$x = 75$$

3. $18 = x(45)$

$$\frac{18}{45} = x$$

$$\frac{2}{5} = x$$

$$x = 40\%$$

4. $x = (0.65)20$

$$x = 13$$

Percent—Proportion Method

A *proportion* is a statement that says that two values expressed in fraction form are equal. Since $\frac{5}{10}$ and $\frac{4}{8}$ both have values of $\frac{1}{2}$, it can be stated that $\frac{5}{10} = \frac{4}{8}$.

In a proportion, the cross products (multiplying across the equal sign) always produce equal answers. In the example of $\frac{5}{10} = \frac{4}{8}$, $5 \times 8 = 10 \times 4$.

You can use this cross-products fact in order to solve a proportion. Suppose $\frac{x}{6} = \frac{4}{15}$. Applying the cross-products fact, you get

$$15x = 6 \times 4$$
$$15x = 24$$
$$x = \frac{24}{15} = \frac{8}{5} \text{ or } 1\frac{3}{5} \text{ or } 1.6$$

You can now apply this to percentage problems using the "is/of" method:

$$\frac{\text{percent number}}{100} = \frac{\text{"is" number}}{\text{"of" number}}$$

For example:

30 is what percent of 50?

Because the percent is the unknown, put an x over the 100. The number 30 is next to the word is, so it goes on top of the next fraction, and 50 is next to the word of, so it goes on the bottom of the next fraction. You now have the following proportion:

$$\frac{x}{100} = \frac{30}{50}$$

At this point, if you recognize that $\frac{30}{50} = \frac{60}{100}$, then you could quickly arrive on the answer of 60%. If you don't recognize this fact, you can continue using the cross-products approach:

$$50x = 3,000$$
$$x = 60$$

Hence, 30 is 60% of 50.

This method works for the three basic types of percent questions:

- 30 is what percent of 50?
- 30 is 20% of what number?
- What number is 30% of 50? (In this type of percent question, it's probably easier to simply multiply the numbers.)

Practice: Percent—Proportion Method

1. 40 is what percent of 200?

2. What percent of 25 is 10?

3. What number is 15% of 30?

4. 60 is 20% of what number?

5. 70% of what number is 35?

Answers: Percent—Proportion Method

1. $\dfrac{x}{100} = \dfrac{40}{200}$

   $\dfrac{x}{100} = \dfrac{20}{100}$

   $x = 20$

   Answer: 20%

   You don't have to work this problem out mechanically, because you can reduce $\dfrac{40}{200}$ to $\dfrac{20}{100}$.

2. $\dfrac{x}{100} = \dfrac{10}{25}$

   $25x = 1{,}000$

   $\dfrac{25x}{25} = \dfrac{\overset{40}{1{,}000}}{25}$

   $x = 40$

   Answer: 40%

   You could solve this problem by observing that $4 \times 25 = 100$, so $\dfrac{40}{100} = \dfrac{10}{25}$.

3. $\dfrac{15}{100} = \dfrac{x}{30}$

   $450 = 100x$

   $\dfrac{450}{100} = \dfrac{100x}{100}$

   $x = 4.5$

   Answer: 4.5

4. $\dfrac{20}{100} = \dfrac{60}{x}$ $\dfrac{20}{100} = \dfrac{60}{x}$

   $20x = 6{,}000$ or $\dfrac{1}{5} = \dfrac{60}{x}$

   $\dfrac{20x}{20} = \dfrac{6{,}000}{20}$ $x = 300$

   $x = 300$

   Answer: 300

5. $\dfrac{70}{100} = \dfrac{35}{x}$ $\dfrac{70}{100} = \dfrac{35}{x}$

     $70x = 3,500$

     or $\dfrac{7}{10} = \dfrac{35}{x}$

     $\dfrac{\cancel{70}x}{\cancel{70}} = \dfrac{3,500}{70}$

     $7x = 350$

     $x = 50$ $x = 50$

Answer: 50

Again, this problem could be solved by observing that $\dfrac{70}{100}$ can be reduced to $\dfrac{35}{50}$.

Finding Percent Increase or Percent Decrease

To find the *percent change* (increase or decrease), use:

$$\text{percent change} = \frac{\text{change}}{\text{starting point}} \text{ then convert to a percentage.}$$

For example:

What is the percent decrease of a $500 item on sale for $400?

You know that the starting point is 500 and the change is 500 – 400 = 100. So,

$$\text{percent change} = \frac{\text{change}}{\text{starting point}} = \frac{100}{500} = \frac{1}{5} = 0.20 = 20\% \text{ decrease}$$

What is the percent increase of Jon's salary if it went from $1,500 a month to $2,000 a month?

You know that the starting point is 1,500 and the change is 2,000 – 1,500 = 500.

$$\text{percent change} = \frac{\text{change}}{\text{starting point}} = \frac{500}{1,500} = \frac{1}{3} = 33\tfrac{1}{3}\% \text{ increase}$$

Note that the terms *percentage rise, percentage difference,* and *percentage change* are the same as *percent change*.

Practice: Finding Percent Increase or Percent Decrease

1. Find the percent decrease from 200 to 180.

2. What is the percent difference between a first month's rent of $750 and a second month's rent of $1,000?

3. What is the percent increase in rainfall from January (2.5 inches) to February (4.0 inches)?

4. What is the percent change from 2,100 to 1,890?

Answers: Finding Percent Increase or Percent Decrease

1. $\dfrac{\text{change}}{\text{starting point}} = \dfrac{20}{200} = \dfrac{1}{10} = 10\%$

2. $\dfrac{\text{change}}{\text{starting point}} = \dfrac{250}{750} = \dfrac{1}{3} = 33\dfrac{1}{3}\%$

3. $\dfrac{\text{change}}{\text{starting point}} = \dfrac{1.5}{2.5} = \dfrac{15}{25} = \dfrac{3}{5} = 60\%$

4. $\dfrac{\text{change}}{\text{starting point}} = \dfrac{210}{2,100} = \dfrac{1}{10} = 10\%$

Powers and Exponents

An *exponent* is a positive or negative number or zero placed above and to the right of a quantity. It expresses the power to which the quantity is to be raised or lowered. In 4^3, 3 is the exponent. It shows that 4 is to be used as a factor three times: $4 \times 4 \times 4$. 4^3 is read as *four to the third power* (or *four cubed*). *Some examples:*

$2^4 = 2 \times 2 \times 2 \times 2 = 16$

$3^2 = 3 \times 3 = 9$

$3^5 = 3 \times 3 \times 3 \times 3 \times 3 = 243$

Remember that $x^1 = x$ and $x^0 = 1$ when x is any number (other than 0). *For example:*

$2^1 = 2 \qquad 3^1 = 3 \quad 4^1 = 4$

$2^0 = 1 \qquad 3^0 = 1 \quad 4^0 = 1$

If the exponent is negative, such as 3^{-2}, then the number and exponent may be dropped under the number 1 in a fraction to remove the negative sign. The number can be simplified as follows:

$$3^{-2} = \dfrac{1}{3^2} = \dfrac{1}{9}$$

A few more examples:

$$2^{-3} = \dfrac{1}{2^3} = \dfrac{1}{8} \qquad 3^{-4} = \dfrac{1}{3^4} = \dfrac{1}{81} \qquad 4^{-2} = \dfrac{1}{4^2} = \dfrac{1}{16}$$

Operations with Powers and Exponents

To *multiply* two numbers with exponents, *if the base numbers are the same,* simply keep the base number and add the exponents. *For example:*

1. $2^3 \times 2^5 = 2^8$ $(2 \times 2 \times 2) \times (2 \times 2 \times 2 \times 2 \times 2) = 2^8$

2. $3^2 \times 3^4 = 3^6$

3. $5^4 \times 5^3 = 5^7$

To *divide* two numbers with exponents, *if the base numbers are the same,* simply keep the base number and subtract the second exponent from the first. *For example:*

1. $3^4 \div 3^2 = 3^2$

2. $4^8 \div 4^5 = 4^3$

3. $\dfrac{9^6}{9^2} = 9^4$

To *multiply or divide* numbers with exponents, *if the base numbers are different,* you must simplify each number with an exponent first and then perform the operation. *For example:*

1. $3^2 \times 2^2 = 9 \times 4 = 36$

2. $6^2 \div 2^3 = 36 \div 8 = 4\dfrac{4}{8} = 4\dfrac{1}{2}$

To *add or subtract* numbers with exponents, *whether the base numbers are the same or different,* you must simplify each number with an exponent first and then perform the indicated operation. *For example:*

1. $3^2 - 2^3 = 9 - 8 = 1$

2. $4^3 + 3^2 = 64 + 9 = 73$

If a *number with an exponent is taken to another power* $(4^2)^3$, simply keep the original base number and multiply the exponents. *For example:*

1. $(4^2)^3 = 4^6$

2. $(3^3)^2 = 3^6$

Practice: Operations with Powers and Exponents

Simplify, but leave with a number and one exponent when possible:

1. $2^4 \times 2^7 =$ 7. $4^2 \times 3^3 =$

2. $3^6 \times 3^4 =$ 8. $2^4 \div 3^2 =$

3. $5^3 \times 5 =$ 9. $(4^2)^4 =$

4. $2^9 \div 2^4 =$ 10. $(5^3)^5 =$

5. $4^6 \div 4^2 =$ 11. $(3^4)^3 =$

6. $5^2 \div 5^4 =$ 12. $(6^2)^3 =$

Answers: Operations with Powers and Exponents

1. 2^{11} 7. $16 \times 27 = 432$

2. 3^{10} 8. $16 \div 9 = 1\frac{7}{9}$

3. $5^3 \times 5 = 5^3 \times 5^1 = 5^4$ 9. 4^8

4. 2^5 10. 5^{15}

5. 4^4 11. 3^{12}

6. 5^{-2} or $\frac{1}{5^2}$ 12. 6^6

Scientific Notation

Very large or very small numbers are sometimes written in *scientific notation*. A number written in scientific notation is a number between 1 and 10 and multiplied by a power of 10. *For example:*

1. 2,100,000 written in scientific notation is 2.1×10^6. Simply place the decimal point to get a number between 1 and 10 and then count the digits to the right of the decimal to get the power of 10.

   2.100,000.   *moved 6 digits to the left*

2. 0.0000004 written in scientific notation is 4×10^{-7}. Simply place the decimal point to get a number between 1 and 10 and then count the digits from the original decimal point to the new one.

   .0000004.   *moved 7 digits to the right*

Notice that numbers greater than 1 have positive exponents when expressed in scientific notation, and positive numbers less than 1 have negative exponents when expressed in scientific notation. That is, if a number expressed in scientific notation has a positive exponent, then its value is greater than 1, and if it has a negative exponent, then it is a positive number but is less than 1.

Practice: Scientific Notation

Change the following to scientific notation:

1. 35,000

2. 1,112,000,000

3. 0.00047

4. 0.00000000327

Change the following from scientific notation:

5. 2.6×10^4

6. 3.11×10^7

7. 6.1×10^{-4}

8. 7.22×10^{-6}

Answers: Scientific Notation

1. 3.5×10^4

2. 1.112×10^9

3. 4.7×10^{-4}

4. 3.27×10^{-9}

5. 26,000

6. 31,100,000

7. 0.00061

8. 0.00000722

Multiplication in Scientific Notation

To *multiply* numbers in *scientific notation,* simply multiply the numbers together to get the first number and add the powers of ten to get the second number. *For example:*

1. $(2 \times 10^2)(3 \times 10^4) =$

$$(\overset{\times}{2 \times 10^2})(\overset{+}{3 \times 10^4}) = 6 \times 10^6$$

2. $(6 \times 10^5)(5 \times 10^7) =$

$$(\overset{\times}{6 \times 10^5})(\overset{+}{5 \times 10^7}) = 30 \times 10^{12}$$

This answer must be changed to scientific notation (first number from 1 to 9).

$30 \times 10^{12} = 3.0 \times 10^{13}$

3. $(4 \times 10^{-4})(2 \times 10^5) =$

$$(\overset{\times}{4 \times 10^{-4}})(\overset{+}{2 \times 10^5}) = 8 \times 10^1$$

Practice: Multiplication in Scientific Notation

1. $(3 \times 10^5)(2 \times 10^7) =$

2. $(3.5 \times 10^2)(2.1 \times 10^4) =$

3. $(5 \times 10^4)(9 \times 10^2) =$

4. $(6 \times 10^8)(4 \times 10^{-2}) =$

5. $(2 \times 10^2)(4 \times 10^4)(5 \times 10^6) =$

6. $(1.6 \times 10^{-3})(4.2 \times 10^{-4}) =$

Answers: Multiplication in Scientific Notation

1. 6×10^{12}

2. 7.35×10^{6}

3. $45 \times 10^{6} = 4.5 \times 10^{7}$

4. $24 \times 10^{6} = 2.4 \times 10^{7}$

5. $40 \times 10^{12} = 4.0 \times 10^{13}$

6. 6.72×10^{-7}

Division in Scientific Notation

To divide numbers in scientific notation, simply divide the numbers to get the first number and subtract the powers of ten to get the second number. *For example:*

1. $(8 \times 10^{5}) \div (2 \times 10^{2}) =$

$$\left(8 \times 10^{5}\right) \div \left(2 \times 10^{2}\right) = 4 \times 10^{3}$$

2. $\dfrac{7 \times 10^{9}}{4 \times 10^{3}} = 1.75 \times 10^{6}$

3. $(6 \times 10^{7}) \div (3 \times 10^{9}) =$

$$\left(6 \times 10^{7}\right) \div \left(3 \times 10^{9}\right) = 2 \times 10^{-2}$$

4. $(2 \times 10^{4}) \div (5 \times 10^{2}) =$

$$\left(2 \times 10^{4}\right) \div \left(5 \times 10^{2}\right) = .4 \times 10^{2}$$

This answer must be changed to scientific notation.

$0.4 \times 10^{2} = 4 \times 10^{1}$

5. $(8.4 \times 10^5) \div (2.1 \times 10^{-4}) =$

$$\overbrace{\left(8.4 \times 10^5\right) \div \left(2.1 \times 10^{-4}\right)}^{\div \quad -} = 4 \times 10^{5-(-4)} = 4 \times 10^9$$

Practice: Division in Scientific Notation

1. $(8 \times 10^7) \div (4 \times 10^3) =$

2. $\dfrac{9.3 \times 10^8}{3.1 \times 10^5} =$

3. $(7.5 \times 10^{12}) \div (1.5 \times 10^{15}) =$

4. $(1.2 \times 10^5) \div (4 \times 10^3) =$

5. $(9 \times 10^2) \div (2 \times 10^8) =$

6. $(6 \times 10^4) \div (2 \times 10^{-3}) =$

Answers: Division in Scientific Notation Problems

1. 2×10^4

2. 3×10^3

3. 5×10^{-3}

4. $0.3 \times 10^2 = 3 \times 10^1$

5. 4.5×10^{-6}

6. 3×10^7 [exponents: $4 - (-3) = 4 + 3 = 7$]

Squares and Cubes

Two specific types of powers should be noted: *squares and cubes.* To *square a number,* just multiply it by itself (the exponent would be 2). For example, 6 squared (written 6^2) is 6×6, or 36. 36 is called a *perfect square* (the square of a whole number).

Here is a list of the first 13 perfect squares.

$$0^2 = 0 \qquad\qquad 7^2 = 49$$
$$1^2 = 1 \qquad\qquad 8^2 = 64$$
$$2^2 = 4 \qquad\qquad 9^2 = 81$$
$$3^2 = 9 \qquad\qquad 10^2 = 100$$
$$4^2 = 16 \qquad\qquad 11^2 = 121$$
$$5^2 = 25 \qquad\qquad 12^2 = 144$$
$$6^2 = 36$$

To *cube a number* just multiply it by itself twice (the exponent would be 3). For example, 5 cubed (written 5^3) is $5 \times 5 \times 5$, or 125. 125 is called a *perfect cube* (the cube of a whole number).

Here is a list of the first 8 perfect cubes.

$$0^3 = 0$$
$$1^3 = 1$$
$$2^3 = 8$$
$$3^3 = 27$$
$$4^3 = 64$$
$$5^3 = 125$$
$$6^3 = 216$$
$$7^3 = 343$$

Practice: Powers and Exponents

Give each answer without exponents:

1. $5^4 =$

2. $2^5 =$

3. $6^1 =$

4. $7^0 =$

5. $5^{-2} =$

Answers: Powers and Exponents

1. $5^4 = 5 \times 5 \times 5 \times 5 = 625$

2. $2^5 = 2 \times 2 \times 2 \times 2 \times 2 = 32$

3. $6^1 = 6$

4. $7^0 = 1$

5. $5^{-2} = \dfrac{1}{5^2} = \dfrac{1}{25}$

Square Roots and Cube Roots

Note that square and cube roots and operations with them are often included in algebra sections, and the following will be discussed further in the algebra section.

Square Roots

To find the *square root* of a number, you want to find some number that, when multiplied by itself, gives you the original number. In other words, to find the square root of 25, you want to find the number that, when multiplied by itself, gives you 25. The square root of 25, then, is 5. The symbol for square root is $\sqrt{\ }$.

Here is a list of the first 11 perfect (whole number) square roots.

$$\sqrt{0} = 0 \qquad\qquad \sqrt{36} = 6$$

$$\sqrt{1} = 1 \qquad\qquad \sqrt{49} = 7$$

$$\sqrt{4} = 2 \qquad\qquad \sqrt{64} = 8$$

$$\sqrt{9} = 3 \qquad\qquad \sqrt{81} = 9$$

$$\sqrt{16} = 4 \qquad\qquad \sqrt{100} = 10$$

$$\sqrt{25} = 5$$

Other roots are similarly defined and identified by the index given. ***Special note:*** If no sign (or a positive sign) is placed in front of the square root, then the positive answer is required. Only if a negative sign is in front of the square root is a negative answer required. This notation is used on most standardized exams and will be adhered to in this book. *For example:*

1. $\sqrt{9} = 3$

   $-\sqrt{9} = -3$

2. $\sqrt{16} = 4$

   $-\sqrt{16} = -4$

   $\sqrt{-16}$ is not a real number.

Cube Roots

To find the *cube root* of a number, you want to find some number that, when multiplied by itself twice, gives you the original number. In other words, to find the cube root of 8, you want to find the number that, when multiplied by itself twice, gives you 8. The cube root of 8, then, is 2, since $2 \times 2 \times 2 = 8$. Notice that the symbol for cube root is the square root sign with a small three (called the *index*) above and to the left $\sqrt[3]{}$. (In square root, an index of two is understood and usually not written.) Following is a list of the first five perfect (whole number) cube roots:

$$\sqrt[3]{0} = 0$$

$$\sqrt[3]{1} = 1$$

$$\sqrt[3]{8} = 2$$

$$\sqrt[3]{27} = 3$$

$$\sqrt[3]{64} = 4$$

Notice that the cube root of a negative number is a real number, but that the square root of a negative number is not a real number:

$\sqrt[3]{-8} = -2$, which is a real number

Approximating Square Roots

To find the square root of a number that is not an exact square, you will need to find an approximate answer by using the procedure explained here:

Approximate $\sqrt{42}$.

The $\sqrt{42}$ is between $\sqrt{36}$ and $\sqrt{49}$: $\sqrt{36} < \sqrt{42} < \sqrt{49}$.

$$\sqrt{36} = 6$$

$$\sqrt{49} = 7$$

Therefore, $6 < \sqrt{42} < 7$, and since 42 is halfway between 36 and 49, $\sqrt{42}$ is approximately halfway between $\sqrt{36}$ and $\sqrt{49}$. To check, multiply: $6.5 \times 6.5 = 42.25$, or about 42.

Square roots of nonperfect squares can be approximated or looked up in tables. You may want to keep these two in mind:

$$\sqrt{2} \approx 1.414 \qquad \sqrt{3} \approx 1.732$$

Practice: Approximating Square Root Problems

1. $\sqrt{22}$

2. $\sqrt{71}$

3. $\sqrt{13}$

4. $\sqrt{\dfrac{400}{24}}$

Answers: Approximating Square Root Problems

1. 4.7

   $\sqrt{16} < \sqrt{22} < \sqrt{25}$

   $4 < \sqrt{22} < 5$

   $4 < 4.7 < 5$

   Check:

   4.7
   $\underline{\times\ 4.7}$
   329
   $\underline{188}$
   $22.09 \approx 22$

2. 8.4

   $\sqrt{64} < \sqrt{71} < \sqrt{81}$

   $8 < \sqrt{71} < 9$

   $8 < 8.4 < 9$

   Check:

   8.4
   $\underline{\times\ 8.4}$
   336
   $\underline{672}$
   $70.56 \approx 71$

3. 3.6   Check:

$\sqrt{9} < \sqrt{13} < \sqrt{16}$ 3.6

$3 < \sqrt{13} < 4$ $\times\,3.6$

$3 < 3.6 < 4$ 216

                              108

                              $12.96 \approx 13$

4. 4.1   Check:

$\sqrt{\dfrac{400}{24}} \approx \sqrt{16.7}$ 4.1

$\sqrt{16} < \sqrt{16.7} < \sqrt{25}$ $\times\,4.1$

$4 < \sqrt{16.7} < 5$ 41

$4 < 4.1 < 5$ 164

                              $16.81 \approx 16.7$

Simplifying Square Roots

Sometimes you will have to simplify square roots or write them in simplest form. In fractions, $\frac{2}{4}$ can be reduced to $\frac{1}{2}$. In square roots, $\sqrt{32}$ can be simplified to $4\sqrt{2}$. To *simplify a square root,* first factor the number under the $\sqrt{\ }$ into a counting number times the largest perfect square number that will divide into the number without leaving a remainder. (Perfect square numbers are 1, 4, 9, 16, 25, 36, 49 . . .). *For example:*

$$\sqrt{32} = \sqrt{16 \times 2}$$

Then take the square root of the perfect square number:

$$\sqrt{16 \times 2} = \sqrt{16} \times \sqrt{2} = 4 \times \sqrt{2}$$

and finally write as a single expression: $4\sqrt{2}$.

Remember that most square roots cannot be simplified, as they are already in simplest form—for example, $\sqrt{7}$, $\sqrt{10}$, or $\sqrt{15}$.

Practice: Simplifying Square Roots

Simplify the following:

1. $\sqrt{18}$

2. $\sqrt{75}$

3. $\sqrt{96}$

4. $\sqrt{50}$

Answers: Simplifying Square Roots

1. $\sqrt{18} = \sqrt{9 \times 2}$
$= \sqrt{9} \times \sqrt{2}$
$= 3 \times \sqrt{2}$
$= 3\sqrt{2}$

2. $\sqrt{75} = \sqrt{25 \times 3}$
$= \sqrt{25} \times \sqrt{3}$
$= 5 \times \sqrt{3}$
$= 5\sqrt{3}$

3. $\sqrt{96} = \sqrt{16 \times 6}$
$= \sqrt{16} \times \sqrt{6}$
$= 4 \times \sqrt{6}$
$= 4\sqrt{6}$

4. $\sqrt{50} = \sqrt{25 \times 2}$
$= \sqrt{25} \times \sqrt{3}$
$= 5 \times \sqrt{2}$
$= 5\sqrt{2}$

Data Analysis Review

Probability

Probability is the numerical measure of the chance of an outcome or event occurring. *When all outcomes are equally likely to occur,* the probability of the occurrence of a given outcome can be found by using the following formula:

$$\text{probability} = \frac{\text{number of favorable outcomes}}{\text{number of possible outcomes}}$$

Examples:

1. Using the spinner below, what is the probability of spinning a 6 in one spin?

   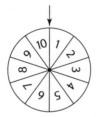

   Since there is only *one* 6 on the spinner out of *ten* numbers and all the numbers are equally spaced, the probability is $\frac{1}{10}$.

2. Using the spinner above, what is the probability of spinning either a 3 or a 5 in one spin?

   Since there are *two favorable outcomes* out of *ten possible outcomes,* the probability is $\frac{2}{10}$, or $\frac{1}{5}$.

   When two events are independent of each other, you need to multiply to find the favorable and/or possible outcomes.

3. What is the probability that both spinners below will stop on a 3 on the first spin?

   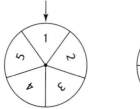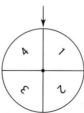

Since the probability that the first spinner will stop on the number 3 is $\frac{1}{5}$ and the probability that the second spinner will stop on the number 3 is $\frac{1}{4}$, and since each event is independent of the other, simply multiply:

$$\frac{1}{5} \times \frac{1}{4} = \frac{1}{20}$$

4. What is the probability that on two consecutive rolls of a die the numbers will be 2 and then 3?

    Since the probability of getting a 2 on the first roll is $\frac{1}{6}$ and the probability of getting a 3 on the second roll is $\frac{1}{6}$, and since the rolls are independent of each other, simply multiply:

    $$\frac{1}{6} \times \frac{1}{6} = \frac{1}{36}$$

5. What is the probability of tossing heads three consecutive times with a two-sided fair coin?

    Since each toss is independent and the probability is $\frac{1}{2}$ for each toss, the probability would be:

    $$\frac{1}{2} \times \frac{1}{2} \times \frac{1}{2} = \frac{1}{8}$$

6. What is the probability of rolling two dice in one toss so that they total 5?

    Since there are six possible outcomes on each die, the total possible outcomes for two dice is $6 \times 6 = 36$. The favorable outcomes are $(1 + 4)$, $(4 + 1)$, $(2 + 3)$, and $(3 + 2)$. These are all the ways of tossing a total of 5 on two dice. Thus, there are four favorable outcomes, which gives the probability of throwing a five as:

    $$\frac{4}{36} = \frac{1}{9}$$

7. Three green marbles, two blue marbles, and five yellow marbles are placed in a jar. What is the probability of selecting at random a green marble on the first draw?

    Since there are ten marbles (total possible outcomes) and three green marbles (favorable outcomes), the probability is $\frac{3}{10}$.

Practice: Probability

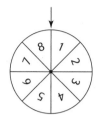

1. Using the equally spaced spinner above, what is the probability of spinning a 4 or greater in one spin?

2. Using the equally spaced spinner above, what is the probability of spinning either a 2 or a 5 on one spin?

3. What is the probability of rolling two dice in one toss so that they total 7?

4. What is the probability of tossing tails four consecutive times with a two-sided fair coin?

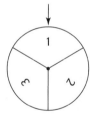
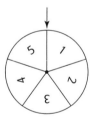

5. What is the probability that each equally spaced spinner above will stop on a 2 on its first spin?

6. In a regular deck of 52 cards, what is the probability of drawing a heart on the first draw? (There are 13 hearts in a deck.)

Answers: Probability

1. Since there are five numbers that are 4 or greater out of the eight numbers and all the numbers are equally spaced, the probability is $\frac{5}{8}$.

2. Since there are two favorable outcomes out of eight possible outcomes, the probability is $\frac{2}{8}$, or $\frac{1}{4}$.

3. Since there are six ways to total 7 on two dice—$(1 + 6)$, $(6 + 1)$, $(2 + 5)$, $(5 + 2)$, $(3 + 4)$, $(4 + 3)$—out of a possible 36 outcomes (6×6), the probability is $\frac{6}{36}$, or $\frac{1}{6}$.

4. Since each toss is independent and the probability is $\frac{1}{2}$ for each toss, the probability would be $\frac{1}{2} \times \frac{1}{2} \times \frac{1}{2} \times \frac{1}{2} = \frac{1}{16}$.

5. Since the probability that the first spinner will stop on the number 2 is $\frac{1}{3}$, and the probability that the second spinner will stop on the number 2 is $\frac{1}{5}$, and since each event is independent of the other, simply multiply:

$$\frac{1}{3} \times \frac{1}{5} = \frac{1}{15}$$

6. Since there are 13 favorable outcomes out of 52 possible outcomes, the probability is $\frac{13}{52}$, or $\frac{1}{4}$.

Combinations and Permutations

If there are a *number of successive choices* to make and the choices are *independent of each other* (order makes no difference), the total number of possible choices *(combinations)* is the product of each of the choices at each stage. *For example:*

1. How many possible combinations of shirts and ties are there if there are five different color shirts and three different color ties?

   To find the total number of possible combinations, simply multiply the number of shirts times the number of ties:

   $5 \times 3 = 15$

If there are a *number of successive choices* to make and the choices are *affected by the previous choice or choices* (dependent upon order), then *permutations* are involved.

2. How many ways can you arrange the letters S, T, O, P in a row?

number of choices for the first letter		number of choices for the second letter		number of choices for the third letter		number of choices for the fourth letter
4	×	3	×	2	×	1

$$4! = 4 \times 3 \times 2 \times 1 = 24$$

The product $4 \times 3 \times 2 \times 1$ can be written 4! (read *4 factorial* or *factorial 4*). Thus, there are 24 different ways to arrange four different letters.

Following is a more difficult type of combination involving permutations.

3. In how many ways can four out of seven books be arranged on a shelf?

    Notice that the order in which the books are displayed makes a difference. The symbol to denote this is $P(n, r)$, which is read as the permutations of n things taken r at a time. The formula used is

    $$P(n,r) = \frac{n!}{(n-r)!}$$

    Since $n = 7$ and $r = 4$, (seven taken three at a time) the equation becomes

    $$\frac{7!}{(7-4)!} = \frac{7!}{3!} = \frac{7 \times 6 \times 5 \times 4 \times 3 \times 2 \times 1}{3 \times 2 \times 1} = 7 \times 6 \times 5 \times 4 = 840$$

4. If, from among five people, three executives are to be selected, how many possible combinations of executives are there? (Notice that the order of selection makes no difference.) The symbol used to denote this situation is $C(n, r)$, which is read as the number of combinations of n things taken r at a time. The formula used is

    $$C(n,r) = \frac{n!}{r!(n-r)!}$$

    Since $n = 5$ and $r = 3$ (five people taken three at a time), then the equation is as follows:

    $$\frac{5!}{3!(5-3)!} = \frac{5 \times \overset{2}{\cancel{4}} \times \cancel{3} \times \cancel{2} \times 1}{\cancel{3} \times \cancel{2} \times 1(\cancel{2} \times 1)} = 10$$

If the problem involves very few possibilities, you may want to actually list the possible combinations.

Practice: Combinations and Permutations Problems

1. How many possible outfits could Tim wear if he has three different color shirts, four different types of slacks, and two pairs of shoes?

2. A three-digit PIN requires the use of the numbers from 0 to 9. How many different possible PINs exist?

3. How many different ways are there to arrange three jars in a row on a shelf?

4. There are nine horses in a race. How many different 1st-, 2nd-, and 3rd-place finishes are possible?

5. A coach is selecting a starting lineup for her basketball team. She must select from among nine players to get her starting lineup of five. How many possible starting lineups could she have?

6. How many possible combinations of *a*, *b*, *c*, and *d* taken two at a time are there?

Answers: Combinations and Permutations Problems

1. To find the total number of possible combinations, simply multiply the numbers together.

   $3 \times 4 \times 2 = 24$

2. Note that each position in the PIN is independent of the others; thus, since each has a possible of ten numbers, $10 \times 10 \times 10 = 1,000$ possible PINs.

3. Since the order of the items is affected by the previous choice(s), the number of different ways equals 3!, or $3 \times 2 \times 1 = 6$ different ways.

4. Since the order in which a horse finishes makes a difference, use the permutations formula with $n = 9$ and $r = 3$.

$$\frac{9!}{(9-3)!} = \frac{9!}{6!} = \frac{9 \times 8 \times 7 \times 6 \times 5 \times 4 \times 3 \times 2 \times 1}{6 \times 5 \times 4 \times 3 \times 2 \times 1} = 9 \times 8 \times 7 = 504$$

5. The order in which players is selected does not matter; thus, use the combinations formula. Since $n = 9$ and $r = 5$ (nine players taken five at a time), the equation is as follows:

$$\frac{9!}{5!(9-5)!} = \frac{9 \times 8 \times 7 \times 6 \times 5 \times 4 \times 3 \times 2 \times 1}{5 \times 4 \times 3 \times 2 \times 1(4)!} =$$

$$\frac{9 \times \overset{2}{8} \times 7 \times \overset{\frac{1}{2}}{6} \times 5 \times 4 \times 3 \times 2 \times 1}{5 \times 4 \times 3 \times 2 \times 1(4 \times 3 \times 2 \times 1)} = 126$$

6. Since $n = 4$ and $r = 2$ (four letters taken two at a time), the equation is as follows:

$$\frac{4!}{2!(4-2)!} = \frac{4!}{2!(2)!} = \frac{\overset{2}{\cancel{4}} \times 3 \times \cancel{2} \times 1}{\cancel{2} \times 1 (\cancel{2} \times 1)} = 6$$

You might simply have listed the possible combinations as *ab, ac, ad, bc, bd,* and *cd.*

Statistics

Some Basics: Measures of Central Tendencies

Any measure indicating a center of a distribution is called a *measure of central tendency.* The three basic measures of central tendency are

- mean (or arithmetic mean)
- median
- mode

Mean

The *mean* (arithmetic mean) is what is usually called the average. The arithmetic mean is the most frequently used measure of central tendency. It is generally reliable, is easy to use, and is more stable than the median. To determine the arithmetic mean, simply total the items and then divide by the number of items. *For example:*

1. What is the arithmetic mean of 0, 12, 18, 20, 31, and 45?

   $0 + 12 + 18 + 20 + 31 + 45 = 126$

   $126 \div 6 = 21$

   The arithmetic mean is 21.

2. What is the arithmetic mean of 25, 27, 27, and 27?

   $25 + 27 + 27 + 27 = 106$

   $106 \div 4 = 26\frac{1}{2}$

   The arithmetic mean is $26\frac{1}{2}$.

3. What is the arithmetic mean of 20 and –10?

   $20 + (–10) = +10$

   $10 ÷ 2 = 5$

   The arithmetic mean is 5.

Practice: Arithmetic Mean Problems

1. Find the arithmetic mean of 3, 6, and 12.

2. Find the arithmetic mean of 2, 8, 15, and 23.

3. Find the arithmetic mean of 26, 28, 36, and 40.

4. Find the arithmetic mean of 3, 7, –5, and –13.

Answers: Arithmetic Mean Problems

1. $21 ÷ 3 = 7$

2. $48 ÷ 4 = 12$

3. $130 ÷ 4 = 32\frac{1}{2}$

4. $–8 ÷ 4 = –2$

Weighted Mean

When one or a number of items is used several times, those items have more "weight." This establishment of relative importance or weighting is used to compute the *weighted mean. For example:*

What is the mean of three tests averaging 70% plus seven tests averaging 85%?

In effect, you have here ten exams, three of which score 70% and seven of which score 85%. Instead of adding all ten scores, to determine the above "weighted mean," simply multiply 3 times 70% to find the total of those items (210); then multiply 7 times 85% to find their total (595). Now add the two totals (210 + 595 = 805) and divide by the number of items overall (10). The weighted mean is, thus, 80.5%.

Practice: Weighted Mean Problems

1. For the first nine months of the year, the average monthly rainfall was 2 inches. For the last three months of that year, rainfall averaged 4 inches per month. What was the mean monthly rainfall for the entire year?

2. Six students averaged 90% on a class test. Four other students averaged 70% on the test. What was the mean score of all ten students?

Answers: Weighted Mean Problems

1. $9 \times 2" = 18"$

    $3 \times 4" = 12"$

    Total = 30" divided by 12 months in all = 2.5" monthly mean

2. $6 \times 90 = 540$

    $4 \times 70 = 280$

    Total = 820 divided by 10 students = 82%

Median

The *median* of a set of numbers arranged in ascending or descending order is the middle number (*if* there is an odd number of items in the set). If there is an even number of items in the set, their median is the arithmetic mean of the middle two numbers. The median is easy to calculate and is not influenced by extreme measurements. *For example:*

1. Find the median of 3, 4, 6, 9, 21, 24, 56.

    9 is the median.

2. Find the median of 4, 5, 6, 10.

    $5\frac{1}{2}$ is the median.

Practice: Median Problems

Find the median of each group of numbers.

1. 9, 3, 5

2. 18, 16, 0, 7, 12

3. 100, 101, 102, 20

4. 71, −5, −3, −100

Answers: Median Problems

1. 5   3,⑤,9

2. 12   0, 7,⑫, 16, 18

3. 100.5   20, 100, 101, 102   (100.5)

4. −4   −100, −5, −3, 71   (−4)

Mode

The set, class, or classes that appear most, or whose frequency is the greatest is the *mode* or modal class. In order to have a mode, there must be a repetition of a data value. (Mode is not greatly influenced by extreme cases but is probably the least important or least used of the three types.) *For example:*

Find the mode of 3, 4, 8, 9, 9, 2, 6, 11

The mode is 9 because it appears more often than any other number.

Practice: Mode Problems

Find the mode of each group of numbers.

1. 2, 2, 3

2. 8, 4, 3, 5, 4, 6

3. 7, 8, 4, −3, 2, −3

4. 100, 101, 100, 102, 100, 101

Answers: Mode Problems

1. 2

2. 4

3. −3

4. 100

Range

For a set of numbers, the *range* is the difference between the largest and the smallest number. The range depends solely on the extreme values. *For example:*

Find the range of the following numbers. 3, 5, 7, 3, 2

$7 - 2 = 5$

The range is 5.

Practice: Range Problems

1. Find the range of 2, 45, 106, 99

2. Find the range of 6, 101, 152, –5

Answers: Range Problems

1. $106 - 2 = 104$
2. $152 - (-5) = 157$

Practice: Measures of Central Tendencies Problems

Find the mean, mode, median, and range of each of the following sets.

1. 7, 8, 8, 14, 18

2. 9, 10, 106, 120, 120

3. –3, –1, 0, 2, 2, 3

Answers: Measure of Central Tendencies Problems

1. Mean = 11

   $55 \div 5 = 11$

   Mode = 8

   Median = 8

   Range = 11

   $18 - 7 = 11$

2. Mean = 73

   $365 \div 5 = 73$

   Mode = 120

   Median = 106

   Range = 111

   $120 - 9 = 111$

3. Mean = 0.5

   $3 \div 6 = 0.5$

   Mode = 2

   Median = 1

   average of 0 and 2

   Range = 6

   $3 - (-3) = 6$

Standard Deviation

The *standard deviation* of a set of data is a measure of how far data values of a population are from the mean value of the population. A small standard deviation indicates that the data values tend to be very close to the mean value. A large standard deviation indicates that the data values are "spread out" from the mean value.

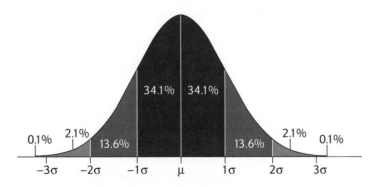

The diagram above represents a set of data that has a normal distribution. In it, μ represents the mean value of the set of data. Each colored band has a width of one standard deviation. For normally distributed data, you will find approximately 68% of all the data values within one standard deviation from the mean. You will find approximately 95.5% of all the data values within two standard deviations from the mean. At three standard deviations from the mean, approximately 99.8% of all the data values are found.

The basic method for calculating the standard deviation for a population is lengthy and time consuming. It involves five steps:

1. Find the mean value for the set of data.
2. For each data value, find the difference between it and the mean value; then square that difference.
3. Find the sum of the squares found in Step 2.
4. Divide the sum found in Step 3 by how many data values there are.
5. Find the square root of the value found in Step 4.

The result found in Step 4 is referred to as the *variance*. The square root of the variance is the standard deviation. *For example:*

Find the variance and standard deviation for the following set of data.

$\{3,7,7,8,10\}$

1. Find the mean value: $\dfrac{3+7+7+8+10}{5} = \dfrac{35}{5} = 7$

2. Find the squares of the differences between the data values and the mean.

Data Value	Mean	Data Value – Mean	(Data Value – Mean)^2
3	7	(–4)	16
7	7	(0)	0
7	7	(0)	0
8	7	(1)	1
10	7	3	9

3. Find the sum of the squares from Step 2: 26.
4. Divide the sum from Step 3 by how many data values there are: $\dfrac{26}{5} = 5.2$. Variance = 5.2.
5. Find the square root of the value found in Step 4: standard deviation $= \sqrt{5.2} \approx 2.28$.

If each data value in this example were increased by the same amount, certain statistical values would be affected while others would not. The statistical values that would be affected are the mean, median, and mode. The statistical values that would not be affected are the range, variance, and standard deviation. The mean, median, and mode would each increase by the amount that each data value was increased. *For example:*

A scientist discovered that the instrument used for an experiment was off by 2 milligrams. If each weight in his experiment needed to be increased by 2 milligrams, then which of the following statistical measures would not be affected?

   I.   mean

  II.   median

 III.   mode

 IV.   range

  V.   standard deviation

  A.   I and II only

  B.   II and III only

  C.   III and IV only

  D.   IV and V only

Answer: D. Only range and standard deviation would not be affected.

Number Sequences

Progressions of numbers are sequences with some patterns. Unless the sequence has a simple repeat pattern (1, 2, 4, 1, 2, 4, . . . or 1, 1, 2, 2, 2, 3, 3, 3, 3, . . .), you should first look for a *common difference between the numbers* to solve the problem. *For example:*

$$\underset{4,\quad\ \ 8,\quad\ 12,\quad\ 16,\quad\ 20,\dots}{\overset{+4\quad\ +4\quad\ +4\quad\ +4}{\frown\ \frown\ \frown\ \frown}}$$

If this does not give the pattern, you may want to take a closer look at the difference between the numbers to see if a *pattern* arises there. *For example:*

$$\underset{1,\quad\ 2,\quad\ 4,\quad\ 7,\quad\ 11,\quad\ 16,\dots}{\overset{+1\quad\ +2\quad\ +3\quad\ +4\quad\ +5}{\frown\ \frown\ \frown\ \frown\ \frown}}$$

If this does not give the pattern, you may want to check to see if the numbers themselves are being added, multiplied, or squared (subtracted or divided is also possible but not as common) to get the following number. *For example:*

1. $(2+3=5)$ $(5+8=13)$

   2,   3,   5,   8,   13,   21,...

            $(3+5=8)$

2. $(2\times4=8)$

   2,   8,   32,   128,...

        $(8\times4=32)$

Finally, if using the actual numbers or the relationships between adjacent numbers doesn't solve the pattern, you should try to find a pattern between adjacent numbers or possibly even the use of more than one operation between adjacent numbers. *For example:*

1.   +2   +2   +2   +2

    1,   5,   3,   7,   5,   9

2. $(0\times1)+1=1$ $(1\times2)+1=3$

    0,   1,   1,   2,   3,   7,   22,...

      $(1\times1)+1=2$ $(2\times3)+1=7$

Multiply adjacent numbers and add 1.

Practice: Number Sequence Problems

Find the next number in each sequence.

1. 37, 35, 32, 28, 23, _____

2. 31, 33, 29, 35, 27, 37, 25, _____

3. 2, 6, 18, 54, _____

4. 0, 10, 19, 27, 34, 40, _____

5. 49, 64, 81, 100, 121, _____

6. 3, 9, 4, 8, 5, 7, 6, _____

7. 1, 3, 2, 5, 9, 44, _____

Answers: Number Sequence Problems

1. 17 (–2, –3, –4, and so on)

2. 39 (+2, –4, +6, –8, and so on, or alternate numbers –2 then +2)

3. 162 (multiplying by 3)

4. 45 (+10, +9, +8, +7, and so on)

5. 144 (consecutive perfect squares)

6. 6 (alternate numbers up 1, down 1) (+6, –5, +4, –3, +2, –1, 0)

7. 395 (multiply adjacent numbers and subtract 1) (very difficult)

Measures

Measurement Systems

Customary System, or English System

Length

12 inches (in.) = 1 foot (ft.)

3 feet = 1 yard (yd.)

36 inches = 1 yard

1,760 yards = 1 mile (mi.)

5,280 feet = 1 mile

Area

144 square inches (sq. in.) = 1 square foot (sq. ft.)

9 square feet = 1 square yard (sq. yd.)

Weight

16 ounces (oz.) = 1 pound (lb.)

2,000 pounds = 1 ton (T)

Capacity

2 cups = 1 pint (pt.)

2 pints = 1 quart (qt.)

4 quarts = 1 gallon (gal.)

4 pecks = 1 bushel

Time

365 days = 1 year

52 weeks = 1 year

10 years = 1 decade

100 years = 1 century

Metric System

Length—meter

Kilometer (km) = 1,000 meters (m)

Hectometer (hm) = 100 meters

Decameter (dam) = 10 meters

10 decimeters (dm) = 1 meter

100 centimeters (cm) = 1 meter

1,000 millimeters (mm) = 1 meter

Volume—liter

1,000 milliliters (ml, or mL) = 1 liter (1, or L)

1,000 liters = 1 kiloliter (kl, or kL)

Mass—gram

1,000 milligrams (mg) = 1 gram (g)

1,000 grams = 1 kilogram (kg)

1,000 kilograms = 1 metric ton (t)

Some approximations

A meter is a little more than a yard.

A kilometer is about 0.6 mile.

A kilogram is about 2.2 pounds.

A liter is slightly more than a quart.

Converting Units of Measure

Examples:

1. If 36 inches equals 1 yard, then 3 yards equals how many inches?

   Intuitively: $3 \times 36 = 108$ inches

   By proportion: $\dfrac{\text{yards}}{\text{inches}} : \dfrac{3}{x} = \dfrac{1}{36}$

   Remember to set the same units across from each other—inches across from inches, yards across from yards. Then solve:

   $$\frac{3}{x} = \frac{1}{36}$$
   $$108 = x$$
   $$x = 108 \text{ inches}$$

2. If 2.2 pounds equals 1 kilogram, then 10 pounds equals approximately how many kilograms?

   Intuitively: $10 \div 2.2 = 4.5$ kilograms

   By proportion: $\dfrac{\text{kilograms}}{\text{pounds}} : \dfrac{1}{2.2} = \dfrac{x}{10}$

   $$2.2x = 10$$
   $$\frac{\cancel{2.2}x}{\cancel{2.2}} = \frac{10}{2.2}$$
   $$x \approx 4.5 \text{ kilograms}$$

3. Change 3 decades into weeks.

   Since 1 decade equals 10 years and 1 year equals 52 weeks, then 3 decades equal 30 years.

   30 years × 52 weeks = 1,560 weeks in 30 years or 3 decades

   Notice that this was converted step-by-step. It could have been done in one step:

   $3 \times 10 \times 52 = 1,560$ weeks

Practice: *Simple Conversion Problems*

1. If 1,760 yards equal 1 mile, how many yards are in 5 miles?

2. If 1 kilometer equals approximately 0.6 mile, approximately how many kilometers are there in 3 miles?

3. How many cups are in 3 gallons?

4. How many ounces are in 6 pounds?

5. If 1 kilometer equals 1,000 meters and 1 decameter equals 10 meters, how many decameters are in

   a. 1 kilometer
   b. 3 kilometers

Answers: *Simple Conversion Problems*

1. $1,760 \times 5 = 8,800$ yards in 5 miles.

$$\frac{\text{yards}}{\text{miles}} : \frac{x}{5} = \frac{1760}{1}$$
$$x = 1,760 \times 5$$
$$x = 8,800 \text{ yards}$$

2.
$$\frac{1}{0.6} = \frac{x}{3}$$
$$\frac{\text{kilometers}}{\text{miles}} : \frac{x}{3} = \frac{1}{0.6}$$
$$0.6x = 3$$
$$\frac{\cancel{0.6}x}{\cancel{0.6}} = \frac{3}{0.6}$$
$$x = 5 \text{ kilometers}$$

3. $4 \times 3 \times 2 \times 2 = 48$ cups in 3 gallons.

   1 gallon = 4 quarts

   Therefore, 3 gallons = 3(4)=12 quarts

   1 quart = 4 cups

   Therefore, 12 quarts = 12(4) = 48 cups

4. $6 \times 16 = 96$ ounces in 6 pounds.

   $$\frac{\text{ounces}}{\text{pounds}} : \frac{x}{6} = \frac{16}{1}$$
   $$x = 6 \times 16$$
   $$x = 96 \text{ ounces}$$

5. a. $\frac{1}{10} = \frac{x}{1,000}$

   1 kilometer = 1,000 meters

   1 decameter = 10 meters

   $$\frac{\text{decameters}}{\text{meters}} : \frac{1}{10} = \frac{x}{1000}$$
   $$10x = 1,000$$
   $$10x = 1,000$$
   $$\frac{\cancel{10}x}{\cancel{10}} = \frac{1,000}{10}$$
   $$x = 100 \text{ decameters}$$

   b. $\frac{1}{10} = \frac{x}{3,000}$

   1 kilometer = 1,000 meters

   Therefore, 3 kilometers = 3,000 meters

   1 decameter = 10 meters

   $$\frac{\text{decameters}}{\text{meters}} : \frac{1}{10} = \frac{x}{3,000}$$
   $$10x = 3,000$$
   $$\frac{\cancel{10}x}{\cancel{10}} = \frac{3,000}{10}$$
   $$x = 300 \text{ decameters}$$

Arithmetic and Data Analysis
Review Test

Questions

Arithmetic

1. The numbers 1, 2, 3, 4, . . . are called _____.

2. The numbers 0, 1, 2, 3, . . . are called _____.

3. The numbers . . . –2, –1, 0, 1, 2, . . . are called _____.

4. Fractions and integers fall into a category called _____

5. $\sqrt{3}$ and π are examples of _____.

6. A prime number is a number that can be divided evenly only by _____.

7. A composite number is divisible by _____.

8. The first four square numbers greater than zero are _____, _____, _____, _____.

9. The first four cube numbers greater than zero are _____, _____, _____, _____.

10. Give the symbol or symbols for each of the following.
    (a) is equal to _____
    (b) is not equal to _____
    (c) is greater than _____
    (d) is less than _____
    (e) is greater than or equal to _____
    (f) is less than or equal to _____
    (g) is parallel to _____

11. "5 times 4" can be written a number of ways. Show three of them.
    _____, _____, _____

12. List the properties that are represented by each of the following.

   (a) $3 + 0 = 3$

   (b) $4 \times 1 = 4$

   (c) $3 + 6 = 6 + 3$

   (d) $4 + (6 + 2) = (4 + 6) + 2$

   (e) $3 + (-3) = 0$

   (f) $4(3 + 5) = 4(3) + 4(5)$

   (g) $7 \times \frac{1}{7} = 1$

   (h) $6 \times 8 = 8 \times 6$

   (i) $(2 \times 6) \times 3 = 2 \times (6 \times 3)$

13. In the number 543,216, which digit is in the ten thousands place?

14. Express 367 in expanded notation.

15. $(4 \times 10^2) + (3 \times 10^0) + (2 \times 10^{-2}) =$

16. Simplify $3[5 + 2(3 - 1)]$.

17. Simplify $2 + 3\{2 + 4[6 + 4(2 + 1)]\}$.

18. Simplify $8 + 2 \times 6 + 10^2 + (2 + 3) \times 5$.

19. Round off 7.1779 to the nearest thousandth.

20. Complete the number line below:

21. $-8 + 5 =$

22. $8 - 17 =$

23. $-6 - 5 =$

24. $12 - (-6) =$

25. $\begin{array}{r} -19 \\ -+24 \\ \hline \end{array}$

26. $12 - (4 - 7 + 6) =$

27. $(-18)(5) =$

28. $-15 \div -3 =$

29. $0 \div 5 =$

30. $\dfrac{8}{0} =$

31. The number 8,424 is divisible by which numbers between 1 and 10?

32. An improper fraction has _____.

33. Change $\dfrac{17}{3}$ to a mixed number.

34. Change $9\dfrac{1}{4}$ to an improper fraction.

35. Reduce $\dfrac{14}{35}$.

36. Change $\dfrac{1}{4}$ to twelfths.

37. List all the factors of 30.

38. Find the greatest common factor of 18 and 24.

39. List the first four multiples of 7.

40. Find the least common multiple of 6 and 8.

41. $\dfrac{3}{7} + \dfrac{4}{5} =$

42. $-\dfrac{6}{7} + \dfrac{1}{4} =$

43. $\dfrac{5}{8} - \dfrac{1}{3} =$

44. $\dfrac{1}{4} - \dfrac{2}{3} =$

45. $3\dfrac{1}{5} + 4\dfrac{3}{8} =$

46. $-5\dfrac{1}{2} + 4\dfrac{1}{4} =$

47. $6\frac{1}{4} - 3\frac{3}{5} =$

48. $\frac{3}{5} \times \frac{25}{36} =$

49. $-\frac{1}{6} \times -\frac{2}{7} =$

50. $8 \times \frac{1}{6} =$

51. $-6\frac{1}{2} \times 2\frac{4}{13} =$

52. $\frac{4}{9} \div \frac{5}{8} =$

53. $\dfrac{\frac{3}{4}}{\frac{4}{5}}$

54. $4\frac{1}{3} \div 3\frac{3}{4} =$

55. Simplify $\dfrac{1}{2 + \dfrac{1}{4 + \frac{1}{2}}}$.

56. Change 0.35 to a fraction in lowest terms.

57. $4.6 + 3.924 + 1.88 =$

58. $6.009 - 4.11 =$

59. $8.9 \times 0.32 =$

60. $23.44 \div 0.4 =$

61. Change $\frac{5}{8}$ to a decimal.

62. Change 0.66 to a fraction in lowest terms.

63. Change 0.6 to a percent.

64. Change 57% to a decimal.

65. Change $\frac{7}{25}$ to a percent.

66. Change 78% to a fraction in lowest terms.

67. What is 45% of 30?

68. 15 is what percent of 120?

69. 21 is 30% of what number?

70. What is the percent increase from 120 to 150?

71. Express 360,000 in scientific notation.

72. Express 0.0002 in scientific notation.

73. $(3 \times 10^5)(2 \times 10^7) =$

74. $(7 \times 10^3)(5 \times 10^8) =$

75. $(1.5 \times 10^{-6})(3 \times 10^8) =$

76. $(9 \times 10^8) \div (3 \times 10^3) =$

77. $\dfrac{9 \times 10^2}{5 \times 10^8} =$

78. $(3 \times 10^7) \div (5 \times 10^{-4}) =$

79. $4^3 =$

80. $8^0 =$

81. $5^{-2} =$

82. $7^3 \times 7^5 =$ (with exponent)

83. $5^8 \div 5^3 =$ (with exponent)

84. $8^2 \times 3^2 =$

85. $2^6 - 5^2 =$

86. $(4^3)^2 =$ (with exponent)

87. $\sqrt{64} =$

88. $\sqrt[3]{27} =$

89. $\sqrt{-25} =$

90. $\sqrt[3]{-64} =$

91. Approximate $\sqrt{50}$ to the nearest tenth.

92. Simplify $\sqrt{60}$.

Data Analysis

1. Using the equally spaced spinner (below), what is the probability of spinning either an A or a B in one spin?

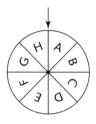

2. What is the probability that equally spaced spinner A will stop on 5 and equally spaced spinner B will stop on 2 if each spinner is given one spin?

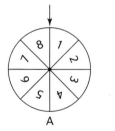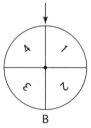

3. What is the probability of rolling two dice on one toss so that the sum is 6?

4. What is the probability of tossing tails five consecutive times with a two-sided fair coin?

5. How many different ways are there to arrange four books in a row on a shelf?

6. If among five people, two game-show contestants must be chosen, how many possible combinations of contestants are there?

7. Find the arithmetic mean, mode, median, and range of the following set of numbers. 7, 4, 3, 9, 6, 8, 9

8. Find the next number in the sequence. 4, 6, 9, 13, 18, _____

9. How many ounces in 12 pounds?

10. If 1 decimeter is 10 centimeters and 1 centimeter is 10 millimeters, then how many millimeters are there in a decimeter?

11. In how many different ways can six of nine books be arranged on a shelf?

Answers

Arithmetic

Page numbers following each answer refer to the review section applicable to this problem type.

1. natural or counting numbers (p. 10)

2. whole numbers (p. 10)

3. integers (p. 10)

4. rational numbers (p. 10)

5. irrational numbers (p. 10)

6. one and itself (p. 10)

7. more than just 1 and itself (p. 10)

8. 1, 4, 9, 16 (p. 10)

9. 1, 8, 27, 64 (p. 10)

10. $(a) =, (b) \neq, (c) >, (d) <, (e) \geq, (f) \leq, (g) \parallel$ (p. 11)

11. 5×4, $5 \cdot 4$, $5(4)$ (p. 11)

12. (a) additive identity (p. 12)

    (b) multiplicative identity (p. 12)

    (c) commutative property of addition (p. 11)

    (d) associative property of addition (p. 12)

    (e) additive inverse (p. 12)

    (f) distributive property of multiplication and addition (p. 13)

    (g) multiplicative inverse (p. 13)

    (h) commutative property of multiplication (p. 12)

    (i) associative property of multiplication (p. 12)

13. 4 (p. 13)

14. $(3 \times 10^2) + (6 \times 10^1) + (7 \times 10^0)$ (p. 14)

15. 403.02 (p. 14)

16. 27 (p. 15)

17. 224 (p. 15)

18. 145 (p. 16)

19. 7.178 (p. 18)

20. $A = -2, B = -1, C = \frac{1}{2}, D = 1\frac{1}{2}$ (p. 19)

21. -3 (p. 20)

22. -9 (p. 21)

23. -11 (p. 21)

24. $+18$ (p. 23)

25. -43 (p. 21)

26. 9 (p. 23)

27. -90 (p. 24)

28. 5 (p. 24)

29. 0 (p. 24)

30. undefined (p. 25)

31. 2, 3, 4, 6, 8, 9 (p. 25)

32. a numerator that is larger than or equal to the denominator (p. 27)

33. $5\frac{2}{3}$ (p. 28)

34. $\frac{37}{4}$ (p. 28)

35. $\frac{2}{5}$ (p. 29)

36. $\frac{3}{12}$ (p. 31)

37. 1, 2, 3, 5, 6, 10, 15, 30 (p. 32)

38. 6 (p. 32)

39. 7, 14, 21, 28 (p. 34)

40. 24 (p. 34)

41. $\frac{43}{35} = 1\frac{8}{35}$ (p. 35)

42. $-\frac{17}{28}$ (p. 37)

43. $\frac{7}{24}$ (p. 38)

44. $-\frac{5}{12}$ (p. 38)

45. $7\frac{23}{40}$ (p. 40)

46. $-1\frac{1}{4}$ (p. 40)

47. $2\frac{13}{20}$ (p. 42)

48. $\frac{5}{12}$ (p. 43)

49. $\frac{1}{21}$ (p. 43)

50. $\frac{4}{3} = 1\frac{1}{3}$ (p. 43)

51. −15 (p. 45)

52. $\frac{32}{45}$ (p. 46)

53. $\frac{15}{16}$ (p. 46)

54. $\frac{52}{45} = 1\frac{7}{45}$ (p. 47)

55. $\frac{9}{20}$ (p. 48)

56. $\frac{7}{20}$ (p. 50)

57. 10.404 (p. 51)

58. 1.899 (p. 51)

59. 2.848 (p. 52)

60. 58.6 (p. 53)

61. 0.625 (p. 53)

62. $\frac{33}{50}$ (p. 50)

63. 60% (p. 54)

64. 0.57 (p. 55)

65. 28% (p. 56)

66. $\frac{39}{50}$ (p. 57)

67. 13.5 or $13\frac{1}{2}$ (p. 58)

68. 12.5% (p. 59)

69. 70 (p. 59)

70. 25% (p. 63)

71. 3.6×10^{5} (p. 66)

72. 2×10^{-4} (p. 66)

73. 6×10^{12} (p. 68)

74. $35 \times 10^{11} = 3.5 \times 10^{12}$ (p. 68)

75. 4.5×10^{2} (p. 68)

76. 3×10^{5} (p. 69)

77. 1.8×10^{-6} (p. 69)

78. $0.6 \times 10^{11} = 6 \times 10^{10}$ (p. 69)

79. 64 (p. 64)

80. 1 (p. 64)

81. $\frac{1}{25}$ or $\frac{1}{5^{2}}$ (p. 64)

82. 7^{8} (p. 65)

83. 5^{5} (p. 65)

84. 576 (p. 65)

85. 39 (p. 65)

86. 4^{6} (p. 65)

87. 8 (p. 72)

88. 3 (p. 73)

89. not a real number (p. 73)

90. −4 (p. 73)

91. 7.1 (p. 73)

92. $2\sqrt{15}$ (p. 75)

Data Analysis

1. $\frac{2}{8} = \frac{1}{4}$ (p. 77)

2. $\frac{1}{32}$ (p. 77)

3. $\frac{5}{36}$ (p. 77)

4. $\frac{1}{32}$ (p. 77)

5. 24 ways (p. 80)

6. 10 possible combinations (p. 83)

7. mean $= 6\frac{4}{7}$, mode = 9, median = 7, range = 6 (p. 83)

8. 24 (p. 90)

9. 192 ounces (p. 92)

10. 100 millimeters (p. 93)

11. 60,480 permutations (p. 80)

Arithmetic Glossary of Terms

additive inverse: The opposite (negative) of the number. Any number plus its additive inverse equals 0.

associative property: Grouping of elements does not make any difference in the outcome. Only true for multiplication and addition.

braces: Grouping symbols used after the use of brackets. Also used to represent a set. { }

brackets: Grouping symbols used after the use of parentheses. [ ]

canceling: In multiplication of fractions, dividing the same number into both a numerator and a denominator.

closure property: When all answers fall into the original set.

combinations: The total number of possible choices when the order in which they occur does not matter.

common denominator: A number that can be divided evenly by all denominators in the problem.

common factors: Factors that are the same for two or more numbers.

common multiples: Multiples that are the same for two or more numbers.

commutative property: Order of elements does not make any difference in the outcome. Only true for multiplication and addition.

complex fraction: A fraction having a fraction or fractions in the numerator and/or denominator.

composite number: A number divisible by more than just 1 and itself (4, 6, 8, 9, . . .). 0 and 1 are *not* composite numbers.

cube (of a number): The result when a number is used as factor three times or when the number is raised to the third power.

cube root: The value that when raised to the third power gives the original number. For example, the cube root of 125 is 5. The cube root symbol is $\sqrt[3]{\ }$, $\sqrt[3]{125} = 5$.

decimal fraction: Fraction with a denominator 10, 100 , 1,000, and so on, written using a decimal point—for example, 0.3, 0.275.

decimal point: A point used to distinguish decimal fractions from whole numbers.

denominator: The bottom symbol or number of a fraction.

108

dependent events: When the outcome of one event has a bearing or effect on the outcome of another event.

difference: The result of subtraction.

distributive property: The process of distributing the number on the outside of the parentheses to each number on the inside: $a(b + c) = ab + ac$.

even number: An integer (positive whole numbers, zero, and negative whole numbers) divisible by 2 with no remainder.

expanded notation: Pointing out the place value of each digit in a number by writing the number as the digit times its place value: $342 = (3 \times 10^2) + (4 \times 10^1) + (2 \times 10^0)$.

exponent: A positive or negative number or zero placed above and to the right of a number. Expresses the power to which the quantity is to be raised or lowered.

factor (noun): A number or symbol that divides without a remainder into another number. For example, 6 is a factor of 24, but 7 is not a factor of 24. 4 is a factor of 4. b is a factor of $5ab$.

factor (verb): To find two or more quantities whose product equals the original quantity.

fraction: A symbol expressing part of a whole. Consists of a numerator and a denominator—for example, $\frac{3}{5}$ or $\frac{9}{4}$.

greatest common factor: The largest factor common to two or more numbers.

hundredth: The second decimal place to the right of the decimal point. For example, 0.08 is eight hundredths.

identity element for addition: 0. Any number added to 0 gives the original number.

identity element for multiplication: 1. Any number multiplied by 1 gives the original number.

improper fraction: A fraction in which the numerator is greater than or equal to the denominator. For example, $\frac{5}{5}$ and $\frac{3}{2}$ are improper fractions.

independent events: When the outcome of one event has no bearing or effect on the outcome of another event.

integer: A whole number, either positive, negative, or zero.

invert: Turn upside down. If you are asked to invert $\frac{2}{3}$, the correct answer is $\frac{3}{2}$.

irrational number: A number that is not rational (cannot be written as a fraction $\frac{x}{y}$, with x a natural number and y an integer)—for example, $\sqrt{3}$ or π.

least common multiple: The smallest multiple that is common to two or more numbers.

lowest common denominator: The smallest number that can be divided evenly by all denominators in the problem. It is the least common multiple of the denominators.

mean (arithmetic): The average of a number of items in a group (total the items and divide by the number of items).

median: The middle item in an ordered group. If the group has an even number of items, the median is the average of the two middle terms.

mixed number: A number containing both a whole number and a fraction—for example, $5\frac{1}{2}$.

mode: The number appearing most frequently in a group.

multiples: Numbers found by multiplying a number by 2, by 3, by 4, and so on.

multiplicative inverse: The reciprocal of the number. Any nonzero number multiplied by its multiplicative inverse equals 1.

natural number: A counting number: 1, 2, 3, 4, and so on.

negative number: A number less than zero.

number line: A visual representation of the positive and negative numbers and zero. The line may be thought of as an infinitely long ruler with negative numbers to the left of zero and positive numbers to the right of zero.

number sequence: A sequence of numbers with some pattern. One number follows another in some defined manner.

numerator: The top symbol or number of a fraction.

odd number: An integer (whole number) not divisible evenly by 2.

operation: Any arithmetic that can be with numbers. This includes, but is not limited to, addition, subtraction, multiplication, division, raising to exponents, finding roots, and finding absolute value.

order of operations: The priority given to an operation relative to other operations. For example, multiplication takes precedence (is performed before) addition.

parentheses: Grouping symbols. ( )

percentage: A common fraction with 100 as its denominator. For example, 37% is $\frac{37}{100}$.

permutations: The total number of possible choices when the order in which they occur matters.

place value: The value given a digit by the position of a digit in the number.

positive number: A number greater than zero.

power: A product of equal factors. $4 \times 4 \times 4 = 4^3$, read "four to the third power" or "the third power of four." *Power* and *exponent* are sometimes used interchangeably.

prime number: A number that can be divided by only itself and one—for example, 2, 3, 5, 7, and so on. 0 and 1 are *not* prime.

probability: The numerical measure of the chance of an outcome or event occurring.

product: The result of multiplication.

proper fraction: A fraction in which the numerator is less than the denominator—for example, $\frac{2}{3}$.

proportion: Written as two equal ratios. For example, 5 is to 4 as 10 is to 8, or $\frac{5}{4} = \frac{10}{8}$.

quotient: The result of division.

range: The difference between the largest and the smallest number in a set of numbers.

ratio: A comparison between two numbers or symbols. May be written $x{:}y$, $\frac{x}{y}$, or x is to y.

rational number: Any value that can be exactly expressed as a fraction $\frac{x}{y}$ with x an integer and y a natural number.

real number: Any rational or irrational number.

reciprocal: The multiplicative inverse of a number. For example, $\frac{2}{3}$ is the reciprocal of $\frac{3}{2}$.

reducing: Changing a fraction into its lowest terms. For example, $\frac{2}{4}$ is reduced to $\frac{1}{2}$.

rounding off: Changing a number to a nearest place value as specified. A method of approximating.

scientific notation: A number between 1 and 10 and multiplied by a power of 10. Used for writing very large or very small numbers—for example, 2.5×10^4.

square (of a number): The result when a number is used as a factor two times or when the number is raised to the second power.

square root: The number that, when multiplied by itself, gives you the original number. For example, 5 is the square root of 25. Its symbol is $\sqrt{}$. $\sqrt{25} = 5$.

standard deviation: The standard deviation of a population is a measure of the deviation of scores from the mean score. It is calculated by taking the positive square root of the variance.

sum: The result of addition.

tenth: The first decimal place to the right of the decimal point. For example, 0.7 is seven tenths.

variance: The variance of a population is a measure of the deviation of scores from the mean score. The variance of a population is calculated by taking each data value, subtracting it from the mean, squaring each difference, adding these squares together, and then dividing the sum by the number of data values.

weighted mean: The mean of a set of numbers that have been weighted (multiplied by their relative importance or times of occurrence).

whole number: 0, 1, 2, 3, and so on.

Algebra

Diagnostic Test

Questions

1. $\{1,3,5\} \cap \{1,2,3\} =$

2. $\{2,5\} \cup \{3,4,5\} =$

3. True or false: $\{3, 4, 6\} = \{4, 3, 6\}$

4. True or false: $\{8, 9, 10\} \sim \{a, b, c\}$

5. Express algebraically: five increased by three times x.

6. Evaluate: $x^2 - 3x - 4$ if $x = 5$.

7. Evaluate: $\dfrac{x}{3} - \dfrac{x+2y}{y}$ if $x = 2$ and $y = 6$.

8. Solve for x: $2x - 9 = 21$.

9. Solve for y: $\dfrac{4}{7}y + 6 = 18$.

10. Solve for x: $8x - 8 = 4x + 3$.

11. Solve for x: $wx + r = t$.

12. Solve for m: x is to y as a is to m.

13. Solve for y: $\dfrac{8}{y} = \dfrac{3}{7}$.

14. Solve this system for x and y:

    $8x + 2y = 7$

    $3x - 4y = 5$

15. $\begin{aligned}4xy^2z \\ -7xy^2z\end{aligned}$

16. $12x + 4x - 23x - (-3x) =$

17. $6x^2y(4xy^2) =$

18. $(2x^3y^4)^3 =$

19. $\dfrac{a^7b^3}{a^2b} =$

20. $\dfrac{-5(a^3b^2)(2a^2b^5)}{a^4b^3} =$

21. $(4x - 7z) - (3x - 4z) =$

22. $(4x + 2y)(3x - y) =$

23. $\dfrac{16x^2y + 18xy^3}{2xy} =$

24. $(x^2 + 3x - 18) \div (x + 6) =$

25. Factor completely: $8x^3 - 12x^2$.

26. Factor: $16a^2 - 81$.

27. Factor: $x^2 - 2x - 63$.

28. Factor: $3a^2 - 4a + 1$.

29. Solve: $m^2 - 2mn - 3n^2$.

30. Solve for r: $r^2 - 10r = -24$.

31. Solve for x: $x^2 - 49 = 0$.

32. Reduce: $\dfrac{x^2 - 3x + 2}{3x - 6}$

113

For questions 33–39, do the arithmetic and simplify the answers.

33. $\dfrac{x^3}{2y} \times \dfrac{5y^2}{6x} =$

34. $\dfrac{x-5}{x} \times \dfrac{x+2}{x^2-2x-15} =$

35. $\dfrac{6x-3}{2} \div \dfrac{2x-1}{x} =$

36. $\dfrac{3x-2}{x+1} - \dfrac{2x-1}{x+1} =$

37. $\dfrac{5}{x} + \dfrac{7}{y} =$

38. $\dfrac{3}{a^3b^5} + \dfrac{2}{a^4b^2} =$

39. $\dfrac{2x}{x-1} - \dfrac{x}{x+2} =$

40. Solve for x: $2x + 3 < 11$.

41. Solve for x: $3x + 4 \geq 5x - 8$.

42. Graph: $\{x: 2 \leq x < 9\}$.

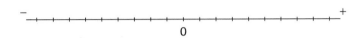

43. Graph: $\{x: -1 < x \leq 6, x \text{ is an integer}\}$.

44. $|-5-4| =$

45. Solve for x: $|x| = 12$.

46. Solve for x: $|x-3| = 10$.

47. Give the coordinates represented by points A and B.

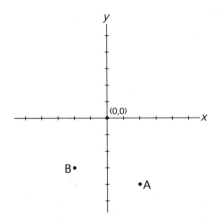

48. Is $x^2 + y = 4$ linear or nonlinear?

49. Graph $y = x + 2$.

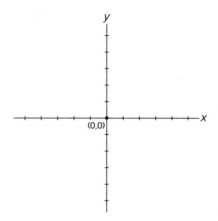

50. Find the slope and y-intercept for the graph of $2x - 3y = 6$.

51. Simplify $\sqrt{18 + 2}$.

52. $\sqrt{3} \times \sqrt{12} =$

53. $\dfrac{\sqrt{27}}{\sqrt{3}} =$

54. $\sqrt{18} + \sqrt{2} =$

In problems 55 through 57, each variable is nonnegative.

55. $\sqrt{36a^2 b^8} =$

56. $\sqrt{50a^3 b^7} =$

57. $\sqrt{5xy} \times \sqrt{8x^2 yz} =$

58. $3\sqrt{2} \times 4\sqrt{5} =$

59. In the binary operation, $*$ is defined for all integers x and y by $x * y = \dfrac{x^2 + y^2}{x^2}$, where $x \neq 0$. What is the value of $3 * {-2}$?

Answers

Page numbers following each answer refer to the review section applicable to this problem type.

1. $\{1, 3\}$ (p. 119)

2. $\{2, 3, 4, 5\}$ (p. 119)

3. true (p. 119)

4. true (p. 119)

5. $5 + 3x$ (p. 120)

6. 6 (p. 122)

7. $\dfrac{-10}{6} = \dfrac{-5}{3} = -1\frac{2}{3}$ (p. 122)

8. $x = 15$ (p. 125)

9. $y = 21$ (p. 125)

10. $x = \dfrac{11}{4} = 2\dfrac{3}{4}$ (p. 125)

11. $x = \dfrac{t-r}{w}$ (p. 130)

12. $m = \dfrac{ay}{x}$ (p. 132)

13. $y = \dfrac{56}{3} = 18\dfrac{2}{3}$ (p. 134)

14. $x = 1, y = -\dfrac{1}{2}$ (p. 136)

15. $-3xy^2z$ (p. 143)

16. $-4x$ (p. 143)

17. $24x^3y^3$ (p. 144)

18. $8x^9y^{12}$ (p. 144)

19. a^5b^2 (p. 145)

20. $-10ab^4$ (p. 145)

21. $x - 3z$ (p. 147)

22. $12x^2 + 2xy - 2y^2$ (p. 148)

23. $8x + 9y^2$ (p. 151)

24. $(x - 3)$ (p. 152)

25. $4x^2(2x - 3)$ (p. 156)

26. $(4a - 9)(4a + 9)$ (p. 157)

27. $(x - 9)(x + 7)$ (p. 158)

28. $(3a - 1)(a - 1)$ (p. 158)

29. $(m + n)(m - 3n)$ (p. 158)

30. $\{6, 4\}$ (p. 163)

31. $\{7, -7\}$ (p. 163)

32. $\dfrac{x-1}{3}$ (p. 169)

33. $\dfrac{5x^2y}{12}$ (p. 170)

34. $\dfrac{x+2}{x(x+3)}$ or $\dfrac{x+2}{x^2+3x}$ (p. 170)

35. $\dfrac{3x}{2}$ (p. 171)

36. $\dfrac{x-1}{x+1}$ (p. 172)

37. $\dfrac{5y+7x}{xy}$ (p. 172)

38. $\dfrac{3a+2b^3}{a^4b^5}$ (p. 172)

39. $\dfrac{x^2+5x}{(x-1)(x+2)}$ (p. 172)

40. $\{x : x < 4\}$ (p. 176)

41. $\{x : x \le 6\}$ (p. 176)

42.

(p. 179)

43.

(p. 179)

44. 9 (p. 180)

45. $|x| = 12$
$x = 12$ or $x = -12$ (p. 180)

46. $|x - 3| = 10$
$x - 3 = 10$ or $x - 3 = -10$
$x = 13$ $\qquad$ $x = -7$
(p. 180)

47. A. $(2, -4)$

B. $(-2, -3)$ (p. 180)

48. nonlinear (p. 185)

49.

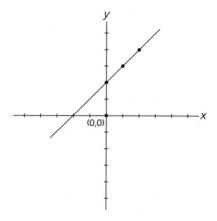

x	y
0	2
1	3
2	4

(p. 185)

50. Slope = $\frac{2}{3}$; y-intercept is -2 or $(0, -2)$ (p. 193)

51. $\sqrt{20} = 2\sqrt{5}$ (p. 204)

52. $\sqrt{36} = 6$ (p. 200)

53. $\sqrt{9} = 3$ (p. 202)

54. $4\sqrt{2}$ (p. 204)

55. $6ab^4$ (p. 200)

56. $5ab^3\sqrt{2ab}$ (p. 200)

57. $\sqrt{40x^3y^2z} = 2xy\sqrt{10xz}$ (p. 205)

58. $12\sqrt{10}$ (p. 205)

59. $\frac{13}{9}$ or $1\frac{4}{9}$ (p. 206)

Algebra Review

Algebra is essentially arithmetic with some of the numbers replaced by letters or variables. The letters or variables are merely substitutes for numbers. Initially, algebra referred to equation solving, but now it encompasses the language of algebra and the patterns of reasoning. The rules for algebra are basically the same as the rules for arithmetic.

Some Basic Language

Understood Multiplication

When two or more letters, or a number and letter(s) are written next to each other, they are *understood to be multiplied*. Thus, $8x$ means 8 times x. ($x8$ is never written.) Or ab means a times b. Or $18ab$ means 18 times a times b.

Parentheses also represent multiplication. Thus, 3(4) means 3 times 4. A raised dot also means multiplication. Thus, $6 \cdot 5$ means 6 times 5.

Letters to Be Aware of

Although they may appear in some texts, we recommend that you never use o, e, or i as variables. (Technically, e and i stand for constants or predetermined numbers, and o is too easily confused with zero.) When using z, you may want to write it as $\bar{z}$ so it is not confused with 2.

Basic Terms in Set Theory

A *set* is a group of objects, numbers, and so on: $\{1, 2, 3\}$

An *element* is a member of a set: $3 \in \{1,2,3\}$

3 is an element of the set of 1, 2, 3.

Special Sets

A *subset* is a set within a set: $\{2,3\} \subset \{1,2,3\}$

The set of 2, 3 is a subset of the set of 1, 2, 3.

The *universal set* is the general category set, or the set of all those elements under consideration.

The *empty set*, or *null set*, is a set with no members: $\emptyset$ or $\{ \}$

Describing Sets

Rule is a method of naming a set by describing its elements.

$\{x \mid x > 3, x \text{ is a whole number}\}$

{all students in the class with blue eyes}

Roster is a method of naming a set by listing its members.

$\{4, 5, 6 \dots\}$

{Fred, Tom, Bob}

Venn diagrams (and Euler circles) are ways of pictorially describing sets.

Types of Sets

Finite sets are countable; they stop: $\{1, 2, 3, 4\}$

Infinite sets are uncountable; they continue forever: $\{1, 2, 3, \dots\}$

Comparing Sets

Equal sets are those that have the exact same members:

$\{1, 2, 3\} = \{3, 2, 1\}$

Equivalent sets are sets that have the same number of members:

$\{1, 2, 3\} \sim \{a, b, c\}$

Operations with Sets

The *union* of two or more sets is all of the members in those sets.

$$\{1,2,3\} \cup \{3,4,5\} = \{1,2,3,4,5\}$$

The union of sets with members 1, 2, 3 and 3, 4, 5 is the set with members 1, 2, 3, 4, 5.

The *intersection* of two or more sets is the set of elements that they share, where they intersect, or overlap.

$$\{1,2,3\} \cap \{3,4,5\} = \{3\}$$

The intersection of a set with members 1, 2, 3 and a set with members 3, 4, 5 is a set with only member 3.

Practice: Set Theory Problems

1. True or false: $3 \in \{\text{prime numbers}\}$

2. True or false: $\{2, 3, 5\} = \{3, 2, 5\}$

3. True or false: $\{1, 2, 3, 4\} \sim \{a, b, c, d\}$

4. True or false: $\{1,5\} \subset \{2,3,4,5\}$

5. $\{3,4\} \cup \{1,2,3\} =$

6. $\{6,7,8\} \cap \{4,5,6\} =$

7. $\{1,2,3\} \cap \{4,5\} =$

Answers: Set Theory Problems

1. True

2. True

3. True

4. False

5. $\{1, 2, 3, 4\}$

6. $\{6\}$

7. $\emptyset$ or $\{\ \}$

Variables and Algebraic Expressions

A *variable* is a symbol used to denote any element of a given set. Often a letter is used to stand for a number. Variables are used to change verbal expressions into *algebraic expressions. For example:*

Verbal Expression	Algebraic Expression
the sum of a number and 7	$n + 7$ or $7 + n$
the number diminished by 10	$n - 10$
seven times a number	$7n$
x divided by 4	$\dfrac{x}{4}$

Key Words Denoting Addition

sum	gain
plus	increase
more than	enlarge
greater than	rise
larger than	grow

Key Words Denoting Subtraction

difference	decrease
minus	drop
lose	lower
less than	diminish
smaller than	reduce
fewer than	

Key Words Denoting Multiplication

product	twice
multiplied by	of
times	

Key Words Denoting Division

quotient	ratio
divided by	half

Practice: Expressing Operations Algebraically Problems

Express each of the following algebraically.

1. a number increased by four

2. five less than a number

3. a number reduced by 12

4. the product of a number and six

5. a number divided by three

6. one half of a number

7. a number multiplied by 14

8. the ratio of five to a number

9. 12 decreased by four times y

10. the product of five and the sum of x and y

11. five times c, decreased by one-third of b

12. the average of x, y, and z

Answers: Expressing Operations Algebraically Problems

1. $n + 4$ or $4 + n$
2. $n - 5$
3. $n - 12$
4. $6n$
5. $\dfrac{n}{3}$
6. $\left(\dfrac{1}{2}\right)n$ or $\dfrac{n}{2}$
7. $14n$
8. $\dfrac{5}{n}$
9. $12 - 4y$
10. $5(x + y)$ or $(x + y)5$
11. $5c - \dfrac{b}{3}$ or $5c - \left(\dfrac{1}{3}\right)b$
12. $\dfrac{(x + y + z)}{3}$

Evaluating Expressions

To *evaluate* an *expression,* just replace the unknowns with grouping symbols, insert the value for the unknowns and do the arithmetic.

Examples:

1. Evaluate: $ab + c$ if $a = 5$, $b = 4$, and $c = 3$.

   $(5)(4) + 3 = 20 + 3$

   $\qquad\qquad = 23$

2. Evaluate: $2x^2 + 3y + 6$ if $x = 2$ and $y = 9$.

   $2(2)^2 + 3(9) + 6 = 2(4) + 27 + 6$

   $\qquad\qquad\qquad = 8 + 27 + 6$

   $\qquad\qquad\qquad = 35 + 6$

   $\qquad\qquad\qquad = 41$

3. Evaluate: $-4p^2 + 5q - 7$ if $p = -3$ and $q = -8$.

   $-4(-3)^2 + 5(-8) - 7 = -4(9) + 5(-8) - 7$

   $\qquad\qquad\qquad\qquad = -36 - 40 - 7$

   $\qquad\qquad\qquad\qquad = -76 - 7$

   $\qquad\qquad\qquad\qquad = -83$

4. Evaluate: $\dfrac{a+c}{5} + \dfrac{a}{b+c}$ if $a = 3$, $b = -2$, and $c = 7$.

   $\dfrac{(3)+(7)}{5} + \dfrac{3}{(-2)+(7)} = \dfrac{10}{5} + \dfrac{3}{5}$

   $\qquad\qquad\qquad\qquad = \dfrac{13}{5}$

   $\qquad\qquad\qquad\qquad = 2\dfrac{3}{5}$

5. Evaluate: $5x^3y^2$ if $x = -2$ and $y = 3$.

   $5(-2)^3(3)^2 = 5(-8)(9)$

   $\qquad\qquad\quad = -40(9)$

   $\qquad\qquad\quad = -360$

Practice: Evaluating Expressions Problems

1. Evaluate: $x^2 + 4x - 7$ if $x = 3$.

2. Evaluate: $y^2 - y + 8$ if $y = 5$.

3. Evaluate: $7s - 2t^2$ if $s = 3$ and $t = 8$.

4. Evaluate: $10m^2 - 5n - 25$ if $m = -6$ and $n = -3$.

5. Evaluate: $\frac{x}{2} + \frac{x+y}{y}$ if $x = 1$ and $y = 4$.

6. Evaluate: $3x^2y^3z$ if $x = 2$, $y = 3$, and $z = -1$.

Answers: Evaluating Expressions Problems

1. Evaluate: $x^2 + 4x - 7$ if $x = 3$.

   $(3)^2 + 4(3) - 7 = 9 + 12 - 7$
   $$= 21 - 7$$
   $$= 14$$

2. Evaluate: $y^2 - y + 8$ if $y = 5$.

   $(5)^2 - 5 + 8 = 25 - 5 + 8$
   $$= 20 + 8$$
   $$= 28$$

3. Evaluate : $7s - 2t^2$ if $s = 3$ and $t = 8$.

   $7(3) - 2(8)^2 = 7(3) - 2(64)$
   $$= 21 - 128$$
   $$= -107$$

4. Evaluate: $10m^2 - 5n - 25$ if $m = -6$ and $n = -3$.

   $10(-6)^2 - 5(-3) - 25 = 10(36) + 15 - 25$
   $$= 360 + 15 - 25$$
   $$= 375 - 25$$
   $$= 350$$

5. Evaluate: $\frac{x}{2} + \frac{x+y}{y}$ if $x = 1$ and $y = 4$.

$\frac{1}{2} + \frac{1+4}{4} = \frac{2}{4} + \frac{5}{4}$ (finding common denominator)

$$= \frac{7}{4}$$

$$= 1\frac{3}{4}$$

6. Evaluate : $3x^2y^3z$ if $x = 2$, $y = 3$, and $z = -1$.

$3(2)^2(3)^3(-1) = 3(4)(27)(-1)$

$$= 12(27)(-1)$$

$$= 324(-1)$$

$$= -324$$

Equations

Solving Equations

An *equation* is a mathematical sentence, a relationship between numbers and/or symbols. Remember that an equation is like a balance scale, with the equal sign (=) being the fulcrum, or center. Thus, if you do the *same thing to both sides* of the equal sign (say, add 5 to each side), the equation will still be balanced.

Examples:

1. $x - 5 = 23$

    To solve the equation $x - 5 = 23$, you must get x by itself on one side; therefore, add 5 to both sides:

    $$\begin{array}{r} x - 5 = 23 \\ \underline{+5 \quad +5} \\ x \quad = 28 \end{array}$$

In the same manner, you may subtract, multiply, or divide *both* sides of an equation by the same (nonzero) number, and the equation will not change. Sometimes you may have to use more than one step to solve for an unknown.

2. $3x + 4 = 19$

    Subtract 4 from both sides to get the $3x$ by itself on one side:

    $$3x + 4 = 19$$
    $$\underline{-4 \quad -4}$$
    $$3x \quad\;\; = 15$$

    Then divide both sides by 3 to get x:

    $$\frac{3x}{3} = \frac{15}{3}$$
    $$x = 5$$

    Remember: Solving an equation is using opposite operations, until the letter is on a side by itself (for addition, subtract; for multiplication, divide; and so on).

    To check, substitute your answer into the original equation.

    $$3x + 4 = 19$$
    $$3(5) + 4 = 19$$
    $$15 + 4 = 19$$
    $$19 = 19$$

3. $\frac{x}{5} - 4 = 2$

    Add 4 to both sides:

    $$\frac{x}{5} - 4 = 2$$
    $$\underline{+4 +4}$$
    $$\frac{x}{5} \quad\;\; = 6$$

    Multiply both sides by 5 to get x:

    $$(5)\frac{x}{5} = (5)6$$
    $$x = 30$$

4. $\frac{3}{5}x - 6 = 12$

   Add 6 to each side:

$$\frac{3}{5}x - 6 = 12$$
$$\underline{\phantom{\frac{3}{5}x}\; +6 \; +6}$$
$$\frac{3}{5}x \qquad = 18$$

   Multiply each side by $\frac{5}{3}$.

$$\left(\frac{5}{3}\right)\frac{3}{5}x = \left(\frac{5}{3}\right)18$$

$$x = \left(\frac{5}{\cancel{3}_1}\right)\frac{\cancel{18}^6}{1}$$

$$x = 30$$

5. $5x = 2x - 6$

   Add $-2x$ to each side:

$$5x = 2x - 6$$
$$\underline{-2x - 2x}$$
$$3x = \qquad -6$$

   Divide both sides by 3:

$$\frac{3x}{3} = \frac{-6}{3}$$
$$x = -2$$

6. $6x + 3 = 4x + 5$

   Add -3 to each side:

$$6x + 3 = 4x + 5$$
$$\underline{\; -3 \qquad\quad -3}$$
$$6x \qquad = 4x + 2$$

Add $-4x$ to each side:

$$-6x = 4x + 2$$
$$\underline{-4x - 4x}$$
$$-2x = \qquad 2$$

Divide each side by 2:

$$\frac{2x}{2} = \frac{2}{2}$$
$$x = 1$$

Practice: Solving Equations Problems

Solve each equation for y.

1. $y + 8 = 19$

2. $y - 9 = 21$

3. $4y + 8 = 32$

4. $-\frac{y}{5} = 8$

5. $-\frac{2}{3}y + 1 = 13$

6. $4y = 52$

7. $7y = 4y - 12$

8. $5y - 4 = 3y + 4$

Answers: Solving Equations Problems

1. $y + 8 = 19$
   $$\underline{\quad -8 \quad -8}$$
   $y \qquad = 11$

2. $y - 9 = 21$
   $$\underline{\quad +9 \quad +9}$$
   $y \qquad = 30$

3. $$4y + 8 = 32$$
$$\underline{-8 \quad -8}$$
$$4y = 24$$

$$\frac{4y}{4} = \frac{24}{4}$$

$$y = 6$$

4. $$-\left(\frac{y}{5}\right) = 8$$

$$\left(\frac{-\cancel{5}^{1}}{1}\right)\left(-\frac{y}{\cancel{5}_{1}}\right) = 8(-5)$$

$$y = -40$$

5. $$-\frac{2}{3}y + 1 = 13$$
$$\underline{\phantom{-\frac{2}{3}y}-1 \quad -1}$$
$$-\frac{2}{3}y = 12$$

$$\left(-\frac{3}{2}\right)\left(-\frac{2}{3}\right)y = 12\left(-\frac{3}{2}\right)$$
$$y = -18$$

6. $$\frac{4y}{4} = \frac{52}{4}$$

$$y = 13$$

7. $$7y = 4y - 12$$
$$\underline{-4y - 4y}$$
$$3y = -12$$

$$\frac{3y}{3} = \frac{-12}{3}$$

$$y = -4$$

8.

$$5y - 4 = 3y + 4$$
$$\underline{ +4 = +4}$$
$$5y = 3y + 8$$
$$5y = -3y + 8$$
$$\underline{-3y = -3y }$$
$$2y = 8$$
$$\frac{2y}{2} = \frac{8}{2}$$
$$y = 4$$

Literal Equations

Literal equations have no numbers, only symbols (letters).

Examples:

1. Solve for Q: $QP - X = Y$.

   First add X to both sides.

   $$QP - X = Y$$
   $$\underline{ + X + X}$$
   $$QP = Y + X$$

   Then divide both sides by P:

   $$\frac{QP}{P} = \frac{Y + X}{P}$$
   $$Q = \frac{Y + X}{P}$$

   Operations opposite to those in the original equation were used to isolate Q. (To remove the $-X$, we *added* a $+X$ to both sides of the equation; since we had Q times P, we *divided* both sides by P.)

2. Solve for y: $\dfrac{y}{x} = c$

   Multiply both sides by x to get y alone:

   $$(x)\frac{y}{x} = (x)c$$
   $$y = xc$$

3. Solve for x: $\dfrac{b}{x} = \dfrac{p}{q}$

To solve this equation quickly, you cross-multiply. To cross-multiply, bring the denominators up next to the opposite side numerators and multiply

$$\frac{b}{x} = \frac{p}{q}$$

$$bq = px$$

Then divide both sides by p to get x alone.

$$\frac{bq}{p} = \frac{px}{p}$$

$$\frac{bq}{p} = x \text{ or } x = \frac{bq}{p}$$

Cross-multiplying can be used only when the format is two fractions separated by an equal sign.

4. Solve for c: $\dfrac{g}{m} = \dfrac{k}{c}$

Cross-multiply:

$$gc = mk$$

Divide both sides by g:

$$\frac{gc}{g} = \frac{mk}{g}$$

Thus,

$$c = \frac{mk}{g}$$

Be aware that cross-multiplying is most effective only when the letter you are solving for is on the bottom (the *denominator*) of a fraction. If it is on top (the *numerator*), it's easier simply to clear the denominator under the unknown you're solving for.

5. Solve for x: $\dfrac{x}{k} = \dfrac{p}{q}$

Multiply both sides by k:

$$(k)\frac{x}{k} = (k)\frac{p}{q}$$

$$x = \frac{kp}{q}$$

In this problem, there was no need to cross-multiply.

Practice: Literal Equations Problems

1. Solve for z: $\dfrac{b}{z} = \dfrac{d}{e}$

2. Solve for q: $\dfrac{m}{n} = \dfrac{r}{q}$

3. Solve for c: $\dfrac{a}{b} = \dfrac{c}{d}$

4. Solve for c: $\dfrac{d}{x} = \dfrac{y}{c}$

Answers: Literal Equations Problems

1. $\dfrac{b}{z} = \dfrac{d}{e}$

   $be = dz$

   $\dfrac{be}{d} = \dfrac{dz}{d}$

   $\dfrac{be}{d} = z$

2. $\dfrac{m}{n} = \dfrac{r}{q}$

   $mq = nr$

   $\dfrac{mq}{m} = \dfrac{nr}{m}$

   $q = \dfrac{nr}{m}$

3. $\dfrac{a}{b} = \dfrac{c}{d}$

   $(d)\dfrac{a}{b} = (d)\dfrac{c}{d}$

   $\dfrac{ad}{b} = c$

4. $\dfrac{d}{x} = \dfrac{y}{c}$

   $dc = yx$

   $\dfrac{dc}{d} = \dfrac{yx}{d}$

   $c = \dfrac{yx}{d}$

Ratios and Proportions

Ratios

A ratio is a method of comparing two or more numbers or variables. Ratios are written as $a{:}b$ or in working form as a fraction, $\dfrac{a}{b}$, and are read as "*a* is to *b*." Notice that whatever comes after the "to" goes second or at the bottom of the fraction.

Proportions

Proportions are written as two ratios (fractions) equal to each other.

Examples:

1. Solve this proportion for x: p is to q as x is to y.

   First, the proportion may be rewritten:

   $$\frac{p}{q} = \frac{x}{y}$$

   Now simply multiply each side by y.

   $$(y)\frac{p}{q} = (y)\frac{x}{y}$$

   $$\frac{yp}{q} = x$$

2. Solve this proportion for t: s is to t as r is to q.

   Rewrite:

   $$\frac{s}{t} = \frac{r}{q}$$

   Cross-multiply:

   $$sq = rt$$

   Divide both sides by r:

   $$\frac{sq}{r} = \frac{rt}{r}$$

   $$\frac{sq}{r} = t$$

Practice: Proportion Problems

1. Solve for p: c is to p as g is to h.

2. Solve for s: t is to q as z is to s.

3. Solve for h: l is to k as h is to d.

4. Solve for b: a is to b as c is to d.

Answers: Proportion Problems

1. $\dfrac{c}{p} = \dfrac{g}{h}$

    $ch = pg$

    $\dfrac{ch}{g} = \dfrac{pg}{g}$

    $\dfrac{ch}{g} = p$

2. $\dfrac{t}{q} = \dfrac{z}{s}$

    $ts = qz$

    $\dfrac{ts}{t} = \dfrac{qz}{t}$

    $s = \dfrac{qz}{t}$

3. $\dfrac{l}{k} = \dfrac{h}{d}$

    $(d)\dfrac{l}{k} = (d)\dfrac{h}{d}$

    $\dfrac{dl}{k} = h$

4. $\dfrac{a}{b} = \dfrac{c}{d}$

    $ad = bc$

    $\dfrac{ad}{c} = \dfrac{bc}{c}$

    $\dfrac{ad}{c} = b$

Solving Proportions for Value

Use the same rule (p. 133) to solve for the unknown. *For example:*

$$\frac{4}{x} = \frac{2}{5}$$

Cross-multiply:

$$(4)(5) = 2x$$
$$20 = 2x$$

Divide both sides by 2:

$$\frac{20}{2} = \frac{2x}{2}$$

$$10 = x$$

Practice: Solving Proportions for Value Problems

Solve for the unknown.

1. $\dfrac{3}{k} = \dfrac{1}{11}$

2. $\dfrac{2}{5} = \dfrac{8}{R}$

3. $\dfrac{14}{5} = \dfrac{7}{t}$

4. $\dfrac{15}{2} = \dfrac{25}{t}$

Answers : Solving Proportions for Value Problems

1. $\dfrac{3}{k} = \dfrac{1}{11}$

   $33 = 1k$ or $33 = k$

2. $\dfrac{2}{5} = \dfrac{8}{R}$

   $2R = 40$

   $\dfrac{2R}{2} = \dfrac{40}{2}$

   $R = 20$

   Note that this problem could have been done intuitively if you noticed that the second ratio (fraction) is four times the first.

   $$\dfrac{2 \times 4}{5 \times 4} = \dfrac{8}{\boxed{20}}$$

3. $\dfrac{14}{5} = \dfrac{7}{t}$

   $14t = 35$

   $\dfrac{14t}{14} = \dfrac{35}{14}$

   $t = \dfrac{35}{14} = 2\dfrac{7}{14} = 2\dfrac{1}{2}$

   Intuitively: $\dfrac{14 \div 2}{5 \div 2} = \dfrac{7}{\boxed{2\frac{1}{2}}}$

4. $\dfrac{15}{2} = \dfrac{25}{t}$

   $15t = 50$

   $\dfrac{15t}{15} = \dfrac{50}{15}$

   $t = \dfrac{50}{15} = 3\dfrac{5}{15} = 3\dfrac{1}{3}$

Solving for Two Unknowns Systems of Equations

If you solve *two equations with the same two unknowns in each,* you can solve for both unknowns. One method is:

a. Multiply one or both equations by some number to make the number in front of one of the letters (unknowns) the same in each equation.

b. Add or subtract the two equations to eliminate one letter.

c. Solve for the other unknown.

d. Insert the value of the first unknown in one of the original equations to solve for the second unknown.

Examples:

1. Solve for x and y:

$$3x + 3y = 24$$
$$2x + y = 13$$

First multiply the bottom equation by 3. Now the y is preceded by a 3 in each equation:

$$3x + 3y = 24 \qquad\qquad 3x + 3y = 24$$
$$3(2x) + 3(y) = 3(13) \qquad\quad 6x + 3y = 39$$

Now you can subtract equations, eliminating the y terms:

$$
\begin{array}{r}
3x + 3y = 24 \\
-6x + -3y = -39 \\
\hline
-3x \qquad\quad = -15
\end{array}
$$

$$\frac{-3x}{-3} = \frac{-15}{-3}$$

$$x = 5$$

Now insert $x = 5$ in one of the original equations to solve for y:

$$2x + y = 13$$
$$2(5) + y = 13$$
$$-10 + y = 13$$
$$
\begin{array}{r}
-10 \qquad -10 \\
\hline
y = 3
\end{array}
$$

Answer: $x = 5$, $y = 3$

Of course, if the number in front of a letter is already the same in each equation, you don't have to change either equation. Simply add or subtract.

2. Solve for x and y: $x + y = 7$

$$x - y = 3$$

$$
\begin{aligned}
x + y &= 7 \\
x - y &= 3 \\
\hline
2x &= 10 \\
\frac{2x}{2} &= \frac{10}{2} \\
x &= 5
\end{aligned}
$$

Now, inserting 5 for x in the first equation gives:

$$
\begin{aligned}
5 + y &= 7 \\
-5 \quad &-5 \\
\hline
y &= 2
\end{aligned}
$$

Answer: $x = 5$, $y = 2$

You should note that this method will not work when the two equations are, in fact, the same equation but written in two different forms as is shown in the next example.

3. Solve for a and b: $3a + 4b = 2$

$$6a + 8b = 4$$

The second equation is actually the first equation multiplied by 2. In this instance, the system does not have a unique solution. Any replacements for a and b that make one of the sentences true, will also make the other sentence true. For example, if $a = 2$ and $b = -1$, then each sentence would be true. If $a = 6$ and $b = -4$, then each sentence would be true. In this situation, the system has an infinite number of solutions for a and b.

4. Solve for p and q: $3p + 4q = 9$

$$2p + 2q = 6$$

Multiply the second equation by 2:

$$(2)2p + (2)2q = (2)6$$
$$4p + 4q = 12$$

Now subtract the equations:

$$
\begin{aligned}
3p + 4q &= 9 \\
(-)4p + 4q &= 12 \\
\hline
-p &= -3 \\
p &= -3
\end{aligned}
$$

Now that you know $p = 3$, you may plug in 3 for p in either of the two original equations to find q.

$$
\begin{aligned}
3p + 4q &= 9 \\
3(3) + 4q &= 9 \\
9 + 4q &= 9 \\
4q &= 0 \\
q &= 0
\end{aligned}
$$

Answer: $p = 3$, $q = 0$

Sometimes a system is more easily solved by the substitution method.

5. Solve for x and y: $x = y + 8$

$$x + 3y = 48$$

From the first equation, substitute $(y + 8)$ for x in the second equation:

$$(y + 8) + 3y = 48$$

Now solve for y. Simplify by combining y's.

$$
\begin{aligned}
4y + 8 &= 48 \\
-8 & -8 \\
\hline
4y &= 40
\end{aligned}
$$

$$\frac{4y}{4} = \frac{40}{4}$$
$$y = 10$$

Now insert $y = 10$ in one of the original equations.

$$x = y + 8$$
$$x = 10 + 8$$
$$x = 18$$

Answer: $y = 10$, $x = 18$

Practice: Systems of Equations Problems

Solve for both unknowns.

1. $6a - 2b = 32$

   $3a + 2b = 22$

2. $3a + 3b = 24$

   $2a + b = 13$

3. $3x + 2y = 10$

   $2x + 3y = 5$

4. $6x + 2y = 24$

   $x = -y + 5$

Answers: Systems of Equations Problems

1. $6a - 2b = 32$

   $3a + 2b = 22$

   Add the two equations:

$$
\begin{array}{r}
6a - 2b = 32 \\
(+)\,3a + 2b = 22 \\
\hline
9a \quad\quad = 54 \\
\dfrac{9a}{9} = \dfrac{54}{9} \\
a = 6
\end{array}
$$

Now plug in 6 for a in one of the original equations.

$$3a + 2b = 22$$
$$3(6) + 2b = 22$$
$$18 + 2b = 22$$
$$\underline{-18 \qquad -18}$$
$$2b = 4$$

$$\frac{2b}{2} = \frac{4}{2}$$
$$b = 2$$

Answer: $a = 6$, $b = 2$

2. $3a + 3b = 24$

   $2a + b = 13$

   Multiply the second equation by 3:

   $$(3)2a + (3)b = (3)13$$
   $$6a + 3b = 39$$

   Subtract the first equation from the second:

   $$6a + 3b = 39$$
   $$\underline{(-)3a + 3b = 24}$$
   $$3a \qquad = 15$$

   $$\frac{3a}{3} = 15$$
   $$a = 5$$

   Now plug in 5 for a in one of the original equations:

   $$2a + b = 13$$
   $$2(5) + b = 13$$
   $$10 + b = 13$$
   $$\underline{-10 \qquad -10}$$
   $$b = 3$$

Answer: $a = 5$, $b = 3$

3. $3x + 2y = 10$

   $2x + 3y = 5$

   Multiply the first equation by 2:

   $$(2)3x + (2)2y = (2)10$$

   $$6x + 4y = 20$$

   Multiply the second equation by 3:

   $$(3)2x + (3)3y = (3)5$$

   $$6x + 9y = 15$$

   Subtract the second equation from the first:

   $$6x + 4y = 20$$
   $$\underline{(-)6x + 9y = 15}$$
   $$-5y = 5$$

   $$\frac{-5y}{-5} = \frac{5}{-5}$$
   $$y = -1$$

   Now plug in –1 for y in one of the original equations:

   $$3x + 2y = 10$$
   $$3x + 2(-1) = 10$$
   $$3x - 2 = 10$$
   $$\underline{+2 \qquad +2}$$
   $$3x = 12$$

   $$\frac{3x}{3} = \frac{12}{3}$$
   $$x = 4$$

   Answer: $y = -1$, $x = 4$

4. $6x + 2y = 24$

   $x = -y + 5$

   Substitute the value of x from the second equation into the first equation:

$$6x + 2y = 24$$
$$6(-y + 5) + 2y = 24$$
$$-6y + 30 + 2y = 24$$
$$-4y + 30 = 24$$
$$\underline{-30 - 30}$$
$$-4y \qquad = -6$$

$$\frac{-4y}{-4} = \frac{-6}{-4}$$

$$y = \frac{3}{2} \text{ or } 1\frac{1}{2}$$

Now plug in $1\frac{1}{2}$ for y in one of the original equations:

$$x = -y + 5$$
$$x = -\left(1\frac{1}{2}\right) + 5$$
$$x = 3\frac{1}{2}$$

Answer: $y = 1\frac{1}{2}$, $x = 3\frac{1}{2}$

Monomials and Polynomials

A *monomial* is an algebraic expression that consists of only one term. (A *term* is a numerical or literal expression with its own sign.) For instance, $9x$, $4a^2$, and $3mpxz^2$ are all monomials.

A *polynomial* consists of two or more terms. For instance, $x + y$, $y^2 - x^2$, and $x^2 + 3x + 5y^2$ are all polynomials.

A *binomial* is a polynomial that consists of exactly two terms. For instance, $x + y$ is a binomial.

A *trinomial* is a polynomial that consists of exactly three terms. For instance, $y^2 + 9y + 8$ is a trinomial.

The number in front of the variable is called the *coefficient*. In $9y$, 9 is the coefficient.

Polynomials are usually arranged in one of two ways.

Ascending order is basically when the power of a term increases for each succeeding term. For example, $x + x^2 + x^3$ or $5x + 2x^2 - 3x^3 + x^5$ are arranged in ascending order.

Descending order is basically when the power of a term decreases for each succeeding term. For example, $x^3 + x^2 + x$ or $2x^4 + 3x^2 + 7x$ are arranged in descending order. Descending order is more commonly used.

Adding and Subtracting Monomials

To *add* or *subtract monomials,* follow the same rules as with signed numbers (p. 22), *provided that the terms are alike.* Notice that you add or subtract the coefficients only and leave the variables the same.

Examples:

1. $15x^2yz$
   $-18x^2yz$
   $-3x^2yz$

2. $3x + 2x = 5x$

3. $9y$
   $-3y$
   $6y$

4. $17q + 8q - 3q - (-4q) =$
   $22q - (-4q) =$
   $22q + 4q = 26q$

Remember that the rules for signed numbers apply to monomials as well.

Practice: Adding and Subtracting Monomials Problems

Perform the indicated operation.

1. $-9m^2s + 5m^2s =$

2. $7qt^2 - 3qt^2 + 20qt^2 =$

3. $18pc$
   $- 7pc$

4. $-7x^2y$
   $--3x^2y$

Answers: Adding and Subtracting Monomials Problems

1. $-4m^2s$

2. $24qt^2$

3. $11pc$

4. $-4x^2y$

Multiplying Monomials

Reminder: The rules and definitions for powers and exponents introduced in arithmetic (pp. 64–65) also apply in algebra. For example, $5 \cdot 5 = 5^2$ and $x \cdot x = x^2$. Similarly, $a \cdot a \cdot a \cdot b \cdot b = a^3b^2$.

To *multiply monomials,* add the exponents of the same bases.

Examples:

1. $(x^3)(x^4) = x^7$

2. $\left(x^2y\right)\left(x^3y^2\right) = x^5y^3$

3. $\left(6k^5\right)\left(5k^2\right) = 30k^7$

4. $-4\left(m^2n\right)\left(-3m^4n^3\right) = 12m^6n^4$

5. $(c^2)(c^3)(c^4) = c^9$

6. $\left(3a^2b^3c\right)\left(b^2c^2d\right) = 3a^2b^5c^3d$

Note that in question 4, the product of –4 and –3 is +12, the product of m^2 and m^4 is m^6, and the product of n and n^3 is n^4, because any monomial having no exponent indicated is assumed to have an exponent of 1.

When monomials are being *raised to a power,* the answer is obtained by multiplying the exponents of each part of the monomial by the power to which it is being raised.

Examples:

1. $(a^7)^3 = a^{21}$

2. $(x^3y^2)^4 = x^{12}y^8$

3. $(2x^2y^3)^3 = (2)^3x^6y^9 = 8x^6y^9$

Practice: Multiplying Monomials Problems

1. $(m^3)(m^{10}) =$

2. $(a^5b^6)(a^4b^2) =$

3. $(5k^2)(8k^4) =$

4. $-2(x^2y^3)(6xy^4) =$

5. $(2x^2)(-4x)(x^3y) =$

6. $(d^4)^5 =$

7. $(c^3d^2)^5 =$

8. $(3a^2bc^3)^2 =$

Answers: Multiplying Monomials Problems

1. m^{13}

2. a^9b^8

3. $40k^6$

4. $-12x^3y^7$

5. $-8x^6y$

6. d^{20}

7. $c^{15}d^{10}$

8. $9a^4b^2c^6$

Dividing Monomials

To *divide monomials,* subtract the exponent of the divisor (denominator) from the exponent of the dividend (numerator) of the same base.

Examples:

1. $\dfrac{y^{15}}{y^4} = y^{11}$ or $y^{15} \div y^4 = y^{11}$

2. $\dfrac{x^5y^2}{x^3y} = x^2y$

3. $\dfrac{36a^4b^6}{-9ab} = -4a^3b^5$ (divide the numbers)

4. $\dfrac{fg^{15}}{g^3} = fg^{12}$

5. $\dfrac{x^5}{x^8} = \dfrac{1}{x^3}$ (may also be expressed x^{-3})

6. $\dfrac{-3(xy)(xy^2)}{xy}$

You can simplify the numerator first:

$$\dfrac{-3(xy)(xy^2)}{xy} = \dfrac{-3(x^2y^3)}{xy} = -3xy^2$$

Or, since the numerator is all multiplication, we can cancel.

$$\dfrac{-3(\cancel{xy})(xy^2)}{\cancel{xy}} = -3xy^2$$

Practice: Dividing Monomials Problems

1. $\dfrac{x^8}{x^3} =$

2. $a^9 \div a^6 =$

3. $\dfrac{m^5n^4}{m^2n^3} =$

4. $\dfrac{-10x^4z^9}{5x^3z^4} =$

5. $\dfrac{x^8y^3}{x^5} =$

6. $(3p^5q^3) \div (12p^4q^9) =$

7. $\dfrac{s^4t^6}{s^7t^3} =$

8. $\dfrac{2(x^2y)(3x^2y^3)}{x^2y^2} =$

Answers: Dividing Monomials Problems

1. x^5

2. a^3

3. m^3n

4. $-2xz^5$

5. x^3y^3

6. $\dfrac{\cancel{3}p^{\frac{1}{3}}\cancel{q^2}}{\underset{4}{\cancel{12}}\ \cancel{p^4}q^{\cancel{8}}} = \dfrac{1p}{4q^6} = \dfrac{p}{4q^6}$ or $0.25pq^{-6}$

7. $\dfrac{t^3}{s^3}$ or $s^{-3}t^3$

8. $\dfrac{2(x^2y)(3x^2y^3)}{x^2y^2} = \dfrac{6x^4y^4}{x^2y^2} = 6x^2y^2$ or $\dfrac{2(\cancel{x^2}y)(3x^2y^{\frac{1}{2}})}{\cancel{x^2}\ y^{\cancel{2}}} = 6x^2y^2$

Adding and Subtracting Polynomials

To *add* or *subtract polynomials,* just arrange *like terms* in columns and then add or subtract. (Or simply add or subtract *like terms* when rearrangement is not necessary.)

Examples:

1. Add:

$$a^2 + \ ab + \ b^2$$
$$\underline{3a^2 + 4ab - 2b^2}$$
$$4a^2 + 5ab - \ b^2$$

2. $(5y - 3x) + (9y + 4x) =$

$$(5y - 3x) + (9y + 4x) = 14y + x \text{ or } x + 14y$$

3. Subtract:

$$a^2 + b^2$$
$$\underline{(-)2a^2 - b^2}$$

Change to an addition problem:

$$a^2 + b^2$$
$$\underline{(+)-2a^2 + b^2}$$
$$-a^2 + 2b^2$$

4. $(3cd - 6mt) - (2cd - 4mt) =$

$(3cd - 6mt) + (-2cd + 4mt) =$

$$(3cd - 6mt) + (-2cd + 4mt) = cd - 2mt$$

5. $3a^2bc + 2ab^2c + 4a^2bc + 5ab^2c =$

$3a^2bc + 2ab^2c$

$\underline{+4a^2bc + 5ab^2c}$

$7a^2bc + 7ab^2c$

or

$$3a^2bc + 2ab^2c + 4a^2bc + 5ab^2c = 7a^2bc + 7ab^2c$$

Practice: Adding and Subtracting Polynomials Problems

Perform the indicated operations and simplify.

1. $\quad 5x^2y^2 - 4ab$

$-6x^2y^2 + 3ab$

$\underline{-2x^2y^2 - \ ab}$

2. $(7gr - 3nt) + (5gr - 2nt) =$

3. $(9kb^2 + 6ht - 3ab) - (4kb^2 - 6ht + 2ab) =$

4. $7xyz^2 + 8x^2yz + 9xy^2z + 8xyz^2 + 3xy^2z - 3x^2yz =$

Answers: Adding and Subtracting Polynomials Problems

1. $-3x^2y^2 - 2ab$

2. $12gr - 5nt$

3. $5kb^2 + 12ht - 5ab$

4. $15xyz^2 + 5x^2yz + 12xy^2z$

Multiplying Polynomials

To *multiply polynomials,* multiply each term in one polynomial by each term in the other polynomial. Then simplify if necessary.

Examples:

$$2x - 2a$$

1. $$\underline{\times\ 3x + a}$$

$$+\ 2ax - 2a^2$$

$$\underline{6x^2 - 6ax}$$

$$6x^2 - 4ax - 2a^2$$

similar to

$$21$$
$$\underline{\times\ 23}$$
$$63$$
$$\underline{42}$$
$$483$$

Or you may wish to use the "F.O.I.L." method with *binomials*. F.O.I.L. stands for "first terms, outside terms, inside terms, last terms." Then simplify if necessary.

2. $(3x + a)(2x - 2a) =$

Multiply *first* terms from each quantity.

$$(\overset{\frown}{3x + a})(2x - 2a) = 6x^2 \underline{\hspace{3cm}}$$

Now *outside* terms.

$$(\overset{\frown}{3x + a})(2x - 2a) = 6x^2 - 6ax \underline{\hspace{2cm}}$$

Now *inside* terms.

$$(3x + \overset{\frown}{a})(2x - 2a) = 6x^2 - 6ax + 2ax \underline{\hspace{1.5cm}}$$

Now *last* terms.

$$(3x + \overset{\frown}{a})(2x - 2a) = 6x^2 - 6ax + 2ax - 2a^2$$

Now simplify.

$$6x^2 - 6ax + 2ax - 2a^2 = 6x^2 - 4ax - 2a^2$$

3. $(x + y)(x + y + z) =$

$$x + y + z$$
$$\underline{\times\ x + y}$$
$$xy + y^2 + yz$$
$$\underline{x^2 + xz + xy}$$
$$x^2 + xz + 2xy + y^2 + yz$$

Practice: Multiplying Polynomials Problems

1. $(2x + y)(3x + 5y) =$

2. $(7a + b)(2a - 3b) =$

3. $(9x + 5)(3x - 2) =$

4. $(-6y + z^2)(2y - 3z) =$

Answers : Multiplying Polynomials Problems

1.
$$
\begin{array}{r}
2x + y \\
\times\ 3x + 5y \\
\hline
+10xy + 5y^2 \\
+\ 6x^2 +\ 3xy \\
\hline
6x^2 + 13xy + 5y^2
\end{array}
$$

2.
$$
\begin{array}{r}
7a +\ b \\
\times\ 2a - 3b \\
\hline
-21ab - 3b^2 \\
+14a^2 +\ 2ab \\
\hline
14a^2 - 19ab - 3b^2
\end{array}
$$

3.
$$
\begin{array}{r}
9x +\ 5 \\
\times\ 3x -\ 2 \\
\hline
-18x - 10 \\
+27x^2 + 15x \\
\hline
27x^2 -\ 3x - 10
\end{array}
$$

4.
$$
\begin{array}{r}
-6y +\ z^2 \\
\times\ 2y - 3z \\
\hline
+18yz - 3z^3 \\
-12y^2 + 2yz^2 \\
\hline
-12y^2 + 2yz^2 + 18yz - 3z^3
\end{array}
$$

or

$-12y^2 + 18yz + 2yz^2 - 3z^3$

Dividing Polynomials by Monomials

To *divide a polynomial* by a monomial, just divide each term in the polynomial by the monomial.

Examples:

1. $(6x^2 + 2x) \div (2x) = \dfrac{6x^2 + 2x}{2x} = \dfrac{6x^2}{2x} + \dfrac{2x}{2x} = 3x + 1$

2. $(16a^7 - 12a^5) \div (4a^2) = \dfrac{16a^7 - 12a^5}{4a^2} = \dfrac{16a^7}{4a^2} - \dfrac{12a^5}{4a^2} = 4a^5 - 3a^3$

Practice: Dividing Polynomials by Monomials Problems

1. $(3x - 9) \div 3 =$

2. $(16x^3 + 4x^2 + 8x) \div (2x) =$

3. $(14a^2b - 8ab + 4a) \div (2a) =$

4. $(84c^2d - 38cd + 18cd^3) \div (2cd) =$

Answers: Dividing Polynomials by Monomials Problems

1. $(3x - 9) \div 3 = \dfrac{3x - 9}{3} = \dfrac{3x}{3} - \dfrac{9}{3} = x - 3$

2. $(16x^3 + 4x^2 + 8x) \div (2x) = \dfrac{16x^3 + 4x^2 + 8x}{2x} = \dfrac{16x^3}{2x} + \dfrac{4x^2}{2x} + \dfrac{8x}{2x}$
$$= 8x^2 + 2x + 4$$

3. $(14a^2b - 8ab + 4a) \div (2a) = \dfrac{14a^2b - 8ab + 4a}{2a} = \dfrac{14a^2b}{2a} - \dfrac{8ab}{2a} + \dfrac{4a}{2a}$
$$= 7ab - 4b + 2$$

4. $(84c^2d - 38cd + 18cd^3) \div (2cd) = \dfrac{84c^2d - 38cd + 18cd^3}{2cd}$
$$= \dfrac{84c^2d}{2cd} - \dfrac{38cd}{2cd} + \dfrac{18cd^3}{2cd}$$
$$= 42c - 19 + 9d^2$$

Dividing Polynomials by Polynomials

To *divide a polynomial by a polynomial,* make sure both are in descending order; then use long division. (***Remember:*** Divide by the first term, multiply, subtract, bring down.)

Examples:

1. Divide $4a^2 + 18a + 8$ by $a + 4$.

    First, divide a into $4a^2$:

    $$a+4\overline{)4a^2+18a+8}^{\,4a}$$

    Now multiply $4a$ times $(a + 4)$:

    $$\begin{array}{r} 4a \\ a+4\overline{)4a^2+18a+8} \\ \underline{4a^2+16a} \end{array}$$

    Now subtract:

    $$\begin{array}{r} 4a \\ a+4\overline{)4a^2+18a+8} \\ \underline{-\left(4a^2+16a\right)} \\ 2a \end{array}$$

    Now bring down the +8:

    $$\begin{array}{r} 4a \\ a+4\overline{)4a^2+18a+8} \\ \underline{-\left(4a^2+16a\right)} \\ 2a+8 \end{array}$$

    Now divide a into $2a$:

    $$\begin{array}{r} 4a+2 \\ a+4\overline{)4a^2+18a+8} \\ \underline{-\left(4a^2+16a\right)} \\ 2a+8 \end{array}$$

    Now multiply 2 times $(a + 4)$:

    $$\begin{array}{r} 4a+2 \\ a+4\overline{)4a^2+18a+8} \\ \underline{-\left(4a^2+16a\right)} \\ 2a+8 \\ \underline{2a+8} \end{array}$$

Now subtract:

$$\begin{array}{r} 4a+2 \\ a+4\overline{)4a^2+18a+8} \\ -\left(4a^2+16a\right) \\ \hline 2a+8 \\ (-)2a+8 \\ \hline 0 \end{array}$$

Therefore, the final answer is:

$$\frac{4a^2+18a+8}{a+4}$$

$$\begin{array}{r} 4a+2 \\ a+4\overline{)4a^2+18a+8} \\ -\left(4a^2+16a\right) \\ \hline 2a+8 \\ -(2a+8) \\ \hline 0 \end{array}$$ similar to $$\begin{array}{r} 23 \\ 53\overline{)1219} \\ (-)106 \\ \hline 159 \\ (-)159 \\ \hline 0 \end{array}$$

2. $(3x^2 + 4x + 1) \div (x + 1) = 3x + 1$

$$\begin{array}{r} 3x+1 \\ x+1\overline{)3x^2+4x+1} \\ (-)3x^2+3x \\ \hline x+1 \\ (-)x+1 \\ \hline 0 \end{array}$$

3. $(2x + 1 + x^2) \div (x + 1) = x + 1$

First change to descending order : $x^2 + 2x + 1$

Then divide:

$$\begin{array}{r} x+1 \\ x+1\overline{)x^2+2x+1} \\ (-)x^2+1x \\ \hline x+1 \\ (-)x+1 \\ \hline 0 \end{array}$$

4. $(m^3 - m) \div (m + 1) = m^2 - m$

   Note: When terms are missing, be sure to leave proper room between terms.

$$\begin{array}{r} m^2 - m \\ m+1\overline{)m^3 + 0m^2 - m} \\ \underline{(-)m^3 + m^2} \\ -m^2 - m \\ \underline{(-)-m^2 - m} \\ 0 \end{array}$$

5. $(10a^2 - 29a - 21) \div (2a - 7) = 5a + 3$

$$\begin{array}{r} 5a + 3 \\ 2a-7\overline{)10a^2 - 29a - 21} \\ \underline{(-)10a^2 - 35a} \\ 6a - 21 \\ \underline{(-)6a - 21} \\ 0 \end{array}$$

   Note that remainders are possible.

6. $(x^2 + 2x + 4) \div (x + 1) = (x+1) + \dfrac{3}{(x+1)}$

$$\begin{array}{r} x + 1 \text{ (with remainder 3)} \\ x+1\overline{)x^2 + 2x + 4} \\ \underline{(-)x^2 + \ x} \\ x + 4 \\ \underline{(-)x + 1} \\ 3 \end{array}$$

   This answer can be rewritten as $(x+1) + \dfrac{3}{(x+1)}$.

Practice: Dividing Polynomials by Polynomials Problems

1. $(x^2 + 18x + 45) \div (x + 3) =$

2. $(21t + 5 + 4t^2) \div (t + 5) =$

3. $(z^3 - 1) \div (z - 1) =$

4. $(t^2 + 4t - 6) \div (t + 2) =$

5. $(14x^2 + 11x + 2) \div (2x + 1) =$

Answers: Dividing Polynomials by Polynomials Problems

1. $(x^2 + 18x + 45) \div (x + 3) = x + 15$

$$
\begin{array}{r}
x+15 \\
x+3{\overline{\smash{\big)}\,x^2+18x+45}} \\
\underline{(-)x^2+\ 3x} \\
15x+45 \\
\underline{(-)15x+45} \\
0
\end{array}
$$

2. $(21t + 5 + 4t^2) \div (t + 5) = 4t + 1$

Reorder: $4t^2 + 21t + 5$

$$
\begin{array}{r}
4t+1 \\
t+5{\overline{\smash{\big)}\,4t^2+21t+5}} \\
\underline{(-)4t^2+20t} \\
t+5 \\
\underline{(-)t+5} \\
0
\end{array}
$$

3. $(z^3 - 1) \div (z - 1) = z^2 + z + 1$

$$
\begin{array}{r}
z^2+z+1 \\
z-1{\overline{\smash{\big)}\,z^3+0z^2+0z-1}} \\
\underline{(-)z^3-\ z^2} \\
z^2+0z \\
\underline{(-)z^2-\ z} \\
z-1 \\
\underline{(-)z-1} \\
0
\end{array}
$$

4. $(t^2 + 4t - 6) \div (t + 2) = t + 2 - \dfrac{10}{t+2}$

$t + 2$ with remainder -10 or $t + 2 - \dfrac{10}{t+2}$

$$t+2\overline{)t^2 + 4t - 6}$$

$\underline{(-)t^2 + 2t}$

$\qquad 2t - 6$

$\qquad \underline{(-)2t + 4}$

$\qquad\qquad -10$

5. $(14x^2 + 11x + 2) \div (2x + 1) = 7x + 2$

$$2x+1\overline{)14x^2 + 11x + 2}$$

$\underline{(-)14x^2 + \ 7x}$

$\qquad\qquad 4x + 2$

$\qquad\quad \underline{(-)4x + 2}$

$\qquad\qquad\qquad 0$

Factoring

To *factor* means to find two or more quantities whose product equals the original quantity.

Factoring out a Common Factor

To *factor out a common factor:*

(a) Find the largest common monomial factor of each term.

(b) Divide the original polynomial by this factor to obtain the second factor. The second factor will be a polynomial.

Examples:

1. $5x^2 + 4x = x(5x + 4)$

2. $2y^3 - 6y = 2y(y^2 - 3)$

3. $x^5 - 4x^3 + x^2 = x^2(x^3 - 4x + 1)$

Practice: Factoring out a Common Factor Problems

Factor the following completely.

1. $a^2 + 26a =$

2. $t^2 - 35t =$

3. $3m^3 + 6m^2 + 9m =$

4. $12p^3 + 24p^2 =$

Answers: Factoring out a Common Factor Problems

1. $a(a + 26)$

2. $t(t - 35)$

3. $3m(m^2 + 2m + 3)$

4. $12p^2(p + 2)$

Factoring the Difference between Two Squares

To *factor the difference between two squares:*

1. Find the square root of the first term and the square root of the second term.

2. Express your answer as the product of: the sum of the quantities from step a, times the difference of those quantities.

Examples:

1. $x^2 - 144 = (x + 12)(x - 12)$

2. $a^2 - b^2 = (a + b)(a - b)$

3. $9y^2 - 1 = (3y + 1)(3y - 1)$

Note: $x^2 + 144$ is *not* factorable.

Practice: Factoring the Difference between Two Squares Problems

Factor the following.

1. $x^2 - 25 =$

2. $p^2 - q^2 =$

3. $144 - h^2 =$

4. $x^2y^2 - z^2 =$

5. $4a^2 - 9 =$

6. $2t^2 - 50 =$

Answers: Factoring the Difference between Two Squares Problems

1. $(x + 5)(x - 5)$
2. $(p + q)(p - q)$
3. $(12 + h)(12 - h)$
4. $(xy + z)(xy - z)$
5. $(2a + 3)(2a - 3)$
6. $2(t^2 - 25) = 2(t + 5)(t - 5)$. First, factor out the greatest common factor of 2; then recognize the difference of squares ($t^2 - 25$).

Factoring Polynomials Having Three Terms of the Form $Ax^2 + Bx + C$

To factor polynomials having three terms of the form $Ax^2 + Bx + C$:

1. Check to see if you can *monomial factor* (factor out common terms). Then if $A = 1$ (that is, the first term is simply x^2), use double parentheses and factor the first term. Place these factors in the left sides of the parentheses. For example, $(x \quad)(x \quad)$.
2. Factor the last term and place the factors in the right sides of the parentheses.

To decide on the signs of the numbers do the following:

If the sign of the last term is *negative:*

1. Find two numbers whose product is the last term and whose *difference* is the *coefficient* (number in front) of the middle term.
2. Give the larger of these two numbers the sign of the middle term and the *opposite* sign to the other factor.

If the sign of the last term is *positive:*

1. Find two numbers whose product is the last term and whose *sum* is the coefficient of the middle term.

2. Give both factors the sign of the middle term.

Examples:

1. Factor $x^2 - 3x - 10$: $x^2 - 3x + 10 = (x - 5)(x + 2)$.

   First, check to see if you can monomial factor (factor out common terms). Since this is not possible, use double parentheses and factor the first term as follows: $(x\ \ )(x\ \ )$. Next, factor the last term, 10, into 2 times 5 (using step b above, 5 must take the negative sign and 2 must take the positive sign, because they will then total the coefficient of the middle term, which is -3) and add the proper signs leaving: $(x - 5)(x + 2)$.

   Multiply *means* (inner terms) and *extremes* (outer terms) to check.

   $$(x-5)(x+2)$$
   $$-5x$$
   $$+2x$$
   $$-3x \text{ (which is the middle term)}$$

   To completely check, multiply the factors together:

   $$x - 5$$
   $$\times x + 2$$
   $$(+)2x - 10$$
   $$x^2 - 5x$$
   $$x^2 - 3x + 10$$

2. Factor $x^2 + 8x + 15$: $x^2 + 8x + 15 = (x + 3)(x + 5)$

   Notice that $3 \times 5 = 15$ and $3 + 5 = 8$, the coefficient of the middle term. Also, note that the signs of both factors are $+$, the sign of the middle term. To check

   $$(x+3)(x+5)$$
   $$+3x$$
   $$+5x$$
   $$+8x \text{ (the middle term)}$$

3. Factor $x^2 - 5x - 14$: $x^2 - 5x - 14 = (x - 7)(x + 2)$

   Notice that $7 \times 2 = 14$ and $7 - 2 = 5$, the coefficient of the middle term. Also, note that the sign of the larger factor, 7, is –, while the other factor, 2, has a + sign. To check

$$(x - 7)(x + 2)$$
$$-7x$$
$$+2x$$
$$-5x \text{ (the middle term)}$$

   If, however, $A \neq 1$ (the first term has a coefficient other than 1), then additional trial and error will be necessary. The next example is this type of problem.

4. Factor $4x^2 + 5x + 1$: $4x^2 + 5x + 1 = (4x + 1)(x + 1)$

   $(2x +)(2x +)$ might work for the first term. But when 1's are used as factors to get the last term $(2x + 1)(2x + 1)$, the middle term comes out as $4x$ instead of $5x$.

$$(2x + 1)(2x + 1)$$
$$+2x$$
$$+2x$$
$$+4x$$

   Therefore, try $(4x +)(x +)$. Now using 1's as factors to get the last terms gives $(4x + 1)(x + 1)$. Checking for the middle term

$$(4x + 1)(x + 1)$$
$$+1x$$
$$+4x$$
$$+5x$$

   Therefore, $4x^2 + 5x + 1 = (4x + 1)(x + 1)$.

5. Factor $4a^2 + 6a + 2$: $4a^2 + 6a + 2 = 2(2a + 1)(a + 1)$

   Factoring out a 2 leaves $2(2a^2 + 3a + 1)$

   Now factor as usual giving $2(2a + 1)(a + 1)$

   To check

$$(2a + 1)(a + 1)$$

$$\underset{}{+1a}$$
$$+2a$$
$$+3a$$

   (the middle term after 2 was factored out)

6. Factor $5x^3 + 6x^2 + x$: $5x^3 + 6x^2 + x = x(5x + 1)(x + 1)$

   Factoring out an x leaves $x(5x^2 + 6x + 1)$

   Now factor as usual giving $x(5x + 1)(x + 1)$

   To check

$$(5x + 1)(x + 1)$$

$$+1x$$
$$+5x$$
$$+6x$$

   (the middle term after x was factored out)

7. Factor $5 + 7b + 2b^2$ (a slight twist): $5 + 7b + 2b^2 = (5 + 2b)(1 + b)$

   To check

$$(5 + 2b)(1 + b)$$

$$+2b$$
$$+5b$$
$$+7b$$

   (the middle term)

Note that $(5 + b)(1 + 2b)$ is incorrect because it gives the wrong middle term.

8. Factor $x^2 + 2xy + y^2$: $x^2 + 2xy + y^2 = (x + y)(x + y)$

To check

$$(x + y)(x + y)$$
$$+xy$$
$$\underline{+xy}$$
$$+2xy \qquad \text{(the middle term)}$$

Note: There are polynomials that are not factorable.

Practice: Factoring Polynomials Problems

Factor each of the following.

1. $x^2 + 8x + 15 =$

2. $x^2 + 2x - 24 =$

3. $r^3 + 14r^2 + 45r =$

4. $x^2 - 16x + 48 =$

5. $1 + 2x + x^2 =$

6. $c^2 - 2cd + d^2 =$

7. $3y^2 + 4yz + z^2 =$

8. $7a^2 - 20a - 3 =$

Answers: Factoring Polynomials Problems

1. $(x + 3)(x + 5)$

2. $(x + 6)(x - 4)$

3. $r(r + 9)(r + 5)$

4. $(x - 4)(x - 12)$

5. $(1 + x)(1 + x)$

6. $(c - d)(c - d)$

7. $(3y + z)(y + z)$

8. $(7a + 1)(a - 3)$

Solving Quadratic Equations

A *quadratic equation* is an equation that could be written as $Ax^2 + Bx + C = 0$ with $A \neq 0$. To solve a quadratic equation using factoring:

1. Put all terms on one side of the equal sign, leaving zero on the other side.

2. Factor.

3. Set each factor equal to zero.

4. Solve each of these equations.

5. Check by inserting your answer in the original equation.

Examples:

1. Solve : $x^2 - 6x = 16$

    Now, following the steps, $x^2 - 6x = 16$ becomes $x^2 - 6x - 16 = 0$.

    Factor: $(x - 8)(x + 2) = 0$

    $x - 8 = 0$

    $\quad x = 8$

    or

    $x + 2 = 0$

    $\quad x = -2$

    Then to check:

    $8^2 - 6(8) = 16$

    $64 - 48 = 16$

    $4 + 12 = 16$

    $16 = 16$

or

$$(-2)^2 - 6(-2) = 16$$

$$4 + 12 = 16$$

$$16 = 16$$

Both values 8 and –2 are solutions to the original equation.

2. Solve: $y^2 = -6y - 5$

Setting the equation equal to zero:

$$y^2 + 6y + 5 = 0$$

Factoring:

$$(y + 5)(y + 1) = 0$$

Setting each factor equal to 0:

$$y + 5 = 0$$

$$y = -5$$

or

$$y + 1 = 0$$

$$y = -1$$

To check:

$$(-5)^2 = -6(-5) - 5$$

$$25 = 30 - 5$$

$$25 = 25$$

or

$$(-1)^2 = -6(-1) - 5$$

$$1 = 6 - 5$$

$$1 = 1$$

A quadratic missing either or both the constant term and/or the term raised to the first power is called an *incomplete quadratic.*

3. Solve: $x^2 - 16 = 0$

   Factor:

   $(x + 4)(x - 4) = 0$

   $x + 4 = 0$

   $x = -4$

   or

   $x - 4 = 0$

   $x = 4$

   To check:

   $(-4)^2 - 16 = 0$

   $16 - 16 = 0$

   $0 = 0$

   or

   $(4)^2 - 16 = 0$

   $16 - 16 = 0$

   $0 = 0$

4. Solve : $x^2 + 6x = 0$

   Factor:

   $x(x + 6) = 0$

   $x = 0$

   or

   $x + 6 = 0$

   $x = -6$

   To check:

   $(0)^2 + 6(0) = 0$

   $0 + 0 = 0$

   $0 = 0$

or

$$(-6)^2 + 6(-6) = 0$$
$$36 + (-36) = 0$$
$$0 = 0$$

5. Solve : $2x^2 + 2x - 1 = x^2 + 6x - 5$

First, simplify by putting all terms on one side and combining like terms:

$$2x^2 + 2x - 1 = x^2 + 6x - 5$$
$$\underline{-x^2 - 6x + 5 \quad -x^2 - 6x + 5}$$
$$x^2 - 4x + 4 = 0$$

Now factor:

$$(x - 2)(x - 2) = 0$$
$$x - 2 = 0$$
$$x = 2$$

To check:

$$2(2)^2 + 2(2) - 1 = (2)^2 + 6(2) - 5$$
$$8 + 4 - 1 = 4 + 12 - 5$$
$$11 = 11$$

Practice: Solving Quadratic Equations Problems

Solve each of the following.

1. $x^2 + 7x = -10$

2. $y^2 - 18y = -45$

3. $x^2 - 25 = 0$

4. $3t^2 + 4t + 1 = 0$

5. $2b^2 - b = 0$

6. $3n^2 - 2n = -1 + 2n^2$

Answers: Solving Quadratic Equations Problems

1. $x^2 + 7x = -10$

    $x^2 + 7x + 10 = 0$

    $(x + 2)(x + 5) = 0$

    $x + 2 = 0$

    $x = -2$

    or

    $x + 5 = 0$

    $x = -5$

2. $y^2 - 18y = -45$

    $y^2 - 18y + 45 = 0$

    $(y - 15)(y - 3) = 0$

    $y - 15 = 0$

    $y = 15$

    or

    $y - 3 = 0$

    $y = 3$

3. $x^2 - 25 = 0$

    $(x + 5)(x - 5) = 0$

    $x + 5 = 0$

    $x = -5$

    or

    $x - 5 = 0$

    $x = 5$

4. $3t^2 + 4t + 1 = 0$

    $(3t + 1)(t + 1) = 0$

    $3t + 1 = 0$

    $3t = -1$

$$t = -\frac{1}{3}$$

or

$$t + 1 = 0$$

$$t = -1$$

5. $\quad 2b^2 - b = 0$

$$b(2b - 1) = 0$$

$$b = 0$$

or

$$2b - 1 = 0$$

$$2b = 1$$

$$b = \frac{1}{2}$$

6. $\quad 3n^2 - 2n = -1 + 2n^2$

$$\underline{-2n^2 \qquad\qquad -2n^2}$$

$$n^2 - 2n = -1$$

$$n^2 - 2n + 1 = 0$$

$$(n - 1)(n - 1) = 0$$

$$n - 1 = 0$$

$$n = 1$$

Algebraic Fractions

Algebraic fractions are fractions using a variable in the numerator or denominator, such as $\frac{3}{x}$. Since division by 0 is impossible, variables in the denominator have certain restrictions. The denominator can *never* equal 0. Therefore in the fractions:

$\frac{5}{x}$, x cannot equal 0 ($x \neq 0$)

$\frac{2}{x-3}$, x cannot equal 3 ($x \neq 3$)

$\frac{3}{a-b}$, $a - b$ cannot equal 0 ($a - b \neq 0$) so a cannot equal b ($a \neq b$)

$\frac{4}{a^2 b}$, a cannot equal 0 and b cannot equal 0 ($a \neq 0$ and $b \neq 0$)

Be aware of these types of restrictions.

Operations with Algebraic Fractions

Reducing Algebraic Fractions

To *reduce an algebraic fraction* to lowest terms, first factor the numerator and the denominator; then cancel (or divide out) common factors.

Examples:

1. Reduce: $\dfrac{4x^3}{8x^2}$

$$\dfrac{\overset{1}{\cancel{4}}x^{\overset{1}{\cancel{3}}}}{\underset{2}{\cancel{8}}\,\cancel{x^2}} = \dfrac{1}{2}x \text{ or } \dfrac{x}{2}$$

2. Reduce: $\dfrac{(3x-3)}{(4x-4)}$

$$\dfrac{(3x-3)}{(4x-4)} = \dfrac{3(x-1)}{4(x-1)} = \dfrac{3\cancel{(x-1)}}{4\cancel{(x-1)}} = \dfrac{3}{4}$$

3. Reduce: $\dfrac{x^2+2x+1}{(3x+3)}$

$$\dfrac{x^2+2x+1}{(3x+3)} = \dfrac{(x+1)(x+1)}{3(x+1)} = \dfrac{\cancel{(x+1)}(x+1)}{3\cancel{(x+1)}} = \dfrac{(x+1)}{3}$$

Warning: Do *not* cancel through an addition or subtraction sign. *For example:*

$$\dfrac{x+1}{x+2} \neq \dfrac{\cancel{x}+1}{\cancel{x}+2} \neq \dfrac{1}{2}$$

or

$$\dfrac{x+6}{6} \neq \dfrac{x+\cancel{6}}{\cancel{6}} \neq x$$

Practice: Reducing Algebraic Fractions Problems

Reduce each of the following.

1. $\dfrac{8a^2b}{12a^3b}$

2. $\dfrac{5xy^3}{10x^3y}$

3. $\dfrac{10x+5}{8x+4}$

4. $\dfrac{x^2-y^2}{x+y}$

5. $\dfrac{a^2+a}{2a^2+4a+2}$

Answers: Reducing Algebraic Fractions Problems

1. $\dfrac{8a^2b}{12a^3b} = \dfrac{\overset{2}{\cancel{8}}\,\cancel{a^2}\,\cancel{b}}{\underset{3}{\cancel{12}}\,a^{\cancel{3}}\,\cancel{b}} = \dfrac{2}{3a}$

2. $\dfrac{5xy^3}{10x^3y} = \dfrac{\overset{1}{\cancel{5}}\,x\,y^{\cancel{3}}}{\underset{2}{\cancel{10}}\,x^{\cancel{3}}\,y} = \dfrac{1y^2}{2x^2}$ or $\dfrac{y^2}{2x^2}$

3. $\dfrac{10x+5}{8x+4} = \dfrac{5(2x+1)}{4(2x+1)} = \dfrac{5\cancel{(2x+1)}}{4\cancel{(2x+1)}} = \dfrac{5}{4}$ or $1\dfrac{1}{4}$

4. $\dfrac{x^2-y^2}{x+y} = \dfrac{(x-y)(x+y)}{x+y} = \dfrac{(x-y)\cancel{(x+y)}}{\cancel{x+y}} = \dfrac{(x-y)}{1} = x-y$

5. $\dfrac{a^2+a}{2a^2+4a+2} = \dfrac{a(a+1)}{2(a^2+2a+1)} = \dfrac{a(a+1)}{2(a+1)(a+1)} = \dfrac{a\cancel{(a+1)}}{2(a+1)\cancel{(a+1)}} =$

$\dfrac{a}{2(a+1)}$

Multiplying Algebraic Fractions

To *multiply algebraic fractions,* first factor the numerators and denominators that are polynomials; then cancel where possible. Multiply the remaining numerators together and denominators together. (If you've canceled properly, your answer will be in reduced form.)

Examples:

1. $\dfrac{2x}{3} \times \dfrac{y}{5} = \dfrac{2xy}{15}$

2. $\dfrac{x^2}{3y} \times \dfrac{2y}{3x} = \dfrac{x^2}{3\cancel{y}} \times \dfrac{2\cancel{y}}{3\cancel{x}} = \dfrac{2x}{9}$

3. $\dfrac{x+1}{5y+10} \times \dfrac{y+2}{x^2+2x+1} = \dfrac{x+1}{5(y+2)} \times \dfrac{y+2}{(x+1)(x+1)} =$

$\dfrac{\overset{1}{\cancel{x+1}}}{5\cancel{(y+2)}} \times \dfrac{\overset{1}{\cancel{y+2}}}{\cancel{(x+1)}(x+1)} = \dfrac{1}{5(x+1)}$

Practice: Multiplying Algebraic Fractions Problems

1. $\dfrac{6x}{11} \times \dfrac{2}{5y} =$

2. $\dfrac{3a^2}{5b} \times \dfrac{2b}{9a} =$

3. $\dfrac{5}{x+1} \times \dfrac{3x+3}{6} =$

4. $\dfrac{x^2-4}{6} \times \dfrac{3y}{2x+4} =$

5. $\dfrac{x^2+4x+4}{x-3} \times \dfrac{5}{3x+6} =$

Answers: Multiplying Algebraic Fractions Problems

1. $\dfrac{6x}{11} \times \dfrac{2}{5y} = \dfrac{12x}{55y}$

2. $\dfrac{3a^2}{5b} \times \dfrac{2b}{9a} = \dfrac{\cancel{3}\,a^{\cancel{2}^{\,1}}}{5\cancel{b}} \times \dfrac{2\cancel{b}}{\cancel{9}\,\cancel{a}_3} = \dfrac{2a}{15}$

3. $\dfrac{5}{x+1} \times \dfrac{3x+3}{6} = \dfrac{5}{x+1} \times \dfrac{3(x+1)}{6} = \dfrac{5}{\cancel{x+1}} \times \dfrac{\cancel{3}^{\,1}\,\cancel{(x+1)}}{\cancel{6}_2} = \dfrac{5}{2} = 2\dfrac{1}{2}$

4. $\dfrac{x^2-4}{6} \times \dfrac{3y}{2x+4} = \dfrac{(x+2)(x-2)}{6} \times \dfrac{3y}{2(x+2)}$

$$= \dfrac{\cancel{(x+2)}(x-2)}{\cancel{6}_2} \times \dfrac{\cancel{3}^{\,1}y}{2\cancel{(x+2)}} = \dfrac{(x-2)y}{4}$$

5. $\dfrac{x^2+4x+4}{x-3} \times \dfrac{5}{3x+6} = \dfrac{(x+2)(x+2)}{x-3} \times \dfrac{5}{3(x+2)}$

$$= \dfrac{(x+2)\cancel{(x+2)}}{x-3} \times \dfrac{5}{3\cancel{(x+2)}} = \dfrac{5(x+2)}{3(x-3)}$$

Dividing Algebraic Fractions

To *divide algebraic fractions,* invert the fraction doing the dividing and multiply. ***Remember:*** You can cancel only after you invert.

Examples:

1. $\dfrac{3x^2}{5} \div \dfrac{2x}{y} = \dfrac{3x^2}{5} \times \dfrac{y}{2x} = \dfrac{3x^{\cancel{2}^{\,1}}}{5} \times \dfrac{y}{2\cancel{x}} = \dfrac{3xy}{10}$

2. $\dfrac{4x-8}{6} \div \dfrac{x-2}{3} = \dfrac{4x-8}{6} \times \dfrac{3}{x-2}$

$$= \dfrac{4(x-2)}{6} \times \dfrac{3}{x-2}$$

$$= \dfrac{4\,\cancel{(x-2)}^{\,1}}{\cancel{6}_2} \times \dfrac{\cancel{3}^{\,1}}{\cancel{x-2}_1} = \dfrac{4}{2} = 2$$

Practice: Dividing Algebraic Fractions Problems

1. $\dfrac{8x^3}{15} \div \dfrac{6x^2}{3} =$

2. $\dfrac{y^2}{5} \div y^2 =$

3. $\dfrac{2x+6}{5} \div \dfrac{x+3}{10} =$

4. $\dfrac{x^2}{x^2+5x+6} \div \dfrac{x}{x+3} =$

Answers: Dividing Algebraic Fractions Problems

1. $\dfrac{8x^3}{15} \div \dfrac{6x^2}{3} = \dfrac{8x^3}{15} \times \dfrac{3}{6x^2} = \dfrac{\overset{4}{\cancel{8}} x^{\overset{1}{\cancel{3}}}}{\underset{5}{\cancel{15}}} \times \dfrac{\overset{1}{\cancel{3}}}{\underset{3}{\cancel{6}} x^{\cancel{2}}} = \dfrac{4x}{15}$

2. $\dfrac{y^2}{5} \div y^2 = \dfrac{y^2}{5} \div \dfrac{y^2}{1} = \dfrac{y^2}{5} \times \dfrac{1}{y^2} = \dfrac{\cancel{y^2}}{5} \times \dfrac{1}{\cancel{y^2}} = \dfrac{1}{5}$

3. $\dfrac{2x+6}{5} \div \dfrac{x+3}{10} = \dfrac{2x+6}{5} \times \dfrac{10}{x+3} = \dfrac{2(x+3)}{5} \times \dfrac{10}{x+3}$

$$= \dfrac{2\cancel{(x+3)}}{\underset{1}{\cancel{5}}} \times \dfrac{\overset{2}{\cancel{10}}}{\cancel{x+3}} = \dfrac{4}{1} = 4$$

4. $\dfrac{x^2}{x^2+5x+6} \div \dfrac{x}{x+3} = \dfrac{x^2}{x^2+5x+6} \times \dfrac{x+3}{x}$

$$= \dfrac{x^{\overset{1}{\cancel{2}}}}{\cancel{(x+3)}(x+2)} \times \dfrac{\cancel{x+3}}{\cancel{x}} = \dfrac{x}{x+2}$$

Adding or Subtracting Algebraic Fractions

To *add or subtract algebraic fractions having a common denominator*, simply keep the denominator and combine (add or subtract) the numerators. Reduce if necessary.

Examples:

1. $\dfrac{4}{x} + \dfrac{5}{x} = \dfrac{4+5}{x} = \dfrac{9}{x}$

2. $\dfrac{x-4}{x+1} + \dfrac{3}{x+1} = \dfrac{x-4+3}{x+1} = \dfrac{x-1}{x+1}$

3. $\dfrac{3x}{y} - \dfrac{2x-1}{y} = \dfrac{3x-(2x-1)}{y} = \dfrac{3x-2x+1}{y} = \dfrac{x+1}{y}$

Practice: Adding or Subtracting Algebraic Fractions Problems

1. $\dfrac{3}{x} + \dfrac{2}{x} =$

2. $\dfrac{x-1}{y} + \dfrac{3x+2}{y} =$

3. $\dfrac{4x-3}{x} - \dfrac{3x-3}{x} =$

4. $\dfrac{6x-3}{x-4} - \dfrac{x+2}{x-4} =$

Answers: Adding or Subtracting Algebraic Fractions Problems

1. $\dfrac{3}{x} + \dfrac{2}{x} = \dfrac{3+2}{x} = \dfrac{5}{x}$

2. $\dfrac{x-1}{y} + \dfrac{3x+2}{y} = \dfrac{x-1+3x+2}{y} = \dfrac{4x+1}{y}$

3. $\dfrac{4x-3}{x} - \dfrac{3x-3}{x} = \dfrac{4x-3-(3x-3)}{x} = \dfrac{4x-3-3x+3}{x} = \dfrac{x}{x} = 1$

4. $\dfrac{6x-3}{x-4} - \dfrac{x+2}{x-4} = \dfrac{6x-3-(x+2)}{x-4} = \dfrac{6x-3-x-2}{x-4} = \dfrac{5x-5}{x-4} = \dfrac{5(x-1)}{x-4}$

To *add or subtract algebraic fractions having different denominators,* first find a lowest common denominator (LCD), change each fraction to an equivalent fraction with the common denominator, then combine each numerator. Reduce if necessary.

Examples:

1. $\dfrac{2}{x} + \dfrac{3}{y} =$

   LCD = xy

   $\dfrac{2}{x} \times \dfrac{y}{y} + \dfrac{3}{y} \times \dfrac{x}{x} = \dfrac{2y}{xy} + \dfrac{3x}{xy} = \dfrac{2y+3x}{xy}$

2. $\dfrac{x+2}{3x} + \dfrac{x-3}{6x} =$

   LCD = $6x$

   $\dfrac{x+2}{3x} \times \dfrac{2}{2} + \dfrac{x-3}{6x} = \dfrac{2x+4}{6x} + \dfrac{x-3}{6x} = \dfrac{2x+4+x-3}{6x} = \dfrac{3x+1}{6x}$

   If there is a common variable factor with more than one exponent, use its greatest exponent.

3. $\dfrac{2}{y^2} - \dfrac{3}{y} =$

   LCD = y^2

   $\dfrac{2}{y^2} - \dfrac{3}{y} \times \dfrac{y}{y} = \dfrac{2}{y^2} - \dfrac{3y}{y^2} = \dfrac{2-3y}{y^2}$

4. $\dfrac{4}{x^3 y} + \dfrac{3}{xy^2} =$

   LCD = $x^3 y^2$

   $\dfrac{4}{x^3 y} \times \dfrac{y}{y} + \dfrac{3}{xy^2} \times \dfrac{x^2}{x^2} = \dfrac{4y}{x^3 y^2} + \dfrac{3x^2}{x^3 y^2} = \dfrac{4y+3x^2}{x^3 y^2}$

5. $\dfrac{x}{x+1} - \dfrac{2x}{x+2} =$

LCD $= (x + 1)(x + 2)$

$$\frac{x}{x+1} \times \frac{(x+2)}{(x+2)} - \frac{2x}{x+2} \times \frac{(x+1)}{(x+1)} =$$

$$\frac{x^2 + 2x}{(x+1)(x+2)} - \frac{2x^2 + 2x}{(x+1)(x+2)} =$$

$$\frac{x^2 + 2x - 2x^2 - 2x}{(x+1)(x+2)} = \frac{-x^2}{(x+1)(x+2)}$$

To find the lowest common denominator, it is often necessary to factor the denominators and proceed as follows.

6. $\dfrac{2x}{x^2-9} - \dfrac{5}{x^2+4x+3} = \dfrac{2x}{(x+3)(x-3)} - \dfrac{5}{(x+3)(x+1)} =$

LCD $= (x + 3)(x - 3)(x + 1)$

$$\frac{2x}{(x+3)(x-3)} \times \frac{(x+1)}{(x+1)} - \frac{5}{(x+3)(x+1)} \times \frac{(x-3)}{(x-3)} =$$

$$\frac{2x^2 + 2x}{(x+3)(x-3)(x+1)} - \frac{(5x-15)}{(x+3)(x-3)(x+1)} =$$

$$\frac{2x^2 + 2x - (5x-15)}{(x+3)(x-3)(x+1)} = \frac{2x^2 + 2x - 5x + 15}{(x+3)(x-3)(x+1)} =$$

$$\frac{2x^2 - 3x + 15}{(x+3)(x-3)(x+1)}$$

Since $2x^2 - 3x + 15$ is not factorable, this is the reduced answer.

Practice: Adding or Subtracting Algebraic Fractions Problems

1. $\dfrac{5}{x} + \dfrac{2}{y} =$

2. $\dfrac{x}{4} - \dfrac{y}{3} =$

3. $\dfrac{y+5}{2y} + \dfrac{y-2}{8y} =$

4. $\dfrac{7}{x} + \dfrac{3}{x^3} =$

5. $\dfrac{3x}{x^2 y} + \dfrac{2x}{xy^2} =$

6. $\dfrac{x}{3x+3} + \dfrac{2x}{x+1} =$

7. $\dfrac{3}{x^2-4}-\dfrac{2x}{x^2+4x+4}=$

8. $\dfrac{1}{x}+\dfrac{1}{y}+\dfrac{1}{z}=$

Answers: Adding or Subtracting Algebraic Fractions Problems

1. $\dfrac{5}{x}+\dfrac{2}{y}=$

   LCD $= xy$

   $\dfrac{5}{x}\times\dfrac{y}{y}+\dfrac{2}{y}\times\dfrac{x}{x}=\dfrac{5y}{xy}+\dfrac{2x}{xy}=\dfrac{5y+2x}{xy}$

2. $\dfrac{x}{4}-\dfrac{y}{3}=$

   LCD $= 12$

   $\dfrac{x}{4}\times\dfrac{3}{3}-\dfrac{y}{3}\times\dfrac{4}{4}=\dfrac{3x}{12}-\dfrac{4y}{12}=\dfrac{3x-4y}{12}$

3. $\dfrac{y+5}{2y}+\dfrac{y-2}{8y}=$

   LCD $= 8y$

   $\dfrac{y+5}{2y}\times\dfrac{4}{4}+\dfrac{y-2}{8y}=\dfrac{4y+20}{8y}+\dfrac{y-2}{8y}=$

   $\dfrac{4y+20+y-2}{8y}=\dfrac{5y+18}{8y}$

4. $\dfrac{7}{x}+\dfrac{3}{x^3}=$

   LCD $= x^3$

   $\dfrac{7}{x}\times\dfrac{x^2}{x^2}+\dfrac{3}{x^3}=\dfrac{7x^2}{x^3}+\dfrac{3}{x^3}=\dfrac{7x^2+3}{x^3}$

5. $\dfrac{3x}{x^2y}+\dfrac{2x}{xy^2}=$

   LCD $= x^2y^2$

   $\dfrac{3x}{x^2}\times\dfrac{y}{y}+\dfrac{2x}{xy^2}\times\dfrac{x}{x}=\dfrac{3xy}{x^2y^2}+\dfrac{2x^2}{x^2y^2}=\dfrac{3xy+2x^2}{x^2y^2}$

6. $\dfrac{x}{3x+3}+\dfrac{2x}{x+1}=\dfrac{x}{3(x+1)}+\dfrac{2x}{x+1}$

   LCD $= 3(x+1)$

   $\dfrac{x}{3(x+1)}+\dfrac{2x}{x+1}\times\dfrac{3}{3}=\dfrac{x}{3(x+1)}+\dfrac{6x}{3(x+1)}=$

   $\dfrac{x+6x}{3(x+1)}=\dfrac{7x}{3(x+1)}$

7. $\dfrac{3}{x^2-4}-\dfrac{2x}{x^2+4x+4}=\dfrac{3}{(x+2)(x-2)}-\dfrac{2x}{(x+2)(x+2)}$

LCD $=(x+2)(x-2)(x+2)$

$\dfrac{3}{(x+2)(x-2)}\times\dfrac{(x+2)}{(x+2)}-\dfrac{2x}{(x+2)(x+2)}\times\dfrac{(x-2)}{(x-2)}=$

$\dfrac{3x+6}{(x+2)(x-2)(x+2)}-\dfrac{2x^2-4x}{(x+2)(x+2)(x-2)}=$

$\dfrac{3x+6-(2x^2-4x)}{(x+2)(x-2)(x+2)}=\dfrac{3x+6-2x^2+4x}{(x+2)(x-2)(x+2)}=$

$\dfrac{-2x^2+7x+6}{(x+2)(x-2)(x+2)}$

Since $-2x^2-7x+6$ is not factorable, this is the reduced answer.

8. $\dfrac{1}{x}+\dfrac{1}{y}+\dfrac{1}{z}=$

LCD $=xyz$

$\dfrac{1}{x}\times\dfrac{yz}{yz}+\dfrac{1}{y}\times\dfrac{xz}{xz}+\dfrac{1}{z}\times\dfrac{xy}{xy}=\dfrac{yz}{xyz}+\dfrac{xz}{xyz}+\dfrac{xy}{xyz}=\dfrac{yz+xz+xy}{xyz}$

Inequalities

An *inequality* is a statement in which the relationships are not equal. Instead of using an equal sign (=) as in an equation, we use > (greater than) and < (less than), or ≥ (greater than or equal to) and ≤ (less than or equal to) or ≠ (not equal to).

Solving Inequalities

When working with inequalities, treat them exactly like equations (*except, if you multiply or divide both sides by a negative number, you must reverse the direction of the sign*).

Examples:

1. Solve for x: $2x+4>6$.

$2x+4>6$

$\quad\underline{-4-4}$

$2x\quad\ >2$

$\dfrac{2x}{2}>\dfrac{2}{2}$

$x>1$

Answers are sometimes written in set builder notation $\{x: x>1\}$ which is read "all x such that x is greater than 1."

2. Solve for x: $-7x > 14$ (divide by -7 and reverse the sign).

$$\frac{-7x}{-7} < \frac{14}{-7}$$
$$x < -2$$

3. Solve for x: $3x + 2 \geq 5x - 10$

$$\begin{array}{r} 3x + 2 \geq 5x - 10 \\ \underline{-2 \qquad -2} \\ 3x \quad\;\; \geq 5x - 12 \\ \underline{-5x \quad -5x} \\ -2x \quad \geq \quad -12 \end{array}$$

Notice opposite operations are used. Divide both sides by -2 and reverse the sign:

$$\frac{-2x}{-2} \leq \frac{-12}{-2}$$
$$x \leq 6$$

In set builder notation : $\{x: x \leq 6\}$

Practice: Solving Inequalities Problems

Solve each of the following for x.

1. $7x + 4 > 32$

2. $\frac{2}{3}x + 5 \leq 17$

3. $3 - 2x > 7$

4. $5x + 6 > 2x + 21$

Answers: Solving Inequalities Problems

1. $7x + 4 > 32$

$$\begin{array}{r} 7x + 4 > 32 \\ \underline{-4 \;\; -4} \\ 7x \quad > 28 \\ \frac{7x}{7} > \frac{28}{7} \\ x > 4 \text{ or } \{x: x > 4\} \end{array}$$

2. $\frac{2}{3}x + 5 \le 17$

$$\underline{\quad -5 \quad -5 \quad}$$

$\frac{2}{3}x \quad \le 12$

$\frac{3}{2} \times \frac{2}{3}x \le \overset{6}{\cancel{12}} \times \frac{3}{\underset{1}{\cancel{2}}}$

$\quad x \le 18$ or $\{x: x \le 18\}$

3. $3 - 2x > 7$

$$\underline{-3 \qquad -3}$$

$-2x > 4$

$\frac{-2x}{-2} < \frac{4}{-2}$

$x < -2$ or $\{x: x < -2\}$

4. $5x + 6 > 2x + 21$

$$\underline{-2x - 6 \quad -2x - 6}$$

$3x \quad > \quad 15$

$\frac{3x}{3} > \frac{15}{3}$

$x > 5 \ \{x: x > 5\}$

Graphing on a Number Line

Integers and real numbers can be represented on a *number line*. The point on this line associated with each number is called the graph of the number. Notice that number lines are spaced equally or proportionately.

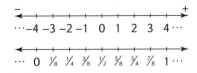

Graphing Inequalities

Examples:

When graphing inequalities involving only integers, dots are used.

1. Graph the set of x such that $1 \le x \le 4$ and x is an integer.

$\{x: 1 \le x \le 4, x \text{ is an integer}\}$

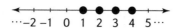

When graphing inequalities involving real numbers, lines, rays, and dots are used. A *dot* is used if the number is included. A *hollow dot* is used if the number is not included.

2. Graph the set of x such that $x \geq 1$. $\{x: x \geq 1\}$

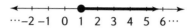

3. Graph the set of x such that $x > 1$. $\{x: x > 1\}$

4. Graph the set of x such that $x < 4$. $\{x: x < 4\}$

This ray is often called an *open ray* or an *open half line*. The hollow dot distinguishes an open ray from a ray.

Intervals

An *interval* consists of all the numbers that lie within two certain boundaries. If the two boundaries, or fixed numbers, are included, then the interval is called a *closed interval*. If the fixed numbers are not included, then the interval is called an *open interval*. If the interval includes only one of the boundaries, then it is called a *half-open interval*.

■ **Closed interval:** $\{x: -1 \leq x \leq 2\}$

■ **Open interval:** $\{x: -1 < x < 2\}$

■ **Half-open interval:** $\{x: -1 < x \leq 2\}$

Practice: Graphing Inequalities Problems

Graph each of the following.

1. $\{x: 2 \le x \le 6, x \text{ is an integer}\}$

2. $\{x: -3 < x < 5, x \text{ is an integer}\}$

3. $\{x: x \ge -2\}$

4. $\{x: x < 3\}$

5. $\{x: x \le -1\}$

Answers: Graphing Inequalities Problems

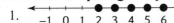

Absolute Value

The numerical value when direction or sign is not considered is called the *absolute value*. The absolute value of x is written $|x|$. The absolute value of a number is always positive except when the number is 0.

$$|0| = 0$$
$$|x| > 0, \text{ when } x \ne 0$$
$$|-x| > 0, \text{ when } x \ne 0$$

Examples:

1. $|4| = 4$

2. $|-6| = 6$

3. $|7 - 9| = |-2| = 2$

4. $3-|-6|=3-6=-3$ (note that absolute value is taken first)

5. $|x|=8$. Solve for x.

   $|x|=8$

   $x= 8$ or x = -8

6. $|2x-1|=7$. Solve for x.

   $|2x-1|=7$

   $2x - 1 = 7$ or $2x - 1 = -7$

   $2x = 8$ or $2x = -6$

   $x = 4$ or $x = -3$

7. $|x|=-3$. There is no solution because the absolute value of any number is never negative.

8. $|2x-1|\geq 0$. The answer is all real numbers, because the absolute value of any number is always positive or zero.

Practice: Absolute Value Problems

1. $|-9|=$

2. $|6|=$

3. $|-3+2|=$

4. $|-6-6|=$

5. $|4-8|=$

6. $|-5|+3=$

7. $9+|-5|=$

8. $6-|-8|=$

9. $|x|=10$

10. $|3x-6|=12$

11. $|2x+3|<0$

12. $|x-4|>0$

Answers: Absolute Value Problems

1. 9
2. 6
3. $|-3+2|=|-1|=1$
4. $|-6-6|=|-12|=12$
5. $|4-8|=|-4|=4$
6. $|-5|+3=5+3=8$
7. $9+|-5|=9+5=14$
8. $6-|-8|=6-8=-2$
9. $x=10$ or $x=-10$
10. $|3x-6|=12$

    $3x-6=12$ or $3x-6=-12$

    $3x=18$ or $3x=-6$

    $x=6$ or $x=-2$

11. No solution

12. Any real number except 4

Analytic Geometry

Coordinate Graphs

Each point on a number line is assigned a number. In the same way, each point in a plane is assigned a pair of numbers. These numbers represent the placement of the point relative to two intersecting lines. In *coordinate graphs*, two perpendicular number lines are used and are called *coordinate axes*. One axis is horizontal and is called the *x-axis*. The other is vertical and is called the *y-axis*. The point of intersection of the two number lines is called the *origin* and is represented by the coordinates (0,0).

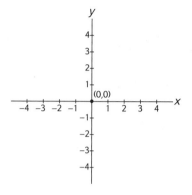

Each point on a plane is located by a unique ordered pair of numbers called the coordinates. Some coordinates are noted below.

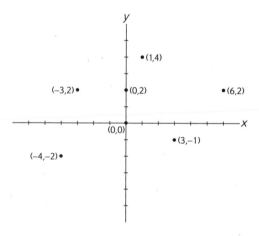

Notice that on the *x*-axis, numbers to the right of 0 are positive and to the left of 0 are negative. On the *y*-axis, numbers above 0 are positive and below 0 are negative. Also, note that the first number in the ordered pair is called the *x-coordinate,* or *abscissa,* while the second number is the *y-coordinate,* or *ordinate.* The *x*-coordinate shows the right or left direction, and the *y*-coordinate shows the up or down direction.

The coordinate graph is divided into four quarters called *quadrants*. These quadrants are labeled below.

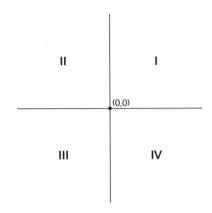

Notice that

> In quadrant I, x is always positive and y is always positive.
>
> In quadrant II, x is always negative and y is always positive.
>
> In quadrant III, x and y are both always negative.
>
> In quadrant IV, x is always positive and y is always negative.

Practice: Coordinate Graph Problems

Identify the points (A, B, C, D, E, and F) on the coordinate graph below.

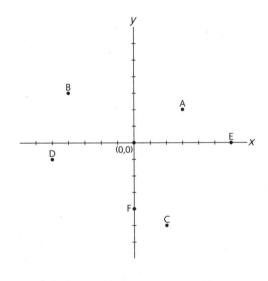

Answers: Coordinate Graph Problems

A. (3,2)

B. (−4,3)

C. (2,−5)

D. (−5,−1)

E. (6,0)

F. (0,−4)

Graphing Equations on the Coordinate Plane

To graph an equation on the coordinate plane, find the solutions by giving a value to one variable and solving the resulting equation for the other value. Repeat this process to find other solutions. (When giving a value for one variable, start with 0, then try 1, and so on.) Then graph the solutions.

Examples:

1. Graph the equation $x + y = 6$.

    If x is 0, then y is 6.

    $(0) + y = 6$

    $y = 6$

    If x is 1, then y is 5.

    $(1) + y = 6$

    $\underline{-1 \qquad -1}$

    $y = 5$

    If x is 2, then y is 4.

    $(2) + y = 6$

    $\underline{-2 \qquad -2}$

    $y = 4$

    Using a simple chart is helpful.

x	y
0	6
1	5
2	4

185

Now plot these coordinates.

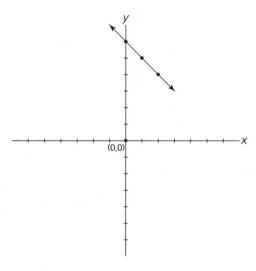

Notice that these solutions, when plotted, form a straight line. Equations whose solution sets form a straight line are called *linear equations*. Equations that have a variable raised to a power, show division by a variable, involve variables with square roots, or have variables multiplied together will not form a straight line when their solutions are graphed. These are called *nonlinear equations*.

2. Graph the equation $y = x^2 + 4$.

If x is 0, then y is 4.

$y = (0)^2 + 4$

$y = 0 + 4$

$y = 4$

If x is 1 or -1, then y is 5.

$y = (1)^2 + 4 \qquad\qquad y = (-1)^2 + 4$

$y = 1 + 4 \qquad\qquad\quad y = 1 + 4$

$y = 5 \qquad\qquad\qquad\quad y = 5$

If x is 2 or -2, then y is 8.

$y = (2)^2 + 4$ $y = (-2)^2 + 4$

$y = 4 + 4$ $y = 4 + 4$

$y = 8$ $y = 8$

Use a simple chart.

x	y
−2	8
−1	5
0	4
1	5
2	8

Now plot these coordinates.

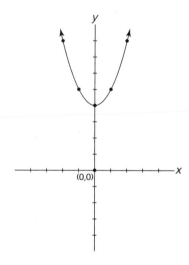

Notice that these solutions, when plotted, give a curved line (nonlinear). The more points plotted, the easier it is to see and describe the solution set.

Practice: Graphing Equations on the Coordinate Plane Problems

State whether the following equations are linear or nonlinear.

1. $x - 5 = 5$

2. $x + 5 = y$

3. $x^2 + y = 3$

4. $xy = 1$

5. $x + \dfrac{5}{y} = 0$

6. $y = x + 7$

Graph each of the following equations.

7. $x - y = 3$

8. $y = x + 2$

9. $y = x^2 + 1$

10. $3x + y = 12$

11. $x + 4 = y + 2x - 3$

12. $y = 4$

Answers: Graphing Equations on the Coordinate Plane Problems

1. linear

2. linear

3. nonlinear

4. nonlinear

5. nonlinear

6. linear

7. $x - y = 3$

x	y
3	0
4	1
5	2

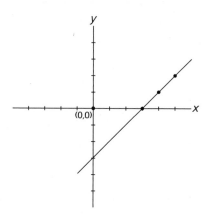

8. $y = x + 2$

x	y
0	2
1	3
2	4

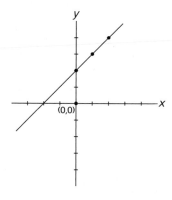

9. $y = x^2 + 1$

   If $x = 0$:

   $y = (0)^2 + 1$

   $y = 0 + 1$

   $y = 1$

   If $x = 1$:

   $y = (1)^2 + 1$

   $y = 1 + 1$

   $y = 2$

   If $x = 2$:

   $y = (2)^2 + 1$

   $y = 4 + 1$

   $y = 5$

   If $x = -1$:

   $y = (-1)^2 + 1$

   $y = 1 + 1$

   $y = 2$

   If $x = -2$:

   $y = (-2)^2 + 1$

   $y = 4 + 1$

   $y = 5$

x	y
−2	5
−1	2
0	1
1	2
2	5

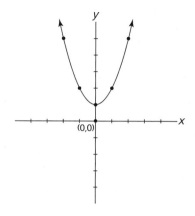

10. $3x + y = 12$

If $x = 0$:

$3(0) + y = 12$

$0 + y = 12$

$y = 12$

If $x = 1$:

$3(1) + y = 12$

$3 + y = 12$

$\underline{-3 \quad\quad -3}$

$y = 9$

If $x = 2$:

$3(2) + y = 12$

$6 + y = 12$

$\underline{-6 \quad\quad -6}$

$y = 6$

x	y
0	12
1	9
2	6

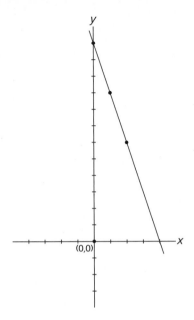

11. $x + 4 = y + 2x - 3$

First simplify by combining like terms:

$$x + 4 = y + 2x - 3$$

$$\underline{-2x \qquad\qquad -2x}$$

$$-x + 4 = y - 3$$

$$\underline{\quad +3 \qquad +3}$$

$$-x + 7 = y$$

or

$$7 = x + y$$

x	y
0	7
1	6
2	5

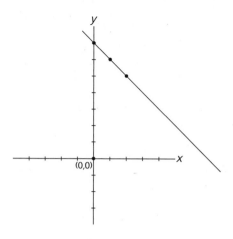

12. $y = 4$

x	y
0	4
1	4
2	4

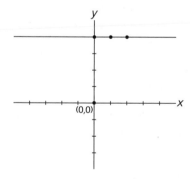

Slope and Intercept of Linear Equations

There are two relationships between the graph of a linear equation and the equation itself that need pointing out. One involves the *slope of the line,* and the other involves the point of intersection of the line with the *y*-axis, known as the *y-intercept.* When a linear equation is written in the $y =$ form, or the $y = mx + b$ form, the m value becomes the slope value for the line, and the b value is the location on the *y*-axis where the line intercepts the *y*-axis. Thus, the $y = mx + b$ form is called the *slope-intercept form* for the equation of a line.

Example:

Rewrite each of the following linear equations in slope-intercept form and identify the slope value and the *y*-intercept location. Also, graph each linear equation.

(a) $x - y = 3$
(b) $y = -2x + 1$
(c) $x - 2y = 4$

Answer:

(a) $x - y = 3$

$$-y = -x + 3$$

$$y = x - 3$$

Slope $= 1$, *y*-intercept $= -3$ or *y*-intercept location $= (0,-3)$

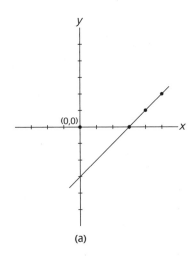

(a)

(b) $y = -2x + 1$ (already in slope-intercept form)

Slope = -2, y-intercept = 1 or y-intercept location = $(0,1)$

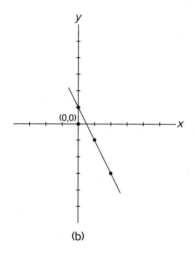

(b)

(c) $x - 2y = 4$

$$-2y = -x + 4$$

$$y = \frac{1}{2}x - 2$$

Slope = $\frac{1}{2}$, y-intercept = -2 or y-intercept location = $(0,-2)$

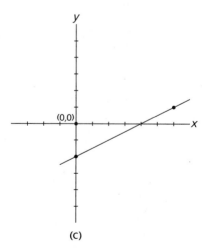

(c)

If you know the ordered pairs of two points on a line, you can evaluate the slope of the line. If (x_1, y_1) and (x_2, y_2) represent any two points on a line, then slope $= \dfrac{y_2 - y_1}{x_2 - x_1}$; that is, $m = \dfrac{y_2 - y_1}{x_2 - x_1}$.

Example:

Find the slope of the line passing through the points (–2,6) and (3,5).

Let $(x_1, y_1) = (-2,6)$ and $(x_2, y_2) = (3,5)$ then $m = \dfrac{5-6}{3-(-2)} = \dfrac{-1}{5} = -\dfrac{1}{5}$.

If the order of the points is reversed; that is, if $(x_1, y_1) = (3,5)$ and $(x_2, y_2) = (-2,6)$ then $m = \dfrac{6-5}{-2-3} = \dfrac{1}{-5} = -\dfrac{1}{5}$.

Therefore, it doesn't matter to which point you give which label when evaluating the slope of the line.

Graphing Linear Equations Using Slope and Intercept

1. Write the equation in slope-intercept form.
2. Locate the *y*-intercept on the graph. (This is one point on the line.)
3. Write the slope as a ratio (fraction) to use to locate other points on the line.
4. Draw the line through the points.

Examples:

1. Graph the equation $2x - y = -4$ using slope and *y*-intercept.

   Answer: $2x - y = -4$ (rewrite in slope-intercept form)

   $$-y = -2x - 4$$

   $$y = 2x + 4 \text{ (slope = 2 and } y\text{-intercept = 4)}$$

   Locate the point (0,4) on the *y*-axis and, from this point, count as shown in the figure:

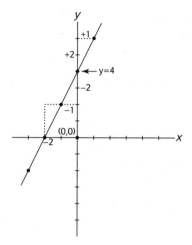

Slope = 2, (rewrite as a ratio) slope = $\frac{2}{1}$ (for every 2 up, go 1 to the right) or slope = $\frac{-2}{-1}$ (for every 2 down, go 1 to the left).

2. Graph the equation $x + 3y = 0$.

   Answer: $x + 3y = 0$ (rewrite in slope-intercept form)

   $3y = -x + 0$

   $y = -\frac{1}{3}x + 0$ (slope = $-\frac{1}{3}$ and y-intercept = 0)

   Locate the point (0,0) on the y-axis and, from this point, count as shown in the figure:

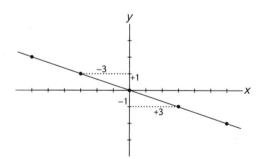

Slope = $-\frac{1}{3}$, slope = $\frac{-1}{3}$ (for every 1 down, go 3 to the right).

Or slope = $\frac{1}{-3}$ (for every 1 up, go 3 to the left).

Graphing Linear Equations Using the *x*-intercept and *y*-intercept

1. Find the *x*-intercept by replacing the y-variable with the value 0; then solve for *x*. (The **x-intercept** of a graph occurs when the graph is on the *x*-axis. When a point is on the *x*-axis, its *y*-coordinate there is 0.)

2. Find the *y*-intercept by replacing the *x*-variable with the value 0; then solve for *y*. (The **y-intercept** of a graph occurs when the graph is on the *y*-axis. When a point is on the *y*-axis, its *x*-coordinate there is 0.)

3. Draw a line passing through the *x*- and *y*-intercepts.

Example:

Graph the linear equation $2x + 3y = 6$ using the *x*-intercept and *y*-intercept.

Answer:

Find the *x*-intercept by replacing y with 0 and solving for *x*.

$$2x + 3(0) = 6$$

$$2x = 6$$

$$x = 3$$

The *x*-intercept is located at (3,0)

Find the *y*-intercept by replacing *x* with 0, and solving for *y*.

$$2(0) + 3y = 6$$

$$3y = 6$$

$$y = 2$$

The *y*-intercept is at (0,2)

Draw the line passing through the *x*- and *y*-intercepts

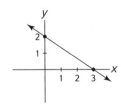

Finding an Equation of a Line

To find an equation of a line when working with ordered pairs, slopes, or intercepts, use the following approach.

1. Find the slope, m (either it is given or you need to calculate it from two given points).

2. Find the y-intercept, b (either it is given or you need to use the equation $y = mx + b$ and substitute the slope value you found in Step 1 and the x- and y-coordinates of any given point).

3. Write the equation of the line in the $y = mx + b$ form using the values found in steps 1 and 2.

Examples:

1. Find an equation of the line with a slope of –4 and a y-intercept of 3.

   You are given that $m = -4$ and that $b = 3$. Therefore, an equation for this line is $y = -4x + 3$.

2. Find an equation for the line passing through (6,4) with a slope of –3.

   You are given that $m = -3$. Use the equation $y = mx + b$. Substitute –3 for m and use the point (6,4) and substitute 6 for x and 4 for y in order to find b.

   $4 = -3(6) + b$

   $4 = -18 + b$

   $22 = b$

   Therefore, an equation for this line is $y = -3x + 22$.

3. Find an equation for a line that passes through the points (5,–4) and (3,–2).

   Find the slope using the two points.

   $$m = \frac{-2-(-4)}{3-5} = \frac{2}{-2} = -1$$

   Use the equation $y = mx + b$. Substitute –1 for m and use one of the two points. You can use either (5,–4) or (3,–2). For this example, use (5,–4). Substitute 5 for x and –4 for y in order to find b.

   $-4 = -1(5) + b$

   $-4 = -5 + b$

   $1 = b$

Therefore, an equation for this line is $y = -x + 1$.

Using the point $(3,-2)$, substitute 3 for x and -2 for y in order to find b.

$3 = -1(-2) + b$

$3 = 2 + b$

$1 = b$

It doesn't matter which of the two points is used in the substitution in order to find b.

Roots and Radicals

Note: This subject is introduced in the Arithmetic Review.

The symbol $\sqrt{}$ is called *a radical sign* and is used to designate *square root.* To designate *cube root,* a small three is placed above the radical sign: $\sqrt[3]{}$. When two radical signs are next to each other, they automatically mean that the two are multiplied. The multiplication sign may be omitted. Note that the square root of a negative number is not possible within the real number system. A completely different system of imaginary numbers is used for roots of negative numbers. The typical standardized exams use only the real number system as general practice. The (so-called) imaginary numbers are multiples of the imaginary unit i: $\sqrt{-1} = i$, $\sqrt{-4} = 2i$, $\sqrt{-9} = 3i$, and so on. The ACT and some college placement exams deal with simple imaginary numbers and their operations.

Simplifying Square Roots

A square root with no sign indicated to its left represents a positive value. A square root with a negative to its left represents a negative value.

In problems 1 through 3, simplify each square root expression.

Examples:

1. $\sqrt{9} = 3$

2. $-\sqrt{9} = -3$

3. $\sqrt{18} = \sqrt{9 \cdot 2} = \sqrt{9} \cdot \sqrt{2} = 3\sqrt{2}$

4. If each variable is nonnegative (not a negative number), $\sqrt{x^2} = x$.

5. If each variable is nonnegative, $\sqrt{x^4} = x^2$.

200

6. If each variable is nonnegative, $\sqrt{x^6 y^8} = \sqrt{x^6}\sqrt{y^8} = x^3 y^4$.

7. If each variable is nonnegative, $\sqrt{25a^4 b^6} = \sqrt{25}\sqrt{a^4}\sqrt{b^6} = 5a^2 b^3$.

8. If x is nonnegative, $\sqrt{x^7} = \sqrt{x^6(x)} = \sqrt{x^6}\sqrt{x} = x^3\sqrt{x}$.

9. If x is nonnegative,
$$\sqrt{x^9 y^8} = \sqrt{x^9}\sqrt{y^8} = \sqrt{x^8(x)}\sqrt{y^8} = x^4\sqrt{x} \cdot y^4 = x^4 y^4\sqrt{x}.$$

10. If each variable is nonnegative,
$$\sqrt{16x^5} = \sqrt{16}\sqrt{x^5} = \sqrt{16}\sqrt{x^4(x)} = 4x^2\sqrt{x}.$$

Practice: Simplifying Square Root Problems

Simplify each of the following. All variables are nonnegative.

1. $\sqrt{36} =$

2. $-\sqrt{49} =$

3. $\sqrt{121} =$

4. $\sqrt{50} =$

5. $\sqrt{72} =$

6. $\sqrt{y^6} =$

7. $\sqrt{x^6 y^{10}} =$

8. $\sqrt{36a^2 b^8} =$

9. $\sqrt{a^9} =$

10. $\sqrt{49a^5 b^4} =$

Answers: Simplifying Square Root Problems

1. 6

2. –7

3. 11

4. $\sqrt{50} = \sqrt{25 \cdot 2} = \sqrt{25} \cdot \sqrt{2} = 5\sqrt{2}$

5. $\sqrt{72} = \sqrt{36 \cdot 2} = \sqrt{36}\sqrt{2} = 6\sqrt{2}$

6. $y^3, y \geq 0$

7. $\sqrt{x^6 y^{10}} = \sqrt{x^6}\sqrt{y^{10}} = x^3 y^5, x \geq 0$ or $\sqrt{x^6 y^{10}} = |x^3| \cdot y^5$

8. $\sqrt{36a^2 b^8} = \sqrt{36}\sqrt{a^2}\sqrt{b^8} = 6ab^4, a \geq 0$ or $6|a|b^4$

9. $\sqrt{a^9} = \sqrt{a^8(a)} = a^4 \sqrt{a}$

10. $\sqrt{49a^5 b^4} = \sqrt{49}\sqrt{a^5}\sqrt{b^4} = \sqrt{49}\sqrt{a^4(a)}\sqrt{b^4} = 7a^2\sqrt{a}(b^2) = 7a^2 b^2 \sqrt{a}$

Operations with Square Roots

You may perform operations under a single radical sign.

Examples:

1. $\sqrt{(5)(20)} = \sqrt{100} = 10$

2. $\sqrt{30 + 6} = \sqrt{36} = 6$

3. $\sqrt{\dfrac{32}{2}} = \sqrt{16} = 4$ (***Note:*** $\sqrt{\dfrac{32}{2}} = \dfrac{\sqrt{32}}{\sqrt{2}}$.)

4. $\sqrt{30 - 5} = \sqrt{25} = 5$

5. $\sqrt{2 + 5} = \sqrt{7}$

You can *add or subtract square roots themselves only if the values under the radical sign are equal.* Then simply add or subtract the coefficients (numbers in front of the radical sign) and keep the original number in the radical sign.

Examples:

1. $2\sqrt{3} + 3\sqrt{3} = (2 + 3)\sqrt{3} = 5\sqrt{3}$

2. $4\sqrt{6} - 2\sqrt{6} = (4 - 2)\sqrt{6} = 2\sqrt{6}$

3. $5\sqrt{2} + \sqrt{2} = 5\sqrt{2} + 1\sqrt{2} = (5 + 1)\sqrt{2} = 6\sqrt{2}$

Note that 1 is understood in $\sqrt{2}$ (in other words, $1\sqrt{2}$).

You *may not add or subtract different square roots.*

Examples:

1. $\sqrt{28} - \sqrt{3} \neq \sqrt{25}$

2. $\sqrt{16} + \sqrt{9} \neq \sqrt{25}$

Practice: Operations under the Radical and Adding and Subtracting Square Roots Problems

1. $\sqrt{(18)(2)} =$

2. $\sqrt{\dfrac{200}{8}} =$

3. $\sqrt{17 + 32} =$

4. $\sqrt{31 - 16} =$

5. $4\sqrt{3} + 2\sqrt{3} =$

6. $12\sqrt{7} - 6\sqrt{7} =$

7. $8\sqrt{11} - \sqrt{11} =$

8. $3\sqrt{5} - 7\sqrt{5} =$

Answers: Operations under the Radical and Adding and Subtracting Square Roots Problems

1. $\sqrt{(18)(2)} = \sqrt{36} = 6$

2. $\sqrt{\dfrac{200}{8}} = \sqrt{25} = 5$

3. $\sqrt{17 + 32} = \sqrt{49} = 7$

4. $\sqrt{31 - 16} = \sqrt{15}$

5. $6\sqrt{3}$

6. $6\sqrt{7}$

7. $7\sqrt{11}$ derived from $8\sqrt{11} - 1\sqrt{11}$

8. $-4\sqrt{5}$ derived from $3\sqrt{5} - 7\sqrt{5} = (3 - 7)\sqrt{5} = -4\sqrt{5}$

Addition and Subtraction of Square Roots after Simplifying

Sometimes after *simplifying the square root(s), addition or subtraction becomes possible.* Always simplify if possible.

Examples:

1. $\sqrt{50} + 3\sqrt{2} =$

   These cannot be added until $\sqrt{50}$ is simplified.

   $\sqrt{50} = \sqrt{25 \cdot 2} = \sqrt{25} \cdot \sqrt{2} = 5\sqrt{2}$

   Now, since both are alike under the radical sign

   $5\sqrt{2} + 3\sqrt{2} = (5+3)\sqrt{2} = 8\sqrt{2}$

2. $\sqrt{300} + \sqrt{12} =$

   Try to simplify each one.

   $\sqrt{300} = \sqrt{100 \cdot 3} = \sqrt{100} \cdot \sqrt{3} = 10\sqrt{3}$

   $\sqrt{12} = \sqrt{4 \cdot 3} = \sqrt{4} \cdot \sqrt{3} = 2\sqrt{3}$

   Now, since both are alike under the radical sign:

   $10\sqrt{3} + 2\sqrt{3} = (10+2)\sqrt{3} = 12\sqrt{3}$

Practice: Addition and Subtraction of Square Roots after Simplifying Problems

1. $4\sqrt{5} - \sqrt{20} =$

2. $\sqrt{18} + \sqrt{32} =$

3. $9\sqrt{7} - \sqrt{28} =$

4. $\sqrt{40} + \sqrt{27} =$

Answers: Addition and Subtraction of Square Roots after Simplifying Problems

1. $4\sqrt{5} - \sqrt{20} =$

   $\sqrt{20} = \sqrt{4 \cdot 5} = \sqrt{4} \cdot \sqrt{5} = 2\sqrt{5}$

   $4\sqrt{5} - 2\sqrt{5} = 2\sqrt{5}$

2. $\sqrt{18} + \sqrt{32} =$

$\left(\sqrt{18} = \sqrt{9\cdot 2} = \sqrt{9}\cdot\sqrt{2} = 3\sqrt{2} \right)$

$\left(\sqrt{32} = \sqrt{16\cdot 2} = \sqrt{16}\cdot\sqrt{2} = 4\sqrt{2} \right)$

$3\sqrt{2} + 4\sqrt{2} = 7\sqrt{2}$

3. $9\sqrt{7} - \sqrt{28} =$

$\left(\sqrt{28} = \sqrt{4\cdot 7} = \sqrt{4}\cdot\sqrt{7} = 2\sqrt{7} \right)$

$9\sqrt{7} - 2\sqrt{7} = 7\sqrt{7}$

4. $\sqrt{40} + \sqrt{27} =$

$\left(\sqrt{40} = \sqrt{4\cdot 10} = \sqrt{4}\cdot\sqrt{10} = 2\sqrt{10} \right)$

$\left(\sqrt{27} = \sqrt{9\cdot 3} = \sqrt{9}\cdot\sqrt{3} = 3\sqrt{3} \right)$

$2\sqrt{10} + 3\sqrt{3}$ cannot be combined

Products of Nonnegative Roots

Remember that in multiplication of roots, the multiplication sign may be omitted. Always simplify the answer when possible.

Examples:

1. $\sqrt{2}\cdot\sqrt{8} = \sqrt{16} = 4$

2. If x is nonnegative,

$$\sqrt{x^3}\cdot\sqrt{x^5} = \sqrt{x^8} = x^4$$

3. If each variable is nonnegative,

$$\sqrt{ab}\cdot\sqrt{ab^3c} = \sqrt{a^2b^4c} = \sqrt{a^2}\sqrt{b^4}\sqrt{c} = ab^2\sqrt{c}$$

4. If each variable is nonnegative,

$$\sqrt{3x}\cdot\sqrt{6xy^2}\cdot\sqrt{2xy} = \sqrt{36x^3y^3} = \sqrt{36}\sqrt{x^3}\sqrt{y^3} =$$
$$\sqrt{36}\sqrt{x^2(x)}\sqrt{y^2(y)} = 6xy\sqrt{xy}$$

5. $2\sqrt{5}\cdot 7\sqrt{3} = (2\cdot 7)\sqrt{5\cdot 3} = 14\sqrt{15}$

Practice: Products of Nonnegative Roots Problems

In the following, all variables are nonnegative.

1. $\sqrt{12} \cdot \sqrt{3} =$

2. $\sqrt{6} \cdot \sqrt{8} =$

3. $\sqrt{y^5} \cdot \sqrt{y^7} =$

4. $\sqrt{x^2 y} \cdot \sqrt{xy^2} =$

5. $\sqrt{abc} \cdot \sqrt{bc} \cdot \sqrt{ac^2} =$

6. $\sqrt{5a^2} \cdot \sqrt{2ab} \cdot \sqrt{10b^2} =$

7. $3\sqrt{2} \cdot 2\sqrt{5} =$

8. $4\sqrt{2} \cdot 5\sqrt{8} =$

Answers: Products of Nonnegative Roots Problems

1. $\sqrt{12} \cdot \sqrt{3} = \sqrt{36} = 6$
2. $\sqrt{6} \cdot \sqrt{8} = \sqrt{48} = \sqrt{16 \cdot 3} = \sqrt{16}\sqrt{3} = 4\sqrt{3}$
3. $\sqrt{y^5} \cdot \sqrt{y^7} = \sqrt{y^{12}} = y^6$
4. $\sqrt{x^2 y} \cdot \sqrt{xy^2} = \sqrt{x^3 y^3} = \sqrt{x^2 (x) y^2 (y)} = xy\sqrt{xy}$

   or

   $\sqrt{x^2 y} \cdot \sqrt{xy^2} = x\sqrt{y} \cdot y\sqrt{x} = xy\sqrt{xy}$
5. $\sqrt{abc} \cdot \sqrt{bc} \cdot \sqrt{ac^2} = \sqrt{a^2 b^2 c^4} = abc^2$
6. $\sqrt{5a^2} \cdot \sqrt{2ab} \cdot \sqrt{10b^2} = \sqrt{100a^3 b^3} = \sqrt{100}\sqrt{a^3}\sqrt{b^3} =$
   $\sqrt{100}\sqrt{a^2 (a)}\sqrt{b^2 (b)} = 10ab\sqrt{ab}$
7. $3\sqrt{2} \cdot 2\sqrt{5} = (3 \cdot 2)\sqrt{2 \cdot 5} = 6\sqrt{10}$
8. $4\sqrt{2} \cdot 5\sqrt{8} = (4 \cdot 5)\sqrt{2 \cdot 8} = 20\sqrt{16} = 20(4) = 80$

"False" Operations

Many standardized exams include a question or two using operations created uniquely *for that particular problem*. The operation may be represented by unusual symbols (such as @ or * or #) and are then defined with standard operations of $+$, $-$, $\times$, $\div$, etc. Don't let these new or different symbols alarm you.

Examples:

1. If $x @ y = \frac{x}{y}$ and $y \neq 0$, then what is $4 @ 2$?

   This operation shows that the first value is divided by the second value. Therefore, $4 @ 2 = \frac{4}{2} = 2$.

   The key to understanding these types of problems is simply understanding the definition of the operation—how to replace, or plug in, values. Notice that the definitions are given in terms of standard operations with which you are familiar.

2. If $x \$ y = x^2 + y^2$, then $2 \$ 5 = ?$

   $2 \$ 5 = (2)^2 + (5)^2 = 4 + 25 = 29$

3. If $a \# b = \frac{a+b}{2}$, $3 \# 5 = ?$

   $3 \# 5 = \frac{3+5}{2} = \frac{8}{2} = 4$

Practice: "False" Operations Problems

1. For all integers a and b, the binary operation $\#$ is defined by $a \# b = ab + b$. What is the value of $5 \# 7$?

2. $x @ y = \frac{x^2 + y^2}{xy}$ for all real numbers x and y such that $xy \neq 0$. What is the value of $2 @ 6$?

3. The operation $\cancel{c}$ is defined for all nonzero numbers x and y by the equation $x \cancel{c} y = (x - y)(x + y)(x)$. What is the value of $5 \cancel{c} 6$?

4. If $a * b$ means that a^2 is greater than b^2, then which of the following relationships must be true?

   I. $a = 0$

   II. $a > b$

   III. $a \neq 0$

5. $[(x)(y)(z)]^\# = x^2 + yz$ for all real numbers x, y, and z. What is the value of $[(3)(4)(5)]^\#$?

6. The operation $\$$ is defined on ordered pairs of numbers as follows:

   $(x, y) \$ (w, z) = (xw, yz)$. What is the value of $(3, 5) \$ (4, 6)$?

7. If $x @ y = xy$, for all positive integers x and y, what is the value of a if $b @ a = b$?

8. If $x \star y = \dfrac{x+y}{5}$, then which of the following must always be true?

   I. $a \star b = b \star a$

   II. $a \star b = a \star a$

   III. $a \star b = b \star b$

Answers: "False" Operations Problems

1. $a \# b = ab + b$

$$5 \# 7 = (5)(7) + 7$$
$$= 35 + 7$$
$$= 42$$

Note that *binary operation* simply means an operation between two values or variables.

2. $x @ y = \dfrac{x^2 + y^2}{xy}$

$$2 @ 6 = \dfrac{(2)^2 + (6)^2}{(2)(6)}$$
$$= \dfrac{4 + 36}{12}$$
$$= \dfrac{40}{12} = \dfrac{10}{3} = 3\dfrac{1}{3}$$

3. $x \not{c} y = (x - y)(x + y)x.$

$$5 \not{c} 6 = (5 - 6)(5 + 6)(5)$$
$$= (-1)(11)(5)$$
$$= -55$$

4. Note that if a^2 is to be greater than b^2, then a^2 must be a positive number, as the smallest value for b^2 is 0. Therefore statement I is false. Statement II is not necessarily true, since a could be -3 and b could be $+2$, yet $a^2 > b^2$. Statement III is true because if $a \neq 0$, a^2 will always be positive.

5. $[(x)(y)(z)]^\# = x^2 + yz$

$$[(3)(4)(5)]^\# = (3)^2 + (4)(5)$$
$$= 9 + 20$$
$$= 29$$

6. $(x, y) \$ (w, z) = (xw, yz)$

   $(3, 5) \$ (4, 6) = (3 \cdot 4, 5 \cdot 6)$

   $\qquad\qquad = (12, 30)$

7. $x @ y = xy$

   $b @ a = ba$

   If $b @ a = b$, then

   $\qquad ba = b$ (divide each side by b)

   $\qquad a = 1$

   Therefore, the value of a is 1.

8. Only I is always true. The sum of $x + y$ equals the sum of $y + x$. Therefore, the original placement of a and b is irrelevant since

   $$\frac{a+b}{5} = \frac{b+a}{5}$$

   Statements II and III are not always true. They are true only if $a = b$.

Algebra Review Test

Questions

1. A set within a set is called a _____.

2. A set with no members is called the _____ or _____.

3. Naming a set by describing its elements is called the _____ method.

4. A method of naming a set by listing its members is called _____.

5. Sets that are countable or stop are called _____.

6. Sets that continue forever are uncountable and are called _____.

7. True or false : $\{1, 2, 3, 4\} = \{a, b, c, d\}$

8. True or false : $\{2, 4, 6\} \sim \{1, 3, 5\}$

9. $\{2,7,8\} \cap \{1,3,8\} =$

10. $\{4,5,6\} \cup \{1,3,5\} =$

11. Express each of the following algebraically.

    a. four more than twice a number
    b. a number decreased by six
    c. a number increased by ten
    d. a number x decreased by four times y

12. Evaluate : $p^2 + 7p - 5$ if $p = 6$

13. Evaluate : $4x^2y^3z^2$ if $x = 2$, $y = 3$, and $z = 4$

14. Evaluate: $\dfrac{xy}{4} - \dfrac{x + yz}{z}$ if $x = 3$, $y = 4$, and $z = 6$

15. Solve for x: $x + 18 = 64$

16. Solve for x: $4x - 8 = 32$

17. Solve for y: $\frac{y}{8} - 3 = 9$

18. Solve for z: $\frac{2}{5}z + 4 = 13$

19. Solve for x: $7x = 4x - 9$

20. Solve for n: $5n + 7 = 3n - 9$

21. Solve for y: $\frac{-y}{6} = 14$

22. Solve for y: $my - n = x$

23. Solve for m: $\frac{m}{n} = a$

24. Solve for x: $\frac{r}{x} = \frac{s}{t}$

25. Solve for x: x is to y as z is to a

26. Solve for x: $\frac{x}{6} = \frac{1}{2}$

27. Solve for c: $\frac{7}{2} = \frac{12}{c}$

28. Solve this system for x and y:

$$x - 2y = 8$$
$$3x + 2y = 4$$

29. Solve this system for a and b:

$$3a + 2b = 1$$
$$2a - 3b = -8$$

30. Solve this system for x and y:

$$y = x + 3$$
$$2x + y = 8$$

31. $12xy$
$\underline{-15xy}$

32. $6qt^2 - 2qt^2 + 6qt^2 =$

33. Simplify: $a \cdot a \cdot a \cdot x \cdot x \cdot y$

34. Simplify: $3(x)(y)(2)(z)$

35. $(y^3)(y^5) =$

36. $(a^2b)(a^3b^4) =$

37. $(-2x^2y)(3x^3y^4) =$

38. $-3(m^3n^3)(-2m^4n^2) =$

39. $(4a^2b^3c^3)(b^3c^2d) =$

40. $(x^7)^4 =$

41. $(a^2b^3)^3 =$

42. $(3x^3y^5)^2 =$

43. $x^5 \div x^2 =$

44. $\dfrac{a^6b^2}{a^4b} =$

45. $\dfrac{14x^6y^4}{2xy} =$

46. $(3p^6q^4) \div (15p^4q^8) =$

47. $\begin{aligned} x^2 + \ & xy + 2y^2 \\ + \ 3x^2 + \ & 5xy + 3y^2 \\ \hline \end{aligned}$

48. $(3x + 7y) + (6x - 2y) =$

49. $(3s^2 + 4st + 13t^2) - (2s^2 + 2st + 3t^2) =$

50. $2a^2b + 3ab^2 + 7a^2b - 5ab^2 =$

51. $(2x + 4)(3x - 1) =$

52. $(a + 3ab + 4)(2a + b) =$

53. $(12a^8 - 8a^7) \div (2a^3) =$

54. $\dfrac{-3(x^2y^3)(-4xy^4)}{2xy^2} =$

55. $(x^2 + 2x + 1) \div (x + 1) =$

56. $(5x^2 + 6x + 1) \div (x + 1) =$

57. $(a^3 - 27) \div (a - 3) =$

58. Factor: $9a - 6$

59. Factor completely: $5x^3 + 10x^2$

60. Factor: $n^2 - 9$

61. Factor: $36a^2 - b^2$

62. Factor completely: $2a^2 - 32$

63. Factor : $x^2 + 3x + 2$

64. Factor : $x^2 - 5x - 6$

65. Factor: $3x^2 - 20x - 7$

66. Factor completely: $x^3 - 4x^2 + 3x$

67. Factor : $24 - 10r + r^2$

68. Factor : $x^2 - 2xy + y^2$

69. Solve for y: $y^2 = 5y - 4$

70. Solve for x: $x^2 - 25 = 0$

71. Solve for x: $x^2 - 5x = 0$

72. Solve for t: $3t^2 + 21t = 2t^2 - 3t + 81$

73. Reduce: $\dfrac{9x^5}{12x^3}$

74. Reduce: $\dfrac{5x - 15}{4x - 12}$

75. Reduce: $\dfrac{x^2 - 9x + 20}{x^2 - x - 12}$

76. $\dfrac{8x^5}{9y^2} \cdot \dfrac{3y^4}{2x^3} =$

77. $\dfrac{x-1}{x} \cdot \dfrac{x+3}{x^2-7x+6} =$

78. $\dfrac{4x^3}{7} \div \dfrac{2x}{9} =$

79. $\dfrac{10y+5}{4} \div \dfrac{2y+1}{2} =$

80. $\dfrac{y+3}{y} + \dfrac{2y+5}{y} =$

81. $\dfrac{4x-5}{x-1} - \dfrac{3x+6}{x-1} =$

82. $\dfrac{7}{x} - \dfrac{6}{y} =$

83. $\dfrac{x-3}{2x} + \dfrac{x+1}{4x} =$

84. $\dfrac{7x}{x^4y^7} + \dfrac{3}{x^6y^2} =$

85. $\dfrac{3x}{x-3} - \dfrac{2x}{x+1} =$

86. $\dfrac{x}{x^2-16} + \dfrac{4x}{x^2+5x+4} =$

87. Solve for x: $5x + 2 > 17$

88. Solve for y: $-4y - 8 \le 12$

89. Solve for x: $5x + 6 \ge 2x + 2$

90. Graph: $\{x: 5 \ge x \ge 3\}$

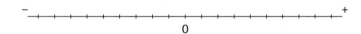

91. Graph: $\{x: -2 \le x < 8, x \text{ is an integer}\}$

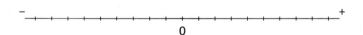

92. Graph: $\{x: x > 1\}$

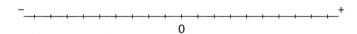

93. Graph: $\{x: x \leq -2\}$

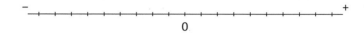

94. $|-6| =$

95. $|3 - 7| =$

96. $5 - |-3| =$

97. Solve for x: $|2x - 7| = 9$

98. Give the coordinates represented by points.

    A.

    B.

    C.

    D.

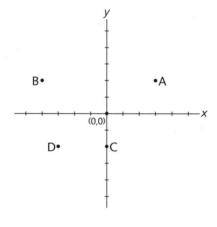

99. Is $x + \dfrac{3}{y} = 5$ linear or nonlinear?

100. Graph $x + y = 9$

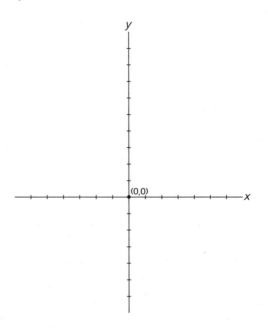

101. Rewrite the equation $3x + 4y = 12$ in slope-intercept form. Then find slope and y-intercept values.

102. For the equation $3x + 4y = 12$, find the x-intercept.

103. Graph $y = x^2 + 3$

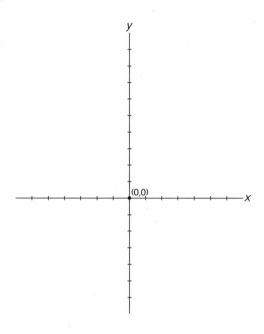

104. $-\sqrt{64} =$

105. $\sqrt{144} =$

106. Simplify: $\sqrt{75} =$

In problems 107 through 121, each variable is nonnegative.

107. $\sqrt{x^8} =$

108. $\sqrt{x^2 y^8} =$

109. $\sqrt{9x^6 y^{10}} =$

110. $\sqrt{y^9} =$

111. $\sqrt{a^3 b^3} =$

112. $\sqrt{27a^3 b^6} =$

113. $\sqrt{(18)(2)} =$

114. $\sqrt{25+4} =$

115. $7\sqrt{5} + 3\sqrt{5} =$

116. $\sqrt{60} + 2\sqrt{15} =$

117. $\sqrt{27} + \sqrt{48} =$

118. $\sqrt{6} \cdot \sqrt{10} =$

119. $\sqrt{x^3 y} \cdot \sqrt{x^2 yz} =$

120. $\sqrt{2xy} \cdot \sqrt{32x^3 y^2} =$

121. $6\sqrt{6} \cdot 2\sqrt{3} =$

122. $a @ b = (a+b)^2$, for all real numbers a and b. What is the value of $5@4$?

Answers

Page numbers following each answer refer to the review section applicable to this problem type.

1. subset (p. 118)

2. empty or null set (p. 118)

3. rule (p. 119)

4. roster (p. 119)

5. finite (p. 119)

6. infinite (p. 119)

7. false (p. 119)

8. true (p. 119)

9. {8} (p. 119)

10. {1, 3, 4, 5, 6} (p. 119)

11. a. $2x + 4$ (p. 120)

    b. $x - 6$ (p. 120)

    c. $x + 10$ (p. 120)

    d. $x - 4y$ (p. 120)

12. 73 (p. 122)
13. 6,912 (p. 122)
14. $-\frac{3}{2}$ or $-1\frac{1}{2}$ (p. 122)
15. $x = 46$ (p. 125)
16. $x = 10$ (p. 125)
17. $y = 96$ (p. 125)
18. $z = \frac{45}{2}$ or $22\frac{1}{2}$ (p. 125)
19. $x = -3$ (p. 125)
20. $n = -8$ (p. 125)
21. $y = -84$ (p. 125)
22. $y = \frac{x+n}{m}$ (p.130)
23. $m = an$ (p. 130)
24. $x = \frac{rt}{s}$ (p. 130)
25. $x = \frac{zy}{a}$ (p. 132)
26. $x = 3$ (p. 134)
27. $c = \frac{24}{7}$ or $3\frac{3}{7}$ (p. 134)
28. $x = 3, y = \frac{-5}{2}$ or $-2\frac{1}{2}$ (p. 136)
29. $a = -1, b = 2$ (p. 136)
30. $x = \frac{5}{3}$ or $1\frac{2}{3}, y = \frac{14}{3}$ or $4\frac{2}{3}$ (p. 136)
31. $-3xy$ (p. 143)
32. $10qt^2$ (p. 143)
33. a^3x^2y (p. 144)
34. $6xyz$ (p. 144)
35. y^8 (p. 144)
36. a^5b^5 (p. 144)
37. $-6x^5y^5$ (p. 144)
38. $6m^7n^5$ (p. 144)
39. $4a^2b^6c^5d$ (p. 144)
40. x^{28} (p. 144)

41. a^6b^9 (p. 144)

42. $9x^6y^{10}$ (p. 144)

43. x^3 (p. 145)

44. a^2b (p. 145)

45. $7x^5y^3$ (p. 145)

46. $\dfrac{p^2}{5q^4}$ or $0.2p^2q^{-4}$ (p. 145)

47. $4x^2 + 6xy + 5y^2$ (p. 147)

48. $9x + 5y$ (p. 147)

49. $s^2 + 2st + 10t^2$ (p. 147)

50. $9a^2b - 2ab^2$ (p. 147)

51. $6x^2 + 10x - 4$ (p. 148)

52. $2a^2 + 6a^2b + 8a + ab + 3ab^2 + 4b$ (p. 148)

53. $6a^5 - 4a^4$ (p. 151)

54. $6x^2y^5$ (p. 151)

55. $(x + 1)$ (p. 152)

56. $(5x + 1)$ (p. 152)

57. $(a^2 + 3a + 9)$ (p. 152)

58. $3(3a - 2)$ (p. 156)

59. $5x^2(x + 2)$ (p. 156)

60. $(n - 3)(n + 3)$ (p. 156)

61. $(6a - b)(6a + b)$ (p. 156)

62. $2(a - 4)(a + 4)$ (p. 156)

63. $(x + 1)(x + 2)$ (p. 158)

64. $(x - 6)(x + 1)$ (p. 158)

65. $(3x + 1)(x - 7)$ (p. 158)

66. $x(x - 3)(x - 1)$ (p. 158)

67. $(6 - r)(4 - r)$ (p. 158)

68. $(x - y)(x - y)$ (p. 158)

69. $y = 1$ or $y = 4$ (p. 163)

70. $x = 5$ or $x = -5$ (p. 163)

71. $x = 0$ or $x = 5$ (p. 163)

72. $t = 3$ or $t = -27$ (p. 163)

73. $\frac{3x^2}{4}$ (p. 169)

74. $\frac{5}{4}$ or $1\frac{1}{4}$ (p. 169)

75. $\frac{x-5}{x+3}$ (p. 169)

76. $\frac{4x^2y^2}{3}$ (p. 170)

77. $\frac{x+3}{x(x-6)}$ or $\frac{x+3}{x^2-6x}$ (p. 170)

78. $\frac{18x^2}{7}$ (p. 171)

79. $\frac{5}{2}$ or $2\frac{1}{2}$ (p. 171)

80. $\frac{3y+8}{y}$ (p. 172)

81. $\frac{x-11}{x-1}$ (p. 172)

82. $\frac{7y-6x}{xy}$ (p. 172)

83. $\frac{3x-5}{4x}$ (p. 172)

84. $\frac{7x^3+3y^5}{x^6y^7}$ (p. 172)

85. $\frac{x^2+9x}{(x-3)(x+1)}$ (p. 172)

86. $\frac{5x^2-15x}{(x+4)(x-4)(x+1)}$ (p. 172)

87. $\{x: x > 3\}$ (p. 176)

88. $\{y: y \geq -5\}$ (p. 176)

89. $\left\{x: x \geq -\frac{4}{3}\right\}$ (p. 176)

90. 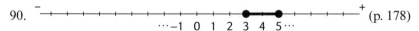 (p. 178)

91. 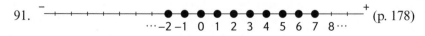 (p. 178)

92. 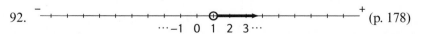 (p. 178)

93. 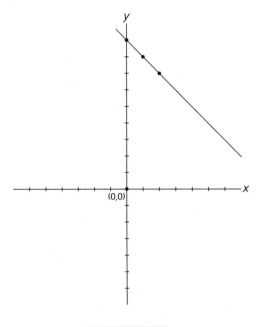 (p. 178)

    ···−4 −3 −2 −1 0 1···

94. 6 (p. 180)

95. 4 (p. 180)

96. 2 (p. 180)

97. $x = 8$ or $x = -1$ (p. 180)

98. A. (3, 2) (p. 182)

    B. (−4, 2) (p. 182)

    C. (0, −2) (p. 182)

    D. (−3, −2) (p. 182)

99. nonlinear (p. 185)

100.

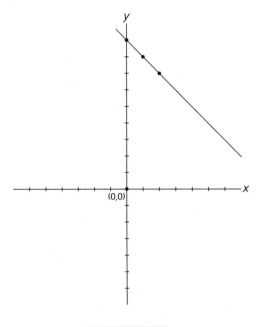

x	y
0	9
1	8
2	7

(p. 185)

101. $y = -\frac{3}{4}x + 3$, slope $= -\frac{3}{4}$, y-intercept $= 3$ or $(0,3)$ (p. 185)

102. 4 or the location $(4, 0)$ (p. 185)

103.

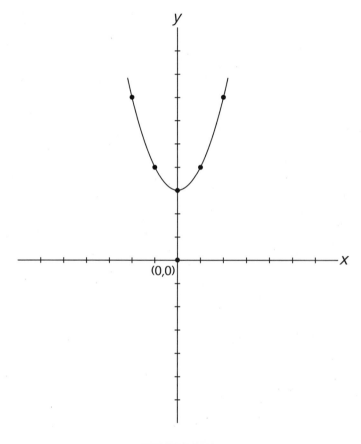

x	y
−2	7
−1	4
0	3
1	4
2	7

(p. 185)

104. -8 (p. 200)

105. 12 (p. 200)

106. $5\sqrt{3}$ (p. 200)

107. x^4 (p. 200)

108. xy^4, $x \geq 0$ (p. 200)

109. $3x^3y^5$; $x, y \geq 0$ (p. 200)

110. $y^4\sqrt{y}$ (p. 200)

111. $ab\sqrt{ab}$ (p. 200)

112. $3ab\sqrt{3ab}$ (p. 200)

113. 6 (p. 200)

114. $\sqrt{29}$ (p. 202)

115. $10\sqrt{5}$ (p. 202)

116. $4\sqrt{15}$ (p. 204)

117. $7\sqrt{3}$ (p. 204)

118. $2\sqrt{15}$ (p. 205)

119. $x^2y\sqrt{xz}$, $y \geq 0$ (p. 205)

120. $8x^2y\sqrt{y}$, $x \geq 0$ (p. 205)

121. $12\sqrt{18} = 36\sqrt{2}$ (p. 205)

122. 81 (p. 206)

Algebra Glossary of Terms

abscissa: The x-coordinate of a point. In the point (3, 2), the abscissa is 3.

absolute value: The numerical value when direction or sign is not considered.

algebra: Arithmetic operations using letters and/or symbols in place of numbers.

algebraic fractions: Fractions using a variable in the numerator and/or denominator.

ascending order: Basically, when the power of a term increases for each succeeding term.

binomial: An algebraic expression consisting of two terms.

Cartesian coordinates: A system of assigning ordered number pairs to points on a plane.

closed interval: An interval that includes both endpoints or fixed boundaries.

coefficient: The number in front of a variable. For example, in $9x$, 9 is the coefficient.

coordinate axes: Two perpendicular number lines used in a coordinate graph.

coordinate graph: Two perpendicular number lines, the x-axis and the y-axis, creating a plane on which each point is assigned a pair of numbers.

cube: The result when a number is multiplied by itself twice. Designated by the exponent 3. (x^3)

cube root: The number that when multiplied by itself twice gives you the original number. For example, 5 is the cube root of 125. Its symbol is $\sqrt[3]{}$. $\sqrt[3]{125} = 5$

denominator: Everything below the fraction bar in a fraction.

descending order: Basically, when the power of a term decreases for each succeeding term.

element: A member of a set.

empty set: A set with no members. Null set.

equal sets: Sets that have exactly the same members.

equation: A balanced relationship between numbers and/or symbols. A mathematical sentence with an equal sign.

equivalent sets: Sets that have the same number of members.

evaluate: To determine the value, or numerical amount.

exponent: A numeral used to indicate the power of a number.

extremes: Outer terms.

factor: To find two or more quantities whose product equals the original quantity.

finite: Countable. Having a definite ending.

F.O.I.L. method: A method of multiplying binomials in which first terms, outside terms, inside terms, and last terms are multiplied.

half-open interval: An interval that includes one endpoint, or one boundary.

imaginary numbers: Square roots of negative numbers. The imaginary unit is i.

incomplete quadratic equation: A quadratic equation missing the constant term and/or the term with the variable raised to the first power.

inequality: A statement in which the relationships are not equal. A mathematical sentence that uses $<$, $\leq$, $>$, $\geq$, or $\neq$.

infinite: Uncountable. Continues forever.

intercepts: The x-intercept of a graph occurs when the graph is on the x-axis. When a point is on the x-axis, its y-coordinate there is 0. The y-intercept of a graph occurs when the graph is on the y-axis. When a point is on the y-axis, its x-coordinate there is 0.

intersection of sets: The set formed by only using the common elements found in each set (the place[s] where the sets overlap).

interval: All the numbers that lie within two certain boundaries.

linear equation: An equation whose solution set forms a straight line when plotted on a coordinate graph.

literal equation: An equation having mostly variables.

means: Inner terms.

monomial: An algebraic expression consisting of only one term.

nonlinear equation: An equation whose solution set does not form a straight line when plotted on a coordinate graph.

null set: A set with no members. Empty set.

number line: A graphic representation of integers and other real numbers. The point on this line associated with each number is called the graph of the number.

numerator: Everything above the fraction bar in a fraction.

open interval: An interval that does not include endpoints or fixed boundaries.

open ray: A ray that does not include its endpoint (an open half line).

ordered pair: Any pair of elements (x, y) having a first element x and a second element y. Used to identify or plot points on a coordinate grid.

ordinate: The y-coordinate of a point. In the point (3, 2), the ordinate is 2.

origin: The point of intersection of the two number lines on a coordinate graph. Represented by the coordinates (0, 0).

polynomial: An algebraic expression consisting of two or more terms.

proportion: Two ratios equal to each other. For example, a is to c as b is to d. Also written as $\frac{a}{c} = \frac{b}{d}$.

quadrants: Four quarters or divisions of a coordinate graph.

quadratic equation: An equation that could be written $Ax^2 + Bx + C = 0$ with $A \neq 0$.

radical sign: The symbol used to indicate a root. For example, $\sqrt{}$ indicates square root, $\sqrt[3]{}$ indicates cube root.

ratio: A method of comparing two or more numbers. For example, $a{:}b$. Often written as a fraction.

ray: A half line that includes its endpoint.

real numbers: The set consisting of all rational and irrational numbers.

roster: A method of naming a set by listing its members.

rule: A method of naming a set by describing its elements.

set: A group of objects, numbers, and so on.

set builder notation: A formal method of describing a set. Often used for inequalities. For example, $\{x{:}\ x > 1\}$, which is read "x such that all x is greater than 1."

simplify: To combine several or many terms into fewer terms.

slope: A value that describes the steepness and direction of a line. If a line has a positive slope, it slants upward toward the right. If a line has a negative slope, it slants downward toward the right. If (x_1, y_1) and (x_2, y_2) represent any two points on a line, then slope $= \frac{y_2 - y_1}{x_2 - x_1}$; that is, $m = \frac{y_2 - y_1}{x_2 - x_1}$.

slope-intercept form: A way to write an equation of a line in order to recognize its slope and y-intercept. When a linear equation is written in $y = mx + b$ form, the m value becomes the slope value for the line, and the b value is the location on the y-axis where the line intercepts the y-axis.

solution set or **solution:** All the answers that satisfy a mathematical sentence.

square: The result when a number is multiplied by itself. Designated by the exponent 2. (x^2)

square root: The number that, when multiplied by itself, gives you the original number. For example, 5 is the square root of 25. Its symbol is $\sqrt{\ }$. $\sqrt{25} = 5$.

subset: A set within a set.

system of equations: Simultaneous equations.

term: A numerical or literal expression with its own sign.

trinomial: An algebraic expression consisting of three terms.

union of sets: The set formed by combining all the elements found in the sets (the place[s] that have elements from either set).

universal set: The general category set, or the set of all those elements under consideration.

unknown: A letter or symbol whose value is not known.

value: Numerical amount.

variable: A symbol used to stand for a number.

Venn diagram: A pictorial description of sets.

x-axis: The horizontal axis in a coordinate graph.

x-coordinate: The first number in the ordered pair. Refers to the distance on the x-axis. Abscissa.

y-axis: The vertical axis in a coordinate graph.

y-coordinate: The second number in the ordered pair. Refers to the distance on the y-axis. Ordinate.

Geometry

Geometry Diagnostic Test

Questions

1. Name any angle of this triangle three different ways.

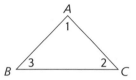

2. A(n) _____ angle measures less than 90 degrees.

3. A(n) _____ angle measures 90 degrees.

4. A(n) _____ angle measures more than 90 degrees but less than 180 degrees.

5. A(n) _____ angle measures 180 degrees.

6. Two angles are complementary when the sum of their measures is _____.

7. Two angles are supplementary when the sum of their measures is _____.

8. In the diagram, find the measure of $\angle a$, $\angle b$, and $\angle c$.

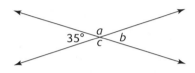

9. In the diagram, find the measure of all remaining angles. $l \parallel m$

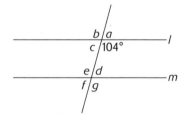

10. Lines that stay the same distance apart and never meet are called _____ lines.

11. Lines that meet to form right angles are called _____ lines.

12. A(n) _____ triangle has three equal sides. Therefore, each interior angle measures _____.

13. In $\triangle ABC$,

    segment BD is a(n) _____

    segment BE is a(n) _____

    segment BF is a(n) _____

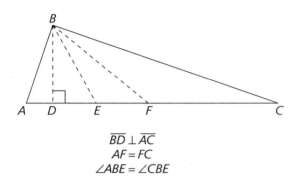

$$\overline{BD} \perp \overline{AC}$$
$$AF = FC$$
$$\angle ABE = \angle CBE$$

14. In the diagram, ABC is an isosceles triangle: $AB = AC$. Find $\angle A$ and $\angle C$.

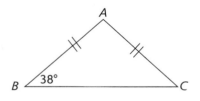

Questions 15 and 16

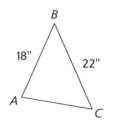

15. In the triangle, AC must be less than _____ inches.

16. In the triangle, which angle is smaller, $\angle A$ or $\angle C$?

17. What is the measure of $\angle ACD$?

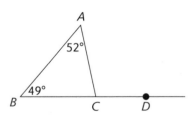

18. What is the length of $\overline{AC}$?

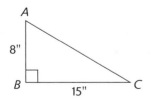

19. What is the length of $\overline{BC}$?

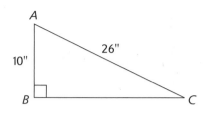

20. What is the value of x?

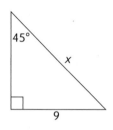

21. What is the value of a?

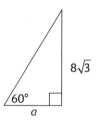

22. Name each of the following polygons.

(A) $AB = BC = AC$
$\angle A = \angle B = \angle C = 60°$

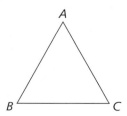

(B) $AB = BC = CD = AD$
$\angle A = \angle B = \angle C = \angle D = 90°$

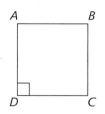

(C) $\overline{AB} \parallel \overline{DC}$
$AB = DC$
$\overline{AD} \parallel \overline{BC}$
$AD = BC$

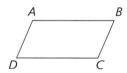

(D) $AB = DC$
$AD = BC$
$\angle A = \angle B = \angle C = \angle D = 90°$

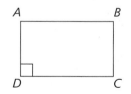

(E) $\overline{AB} \parallel \overline{DC}$

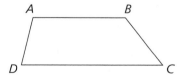

23. For which of the following quadrilaterals *must* the following be true?

Property	Square	Rectangle	Rhombus	Parallelogram	Trapezoid
Diagonals are equal					
Diagonals bisect each other					
Diagonals are perpendicular					
Diagonals bisect the angles					
All sides are equal in length					
All angles are equal in measure					
Opposite angles are equal in measure					
Opposite sides are equal in length					
At least one pair of opposite sides are parallel					
At least two pairs of consecutive angles are supplementary					

Questions 24–25 relate to the following figure:

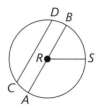

24. Fill in the blanks for circle *R*.

   (A) $\overline{RS}$ is called a

   _____.

   (B) $\overline{AB}$ is called a

   _____.

   (C) $\overline{CD}$ is called a

   _____.

25. In the circle, if $\overset{\frown}{BS} = 62°$, what is the measure of $\angle BRS$?

26. In this circle, if $\overset{\frown}{BS} = 62°$, what is the measure of $\angle BCS$?

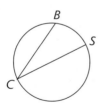

27. Find the area and circumference for the circle $O\left(\pi \approx \frac{22}{7}\right)$.

   (A) area = _____

   (B) circumference =

   _____

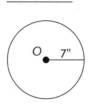

28. Find the area and perimeter of the trapezoid.

   (A) area = _____

   (B) perimeter = _____

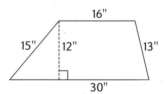

29. Find the area and perimeter of the figure (*ABCD* is a parallelogram).

   (A) area = _____

   (B) perimeter = _____

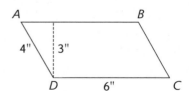

30. Find the volume of the right circular cylinder (use 3.14 for π).

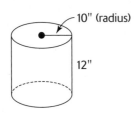

10" (radius)

12"

31. What is the surface area and volume of the cube?

(A) surface area = _____

(B) volume = _____

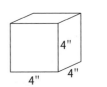

4"

4"

4"

Answers

Page numbers following each answer refer to the review section applicable to this problem type.

1. $\angle 3$, $\angle CBA$, $\angle ABC$, $\angle B$ (p. 238)

   $\angle 1$, $\angle BAC$, $\angle CAB$, $\angle A$ (p. 238)

   $\angle 2$, $\angle ACB$, $\angle BCA$, $\angle C$ (p. 238)

2. acute (p. 239)

3. right (p. 239)

4. obtuse (p. 239)

5. straight (p. 239)

6. $90°$ (p. 241)

7. $180°$ (p. 241)

8. $a = 145°$

   $b = 35°$

   $c = 145°$ (p. 241)

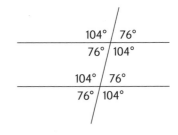

145°

35°   35°

145°

9. $\angle a$, $\angle c$, $\angle d$, $\angle f = 76°$

   $\angle b$, $\angle e$, $\angle g = 104°$ (p. 247)

104° / 76°

76° / 104°

104° / 76°

76° / 104°

10. parallel (p. 247)

11. perpendicular (p. 246)

12. equilateral, 60° (p. 252)

13. segment BD is an altitude

    segment BE is an angle bisector

    segment BF is a median

    (pp. 255–256)

14. $38° + 38° + x° = 180°$

    $76° + x° = 180°$

    $x° = 104°$

    $\angle A = 104°$

    $\angle C = 38°$

    (p. 253)

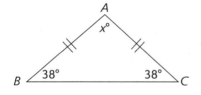

15. 40 inches. Since $AB + BC = 40$ inches, then $AC < AB + BC$ and $AC < 40$ inches (p. 258)

16. $\angle C$ must be the smaller angle, since it is opposite the shorter side AB. (p. 258)

17. $\angle ACD = 101°$ (p. 259)

18. $AC = 17$ inches (p. 262)

19. $BC = 24$ inches. Since 5, 12, 13 is a Pythagorean triple, doubled is 10, 24, 26. (p. 262)

20. $x = 9\sqrt{2}$. Since this is an isosceles right triangle, the ratio of the sides is $x, x, x\sqrt{2}$. (p. 265)

21. $a = 8$. Since this is a 30-60-90 right triangle, the ratio of the sides is $x, x\sqrt{3}, 2x$. (p. 267)

22. (A) equilateral triangle or equiangular triangle (p. 252)

    (B) square (p. 270)

    (C) parallelogram (p. 271)

    (D) rectangle (p. 270)

    (E) trapezoid (p. 272)

23.

Property	Square	Rectangle	Rhombus	Parallelogram	Trapezoid
Diagonals are equal	✓	✓			
Diagonals bisect each other	✓	✓	✓	✓	
Diagonals are perpendicular	✓		✓		
Diagonals bisect the angles	✓		✓		
All sides are equal in length	✓		✓		
All angles are equal in measure	✓	✓			
Opposite angles are equal in measure	✓	✓	✓	✓	
Opposite sides are equal in length	✓	✓	✓	✓	
At least one pair of opposite sides are parallel	✓	✓	✓	✓	✓
At least two pairs of consecutive angles are supplementary	✓	✓	✓	✓	✓

(pp. 270–272)

24. (A) radius (p. 281)

    (B) diameter (p. 282)

    (C) chord (p. 283)

25. 62° (p. 286)

26. 31° (p. 287)

27. (A) area = πr^2

    $= \pi(7^2)$

    $= \frac{22}{7}(7)(7)$

    = 154 square inches
    (p. 285)

    (B) circumference = πd

    $= \pi(14)$

    $= \frac{22}{7}(14)$

    = 44 inches
    (p. 284)

    d = 14 inches, since
    r = 7 inches.

28. (A) area $= \frac{1}{2}(a+b)h$

    $= \frac{1}{2}(16+30)12$

    $= \frac{1}{2}(46)12$

    $= 23(12)$

    = 276 square inches
    (p. 278)

    (B) perimeter = 16 + 13 + 30
    + 15 = 74 inches (p. 277)

29. (A) area = bh

    = 6(3)

    = 18 square inches
    (p. 278)

    (B) perimeter = 6 + 4 + 6 + 4
    = 20 inches (p. 277)

30. Volume = (area of base)
    (height)

    $= (\pi r^2)h$

    $= (\pi \times 10^2)(12)$

    $\approx 3.14(100)(12)$

    $\approx 314(12)$

    $\approx 3{,}768$ cubic inches
    (p. 291)

31. (A) All six surfaces have an
    area of 4×4, or 16 square
    inches, since each surface is a
    square. Therefore, 16(6) = 96
    square inches in the surface
    area. (p. 292)

    (B) Volume = side × side ×
    side, or $4^3 = 4 \times 4 \times 4 = 64$
    cubic inches. (p. 290)

Geometry Review

Plane geometry is the study of shapes and figures in two dimensions (the plane). Plane figures have only length and width.

Solid geometry is the study of shapes and figures in three dimensions. Solid figures have length, width, and thickness.

A *point* is the most fundamental idea in geometry. It is represented by a dot and named by a capital letter.

Angles

An *angle* is formed by two rays that have the same endpoint. That point is called the *vertex;* the rays are called the *sides* of the angle. An angle is measured in degrees from 0 to 360. The number of degrees indicates the size of the angle or the difference in direction of the two rays.

In the diagram, the angle is formed by rays $\overrightarrow{AB}$ and $\overrightarrow{AC}$. A is the vertex. $\overrightarrow{AB}$ and $\overrightarrow{AC}$ are the sides of the angle.

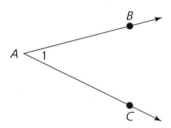

The symbol $\angle$ is used to denote an angle. The symbol $m\angle$ is sometimes used to denote the measure of an angle.

An angle can be named in various ways:

- By the letter of the vertex; therefore, the angle above could be named $\angle A$.
- By the number (or small letter) in its interior; therefore, the angle above could be named $\angle 1$.
- By the letters of the three points that formed it; therefore, the angle above could be named $\angle BAC$ or $\angle CAB$. The center letter is always the letter of the vertex.

Types of Angles

Right Angle

A *right angle* has a measure of 90°. A small square in the interior of an angle designates the fact that a right angle is formed.

In the diagram, $\angle ABC$ is a right angle.

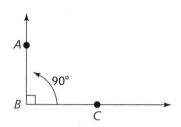

Acute Angle

Any angle whose measure is less than 90° is called an *acute angle*.

In the diagram, $\angle b$ is acute.

Obtuse Angle

Any angle whose measure is larger than 90° but smaller than 180° is called an *obtuse angle*.

In the diagram, $\angle 4$ is an obtuse angle.

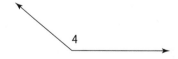

Straight Angle

A *straight angle* has a measure of 180°.

In the diagram, $\angle BAC$ is a straight angle (often called a *line*).

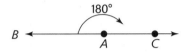

Practice: Angle Problems

Name the angles.

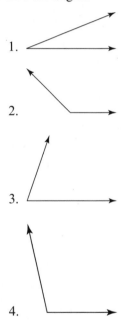

1.

2.

3.

4.

What kind of angle is formed between the hands of a clock (measured clockwise) when it is

   5. 6 o'clock

   6. 2 o'clock

   7. 3 o'clock

   8. 8 o'clock

Answers: Angle Problems

1. an acute angle

2. an obtuse angle

3. an acute angle

4. an obtuse angle

5. a straight angle

6. an acute angle

7. a right angle

8. an obtuse angle

Pairs of Angles

Adjacent Angles

Adjacent angles are any angles that share a common side and a common vertex but do not share any interior points.

In the diagram, ∠1 and ∠2 are adjacent angles. But ∠1 and ∠*ABC* are not adjacent angles since they share interior points (for example, point *E* is in the interior of each angle).

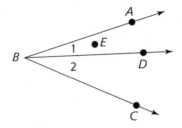

Vertical Angles

If two straight lines intersect, they do so at a point. Four angles are formed. Those angles opposite each other are called *vertical angles.* Those angles sharing a common side and a common vertex are, again, *adjacent angles.* Vertical angles are always equal in measure.

In the diagram, line *l* and line *m* intersect at point *Q*. $\angle 1$, $\angle 2$, and $\angle 3$, and $\angle 4$ are formed.

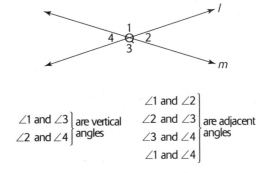

$\left. \begin{array}{l} \angle 1 \text{ and } \angle 3 \\ \angle 2 \text{ and } \angle 4 \end{array} \right\}$ are vertical angles $\left. \begin{array}{l} \angle 1 \text{ and } \angle 2 \\ \angle 2 \text{ and } \angle 3 \\ \angle 3 \text{ and } \angle 4 \\ \angle 1 \text{ and } \angle 4 \end{array} \right\}$ are adjacent angles

Therefore,

$$\angle 1 = \angle 3$$
$$\angle 2 = \angle 4$$

Complementary Angles

Two angles whose sum is 90° are called *complementary angles*.

In the diagram, since $\angle ABC$ is a right triangle, $\angle 1 + \angle 2 = 90°$.

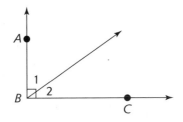

Therefore, $\angle 1$ and $\angle 2$ are complementary angles. If $\angle 1 = 55°$, its complement, $\angle 2$, would be $90° - 55° = 35°$.

Supplementary Angles

Two angles whose sum is 180° are called *supplementary angles*. Two adjacent angles that form a straight line are supplementary.

In the diagram, since ∠*ABC* is a straight angle, ∠3 + ∠4 = 180°.

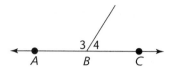

Therefore, ∠3 and ∠4 are supplementary angles. If ∠3 = 122°, its supplement, ∠4, would have a measure of: 180° – 122° = 58°.

Angle Bisector

A ray from the vertex of an angle that divides the angle into two angles of equal measure is called an *angle bisector.*

In the diagram, $\overrightarrow{AB}$ is the angle bisector of ∠*CAD*.

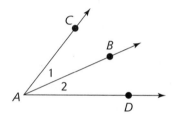

Therefore, ∠1 = ∠2.

Practice: Angle Problems

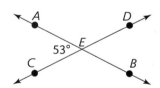

1. In the figure above, if lines *AB* and *CD* intersect at *E*, and if ∠*AEC* measures 53°, how many degrees are there in ∠*BED*?

2. Find the complement of the following angles.

   (a) 17°
   (b) *t*°

3. Find the supplement of the following angles.

    (a) 124°

    (b) $(x + 9)°$

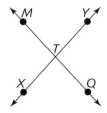

4. In the figure box above, $\angle XTM$ and $\angle$ _____ are *vertical* angles.

5. Find the complement of an angle whose measure is

    (a) $74\frac{1}{2}°$

    (b) $(q - 5)°$

6. Find the supplement of an angle whose measure is

    (a) 180°

    (b) $(m - 30)°$

Answers: Angle Problems

1. Since $\angle AEC$ and $\angle BED$ are vertical angles, $\angle BED = 53°$.

2. (a) $90° - 17° = 73°$

    (b) $(90 - t)°$

3. (a) $180° - 124° = 56°$

    (b) $180° - (x + 9)° = 180° - x° - 9° = (171 - x)°$

4. YTQ

5. (a) $90° - 74\frac{1}{2}° = 15\frac{1}{2}°$

    (b) $90° - (q - 5)° = 90° - q° + 5° = (95 - q)°$

6. (a) $180° - 180° = 0°$

    (b) $180° - (m - 30)° = 180° - m° + 30° = (210 - m)°$

Lines

Straight Lines

A *straight line* is often described as the shortest path connecting two points. It continues forever in both directions. A line consists of an infinite number of points and is named by any two points on the line. (*Line* means straight line.) The symbol ⟷ written on top of the two letters is used to denote that line.

This is line *AB*.

It is written $\overleftrightarrow{AB}$.

A line may also be named by one small letter. This is line *l*.

Line Segments

A *line segment* is a piece of a line. It has two endpoints and is named by its two endpoints. Sometimes the symbol —, written on top of the two letters is used to denote that line segment.

This is line segment *CD*. It is written $\overline{CD}$ or *CD*. (Although there is a technical difference, most standardized exams use one form consistently in context.)

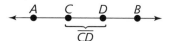

Note that it is a piece of $\overleftrightarrow{AB}$.

A midpoint of a line segment is the halfway point, or the point equidistant from the endpoints.

Rays

A ray has only one endpoint (or origin) and continues forever in one direction. A ray could be thought of as a half-line with an endpoint. It is named by the letter of its endpoint and any other point on the ray. The ray symbol → written on top of the two letters is used to denote that ray.

This is ray *AB*.

It is written $\overrightarrow{AB}$.

This is ray *BC*.

It is written $\overrightarrow{BC}$.

When writing a ray, begin with the endpoint, then name another point through which it passes. In the following figure, even though the ray is going to the left, it is written as $\overrightarrow{BC}$.

Types of Lines

Intersecting Lines

Two or more lines that meet at a point are called *intersecting lines*. That point would be on each of those lines.

In the diagram, lines *l* and *m* intersect at *Q*.

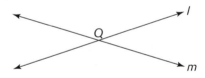

Perpendicular Lines

Two lines that meet to form right angles (90°) are called *perpendicular lines*. The symbol ⊥ is used to denote perpendicular lines.

In the diagram, *l* ⊥ *m*.

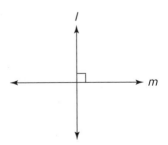

Parallel Lines

Two or more lines that remain the same distance apart at all times are called *parallel lines.* Parallel lines never meet. The symbol ‖ is used to denote parallel lines.

In the diagram, $l \parallel m$.

Parallel Lines Cut by Transversal

When two parallel lines are both intersected by a third line, it is termed *parallel lines cut by a transversal.* In the diagram below, line *n* is the transversal, and lines *m* and *l* are parallel. Eight angles are formed. There are many facts and relationships about these angles.

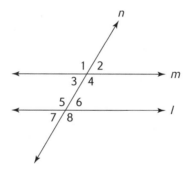

- **Adjacent angles:** Angles 1 and 2 are adjacent and they form a straight line; therefore, they are supplementary: $\angle 1 + \angle 2 = 180°$. Likewise:

  $\angle 2 + \angle 4 = 180°$

  $\angle 3 + \angle 4 = 180°$

  $\angle 1 + \angle 3 = 180°$

  $\angle 5 + \angle 6 = 180°$

  $\angle 7 + \angle 8 = 180°$

  $\angle 5 + \angle 7 = 180°$

  $\angle 6 + \angle 8 = 180°$

- **Vertical angles:** Angles 1 and 4 are vertical angles; therefore, they are equal: $\angle 1 = \angle 4$. Likewise:

  $\angle 2 = \angle 3$

  $\angle 5 = \angle 8$

  $\angle 7 = \angle 6$

- **Corresponding angles:** If you could physically pick up line *l* and place it on line *m*, the angles that would coincide with each other would be equal in measure. They are called corresponding angles. Therefore:

  $\angle 1 = \angle 5$

  $\angle 2 = \angle 6$

  $\angle 3 = \angle 7$

  $\angle 4 = \angle 8$

- **Alternate interior and exterior angles:** Alternate angles are on the opposite sides of the transversal. Interior angles are those contained within the parallel lines. Exterior angles are those on the outsides of the parallel lines. Therefore:

  $\angle 3$ and $\angle 6$ are alternate interior angles and $\angle 3 = \angle 6$.

  $\angle 4$ and $\angle 5$ are alternate interior angles and $\angle 4 = \angle 5$.

  $\angle 2$ and $\angle 7$ are alternate exterior angles and $\angle 2 = \angle 7$.

  $\angle 1$ and $\angle 8$ are alternate exterior angles and $\angle 1 = \angle 8$.

- **Consecutive interior angles:** Consecutive interior angles are on the same side of the transversal. Therefore:

  $\angle 3$ and $\angle 5$ are consecutive interior angles, and $\angle 3 + \angle 5 = 180°$.

  $\angle 4$ and $\angle 6$ are consecutive interior angles, and $\angle 4 + \angle 6 = 180°$.

  The sum of the measures of each pair of consecutive angles = 180°.

  Using all these facts, if you're given the measure of one of the eight angles, the other angle measures can all be determined.

  For example:

  $\angle a + 83° = 180°$

  $\left.\begin{array}{l}\angle a = 97° \\ \angle b = 97°\end{array}\right\}$ vertical angles

  $\left.\begin{array}{l}\angle c = 83° \\ \angle d = 83°\end{array}\right\}$ alternate interior angles

  $l \parallel m$

$\angle e = 97°$
$\angle f = 97°$ } vertical angles

$\angle g = 83°$ } alternate exterior angles

Note that since the lines are parallel, you can *see* which angles are equal, even if you cannot remember the rules.

Practice: Parallel Lines Cut by Transversal Problems

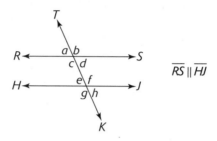

$\overline{RS} \parallel \overline{HJ}$

1. In the figure above, name all the pairs of the following types of angles.

    (a)   vertical angles
    (b)   consecutive interior angles
    (c)   corresponding angles
    (d)   alternate interior angles

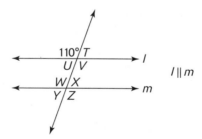

$l \parallel m$

2. In the figure above, find the measure of the angles T, U, V, W, X, Y, and Z.

249

Answers: Parallel Lines Cut by Transversal Problems

1. (a) Vertical angles are a and d, b and c, e and h, f and g.

   (b) Consecutive interior angles are c and e, d and f.

   (c) Corresponding angles are a and e, c and g, b and f, d and h.

   (d) Alternate interior angles are c and f, d and e.

2. Angles V, W, and Z all have measures of 110°.

   Angles T, U, X, and Y all have measures of 70°.

Polygons

Closed shapes, or figures in a plane, with three or more sides are called *polygons*. (*Poly* means "many," and *gon* means "sides." Thus, *polygon* means "many sides." A plane is often described as a flat surface.) Examples of polygons are:

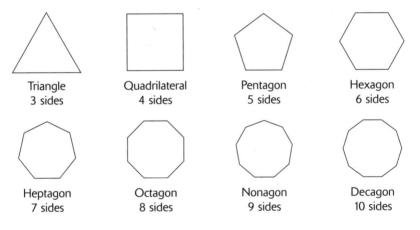

Triangle	Quadrilateral	Pentagon	Hexagon
3 sides	4 sides	5 sides	6 sides
Heptagon	Octagon	Nonagon	Decagon
7 sides	8 sides	9 sides	10 sides

Regular Polygons

Regular means all sides have the same length and all angles have the same measure. A regular three-sided polygon is the equilateral triangle. A regular four-sided polygon is the square. There are no other special names. Other polygons will just be described as regular, if they are. For example, a regular five-sided polygon is called a regular pentagon. A regular six-sided polygon is called a regular hexagon.

Diagonals of Polygons

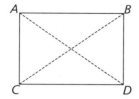

A *diagonal of a polygon* is a line segment that connects one vertex with another vertex and is not itself a side. ($\overline{AD}$ and $\overline{BC}$ are both diagonals.)

Convex Polygons

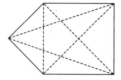

A convex polygon has all diagonals within the figure. Also, all interior angles are less than 180°.

Concave Polygons

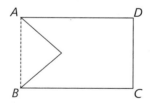

A concave polygon (caves in) has at least one diagonal outside the figure. Also, at least one interior angle is greater than 180°. ($\overline{AB}$ is the diagonal.)

Triangles

This section deals with those polygons having the fewest number of sides. A triangle is a three-sided polygon. It has three angles in its interior. The sum of the measure of these angles is always 180°. The symbol for triangle is △. A triangle is named by the three letters of its vertices.

This is $\triangle ABC$.

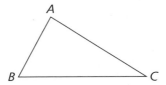

Types of Triangles by Sides

Equilateral Triangles

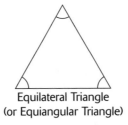

Equilateral Triangle
(or Equiangular Triangle)

A triangle having all three sides equal in measure is called an *equilateral triangle*. *Note:* By angles, this would be called an *equiangular triangle*—all angles are equal (60° each).

Isosceles Triangles

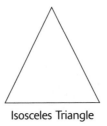

Isosceles Triangle

A triangle having two equal sides, or two equal (congruent) angles, is called an *isosceles triangle*.

Scalene Triangles

Scalene Triangle

A triangle having no equal sides, or no equal angles, is called a *scalene triangle*.

Types of Triangles by Angles

Right Triangles

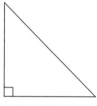

Right Triangle

A triangle having a right (90°) angle in its interior is called a *right triangle*.

Obtuse Triangles

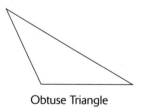

Obtuse Triangle

A triangle having an obtuse angle (greater than 90° but less than 180°) in its interior is called an *obtuse triangle*.

Acute Triangles

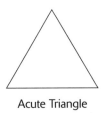

Acute Triangle

A triangle having all acute angles (less than 90°) in its interior is called an *acute triangle*.

Examples: Triangle Problems

1. Two angles of a triangle measure 45° and 85°. How many degrees are there in the third angle?

   Answer: The angles of a triangle add up to 180°. The sum of 45° and 85° is 130°. Therefore, the remaining angle must be 180° – 130° = 50°.

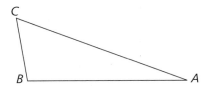

2. In $\triangle ABC$ above, $\angle C$ is three times $\angle A$ and $\angle B$ is five times $\angle A$. Find the number of degrees in each angle of the triangle.

   Answer: Let y equal the number of degrees in $\angle A$. Then $3y$ equals the number of degrees in $\angle C$, and $5y$ equals the number of degrees in $\angle B$. Since the sum of the angles of the triangle is 180°, we can say

   $y + 3y + 5y = 180$

   $\dfrac{9y}{9} = \dfrac{180}{9}$

   $y = 20° \ (\angle A)$

   $3y = 60° \ (\angle C)$

   $5y = 100° \ (\angle B)$

   Notice that 20° + 60° + 100° = 180°.

Facts about Triangles

Base and Height

Any side of a triangle can be called a *base*. With each base, there is an associated *altitude* (or *height*). Each altitude is the *perpendicular* segment from a vertex perpendicular to its opposite side or the extension of the opposite side.

In this diagram of $\triangle ABC$, $\overline{BC}$ is the base and $\overline{AE}$ is the height. $\overline{AE} \perp \overline{BC}$.

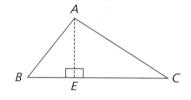

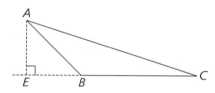

In this diagram of $\triangle ABC$, $\overline{BC}$ is the base and $\overline{AE}$ is the height. Notice that base $\overline{BC}$ had to be extended in order to be able to draw the height from vertex A.

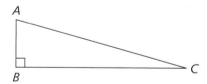

In this diagram of $\triangle ABC$, $\overline{BC}$ is the base and $\overline{AB}$ is the height. In a right triangle, either of the sides that form the right angle can be called the base and the other side can then be called the height to that base.

Median

Every triangle has three medians. A *median* is a line segment drawn from a vertex to the midpoint of the opposite side.

In this diagram of $\triangle ABC$, E is the midpoint of $\overline{BC}$. Therefore, $BE = EC$. $\overline{AE}$ is a median of $\triangle ABC$.

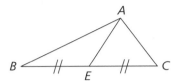

Angle Bisectors

Every triangle has three *angle bisectors*. The angle bisector divides an angle into two smaller angles that are equal in measure.

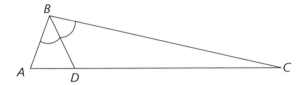

In this diagram of $\triangle ABC$, segment BD is an angle bisector of $\angle ABC$ because $m\angle ABD = m\angle CBD$.

In the following diagram of $\triangle QRS$, $\overline{QX}$ is an altitude ($\overline{QX} \perp \overline{RS}$), $\overline{QY}$ is an angle bisector ($\angle RQY = \angle SQY$), and $\overline{QZ}$ is a median (RZ= SZ). Generally, from one vertex of a triangle, the altitude, angle bisector, and median are different segments.

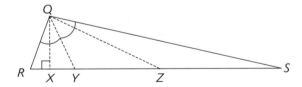

An interesting fact: In any triangle, if one segment is any two of the three special segments in a triangle (altitude, median, angle bisector), then it is automatically the third one, and the triangle is isosceles. The vertex from which the segments are drawn becomes the vertex of the isosceles triangle, and it is at the vertex of the isosceles triangle where the equal sides meet.

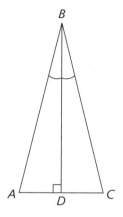

In this diagram of $\triangle ABC$, segment BD is an angle bisector and an altitude. This means that segment BD is also a median, hence $AD = CD$. It also means that $\triangle ABC$ is isosceles with the sides AB and BC being the equal sides of the isosceles triangle.

Angles Opposite Equal Sides

Angles that are opposite from equal sides are also equal.

In the diagram of $\triangle ABC$:

> $\angle A$ is opposite from side BC.
>
> $\angle B$ is opposite from side AC.
>
> $\angle C$ is opposite from side AB.

Therefore, if $AB = AC$, then $\angle C = \angle B$.

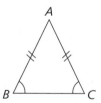

Angles of an Isosceles Triangle

In an isosceles triangle, since two of the sides are equal, the angles opposite those sides are equal. There are always two equal sides in an isosceles triangle.

Angles of an Equilateral Triangle

In an equilateral triangle, because all three sides are equal, all three angles will be equal; they are opposite equal sides. If all three angles are equal and their sum is 180°, the following must be true.

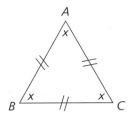

$$x + x + x = 180°$$
$$3x = 180°$$
$$x = 60°$$

Every angle of an equilateral triangle always has a measure of 60°.

Unequal Angles

In any triangle, the longest side is always opposite from the largest angle. Likewise, the shortest side is always opposite from the smallest angle. In a right triangle, the longest side will always be opposite from the right angle, because the right angle will be the largest angle in the triangle.

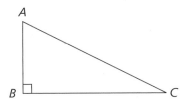

$\overline{AC}$ is the longest side of right triangle ABC.

Adding Sides of a Triangle

The sum of the lengths of any two sides of a triangle must be larger than the length of the third side.

In the diagram of $\triangle ABC$:

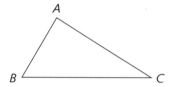

$AB + BC > AC$

$AB + AC > BC$

$AC + BC > AB$

Exterior Angles

If one side of a triangle is extended, the exterior angle formed by that extension is equal to the sum of its remote (farthest away) interior angles.

In the diagram of $\triangle ABC$, side BC is extended to D. $\angle ACD$ is the exterior angle formed.

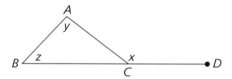

Find x if $y = 82°$ and $z = 41°$.

$\angle x = \angle y + \angle z$

$x = 82° + 41°$

$x = 123°$

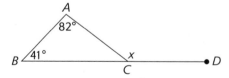

Practice: Triangle Problems

1. Two angles of a triangle measure 50° and 60°. How many degrees are there in the third angle?

2. One of the angles in a right triangle measures 35°. What is the measure of the other acute angle?

3. In an isosceles triangle, one of the angles opposite an equal side is 20°. What is the measure of each of the other two angles?

4. In △ABC, the measure of ∠A is twice the measure of ∠B. The measure of ∠C is three times the measure of ∠B. What is the measure of each of the three angles?

5. In the figure on the right, which side is the largest?

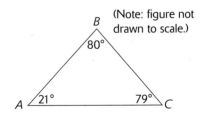

(Note: figure not drawn to scale.)

6. Which of the following measures could be the sides of a triangle?

2, 3, 4
2, 2, 5
4, 3, 7
3, 4, 5
3, 3, 6
1, 2, 3

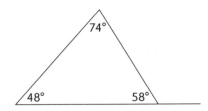

7. What is the measure of the exterior angle of the triangle above?

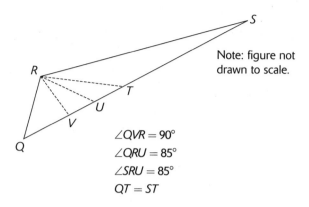

Note: figure not drawn to scale.

$\angle QVR = 90°$
$\angle QRU = 85°$
$\angle SRU = 85°$
$QT = ST$

8. In the figure above, identify which segment is

   (a)   a median
   (b)   an altitude (or height)
   (c)   an angle bisector

Answers: Triangle Problems

1. Since the measure of the three angles of a triangle must total 180°, there are 70° in the third angle.

2. Since, in a right triangle, one of the angles is 90° and the sum of the three angles in a triangle is 180°, the remaining acute angle must be 55°.

3. Since equal sides of a triangle have their opposite angles equal, the other two angles measure 20° and 140°.

4. Let the smallest angle equal x. Therefore, the larger angle equals $2x$, and the largest angle equals $3x$. Their total is $6x$, which equals 180°.

   $6x = 180°$

   $x = 30° \ (\angle B)$

   $2x = 60° \ (\angle A)$

   $3x = 90° \ (\angle C)$

5. Side AC is largest, since in any triangle, the largest side is opposite the largest angle.

6. Since the sum of any two sides of a triangle must be greater than its third side, 2, 2, 5; 4, 3, 7; 3, 3, 6; and 1, 2, 3 cannot be sides of a triangle. The two other sets can.

7. Since an exterior angle of a triangle always equals the sum of its remote two interior angles, the exterior angle measures 122°.

8. (a) $\overline{RT}$ is a median. A median goes from a vertex to the midpoint of the opposite side. Since $QT = ST$, you know that T is the midpoint of $\overline{QS}$.

   (b) $\overline{RV}$ is an altitude (or height). An altitude goes from a vertex and makes a 90° angle with the opposite side or the extension of the opposite side and $\angle QVR = 90°$.

   (c) $\overline{RU}$ is an angle bisector. An angle bisector divides the angle it is in into two smaller but equal angles. Since $\angle SRU = 85°$ and $\angle QRU = 85°$, then $\angle SRU = \angle QRU$. Therefore, $\angle QRT$ has been bisected.

Pythagorean Theorem

In any right triangle, the relationship between the lengths of the sides is stated by the *Pythagorean theorem*. The parts of a right triangle are:

$\angle C$ is the right angle.

The side opposite the right angle is called the *hypotenuse* (side c). (The hypotenuse will always be the longest side.)

The other two sides are called the *legs* (sides a and b).

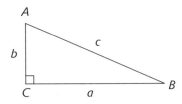

The three lengths a, b, and c will always be numbers such that

$$a^2 + b^2 = c^2$$

For example: If $a = 3$, $b = 4$, and $c = 5$,

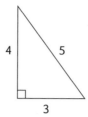

$$a^2 + b^2 = c^2$$
$$3^2 + 4^2 = 5^2$$
$$9 + 16 = 25$$
$$25 = 25$$

Therefore, 3-4-5 is called *a Pythagorean triple.* There are other values for *a*, *b*, and *c* that will always work. Some are: 5-12-13 and 8-15-17. Any multiple of one of these triples will also work. For example, using the 3-4-5: 6-8-10, 9-12-15, and 15-20-25 will also be Pythagorean triples.

If perfect squares are known, the lengths of these sides can be determined easily. A knowledge of the use of algebraic equations can also be used to determine the lengths of the sides.

Examples: Pythagorean Theorem Problems

1. Find x in this right triangle.

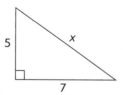

Answer: $a^2 + b^2 = c^2$

$$5^2 + 7^2 = x^2$$
$$25 + 49 = x^2$$
$$\sqrt{74} = x$$

2. Find x in this right triangle.

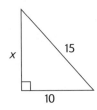

Answer: $a^2 + b^2 = c^2$

$$x^2 + 10^2 = 15^2$$

$$x^2 + 100 = 225$$

$$x = \sqrt{125}$$

$$x = \sqrt{25} \times \sqrt{5}$$

$$x = 5\sqrt{5}$$

Practice: Pythagorean Theorem Problems

1. Find x in this right triangle.

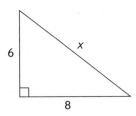

2. Find y in this right triangle.

3. If the two legs of a right triangle measure 5 and 9, what is the length of the hypotenuse?

Answers: Pythagorean Theorem Problems

1. $6^2 + 8^2 = x^2$

    $36 + 64 = x^2$

      $100 = x^2$

       $10 = x$

2. $y^2 + 7^2 = 12^2$

    $y^2 + 49 = 144$

       $y^2 = 95$

       $y = \sqrt{95}$

3. $5^2 + 9^2 = x^2$

    $25 + 81 = x^2$

      $106 = x^2$

    $\sqrt{106} = x$

Special Triangles

Isosceles Right Triangles (45°-45°-90° Right Triangles)

An *isosceles right triangle* has the characteristics of both the isosceles and the right triangles. It will have two equal sides, two equal angles, and one right angle. (The right angle cannot be one of the equal angles or the sum of the angle measures will be more than 180°.)

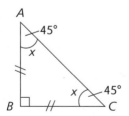

Therefore, in the diagram, $\triangle ABC$ is an isosceles right triangle. And the following must always be true:

$$x + x + 90° = 180°$$
$$2x = 90°$$
$$x = 45°$$

$\triangle ABC$ is isosceles

$AB = BC$

$\angle A = \angle C$

$\angle B = 90°$

The ratio of the sides of an isosceles right triangle is always 1, 1, $\sqrt{2}$, or $x, x, x\sqrt{2}$.

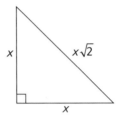

Example:

If one of the equal sides of an isosceles right triangle is 3, what is the measure of the other two sides?

Using the ratio $x, x, x\sqrt{2}$, the measure of the sides must be 3, 3, $3\sqrt{2}$.

Practice: Isosceles Right Triangle Problems

1. If one of the equal sides of an isosceles right triangle is 4, what is the measure of the other two sides?

2. If the longest side of an isosceles right triangle is $5\sqrt{2}$, what is the measure of each of the two equal sides?

3. What is the measure of sides x and y in the triangle above?

Answers: Isosceles Right Triangle Problems

1. The sides of an isosceles right triangle are always in the ratio x, x, $x\sqrt{2}$. Therefore, the other two sides are 4 and $4\sqrt{2}$.

2. The two equal sides each equal 5.

3. Since one angle measures 90° and another measures 45°, the third angle must also measure 45°: $180 - (90 + 45) = 45$. Therefore, we have an isosceles right triangle with the ratio of sides x, x, $x\sqrt{2}$. Since one equal side is 6, the other must be 6, and the longest side is then $6\sqrt{2}$.

30°-60°-90° Right Triangles

A 30°-60°-90° *right triangle* has a unique ratio of its sides. It is a commonly referred-to triangle. The ratio of the sides of a 30°-60°-90° right triangle are 1, $\sqrt{3}$, 2 or x, $x\sqrt{3}$, $2x$ placed as follows.

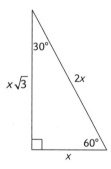

The side opposite 30° is 1 or x.

The side opposite 60° is $\sqrt{3}$ or $x\sqrt{3}$.

The side opposite 90° is the longest side (hypotenuse), 2 or $2x$.

Examples:

1. If the shortest side of a 30°-60°-90° right triangle is 4, what is the measure of the other sides?

    Using the ratio x, $x\sqrt{3}$, $2x$ the measure is 4, $4\sqrt{3}$, 8.

    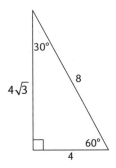

2. In the triangle below, find the remaining sides.

    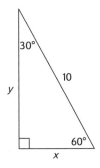

    x is half of the hypotenuse, or 5. The side opposite 60° is $x\sqrt{3}$ or $5\sqrt{3}$.

    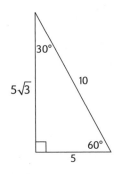

Practice: 30°-60°-90° Right Triangle Problems

1. If the longest side of a 30°-60°-90° right triangle is 12, what are the measures of the other sides?

2. If one angle of a right triangle is 30° and the measure of the shortest side is 7, what is the measure of the remaining two sides?

Answers: 30°-60°-90° Right Triangle Problems

1. Since the ratio of the sides of a 30°-60°-90° right triangle are $x, x\sqrt{3}, 2x$ and the longest side, $2x$, is 12, then the shortest side, x, is 6, and the third side is $6\sqrt{3}$.

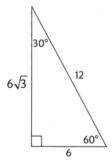

2. If one angle of a right triangle is 30°, then the other angle must be 60°. Hence, you have a 30°-60°-90° right triangle. Using the ratio $x, x\sqrt{3}, 2x,$ with $x = 7, 2x = 14,$ and the third side equals $7\sqrt{3}$.

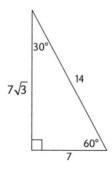

Quadrilaterals

A polygon having four sides is called a *quadrilateral*. There are four angles in its interior. The sum of the measures of these interior angles will always be 360°. A quadrilateral is named by using the four letters of its vertices named in order either clockwise or counterclockwise.

This is quadrilateral *ABCD*.

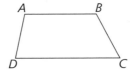

Types of Quadrilaterals

Square

The *square* has four equal sides and four right angles.

Its opposite sides are parallel.

Diagonals of a square are equal, bisect each other, are perpendicular to each other, and bisect the angles through which they pass.

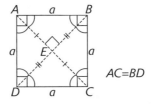

$AC=BD$

Rectangle

The *rectangle* has opposite sides equal and parallel and four right angles.

Diagonals of a rectangle are equal and bisect each other.

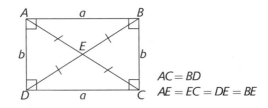

$AC = BD$
$AE = EC = DE = BE$

Parallelogram

The *parallelogram* has opposite sides equal and parallel, opposite angles equal, and consecutive angles supplementary. Diagonals of a parallelogram bisect each other but are not necessarily equal. If the diagonals of a parallelogram are equal, it becomes a rectangle.

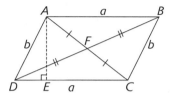

In parallelogram ABCD,

$\angle A = \angle C$

$\angle B = \angle D$

$\angle A + \angle B = 180°$

$\angle A + \angle D = 180°$

$\angle B + \angle C = 180°$

$\angle C + \angle D = 180°$

$\overline{AE}$ is a height (or altitude) in this parallelogram, where $\overline{AE} \perp \overline{CD}$.

Rhombus

The *rhombus* is a parallelogram with four equal sides but not necessarily four equal angles.

Diagonals of a rhombus are not necessarily equal, but they do bisect each other, are perpendicular to each other, and bisect the angles through which they pass.

In the figure, $\overline{BE} \perp \overline{AD}$, so $\overline{BE}$ can be considered a height (or altitude) of the rhombus.

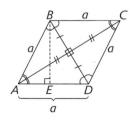

Trapezoid

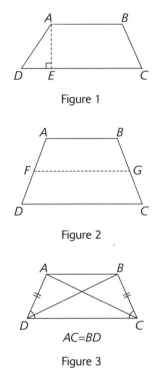

Figure 1

Figure 2

Figure 3

The *trapezoid* has only one pair of parallel sides. In Figure 1, $\overline{AB} \parallel \overline{DC}$.

The parallel sides are called the *bases*. $\overline{AB}$ and $\overline{DC}$ are the bases. The non-parallel sides are called the *legs*. $\overline{AD}$ and $\overline{BC}$ are legs.

A height (or altitude) in a trapezoid is a segment perpendicular to the parallel sides. In Figure 1, $\overline{AE}$ is a height of trapezoid $ABCD$.

The *median* of a trapezoid is a line segment that is parallel to the bases and bisects the legs (connects the midpoints of the legs). In Figure 2, $\overline{FG}$ is the median.

Figure 3 is an *isosceles trapezoid* (one in which the legs are equal). The diagonals are equal in length but do not bisect each other. Each pair of angles on the same base are equal in measure.

Comparing Quadrilaterals

A *parallelogram* is a quadrilateral with opposite sides and angles equal.

A *rectangle* is a parallelogram with right angles.

A *rhombus* is a parallelogram with equal sides.

A *square* is a rhombus with right angles.

A *trapezoid* is a quadrilateral with only one pair of parallel sides.

A Summary of Diagonals, Sides, and Angles of Special Quadrilaterals

The bases of a trapezoid are never equal to each other. The diagonals of a trapezoid do not bisect each other. In all trapezoids, the angles that share the same leg are supplementary.

In isosceles trapezoids, diagonals have the same length and angles that share the same base have equal measures.

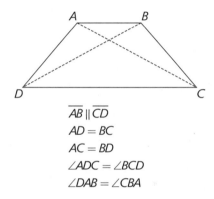

$$\overline{AB} \parallel \overline{CD}$$
$$AD = BC$$
$$AC = BD$$
$$\angle ADC = \angle BCD$$
$$\angle DAB = \angle CBA$$

A parallelogram's diagonals bisect each other. Both pairs of opposite sides in a parallelogram are parallel and equal in length. Both pairs of opposite angles in a parallelogram are equal in measure.

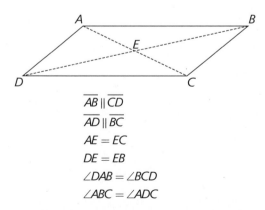

$$\overline{AB} \parallel \overline{CD}$$
$$\overline{AD} \parallel \overline{BC}$$
$$AE = EC$$
$$DE = EB$$
$$\angle DAB = \angle BCD$$
$$\angle ABC = \angle ADC$$

A rectangle's diagonals are equal in measure and bisect each other. The opposite sides of a rectangle are equal in measure and are parallel to one another. All the angles of a rectangle are equal in measure and are each 90°.

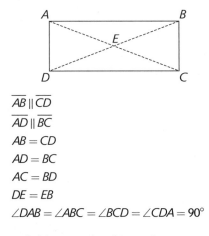

$\overline{AB} \parallel \overline{CD}$

$\overline{AD} \parallel \overline{BC}$

$AB = CD$

$AD = BC$

$AC = BD$

$DE = EB$

$\angle DAB = \angle ABC = \angle BCD = \angle CDA = 90°$

A rhombus's diagonals bisect each other and are perpendicular to one another. The diagonals bisect the angles through which they pass. All sides in a rhombus are equal in measure. Opposite sides in a rhombus are parallel to one another. Opposite angles in a rhombus are equal in measure.

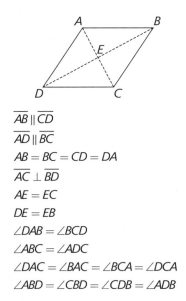

$\overline{AB} \parallel \overline{CD}$

$\overline{AD} \parallel \overline{BC}$

$AB = BC = CD = DA$

$\overline{AC} \perp \overline{BD}$

$AE = EC$

$DE = EB$

$\angle DAB = \angle BCD$

$\angle ABC = \angle ADC$

$\angle DAC = \angle BAC = \angle BCA = \angle DCA$

$\angle ABD = \angle CBD = \angle CDB = \angle ADB$

A square has all of the properties of both the rectangle and the rhombus.

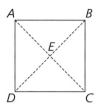

$\overline{AB} \parallel \overline{CD}$

$\overline{AD} \parallel \overline{BC}$

$AB = BC = CD = DA$

$AC = BD$

$AE = EC = DE = EB$

$\overline{AC} \perp \overline{BD}$

$\angle DAB = \angle BCD = \angle ABC = \angle ADC = 90°$

$\angle DAC = \angle BAC = \angle BCA = \angle DCA = \angle ABD = \angle CBD = \angle CDB = \angle ADB = 45°$

Practice: Polygon Problems

Identify the following figures with their most special or descriptive names.

1.

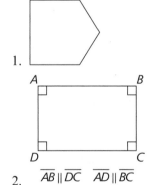

2. $\overline{AB} \parallel \overline{DC}$ $\overline{AD} \parallel \overline{BC}$

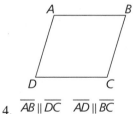

4. $\overline{AB} \parallel \overline{DC}$ $\overline{AD} \parallel \overline{BC}$

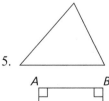

5.

3.

6. $AB = BC = CD = DA$

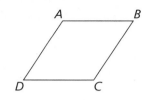

7. $AB = BC = CD = DA$

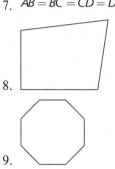

8.

9.

10.

All sides and angles are equal.

True or False:

11. A square must be a parallelogram.

12. A rhombus must be a rectangle.

13. A parallelogram must be a rectangle.

Answers: Polygon Problems

1. Pentagon
2. Rectangle
3. Hexagon
4. Parallelogram
5. Triangle
6. Square
7. Rhombus

8. Quadrilateral
9. Octagon
10. Regular pentagon
11. True
12. False
13. False

Sum of the Interior Angles of a Polygon

The *sum of the interior angles* in any polygon can be determined by using this formula : $(n - 2)180°$, where *n* is the number of sides in the polygon. *For example:*

The triangle (3 sides):

- $(n - 2)180°$
- $(3 - 2)180°$
- $(1)180° = 180°$

The quadrilateral (4 sides):

- $(n - 2)180°$
- $(4 - 2)180°$
- $(2)180° = 360°$

The pentagon (5 sides):

- $(n - 2)180°$
- $(5 - 2)180°$
- $(3)180° = 540°$

Practice: Sum of the Interior Angles of a Polygon Problems

1. Find the sum of the interior angles of a hexagon.

2. Find the degree measure of an angle of a regular nonagon.

Answers: Sum of the Interior Angles of a Polygon Problems

1. Since a hexagon has six sides, use $n = 6$.

   $(n - 2)180°$

   $(6 - 2)180°$

   $(4)180° = 720°$

2. A regular nonagon has nine equal angles. First find the total degree measure.

   $(n - 2)180°$

   $(9 - 2)180°$

   $(7)180° = 1,260°$

   Now to find one angle, divide the total by 9, the number of angles.

   $$\frac{1,260°}{9} = 140°$$

Perimeter and Area of Polygons

Perimeter of Polygons

Perimeter means the total distance all the way around the outside of any polygon. The perimeter of any polygon can be determined by adding up the lengths of all the sides. The total distance around will be the sum of all sides of the polygon. No special formulas are really necessary, although two are commonly seen.

Perimeter of a square = 4*s*, where *s* = length of side.

Perimeter of a parallelogram (rectangle and rhombus) = 2*l* + 2*w* or 2(*l* + *w*), where *l* = length and *w* = width.

Area of Polygons

Area (*A*) means the amount of space inside the polygon. The formulas for each area are as follows:

Triangle: $A = \frac{1}{2}bh$

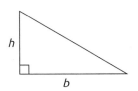 or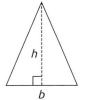

For example:

$A = \frac{1}{2}bh$

$A = \frac{1}{2}(24)(18) = 216$ square inches

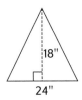

Square or rectangle: $A = lw$

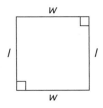 or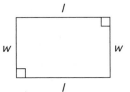

For example:

$A = lw = (4)(4) = 16$ square inches

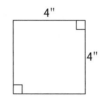

$A = lw = (12)(5) = 60$ square inches

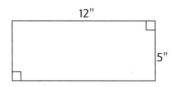

Parallelogram: $A = bh$

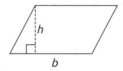

For example:

$A = bh$

$A = (10)(5) = 50$ square inches

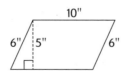

Trapezoid: $A = \frac{1}{2}(b_1 + b_2)h$

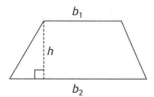

For example:

$$A = \frac{1}{2}(b_1 + b_2)h$$

$$A = \frac{1}{2}(8 + 12)7$$

$$A = \frac{1}{2}(20)7 = 70 \text{ square inches}$$

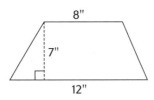

Practice: Perimeter and Area of Polygons Problems

1. $P =$

   $A =$

2. $P =$

   $A =$

3. $P =$

   $A =$

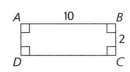

4. $P =$

   $A =$

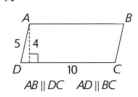

$AB \parallel DC \quad AD \parallel BC$

5. $P =$

   $A =$

6. $P =$

   $A =$

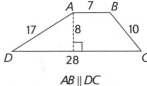

$AB \parallel DC$

Answers: Perimeter and Area of Polygons Problems

1. $P = 15 + 13 + 14 = 42$

   $A = \frac{1}{2}bh = \frac{1}{2}(14)(12) = 84$

2. $P = 6 + 8 + 10 = 24$

   $A = \frac{1}{2}bh = \frac{1}{2}(8)(6) = 24$

3. $P = 10 + 10 + 2 + 2 = 24$

   $A = bh = (10)(2) = 20$

4. $P = 10 + 10 + 5 + 5 = 30$

   $A = bh = (10)(4) = 40$

5. $P = 5 + 5 + 5 + 5 = 20$

   $A = bh = (4)(5) = 20$

6. $P = 17 + 7 + 10 + 28 = 62$

   $A = \frac{1}{2}(b_1 + b_2)h = \frac{1}{2}(7 + 28)(8) = (4)(35) = 140$

Circles

In a plane, the set of all points equidistant from a given point is called a *circle*. Circles are named by the letter of their center point.

This is circle M. M is the center point, since it is the same distance away from any point on the circle.

Parts of a Circle

Radius

The *radius* is a line segment whose endpoints lie one at the center of the circle and one on the circle. A *radius* of a circle can either be the segment that joins the center to any point on the circle or the length of that segment. It is in the context of use that you will know which meaning is being used.

$\overline{MA}$ is a radius.

$\overline{MB}$ is a radius.

In any circle, all radii (plural) are the same length.

Diameter

A *diameter* of a circle can either be the segment that joins any two points on a circle and passes through the center of the circle or the length of that segment. It is in the context of use that you will know which meaning is being used.

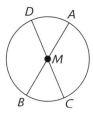

$\overline{AB}$ is a diameter.

$\overline{CD}$ is a diameter.

In any circle, all diameters are the same length. Each diameter equals two radii in length.

Chord

A *chord* of a circle is a line segment whose endpoints lie on the circle.

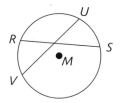

$\overline{RS}$ is a chord.

$\overline{UV}$ is a chord.

The diameter is the longest chord in any circle.

Arc

An arc is a portion of a circle between two points on the circle. It can be measured in two ways. One measure is in degrees. The full rotation of a circle is said to have 360°. Another measure is its length. This would be a portion of the circumference of the circle. The symbol ⌢ is used to denote an arc. It is written on top of the two endpoints that form the arc. Usually it is in the context of use that you would know whether the measure is intended to be a degree measure or a length measure.

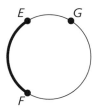

This is $\overset{\frown}{EF}$.

Minor $\overset{\frown}{EF}$ is the shorter arc between E and F.

Major $\overset{\frown}{EGF}$ is the longer arc between E and F. When an arc involves half or more than half of a circle, three letters must be used with the first and third indicating the ends of the arc and the middle letter indicating an additional point through which the arc passes.

When $\overset{\frown}{EF}$ is written, the minor arc is assumed.

Practice: Parts of a Circle Problems

Match the parts of the following circle with center O.

1. Radius

2. Diameter

3. Chord

4. Name of circle

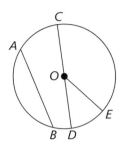

Answers: Parts of a Circle Problems

1. $\overline{OE}$, $\overline{OD}$, and $\overline{OC}$ 3. $\overline{AB}$ and $\overline{CD}$

2. $\overline{CD}$ 4. O

Circumference and Area of a Circle

Circumference

Circumference is the distance around the circle. Since the circumference of any circle divided by its diameter yields the same value, the Greek letter π (pi) is used to represent that value. In fractional or decimal form, the commonly used approximations of π are $\pi \approx 3.14$ or $\pi \approx \frac{22}{7}$. Use either value in your calculations. The formula for circumference is: $C = \pi d$ or $C = 2\pi r$. *For example:*

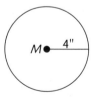

In circle M, $d = 8$, since $r = 4$.

$C = \pi d$

$C = \pi(8)$

$C \approx 3.14(8)$

$C \approx 25.12$ inches

284

Area

The *area* of a circle can be determined by: $A = \pi r^2$. *For example:*

In circle M, $r = 5$, since $d = 10$.

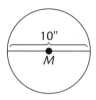

$A = \pi r^2$

$A = \pi(5^2)$

$A \approx 3.14(25)$

$A \approx 78.5$ square inches

Practice: Circumference and Area of a Circle Problems

Find the area and circumference (leave in terms of π) of each circle from the given radius or diameter.

1. $A =$

   $C =$

   Find the radius.

   3. $A = 49\pi$ square inches

   4. $C = 60\pi$ inches

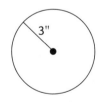

2. $A =$

   $C =$

Answers: Circumference and Area of a Circle Problems

1. $A = \pi r^2$

   $A = \pi(3)^2$

   $A = 9\pi$ square inches

   $C = 2\pi r$

   $C = 2\pi(3)$

   $C = 6\pi$ inches

2. $A = \pi r^2$

   $A = \pi(8)^2$

   $A = 64\pi$ square inches

   $C = 2\pi r$

   $C = 2\pi(8)$

   $C = 16\pi$ inches

   or

   $C = \pi d$

   $C = 16\pi$ inches

3. $A = \pi r^2$

   $49\pi = \pi r^2$

   $49 = r^2$

   7 inches $= r$

4. $C = 2\pi r$

   $60\pi = 2\pi r$

   $60 = 2r$

   30 inches $= r$

   or

   $C = \pi d$

   $60\pi = \pi d$

   $60 = d$

   30 inches $= r$

Angles in a Circle

Central Angles

Central angles are angles formed by any two radii in a circle. The vertex is the center of the circle. A central angle is equal to the measure of its intercepted arc. *For example:*

In circle O, $\overset{\frown}{AB} = 75°$. Therefore, $\angle AOB = 75°$. ($m\overset{\frown}{AB}$ is sometimes used to denote the measure of arc AB when its answer is meant to be in degrees.)

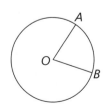

Inscribed Angles

Inscribed angles have their vertex on the circle and have chords as their sides. An inscribed angle is equal to one-half the measure of its intercepted arc. *For example:*

In circle O, $\overset{\frown}{CD} = 90°$.

Therefore, $\angle CED = 45°$.

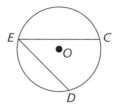

In general as the vertex moves farther away from the arc, the angle measure gets smaller. The closer the vertex is to the arc, the larger the size of the angle. *For example:*

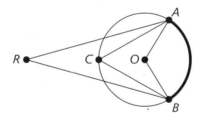

Practice: Angles in a Circle Problems

1. Find the measure of $\angle x$ in circle A.

2. Find the measure of $\angle y$ in circle A.

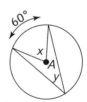

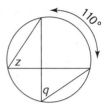

3. Find the measure of $\angle z$.

4. Find the measure of $\angle q$.

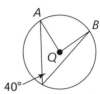

5. Find the measure of $\widehat{AB}$ of circle Q.

6. Find the measure of $\angle AQB$ in circle Q.

Answers: Angles in a Circle Problems

1. Since $\angle x$ is a central angle, it equals the measure of the arc it intercepts, or 60°.

2. Since $\angle y$ is an inscribed angle, it equals one-half the arc it intercepts, or 30°.

3. $\angle z$, an inscribed angle, equals one-half 110°, or 55°.

4. $\angle q$, an inscribed angle, equals one-half 110°, or 55°.

5. $\widehat{AB}$ is twice the inscribed angle which intercepts $\widehat{AB}$.
   Thus, $2 \times 40° = 80°$.

6. The measure of central angle AQB equals the measure of the arc it intercepts, or 80°.

Concentric Circles

Circles with the same center are called *concentric circles.*

Tangents to a Circle

A line that touches a circle at only one point is called a *tangent* or tangent line. This line cannot be in the interior of the circle. Two tangent segments sharing the same exterior point of a circle with their other endpoints on the circle are:

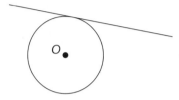

- Equal in length. ($AB = AC$)
- Perpendicular to a radius that meets at that point. $\overline{AB} \perp \overline{OB}$ and $\overline{AC} \perp \overline{OC}$.

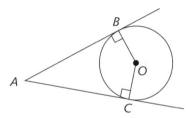

Congruence and Similarity

Two plane geometric figures are said to be *congruent* if they are identical in size and shape. They are said to be *similar* if they have the same shape. Similar shapes have corresponding sides in proportion. Thus, if two shapes are identical, then they are also (trivially) similar. *For example:*

All squares are similar.

These triangles are congruent.

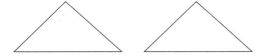

Volumes of Solid Figures

Three of the most common solid geometric figures are the cube, the rectangular solid, and the cylinder. Each of these figures may be thought of as the three-dimensional extensions of three flat two-dimensional figures, namely the square, the rectangle, and the circle.

The *volume* of a solid is the number of cubic units of space the figure contains. Volume is always labeled *cubic* units. The formula for the volume of each shape is different, but in general, it is the area of the base times the height.

Volume of a Cube

The formula for the volume of a cube is $V = s \times s \times s = s^3$.

Volume of a Rectangular Solid

The formula for the volume of a rectangular solid is $V = (lw)(h) = lwh$.

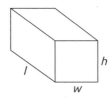

Volume of a Right Circular Cylinder (Circular Bases)

The formula for the volume of a right circular cylinder (circular bases) is
$V = (\pi r^2)h = \pi r^2 h$.

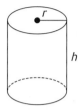

Practice: Volumes of Solid Figures Problems

Find the volumes of the solid figures below whose dimensions are indicated.

1. Rectangular solid

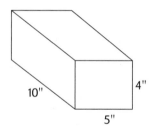

2. Cube

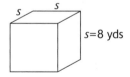

3. Cylinder

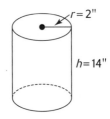

Answers: Volumes of Solid Figures Problems

1. $V = lwh = (10)(5)(4) = 200$ cubic inches

2. $V = s^3 = 8 \times 8 \times 8 = 512$ cubic yards

3. $V = \pi r^2 h \approx \dfrac{22}{\cancel{7}} \times \dfrac{2}{1} \times \dfrac{2}{1} \times \dfrac{\overset{2}{\cancel{14}}}{1} = 22(8) = 176$ cubic inches

Surface Areas of Solid Figures

Surface Area of a Rectangular Solid

To find the *surface area of a rectangular solid,* proceed as follows:

Area of side 1 = 3×4 = 12 square inches
Area of side 2 = 5×3 = 15 square inches
Area of side 3 = 5×4 = 20 square inches

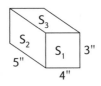

Since there are two of each of these sides:

Surface area = 2(12) + 2(15) + 2(20)
= 24 + 30 + 40
= 94 square inches

Surface Area of a Right Circular Cylinder

To determine the *surface area of a right circular cylinder*, it is best envisioned "rolled out" onto a flat surface as below.

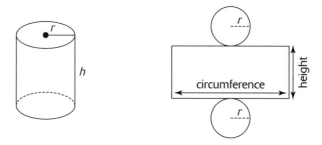

Now find the area of each individual piece. The area of each circle equals πr^2. Note that the length of the rectangle equals the circumference of the circle. The rectangle's area equals circumference times height. Adding the three parts gives the surface area of the cylinder: *For example:*

Find the surface area of a cylinder with radius 5 feet and height 12 feet.

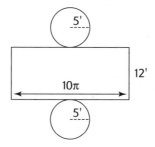

The area of the top circle $= \pi(r^2) = \pi(5^2) = 25\pi$ square feet.

The area of the bottom circle is the same, 25π square feet.

The length of the rectangle is the circumference of the circle, or $2\pi r = 2\pi(5) = 10\pi$.

Therefore, the area of the rectangle equals its height times 10π or $12 \times 10\pi = 120\pi$ square feet.

Totaling all the pieces gives $25\pi + 25\pi + 120\pi = 170\pi$ square feet.

Practice: Volumes and Surface Areas of Solids Problems

1. What is the volume of a cube whose side is $5\frac{1}{2}$ inches?

2. If a rectangular solid has a length of 4 inches, a width of 3 inches, and a height of 2 feet, find its volume.

3. Given that a cylinder's height is 42 inches and its radius is 3 inches, determine its volume.

4. Find the surface area of a rectangular solid that measures 4 inches by 7 inches by 6 inches.

5. Find the surface area of a right regular cylinder that has a height of 20 inches and a radius of 4 inches.

Answers: Volumes and Surface Areas of Solids Problems

1. $166\frac{3}{8}$ cubic inches

$$V = s^3 = 5\frac{1}{2} \times 5\frac{1}{2} \times 5\frac{1}{2} = \frac{11}{2} \times \frac{11}{2} \times \frac{11}{2} = \frac{1,331}{8} = 166\frac{3}{8} \text{ cubic inches}$$

2. 288 cubic inches

$$V = l \times w \times h = 4 \times 3 \times 24 = 288 \text{ cubic inches}$$

Note: The 2 feet had to be converted to 24 inches so that all dimensions would be expressed in the same units.

3. 1,188 cubic inches

$$V = \pi r^2 h \approx \frac{22}{\cancel{7}} \times \frac{3}{1} \times \frac{3}{1} \times \frac{\overset{6}{\cancel{42}}}{1} = 1,188 \text{ cubic inches}$$

4. 188 square inches

Area of side 1 = $4 \times 6 = 24$ square inches

Area of side 2 = $6 \times 7 = 42$ square inches

Area of side 3 = $4 \times 7 = 28$ square inches

Surface area = $2(24) + 2(42) + 2(28)$

$= 48 + 84 + 56$

$= 188$ square inches

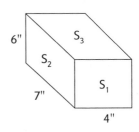

5. 192π square inches

Area of top circle $= \pi r^2 = 16\pi$ square inches

Area of bottom circle $= \pi r^2 = 16\pi$ square inches

Area of rectangle $= 20 \times$ circumference

$$= 20 \times 2\pi r$$

$$= 20 \times 2\pi(4)$$

$$= 20 \times 8\pi \text{ square inches}$$

$$= 160\pi \text{ square inches}$$

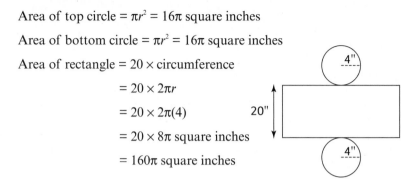

Adding all the pieces, total surface area is 192π square inches.

Geometry Formulas With Which You Should Be Familiar

Shape	Illustration	Perimeter	Area
Square		$P = 4a$	$A = a^2$
Rectangle		$P = 2b + 2h$ or $P = 2(b + h)$	$A = bh$
Parallelogram		$P = 2a + 2b$ or $P = 2(a + b)$	$A = bh$
Triangle		$P = a + b + c$	$A = \dfrac{bh}{2}$ or $A = \dfrac{1}{2}bh$
Rhombus		$P = 4a$	$A = ah$
Trapezoid		$P = b_1 + b_2 + x + y$	$A = \dfrac{h(b_1 + b_2)}{2}$ or $A = \dfrac{1}{2}h(b_1 + b_2)$
Circle		$C = \pi d$ or $C = 2\pi r$	$A = \pi r^2$

(continued)

Geometry Formulas With Which You Should Be Familiar

Shape	Illustration	Surface Area	Volume
Cube		$SA = 6a^2$	$V = a^3$
Rectangular Prism		$SA = 2(lw+lh+wh)$ or $SA =$ (Perimeter of the Base)h + 2(Area of the Base)	$V = lwh$ or $V =$ (Area of the Base)h
Prisms in general		$SA =$ (Perimeter of the Base)h + 2(Area of the Base)	$V =$ (Area of the Base)h
Cylinder		$SA =$ (Perimeter of the Base or Circumference)h + 2(Area of the Base) or $SA = 2\pi rh + 2\pi r^2$ or $SA = 2\pi r(h + r)$	$V =$ (Area of the Base)h or $V = \pi r^2 h$
Sphere	(label radius as r)	$SA = 4\pi r^2$	$V = \dfrac{4}{3}\pi r^3$

Right Triangle

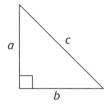

Pythagorean theorem: The sum of the squares of the legs of a right triangle equals the square of the hypotenuse ($a^2 + b^2 = c^2$).

Geometry Review Test

Questions

1. The study of shapes and figures in two dimensions is called
   _____.

2. The study of shapes and figures in three dimensions is called
   _____.

3. An angle is formed by two rays that have the same endpoint; that
   endpoint is called the _____.

4. Which of the following name the same angle in the triangle?

   (A) $\angle A$, $\angle ACB$, and $\angle CAB$
   (B) $\angle ACB$ and $\angle CAB$
   (C) $\angle A$, $\angle 1$, $\angle B$
   (D) $\angle A$, $\angle CAB$, and $\angle 1$
   (E) $\angle ACB$, $\angle 1$, and $\angle B$

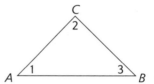

5. A right angle measures _____.

6. An acute angle measures _____.

7. An obtuse angle measures _____.

8. A straight angle measures _____.

9. Two angles next to each other, sharing a common side and vertex,
   are called _____.

10. In the diagram

    (A) $\angle 1 = \angle 3$
    (B) $\angle 1 = \angle 2$ and $\angle 3 = \angle 4$
    (C) $\angle 2 = \angle 4$ and $\angle 2 = \angle 3$
    (D) $\angle 1 = \angle 2$ and $\angle 3 = \angle 2$
    (E) $\angle 1 = \angle 4$ and $\angle 2 = \angle 3$

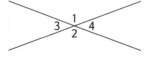

11. Two angles the sum of whose measures is 90° are said to be
    _____ to each other.

12. Two angles the sum of whose measures is 180° are said to be _____ to each other.

13. An angle bisector _____.

14. A _____ is often described as the path joining two points; it goes forever in two opposite directions.

15. A part of a line with two endpoints is called _____.

16. A part of a line that continues in one direction and has only one endpoint is called _____.

17. If two lines meet at a point they are called _____ lines.

18. Two lines that meet at right angles are _____ to each other.

19. Two or more lines that remain the same distance apart at all times are called _____

20. In the diagram _____. $l \parallel m$

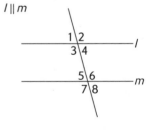

   I.   ∠1 = ∠2 = ∠4 = ∠5

   II. ∠1 = ∠4 = ∠5 = ∠8

  III. ∠2 = ∠3 = ∠6 = ∠7

  IV. ∠5 = ∠8 only

   V. ∠5 = ∠6 = ∠8

  (A) I and V

  (B) II

  (C) III

  (D) II and III

  (E) II and IV

For questions 21 through 28, name the following.

21. A three-sided polygon. _____

22. A four-sided polygon. _____

23. A five-sided polygon. _____

24. A six-sided polygon. _____

25. A seven-sided polygon. _____

26. An eight-sided polygon. _____

27. A nine-sided polygon. _____

28. A ten-sided polygon. _____

29. If all sides and angles have the same measure, the polygon is called _____.

30. In a polygon, a line segment that connects one vertex to another but is not the side of the polygon is called a _____.

31. The polygon below is called a _____ polygon.

32. The sum of the measures of the interior angles of any triangle is _____.

33. If all sides of a triangle are equal, the triangle is _____.

34. A triangle that has two equal sides is called _____.

35. A triangle whose three sides are of different lengths is called _____.

36. A triangle having a 90° angle is called _____.

37. A triangle containing an angle greater than 90° is called _____.

38. If all angles in a triangle are less than 90°, then the triangle is called _____.

39. In a triangle, a line segment drawn from a vertex to the midpoint of the opposite side is called _____.

40. If two angles of a triangle measure 43° each, what is the measure of the third angle? _____

41. The longest side of △ABC is _____.

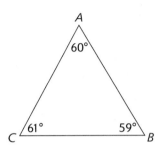

42. A triangle can have sides of length 2, 2, and 5. True or false?

43. Find the measure of ∠z in the triangle shown below. ∠z = _____.

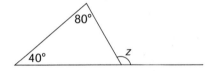

44. Find the length of side c in right triangle ABC.

    c = _____

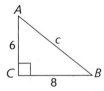

45. Find the length of side r in right △QRS.

    r = _____

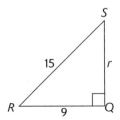

46. Find x, y, and z in the triangle shown at the right.

    $x =$ _____

    $y =$ _____

    $z =$ _____

47. Find a, b, and c in the triangle shown at the right.

    $a =$ _____

    $b =$ _____

    $c =$ _____

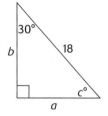

For questions 48 through 51, name the following figures.

48. _____

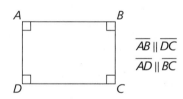

$\overline{AB} \parallel \overline{DC}$

$\overline{AD} \parallel \overline{BC}$

49. _____

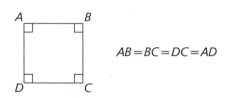

$AB = BC = DC = AD$

50. _____

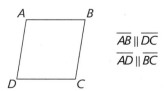

$\overline{AB} \parallel \overline{DC}$

$\overline{AD} \parallel \overline{BC}$

51. _____

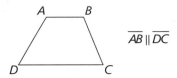

$\overline{AB} \parallel \overline{DC}$

52. What is the sum of the measures of the interior angles of a heptagon? _____

53. Find the area of $\triangle ABC$.

   area = _____

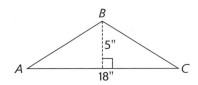

54. Find the area and perimeter of square $ABCD$.

   area = _____

   perimeter = _____

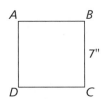

55. Find the area and perimeter of rectangle $ABCD$.

   area = _____

   perimeter = _____

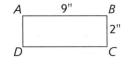

56. Find the area of parallelogram *ABCD*.

    area = _____

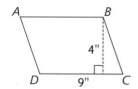

57. Find the area of trapezoid *ABCD*.

    area = _____

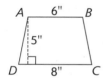

In the circle below

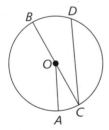

58. $\overline{OA}$ is called a _____ of circle *O*.

59. $\overline{BC}$ is called a _____ of circle *O*.

60. $\overline{DC}$ is called a _____ of circle *O*.

61. Find the area and circumference of circle *A* (in terms of π).

    area = _____

    circumference = _____

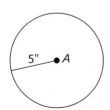

62. In the circle shown below, if $\overset{\frown}{AB} = 50°$, then the measure of the central angle $AOB =$ _____.

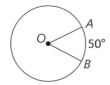

63. In the circle shown at the right, if $\overset{\frown}{AB} = 100°$, then the measure of the inscribed angle $ADB =$ _____

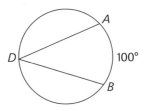

64. Circles with the same center are called _____.

65. A line that touches a circle at one point is called _____.

66. Polygons that are the same shape, but different in size are called _____.

67. Polygons that are exactly the same in shape and size are called _____.

For questions 68 through 70, find the volumes and surface areas of the figures below.

68. volume = _____

    surface area = _____

cube

69. volume = _____

surface area = _____

rectangular solid

70. volume = _____

surface area = _____

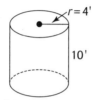

right circular cylinder

Answers

Page numbers following each answer refer to the review section applicable to this problem type.

1. plane geometry (p. 238)

2. solid geometry (p. 238)

3. vertex (p. 238)

4. (D) $\angle A$, $\angle CAB$, $\angle 1$ (p. 238)

5. 90° (p. 239)

6. less than 90° (p. 239)

7. greater than 90° but less than 180° (p. 239)

8. 180° (p. 240)

9. adjacent angles (p. 241)

10. (B) $\angle 1 = \angle 2$ and $\angle 3 = \angle 4$ (p. 241)

11. complementary (p. 242)

12. supplementary (p. 242)

13. divides an angle into two angles of equal measure (p. 243)

14. a line (p. 245)

15. a line segment (p. 245)

16. a ray (p. 245)

17. intersecting (p. 246)

18. perpendicular (p. 246)

19. parallel lines (p. 247)

20. (D) II and III (p. 247)

21. triangle (p. 250)

22. quadrilateral (p. 250)

23. pentagon (p. 250)

24. hexagon (p. 250)

25. heptagon or septagon (p. 250)

26. octagon (p. 250)

27. nonagon (p. 250)

28. decagon (p. 250)

29. regular (p. 250)

30. diagonal (p. 251)

31. concave (p. 251)

32. 180° (p. 251)

33. equilateral (p. 252)

34. isosceles (p. 252)

35. scalene (p. 253)

36. a right triangle (p. 253)

37. an obtuse triangle (p. 253)

38. an acute triangle (p. 254)

39. a median (p. 255)

40. 94° (p. 251)

41. $\overline{AB}$ (p. 258)

42. false (p. 258)

43. 120° (p. 259)

44. 10 (p. 265)

45. 12 (p. 265)

46. $x = 45°$, $y = 8$, $z = 8\sqrt{2}$ (p. 265)

47. $a = 9$, $b = 9\sqrt{3}$, $c = 60°$ (p. 267)

48. rectangle (p. 270)

49. square (p. 270)

50. parallelogram (p. 271)

51. trapezoid (p. 272)

52. 900° (p. 276)

53. 45 square inches (p. 277)

54. area = 49 square inches

    perimeter = 28 inches (p. 277)

55. area = 18 square inches

    perimeter = 22 inches (p. 277)

56. 36 square inches (p. 277)

57. 35 square inches (p. 277)

58. radius (p. 281)

59. diameter (could be called a chord) (p. 282)

60. chord (p. 283)

61. area = 25π square inches

    circumference = 10π inches (p. 284)

62. 50° (p. 286)

63. 50° (p. 287)

64. concentric circles (p. 288)

65. a tangent line (p. 289)

66. similar (p. 289)

67. congruent (p. 289)

68. volume = 216 cubic feet (p. 290)

    surface area = 216 square feet (p. 292)

69. volume = 60 cubic feet (p. 290)

    surface area = 94 square feet (p. 292)

70. volume = 160π cubic feet (p. 291)

    surface area = 112π square feet (p. 293)

Geometry Glossary of Terms

acute angle: An angle whose measure is less than 90°.

acute triangle: A triangle containing all acute angles.

adjacent angles: Angles that share a common side and a common vertex but do not have any common interior points.

angle: Formed by two rays with a common endpoint.

angle bisector: A line, ray, or segment that divides an angle into two smaller angles equal in measure.

arc: The set of points on a circle that lie in the interior of a central angle.

area: The space within a shape; measured in square units.

bisects: Divides into two equal parts.

central angle: An angle whose vertex is the center of the circle. The measure of a central angle is equal to the measure of its arc.

chord: A line segment joining any two points on a circle.

circle: In a plane, the set of points all equidistant from a given point.

circumference: The distance around a circle; equals two times π times the radius or π times the diameter ($C = 2\pi r$ or πd).

complementary angles: Two angles the sum of whose measures is 90°.

concave polygon: A polygon that contains at least one diagonal outside the figure.

concentric circles: Circles with the same center.

congruent: Exactly alike. Identical in shape and size.

consecutive: Next to each other.

convex polygon: A polygon in which all diagonals lie within the figure.

corresponding: In the same position. Coinciding.

cube: A six-sided solid. All sides are equal squares and all edges are equal.

decagon: A plane closed figure with ten sides and ten angles.

degree: A unit of measurement of an angle.

diagonal of a polygon: A line segment that connects one vertex to another vertex and is not a side of the polygon.

diameter: Either a segment that joins any two points on a circle and passes through the center of the circle or the length of that segment. It is in the context of use that you will know which meaning is being used. A diameter is the longest chord in a circle.

equilateral triangle: A triangle in which all three angles are equal in measure and all three sides have the same length.

exterior angle: An angle formed outside the polygon by extending one side. In a triangle, the measure of an exterior angle equals the sum of the measures of the two remote interior angles.

height (or altitude): A segment drawn from a point and is perpendicular to a base or an extension of a base or a segment drawn that is perpendicular to each of two parallel lines.

heptagon or septagon: A plane closed figure with seven sides and seven angles.

hexagon: A plane closed figure with six sides and six angles.

hypotenuse: In a right triangle, the side opposite the 90° angle.

inscribed angle: An angle with its vertex on a circle and has chords as its sides. The vertex is where the chords intersect. The measure of an inscribed angle is equal to one-half the measure of its intercepted arc.

interior angles: Angles formed inside the shape or within two parallel lines.

intersecting lines: Lines that meet at a point.

isosceles right triangle: A triangle having two equal sides, two equal angles, and one 90° angle. Its sides are always in the ratio $1 : 1 : \sqrt{2}$.

isosceles triangle: A triangle having two equal sides (and, thus, two equal angles across from those sides).

legs: In a right triangle, the two sides forming the 90° angle. In a trapezoid, the nonparallel sides.

line (straight line): The path joining two points, it goes forever in two opposite directions.

line segment: A part of a line; has two endpoints.

median: In a triangle, a line segment drawn from a vertex to the midpoint of the opposite side. In a trapezoid, a line segment parallel to the bases and bisecting the legs.

midpoint: The halfway point of a line segment, equidistant from each endpoint.

minute: A subdivision of an angle; $\frac{1}{60}$ degree.

nonagon: A plane closed figure with nine sides and nine angles.

obtuse angle: An angle greater than 90° but less than 180°.

obtuse triangle: A triangle containing an obtuse angle.

octagon: A plane closed figure with eight sides and eight angles.

parallel lines: Two or more lines, always the same distance apart. Parallel lines never meet.

parallelogram: A four-sided plane closed figure having opposite sides equal and parallel. (Opposite angles are equal, and consecutive angles are supplementary.)

pentagon: A five-sided plane closed figure. The sum of its five angles is 540°.

perimeter: The total distance around any figure. In a circle, this is referred to as the *circumference.*

perpendicular lines: Two lines that intersect at right angles.

pi (π): A constant used in determining a circle's area or circumference. Commonly used approximations for π are 3.14 and $\frac{22}{7}$.

plane: Often described as a flat surface, it is determined by three non-collinear points.

plane figure: Any shape that can be drawn on a plane. (A two-dimensional figure.)

plane geometry: The study of shapes and figures in two dimensions.

point: A basic element of geometry, a location. If two lines intersect, they do so at a point.

polygon: A many-sided plane closed figure. Triangle, quadrilateral, pentagon, and so on are examples of polygons.

prism: A three-dimensional shape bounded by congruent parallel bases and a set of parallelograms formed by joining the corresponding vertices of the bases.

Pythagorean theorem: A theorem that applies to right triangles. The sum of the squares of a right triangle's two legs equals the square of the hypotenuse ($a^2 + b^2 = c^2$).

quadrilateral: A four-sided plane closed figure. The sum of its four angles equals 360°.

radii: Plural of *radius.*

radius: Either the segment that joins the center of a circle to any point on the circle or the length of that segment. It is in the context of use that you will know which meaning is being used.

ray: A half-line that continues forever in one direction and has one endpoint.

rectangle: A four-sided plane closed figure having opposite sides equal and parallel and four right angles.

regular polygon: A polygon in which sides and angles are all equal. For example, a regular pentagon has five equal angles and five equal sides.

rhombus: A parallelogram with four equal sides.

right angle: An angle whose measure is equal to 90°.

right circular cylinder: A solid shaped like a can whose circular bases meet the remaining side at right angles.

right triangle: A triangle containing a 90° angle.

scalene triangle: A triangle having none of its sides equal (or angles equal).

similar: Having the same shape but not the same size. Similar figures have angles in the same positions equal in measure and sides in the same positions proportional in measure.

solid geometry: The study of shapes and figures in three dimensions: length, width, and thickness.

square: A four-sided plane closed figure having equal sides and four right angles. Its opposite sides are parallel.

straight angle: An angle equal to 180° and is often referred to as a line.

straight line: The path joining two points, it goes forever in two opposite directions.

supplementary angles: Two angles the sum of whose measures is 180°.

surface area: The sum of the areas of all the surfaces of a three-dimensional figure.

tangent to a circle: A line, line segment, or ray that touches a circle at one point (cannot go within the circle).

transversal: A line crossing two or more parallel or nonparallel lines in a plane.

trapezoid: A four-sided plane closed figure with only one pair of parallel sides, called *bases*.

triangle: A three-sided plane closed figure. It contains three angles the sum of whose measures is 180°.

vertex: The point at which two rays meet and form an angle, or the point at which two sides meet in a polygon.

vertical angles: The opposite angles formed by the intersection of two lines. Vertical angles are equal in measure.

vertices: Plural of *vertex.*

volume: Capacity to hold, measured in cubic units. Volume of rectangular prism = length times width times height.

Word Problems

Diagnostic Test

Questions

1. What is the simple interest on $2,500 invested at an annual rate of 8% over three years?

2. A map's key shows that 1 inch = 25 miles. How many inches apart on the map will two cities be if they are exactly 12 miles apart?

3. A plane flies from Los Angeles to Denver, a distance of 1,120 miles, at 280 miles per hour. A train from Denver to Los Angeles travels at a rate of 70 miles per hour. Assuming the train also travels 1,120 miles, if a passenger took the plane to Denver and then returned to Los Angeles on the train, how long did the entire trip take?

4. In order to pass an examination, a student must answer exactly 30 questions correctly to obtain the minimum passing grade of 60%. How many questions are on the examination?

5. Last year, Tom's income was $36,000. This year, he was given a new position with the company with a salary of $48,000. What was the percent increase in Tom's salary?

6. If one number is 4 times as large as another number and the smaller number is decreased by 2, the result is 14 less than the larger number. What are the two numbers?

7. Fred is six years older than Sylvia. In two years, the sum of their ages will be 18. How old is Sylvia now?

8. The length of a rectangle is three inches more than the width. If the perimeter of the rectangle is 26 inches, what are the measures of length and width?

9. Adam can do a job in five hours, and Jennifer can do the same job in six hours. If they work together, how long will the job take them?

10. Nuts costing 70¢ per pound are mixed with nuts costing 40¢ per pound to produce 20 pounds of mixture worth 50¢ per pound. How much of each type is used?

Answers

Page numbers following each answer refer to the review section applicable to this problem type.

1. $600 (p. 320)

2. 0.48 inches (p. 326)

3. 20 hours (p. 329)

4. 50 questions (p. 332)

5. $33\frac{1}{3}\%$ (p. 336)

6. 4 and 16 (p. 339)

7. 4 years old (p. 343)

8. 8 inches and 5 inches (p. 347)

9. $2\frac{8}{11}$ hours (p. 351)

10. $6\frac{2}{3}$ pounds of 70¢ nuts

    $13\frac{1}{3}$ pounds of 40¢ nuts
    (p. 355)

Word Problems Review

Word problems are often the nemesis of even the best math student. For many, the difficulty is not the computation. The problems stem from what is given and what is being asked.

Solving Technique

There are many types of word problems involving arithmetic, algebra, geometry, and combinations of each with various twists. It is most important to have a systematic technique for solving word problems. Here is such a technique:

1. **Identify what is being asked.**

   What are you ultimately trying to find? How far a car has traveled? How fast a plane flies? How many items can be purchased? Whatever it is, find it and then *circle it.* This helps insure that you're solving for what is being asked.

2. **Underline and pull out information you are given in the problem.**

   Draw a picture if you can. This helps you know what you have and will point you to a relationship or equation. Note any key words in the problem (see the "Key Words and Phrases" section, later in this chapter).

3. **If you can, set up an equation or some straightforward system with the given information.**

4. **Identify whether all the given information is necessary to solve the problem.**

   Occasionally you may be given more than enough information to solve a problem. Choose what you need and don't spend needless energy on irrelevant information.

5. **Carefully solve the equation or work the necessary computation.**

   Be sure that you're working in the same units. For example, you may have to change feet into inches, pounds into ounces, and so on, in order to keep everything consistent.

6. **Double-check that you answered the question.**

   One of the most common errors in answering word problems is the failure to answer what was actually being asked.

7. **Ask yourself whether your answer is reasonable.**

   Check to make sure that an error in computation or a mistake in setting up your equation did not give you a ridiculous answer.

Key Words and Phrases

In working with word problems, some words or phrases give clues as to how the problem should be solved. The most common words or phrases are listed in the following sections.

Add

- **Sum:** As in *the sum of 2, 4, and 6.*
- **Total:** As in *the total of the first six payments.*
- **Addition:** As in *a recipe calls for the addition of 5 pints.*
- **Plus:** As in *3 liters plus 2 liters.*
- **Increase:** As in *her pay was increased by $15.*
- **More than:** As in *this week the enrollment was eight more than last week.*
- **Added to:** As in *if you added $3 to the cost. . . .*
- **Successive:** As in *the total of six successive payments.*

Subtract

- **Difference:** As in *what is the difference between. . . .*
- **Fewer:** As in *there were 15 fewer men than women.*
- **Remainder:** As in *how many are left or what quantity remains.*
- **Less than:** As in *a number is five less than another number.*
- **Reduced by:** As in *the budget was reduced by $5,000.*
- **Decreased:** As in *if he decreased the speed of his car by 10 miles per hour. . . .*
- **Minus:** As in *some number minus 9 is. . . .*

Multiply

- **Product:** As in *the product of 8 and 5 is. . . .*
- **Of:** As in *one-half of the group.*
- **Times:** As in *five times as many girls as boys.*
- **At:** As in *the cost of 10 yards of material at 70¢ a yard is. . . .*
- **Total:** As in *if you spend $15 a week on gas, what is the total for a three week period.*
- **Twice:** As in *twice the value of some number.*

Divide

- **Quotient:** As in *the final quotient is. . . .*
- **Divided by:** As in *some number divided by 12 is. . . .*
- **Divided into:** As in *the group was divided into. . . .*
- **Ratio:** As in *what is the ratio of. . . .*
- **Half:** As in *half the profits are. . . .*

As you work a variety of word problem types, you will discover more key words.

A final reminder: Be sensitive to what each of these questions is asking. What time? How many? How much? How far? How old? What length? What is the ratio?

Simple Interest

Example:

> How much simple interest will an account earn in five years if $500 is invested at 8% interest per year?
>
> First circle what you must find—*interest.* Now use the following equation:
>
> Interest = principal × rate × time
>
> $I = prt$
>
> Simply plug into the equation:
>
> $I = \$500 \times 0.08 \times 5$
>
> $I = \$200$
>
> Note that both rate and time are in yearly terms (annual rate and years).

Practice: Simple Interest Problems

1. What is the simple interest on $5,000 invested at an annual rate of 6% over four years?

2. What is the simple interest on a loan of $10,000 at a $6\frac{1}{2}\%$ annual rate over five years?

3. What is the simple interest on $4,000 at a 4% semiannual rate over three years?

4. A woman invests $30,000 in a mutual fund that pays 3% quarterly. What is her simple interest dividend for nine months?

5. An investment group receives $3,600 simple interest for a three-year investment of $10,000. If the interest rate has remained stable throughout the investment period, what interest rate is the group receiving?

Answers: Simple Interest Problems

1. What is the simple interest on $5,000 invested at an annual rate of 6% over four years?

   First, circle what you must find: *simple interest.* Now, using the information given in the problem, plug into the equation:

   $I = prt$

   $I = \$5,000 \times 0.06 \times 4$

   $I = \$1,200$

   Therefore, the simple interest is $1,200.

2. What is the simple interest on a loan of $10,000 at a $6\frac{1}{2}$% annual rate over five years.

   First, circle what you must find: *simple interest.* Now, using the information given in the problem, plug into the equation:

   $I = prt$

   $I = \$10,000 \times 0.065 \times 5$

   $I = \$3,250$

   Therefore, the simple interest is $3,250.

3. What is the simple interest on $4,000 at a 4% semiannual rate over three years?

   First, circle what you must find in the problem: *simple interest.* However, note that the 4% figure is a *semiannual* rate. Therefore, before plugging into the $I = prt$ equation, you have to change the rate to an annual rate. Because *semiannual* means "every half-year," the annual rate would be twice 4%, or 8%. Thus,

$I = prt$

$I = \$4,000 \times 0.08 \times 3$

$I = \$960$

Therefore, the simple interest is $960.

4. A woman invests $30,000 in a mutual fund that pays 3% quarterly. What is her simple interest dividend for nine months?

First, circle what you must find in the problem: *simple interest dividend*. However, note that the 3% rate is a quarterly rate; thus, the annual rate would be $4 \times 3\%$, or 12%. Also, note that the time is nine months, or $\frac{3}{4}$ of a year. Thus,

$I = prt$

$I = \$30,000 \times 0.12 \times \frac{3}{4}$

$I = \$2,700$

Therefore, simple interest for nine months is $2,700.

5. An investment group receives $3,600 simple interest for a three-year investment of $10,000. If the interest rate has remained stable throughout the investment period, what interest rate is the group receiving?

First, circle what you must find: *interest rate*. Now, plug into the equation:

$$I = prt$$

$$\$3,600 = \$10,000 \times r \times 3$$

$$\frac{\$3,600}{3} = \frac{\$10,000 \times r \times 3}{3}$$

$$\$1,200 = \$10,000r$$

$$\frac{\$1,200}{\$10,000} = \frac{\$10,000r}{\$10,000}$$

$$0.12 = r$$

Therefore, the simple interest rate is 12%.

Compound Interest

Example:

What will be the final value after three years on an original investment of $1,000 if a 12% annual interest rate is compounded yearly?

First, circle what you must find: *final total.* Note that interest will be compounded each year. Therefore, the solution has three parts, one for each year.

Total for first year:

$I = prt$

$I = \$1,000 \times 0.12 \times 1$

$I = \$120$

Thus, the total after one year is $1,000 + $120 = $1,120.

Total for second year:

$I = prt$

$I = \$1,120 \times 0.12 \times 1$

$I = \$134.40$

Note that the principal at the beginning of the second year was $1,120. Thus, the total after two years is $1,120 + $134.40 = $1,254.40.

Total for third year:

$I = prt$

$I = \$1,254.40 \times 0.12 \times 1$

$I = \$150.53$

Note that the principal at the beginning of the second year was $1,254.40. Thus, the total after three years is $1,254.40 + $150.53 = $1,404.93.

Practice: Compound Interest Problems

1. Find the total interest on $140 at a 5% annual rate for two years if interest is compounded annually.

2. Dana deposited $1,000 in the Great Island Bank for her trip to Tahiti. If interest is compounded annually at 8%, how much will be in her account at the end of two years?

3. If the beginning balance of a savings account is $200 and interest is paid semiannually at a 5% semiannual rate, what is the ending balance after two years?

4. Arnie invests $5,000 in a stock that pays dividends of 20% annually. Arnie always reinvests his dividends into his stock. How much stock value will Arnie have after four years?

5. Stacy invests $3,000 for three years at an annual rate of 8%. Find her total after three years if the interest is compounded annually.

Answers: Compound Interest Problems

1. Find the total interest on $140 at a 5% annual rate for two years if interest is compounded annually.

   First, circle what you must find: *total interest.* Now, figure the interest for the first year:

   $I = prt$

   $I = \$140 \times 0.05 \times 1$

   $I = \$7$

   Now, add the interest from the first year ($7) to the second-year principal ($140) to find the second-year interest:

   $I = prt$

   $I = \$147 \times 0.05 \times 1$

   $I = \$7.35$

   Now, add the first-year interest ($7), to the second-year interest ($7.35) to get the total interest paid: $14.35.

2. Dana deposited $1,000 in the Great Island Bank for her trip to Tahiti. If interest is compounded annually at 8%, how much will be in her account at the end of two years?

First, circle what you must find: *how much will be in her account after two years* (or the total principal after two years). Now, figure the interest for the first year:

$I = prt$

$I = \$1,000 \times 0.08 \times 1$

$I = \$80$

Thus, the amount in savings after one year will be $\$1,000 + \$80 = \$1,080$.

A faster way to find the total (with interest) is to simply multiply the principal by 1.08 (if the interest rate is 8%). If the interest rate were, say, 12%, then you could simply multiply the principal by 1.12, and so on. Therefore, using this method to find the amount at the end of the second year:

$p \times 1.08 =$

$\$1,080 \times 1.08 = \$1,166.40$

Therefore, there will be $\$1,166.40$ in the account at the end of two years.

3. If the beginning balance of a savings account is $200 and interest is paid semiannually at a 5% semiannual rate, what is the ending balance after two years?

   First, circle what you must find: *the ending balance after two years.* Note how interest is paid: semiannually at 5%. Thus,

   After $\frac{1}{2}$ year: $\$200 \times 1.05 = \$210$ in account

   After 1 year: $\$210 \times 1.05 = \$220.50$ in account

   After $1\frac{1}{2}$ years: $\$220.50 \times 1.05 = \$231.53$ in account

   After 2 years: $\$231.53 \times 1.05 = \$243.11$ in account

   Therefore, the ending balance is $\$243.11$ after two years.

4. Arnie invests $5,000 in a stock that pays dividends of 20% annually. Arnie always reinvests his dividends into his stock. How much stock value will Arnie have after four years?

   First, circle what you must find: *how much stock . . . after four years* (total). Arnie will have:

   After the first year: $\$5,000 \times 1.20 = \$6,000$ worth of stock

After the second year: $6,000 × 1.20 = $7,200 worth of stock

After the third year: $7,200 × 1.20 = $8,640 worth of stock

After the fourth year: $8,640 × 1.20 = $10,368 worth of stock

Therefore, after four years, Arnie will have $10,368 worth of stock.

5. Stacy invests $3,000 for three years at an annual rate of 8%. Find her total after three years if the interest is compounded annually.

First, circle what you must find: *total after three years.* Stacy will have:

After the first year: $3,000 × 1.08 = $3,240

After the second year: $3,240 × 1.08 = $3,499.20

After the third year: $3,499.20 × 1.08 = $3,779.14

Therefore, Stacy will have a total of $3,779.14 after three years.

Ratio and Proportion

Example:

If Arnold can type 600 pages of manuscript in 21 days, how many days will it take him to type 230 pages if he works at the same rate?

First, circle what you're asked to find: *how many days.* One simple way to work this problem is to set up a framework (proportion) using the categories given in the equation. Here, the categories are pages and days. Therefore, a framework may be

$$\frac{\text{Pages}}{\text{Days}} = \frac{\text{Pages}}{\text{Days}}$$

Note that you also may have used

$$\frac{\text{Days}}{\text{Pages}} = \frac{\text{Days}}{\text{Pages}}$$

The answer will still be the same. Now, simply plug into the equation for each instance:

$$\frac{600}{21} = \frac{230}{x}$$

Cross-multiply:

$$600x = 21 \times 230$$

$$600x = 4,830$$

$$\frac{600x}{600} = \frac{4,830}{600}$$

$$x = 8\frac{1}{20}$$

Therefore, it will take Arnold 8 days, 1 hour, and 12 minutes $(8\frac{1}{20})$ days to type 230 pages.

Practice: Ratio and Proportion Problems

1. A map's key shows that 1 inch = 35 miles. How many inches apart on the map will two cities be if they are exactly 7 miles apart?

2. If eight pounds of apples cost 98¢, at the same rate, how much will 12 pounds of apples cost?

3. If a girl can run m miles in h hours, at the same rate, how long will it take her to run k miles?

4. It takes q hours to drain a pool containing x gallons of water. If the pool contains y gallons of water, how long will it take to drain at the same rate?

5. In six years, a man was able to build 58 violins. Considering that he works at the same speed, how many complete violins can he build in 11 years?

Answers: Ratio and Proportion Problems

1. A map's key shows that 1 inch = 35 miles. How many inches apart on the map will two cities be if they are exactly 7 miles apart?

First, circle what you must find in the problem: *how many inches apart*. Now, using the information given in the problem, construct a framework for a proportion and plug into it:

$$\frac{\text{miles}}{\text{hours}} = \frac{\text{miles}}{\text{hours}}$$

$$\frac{35}{1} = \frac{7}{x}$$

Cross-multiply:

$$35x = 7$$

$$\frac{35x}{35} = \frac{7}{35}$$

$$x = \frac{1}{5}$$

The two cities will be $\frac{1}{5}$ of an inch apart.

2. If 8 pounds of apples cost 98¢, at the same rate, how much will 12 pounds of apples cost?

First, circle what you must find: *how much will 12 pounds of apples cost*. Now, using the information given in the problem, set up a framework for a proportion and plug into it:

$$\frac{\text{pounds}}{\text{price}} = \frac{\text{pounds}}{\text{price}}$$

$$\frac{8}{98¢} = \frac{12}{x}$$

Cross-multiply:

$$8x = 98 \times 12$$

$$\frac{8x}{8} = \frac{1{,}176}{8}$$

$$x = 147¢$$

The answer is 147¢, or $1.47.

3. If a girl can run m miles in h hours, at the same rate, how fast will she run k miles?

First, circle what you must find: *how fast will she run k miles* (how many hours). Now using the information given in the problem, set up a framework for a proportion and plug into it:

$$\frac{\text{miles}}{\text{hours}} = \frac{\text{miles}}{\text{hours}}$$

$$\frac{m}{h} = \frac{k}{x}$$

Cross-multiply:

$$mx = kh$$

$$\frac{mx}{m} = \frac{kh}{m}$$

$$x = \frac{kh}{m} \text{ or } \frac{hk}{m}$$

It will take her $\frac{kh}{m}$ or $\frac{hk}{m}$ hours to run k miles.

4. It takes q hours to drain a pool containing x gallons of water. If the pool contains y gallons of water, how long will it take to drain at the same rate?

First, circle what you must find: *how long* (time). Now, using the information given in the problem, set up a proportion and plug in:

$$\frac{\text{hours}}{\text{gallons}} = \frac{\text{hours}}{\text{gallons}}$$

$$\frac{q}{x} = \frac{?}{y}$$

Cross-multiply:

$qy = x(?)$

$\dfrac{qy}{x} = \dfrac{x(?)}{x}$

$\dfrac{qy}{x}$ or $\dfrac{yq}{x} = ?$

It will take $\dfrac{qy}{x}$ or $\dfrac{yq}{x}$ hours to drain y gallons of water.

Careful: Notice that, because x was in the problem, we used ? for the unknown quantity.

5. In six years, a man was able to build 58 violins. Considering that he works at the same speed, how many complete violins can he build in 11 years?

    First, circle what you must find in the problem: *how many complete violins* (note the word *complete*). Now, using the information given in the problem, set up a proportion and plug in:

    $\dfrac{\text{violins}}{\text{years}} = \dfrac{\text{violins}}{\text{years}}$

    $\dfrac{58}{6} = \dfrac{x}{11}$

    Cross-multiply:

    $638 = 6x$

    $\dfrac{638}{6} = \dfrac{6x}{6}$

    $106.33 \approx x$

    Therefore, he can build 106 complete violins.

Motion

Example:

How long will it take a bus traveling 72 km/hr to go 36 kilometers?

First, circle what you're trying to find: *how long will it take* (time). Motion problems are solved by using the following equation:

distance = rate × time

$d = rt$

Therefore, simply plug into the equation:

$d = rt$

$36 = 72t$

$\dfrac{36}{72} = \dfrac{72t}{72}$

$\dfrac{1}{2} = t$

Therefore, it will take one-half hour for the bus to travel 36 kilometers at 72 km/hr.

Practice: Motion Problems

1. How many miles will a speedboat travel going 80 mph for $2\frac{1}{2}$ hours?

2. How long will it take a car averaging 55 mph to travel a distance of 594 miles?

3. What is the average speed of a train (in miles per hour) if it takes three complete days to travel 3,600 miles?

4. A plane flies from New York to Chicago (a distance of 1,600 miles) at 400 mph. Returning from Chicago to New York, it flies into a headwind and averages only 320 mph. How many hours total was the plane in the air for the entire trip?

5. Frank rows a boat at 5 mph but travels a distance of only 7 miles in two hours. How fast was the current moving against him?

Answers: Motion Problems

1. How many miles will a speedboat travel going 80 mph for $2\frac{1}{2}$ hours?

    First, circle what you must find: *how many miles.* Now, using the information given in the problem, plug into the equation:

    $d = rt$

    $d = 80 \times 2.5$

    $d = 200$ miles

    Thus, the speedboat will travel 200 miles.

2. How long will it take a car averaging 55 mph to travel a distance of 594 miles?

   First, circle what you must find: *how long will it take* (time). Now, using the information given in the problem, plug into the equation:

   $d = rt$

   $594 = 55 \times t$

   $\dfrac{594}{55} = \dfrac{55 \times t}{55}$

   $10.8 = t$

   Therefore, it will take 10.8 hours, or 10 hours and 48 minutes.

3. What is the average speed of a train (in miles per hour) if it takes three complete days to travel 3,600 miles?

   First, circle what you must find: *average speed.* Note that the time is given to you in days, but because you're looking for an answer in terms of miles per hour, you need to convert those three days to hours. With 24 hours per day, 3 days is 72 hours. Now, using the information given in the problem, plug into the equation.

   $d = rt$

   $3,600 = r \times 72$

   $\dfrac{3,600}{72} = \dfrac{r \times 72}{72}$

   $50 = r$

   The average speed of the train is 50 mph.

4. A plane flies from New York to Chicago (a distance of 1,600 miles) at 400 mph. Returning from Chicago to New York, it flies into a headwind and averages only 320 mph. How many hours total was the plane in the air for the entire trip?

   First, circle what you must find: *how many hours was the plane in the air* (time). Note that this is a two-part question, because the time each way will be different. First, to find the time going to Chicago, plug into the equation:

   $d = rt$

   $1,600 = 400 \times t$

   $\dfrac{1,600}{400} = \dfrac{400 \times t}{400}$

   $4 = t$

Thus, it took four hours to fly from New York to Chicago. Now, returning to New York:

$$d = rt$$
$$\frac{1,600}{320} = \frac{320 \times t}{320}$$
$$5 = t$$

Because returning took five hours of flying time, the total time in the air was 4 hours + 5 hours = 9 hours.

5. Frank rows a boat at 5 mph but travels a distance of only 7 miles in two hours. How fast was the current moving against him?

First, circle what you must find: *how fast was the current moving against him.* Using the information given in the problem, plug into the equation. Note that Frank traveled 7 miles in two hours.

$$d = rt$$
$$7 = r \times 2$$
$$3.5 = r$$

Therefore, Frank's actual speed in the water was $3\frac{1}{2}$ mph. If Frank rows at 5 mph, to find the current against him simply subtract:

Frank's speed – actual speed in water = speed of the current

5 mph – 3.5 mph = 1.5 mph

The current was going 1.5 mph against him.

Percent

Example:

Thirty students are awarded doctoral degrees at the graduate school, and this number comprises 40% of the total graduate student body. How many graduate students were enrolled?

First, circle what you must find in the problem: *how many graduate students.* The percentage equation is as follows:

$$\frac{\text{is}}{\text{of}} = \%$$

Try rephrasing the question into a simple sentence. For example, in this case 30 is 40% of what total?

Note that the 30 sits next to the word *is;* therefore, 30 is the "is" number; 40 is the percent. Notice that *what total* sits next to the word *of.* Therefore, plugging into the equation,

$$\frac{\text{is}}{\text{of}} = \%$$

$$\frac{30}{x} = \frac{40}{100}$$

Cross-multiply:

$$40x = 3,000$$

$$\frac{40x}{40} = \frac{3,000}{40}$$

$$x = 75$$

Therefore, the total graduate enrollment was 75 students.

Practice: Percent Problems

1. In a school of 300 students, 60 do not sign up for after-school sports. What percent of the school signs up for after-school sports?

2. In order to pass an examination, a student must correctly answer at least nine questions in order to receive the minimum passing grade of 75%. How many questions are on the examination?

3. Seventy million Americans are registered voters. Sixty percent are registered Democrats, and the rest are either registered Republicans or uncommitted. If 10 percent of the total registered voters are uncommitted, how many registered voters are registered Republicans?

4. 55% of 800 people polled answered vanilla when asked their favorite ice-cream flavor. What percent of those polled answered chocolate as their favorite?

5. A 200-square-yard playground is to be constructed. Exactly 40% must be grass, 30% must be sand, and the remaining percentage must be asphalt. What are the square-yard specifications for grass, sand, and asphalt?

6. A U.S. postage-stamp collection was offered for sale at a stamp show for $800 but went unsold. Its owner resubmitted the collection for sale at the next stamp show but dropped his asking price 30%. The collection, however, still did not sell, so the owner offered an additional discount of 25% off the new asking price. What was the final price of the postage-stamp collection?

333

Answers: Percent Problems

1. In a school of 300 students, 60 do not sign up for after-school sports. What percent of the school signs up for after-school sports?

    First, circle what you must find in this problem: *what percent . . . signs up*. Now, using the information given in the problem, plug into the equation. Note that since 60 students do *not* sign up for after-school sports, the number that *does* sign up must be the total number of students minus 60, or 300 – 60 = 240 students. The problem may now be reworded as *240 students is what percent of 300*.

    $$\frac{is}{of} = \%$$
    $$\frac{240}{300} = \frac{x}{100}$$

    Cross-multiply:

    $$24{,}000 = 300x$$
    $$\frac{24{,}000}{300} = \frac{300x}{300}$$
    $$80 = x$$

    Therefore, 80% of the school signs up for after-school sports.

2. In order to pass an examination, a student must correctly answer at least nine questions in order to receive the minimum passing grade of 75%. How many questions are on the examination?

    First, circle what you're looking for: *how many questions are on the examination*. To plug into the equation, this problem may be reworded as *nine questions is 75% of how many questions*. Now, plug in the numbers:

    $$\frac{is}{of} = \%$$
    $$\frac{9}{x} = \frac{75}{100}$$

    Cross-multiply:

    $$900 = 75x$$
    $$\frac{900}{75} = \frac{75x}{75}$$
    $$12 = x$$

    Therefore, there are 12 questions on the test.

3. Seventy million Americans are registered voters. Sixty percent are registered Democrats, and the rest are either registered Republicans or

uncommitted. If 10 percent of the total registered voters are uncommitted, how many registered voters are registered Republicans?

First, circle what you're asked to find: *how many . . . are registered Republicans.* Note that if 60% are Democrats and 10% are uncommitted, then 30% must be Republicans. Now you may restate the question as *how much is 30% of 70 million voters.* Now plug into the equation:

$$\frac{\text{is}}{\text{of}} = \%$$
$$\frac{x}{70 \text{ million}} = \frac{30}{100}$$

Cross-multiply:

$$100x = 2,100 \text{ million}$$
$$x = 21 \text{ million}$$

In this problem, because you're finding 30% of 70 million, you could simply multiply: 0.30×70 million $= 21$ million. Therefore, there are 21 million registered Republicans.

4. 55% of 800 people polled answered vanilla when asked their favorite ice-cream flavor. What percent of those polled answered chocolate as their favorite?

   Be careful. Note here that just because 55% like vanilla that doesn't mean that *all* the remaining 45% like chocolate. There are many ice-cream flavors to choose from, and the remaining 45% could be divided among chocolate, strawberry, pistachio, and so on. Thus, there is not enough information to determine an answer. This type of question appears occasionally.

5. A 200-square-yard playground is to be constructed. Exactly 40% must be grass, 30% must be sand, and the remaining percentage must be asphalt. What are the square-yard specifications for grass, sand, and asphalt?

   Note that this "three-part" question may be rephrased as:

   For the grass, what is 40% of 200?

   For the sand, what is 30% of 200?

   For the asphalt, what is 30% of 200?

   30% is the remaining percentage for the asphalt.

   Using the equation, for the grass:

$$\frac{is}{of} = \%$$
$$\frac{x}{200} = \frac{40}{100}$$

Cross-multiply:

$100x = 8,000$

$x = 80$ square yards of grass

For the sand:

$$\frac{x}{200} = \frac{30}{100}$$

Cross-multiply:

$100x = 6,000$

$x = 80$ square yards of grass

For the asphalt: 60 square yards of asphalt (because the percentage of asphalt is the same as the percentage of sand).

6. A U.S. postage-stamp collection was offered for sale at a stamp show for $800 but went unsold. Its owner resubmitted the collection for sale at the next stamp show but dropped his asking price 30%. The collection, however, still did not sell, so the owner offered an additional discount of 25% off the new asking price. What was the final price of the postage-stamp collection?

The original price was $800. A 30 percent drop in price is 30% of $800 = 0.30 × 800 = $240 off. The new price therefore is $800 − $240 = $560. Because the collection still did not sell (at $560), an additional 25% discount was offered:

25% of $560 = 0.25 × 560 = $140 off

Therefore the final asking price is $560 − $140 = $420.

Percent Change

Example:

Last year, Harold earned $250 a month at his after-school job. This year, his after-school earnings have increased to $300 per month. What is the percent increase in his monthly after-school earnings?

First, circle what you're looking for: *percent increase.*

Percent change (percent increase, percentage rise, percent difference, percent decrease, and so on) is always found by using the following equation:

$$\text{percent change} = \frac{\text{change}}{\text{starting point}}; \text{ then convert to a percent.}$$

Therefore,

$$\text{percent change} = \frac{\$300 - \$250}{\$250}$$

$$= \frac{\$50}{\$250}$$

$$= \frac{1}{5} = 0.20, \text{ or } 20\%$$

The percent increase in Harold's after-school salary was 20%.

Practice: Percent-Change Problems

1. Last year Hank's income was $36,000. This year it rose to $45,000. What was the percent increase in Hank's salary?

2. A five-year study showed that the population of Hicksville, New York, fell from 65,000 in 1975 to 48,750 in 1980. What was the percent decrease in population over those five years?

3. Last year's Dow Jones averaged 9,000. This year's index averaged 10,800. What was the percentage rise in the average Dow Jones index over those years?

4. Economic indicators predict 12% inflation over the next 12 months. If that's true, how much must a $20,000 salary be increased to keep up with inflation?

5. Due to 5% inflation, a woman's monthly salary was increased $800 to exactly keep up with the economy. What is the woman's new monthly salary? (Hint: First find her initial monthly salary.)

Answers: Percent Change Problems

1. Last year Hank's income was $36,000. This year it rose to $45,000. What was the percent increase in Hank's salary?

First, circle what you must find: *percent increase.* Now, using the information given in the problem, plug into the equation:

$$\text{percent increase} = \frac{\text{change}}{\text{starting point}}; \text{ then convert to a percent.}$$

$$= \frac{\$45,000 - \$36,000}{\$36,000}$$

$$= \frac{\$9,000}{\$36,000}$$

$$= 0.25, \text{ or } 25\%$$

The percent increase was 25%.

2. A five-year study showed that the population of Hicksville, New York, fell from 65,000 in 1975 to 48,750 in 1980. What was the percent decrease in population over those five years?

First, circle what you must find: *percent decrease.* Now, using the information given in the problem, plug into the equation:

$$\text{percent decrease} = \frac{\text{change}}{\text{starting point}}; \text{ then convert to a percent.}$$

$$= \frac{65,000 - 48,750}{65,000}$$

$$= \frac{16,250}{65,000}$$

$$= 0.25, \text{ or } 25\%$$

The percent decrease was 25%. Note that the fact that the study was a five-year study had no bearing on the answer.

3. Last year's Dow Jones averaged 9000. This year's index averaged 10,800. What was the percentage rise in the average Dow Jones index over those years?

First, circle what you must find: *percentage rise.* Now, using the information given in the problem, plug into the equation:

$$\text{percentage rise} = \frac{\text{change}}{\text{starting point}}; \text{ then convert to a percent.}$$

$$= \frac{10,800 - 9,000}{9,000}$$

$$= \frac{1,800}{9,000}$$

$$= 0.20, \text{ or } 20\%$$

The percentage rise in the average Dow Jones was 20%.

4. Economic indicators predict 12% inflation over the next 12 months. If that's true, how much must a $20,000 salary be increased to keep up with inflation?

First, circle what you must find: *how much must a . . . salary be increased.* Now, using the information given in the problem, you could simply multiply: $0.12 \times 20,000 = 2,400$. Or, if you want to plug into the standard equation:

$$\text{percentage rise} = \frac{\text{change}}{\text{starting point}}; \text{ then convert to a percent.}$$

$$12\% = \frac{x}{\$20,000}$$

$$\frac{0.12}{1} = \frac{x}{\$20,000}$$

$$0.12 \times \$20,000 = x$$

$$\$2,400 = x$$

The salary must be increased $2,400.

5. Due to 5% inflation, a woman's monthly salary was increased $800 to exactly keep up with the economy. What is the woman's new monthly salary? (***Hint:*** First find her initial monthly salary.)

First, circle what you must find: *new monthly salary.* Now, using the information given in the problem, plug into the equation:

$$\text{percentage rise} = \frac{\text{change}}{\text{starting point}}; \text{ then convert to a percent.}$$

$$5\% = \frac{\$800}{x}$$

$$\frac{0.05}{1} = \frac{\$800}{x}$$

$$0.05x = \$800$$

$$\frac{0.05x}{0.05} = \frac{\$800}{0.05}$$

$$x = \$16,000$$

Thus, $16,000 is her *starting* monthly salary. Adding the change of $800 (increase), her *new* monthly salary is $16,800.

Number

Examples:

1. One number exceeds another number by 5. If the sum of the two numbers is 39, find the smaller number.

First, circle what you're looking for: *the smaller number.* Now, let the smaller number equal x. Therefore, the larger number equals $x + 5$. Now, use the problem to set up an equation:

$$\underbrace{\text{If the sum of the two numbers}}_{x+(x+5)}\ \underbrace{\text{is}}_{=}\ \underbrace{39}_{39}\ldots$$

$$2x + 5 = 39$$

$$2x + 5 - 5 = 39 - 5$$

$$2x = 34$$

$$\frac{2x}{2} = \frac{34}{2}$$

$$x = 17$$

Therefore, the smaller number is 17.

2. If one number is three times as large as another number and the smaller number is increased by 19, the result is 6 less than twice the larger number. What is the larger number?

   First, circle what you must find: *the larger number.* Let the smaller number equal x. Therefore, the larger number will be $3x$. Now, using the problem, set up an equation:

$$\text{The}\ \underbrace{\text{smaller number}}_{x}\ \underbrace{\text{increased by}}_{+}\ \underbrace{19}_{19}\ \underbrace{\text{is}}_{=}\ \underbrace{\text{6 less than twice the larger number.}}_{2(3x)-6}$$

$$x + 19 = 6x - 6$$

$$-x + x + 19 = -x + 6x - 6$$

$$19 = 5x - 6$$

$$19 + 6 = 5x - 6 + 6$$

$$25 = 5x$$

$$5 = x$$

Therefore, the larger number, $3x$, will be $3 \times 5 = 15$.

3. The sum of three consecutive integers is 306. What is the largest integer?

   First, circle what you must find: *the largest integer.* Let the smallest integer equal x; let the next integer equal $x + 1$; let the largest integer equal $x + 2$. Now, use the problem to set up an equation:

$$\underbrace{\text{The sum of three consecutive integers}}_{x+(x+1)+(x+2)} \; \underbrace{\text{is}}_{=} \; \underbrace{306.}_{306}$$

$$3x + 3 = 306$$
$$3x + 3 - 3 = 306 - 3$$
$$3x = 303$$
$$\frac{3x}{3} = \frac{303}{3}$$
$$x = 101$$

Therefore, the largest integer, $x + 2$, will be $101 + 2 = 103$.

Practice: Number Problems

1. The sum of three consecutive integers is 51. What is the largest integer?

2. The sum of three consecutive even integers is 612. What is the smallest integer?

3. Two integers total 35. One integer is 23 larger than the other. What are the two integers?

4. The difference between $\frac{1}{2}$ of a number and $\frac{1}{3}$ of the same number is 8. What is the number?

5. If one number is twice as large as another number and the smaller number is increased by 8, the result is 4 less than the larger number. What is the larger number?

Answers: Number Problems

1. The sum of three consecutive integers is 51. What is the largest integer?

   First, circle what it is you must find: *the largest integer.* Let the consecutive integers equal x, $x + 1$, and $x + 2$. Now, use the problem to set up an equation:

$$\underbrace{\text{The sum of three consecutive integers}}_{x+(x+1)+(x+2)} \; \underbrace{\text{is}}_{=} \; \underbrace{51.}_{51}$$

$$3x + 3 = 51$$
$$3x + 3 - 3 = 51 - 3$$

$$3x = 48$$

$$\frac{3x}{3} = \frac{48}{3}$$

$$x = 16$$

Therefore, the largest integer, $x + 2$, will be $16 + 2 = 18$.

2. The sum of three consecutive even integers is 612. What is the smallest integer?

First, circle what you must find: *the smallest integer.* Let the three integers equal x, $x + 2$, and $x + 4$ (because consecutive even numbers increase by 2). Now, use the problem to set up an equation.

$$\underbrace{\text{The sum of three consecutive even integers}}_{x+(x+2)+(x+4)} \underbrace{\text{is}}_{=} \underbrace{612.}_{612}$$

$$3x + 6 = 612$$

$$3x + 6 - 6 = 612 - 6$$

$$3x = 606$$

$$\frac{3x}{3} = \frac{606}{3}$$

$$x = 202$$

Therefore, the smallest integer, x, is 202.

3. Two integers total 35. One integer is 23 larger than the other. What are the two integers?

First, circle what you must find: *the two integers.* Let the smaller integer equal x. Therefore, the larger integer equals $x + 23$. Now, use the problem to set up an equation:

$$\underbrace{\text{Two integers}}_{x+(x+23)} \underbrace{\text{total}}_{=} \underbrace{35.}_{35}$$

$$2x + 23 = 35$$

$$2x + 23 - 23 = 35 - 23$$

$$2x = 12$$

$$\frac{2x}{2} = \frac{12}{2}$$

$$x = 6$$

Therefore, one integer, x, is 6 and the other integer, $x + 23$, is 29.

4. The difference between $\frac{1}{2}$ of a number and $\frac{1}{3}$ of the same number is 8. What is the number?

First, circle what you must find: *the number.* Therefore, let the number equal x. Now use the problem to set up an equation:

$\underbrace{\text{The difference between } \tfrac{1}{2} \text{ of a number and } \tfrac{1}{3} \text{ of the same number}}_{\left(\frac{1}{2}\right)x - \left(\frac{1}{3}\right)x}$ $\underbrace{\text{is}}$ $\underbrace{8.}$ $= 8$

$$\frac{x}{2} - \frac{x}{3} = 8$$

Using a common denominator:

$$\frac{3x}{6} - \frac{2x}{6} = 8$$
$$\frac{x}{6} = 8$$
$$(6)\frac{x}{6} = (6)8$$
$$x = 48$$

The number is 48.

5. If one number is twice as large as another number and the smaller number is increased by 8, the result is 4 less than the larger number. What is the larger number?

First, circle what you must find: *the larger number.* Now let x denote the smaller number. Therefore, the larger number will be $2x$, because it is twice as large as x. Now use the problem to set up an equation.

$\underbrace{\text{If the smaller number is increased by 8}}_{x+8},$ $\underbrace{\text{the result}}_{=}$ $\underbrace{\text{is 4 less than the larger number.}}_{2x-4}$

$$-x + x + 8 = 2x - x - 4$$
$$8 = x - 4$$
$$8 + 4 = x - 4 + 4$$
$$12 = x$$

Thus, the larger number, $2x$, is 24.

Age

Examples:

1. Tom and Phil are brothers. Phil is 35 years old. Three years ago, Phil was four times as old as Tom was then. How old is Tom now?

First, circle what it is you must ultimately find: *Tom now.* Therefore, let t be Tom's age now. Then, three years ago, Tom's age would be $t - 3$. Four times Tom's age three years ago would be $4(t - 3)$. Phil's age three years ago would be $35 - 3 = 32$. A simple chart may also be helpful.

	Now	3 Years Ago
Phil	35	32
Tom	t	$t - 3$

Now, use the problem to set up an equation:

Three years ago Phil was four times as old as his brother was then.
$$32 = 4 \text{ times} \quad (t-3)$$

$$\frac{32}{4} = \frac{4(t-3)}{4}$$

$$8 = t - 3$$

$$8 + 3 = t - 3 + 3$$

$$11 = t$$

Therefore, Tom is now 11.

2. Lisa is 16 years younger than Kathy. If the sum of their ages is 30, how old is Lisa?

First, circle what you must find: *Lisa.* Let Lisa equal x. Therefore, Kathy is $x + 16$. (Note that because Lisa is 16 years *younger* than Kathy, you must *add* 16 years to Lisa to denote Kathy's age.) Now use the problem to set up an equation:

If the sum of their ages is 30 ...
$$\text{Lisa} + \text{Kathy} = 30$$

$$x + (x + 16) = 30$$

$$2x + 16 = 30$$

$$2x + 16 - 16 = 30 - 16$$

$$2x = 14$$

$$\frac{2x}{2} = \frac{14}{2}$$

$$x = 7$$

Therefore, Lisa is 7 years old.

Practice: Age Problems

1. Clyde is four times as old as John. If the difference between their ages is 39 years, how old is Clyde?

2. Sylvia is 20 years older than Jan. If the sum of their ages is 48 years, how old is Jan?

3. Sheila is three times as old as Kim. The sum of their ages is 24 years. How old is Sheila?

4. In eight years, Joy will be three times as old as she is now. How old is Joy now?

5. Matt is six years older than Hector. In two years, Matt will be twice as old as Hector. How old is Hector now?

Answers: Age Problems

1. Clyde is four times as old as John. If the difference between their ages is 39 years, how old is Clyde?

First, circle what you must find in this problem: *Clyde*. Let John (the smaller of the two ages) equal x. Therefore, Clyde equals $4x$. Now use the problem to set up an equation:

$$\underbrace{\underbrace{\text{If the difference between their ages}}_{\text{Clyde} - \text{John}} \underbrace{\text{is}}_{=} \underbrace{39}_{39} \ldots}$$

$$4x - x = 39$$
$$3x = 39$$
$$\frac{3x}{3} = \frac{39}{3}$$
$$x = 13$$

Therefore, Clyde, $4x$, is $4 \times 13 = 52$ years old.

2. Sylvia is 20 years older than Jan. If the sum of their ages is 48 years, how old is Jan?

First, circle what you must find in this problem: *Jan*. Let Jan (the younger of the two ages) equal x. Therefore, Sylvia equals $x + 20$. Now, use the problem to set up an equation:

$$\underbrace{\text{If the sum of their ages}}_{\text{Jan} + \text{Sylvia}} \underbrace{\text{is}}_{=} \underbrace{48}_{48} \dots$$

$$x + (x + 20) = 48$$

$$2x + 20 = 48$$

$$2x + 20 - 20 = 48 - 20$$

$$2x = 28$$

$$\frac{2x}{2} = \frac{28}{2}$$

$$x = 14$$

Therefore, Jan is 14 years old.

3. Sheila is three times as old as Kim. The sum of their ages is 24 years. How old is Sheila?

   First, circle what you must find in the problem: *Sheila.* Now let Kim (the younger of the two ages) equal x. Therefore, Sheila equals $3x$. Now, use the problem to set up an equation:

$$\underbrace{\text{The sum of their ages}}_{\text{Sheila} + \text{Kim}} \underbrace{\text{is}}_{=} \underbrace{24}_{24} \dots$$

$$3x + x = 24$$

$$4x = 24$$

$$\frac{4x}{4} = \frac{24}{4}$$

$$x = 6$$

Therefore, Sheila, $3x$, is $3 \times 6 = 18$ years old.

4. In eight years, Joy will be three times as old as she is now. How old is Joy now?

   First, circle what you must find: *Joy now.* You may want to set up a chart for this problem.

	Now	**In Eight Years**
Joy	x	$x + 8$

Let Joy's age now equal x. Therefore Joy's age eight years from now will be $x + 8$. Now, use the problem to set up an equation:

In eight years, Joy will be three times as old as she is now.
$$\underbrace{x+8}_{} \quad \underbrace{=}_{} \quad \underbrace{3}_{} \quad \underbrace{\text{times}}_{} \quad \underbrace{x}_{}$$

$$x + 8 - x = 3x - x$$
$$8 = 2x$$
$$\frac{8}{2} = \frac{2x}{2}$$
$$4 = x$$

Therefore, Joy's age now is 4 years old.

5. Matt is six years older than Hector. In two years, Matt will be twice as old as Hector. How old is Hector now?

First, circle what you must find: *Hector now.* Let Hector now equal x. Therefore, Matt now equals $x + 6$. You may want to set up a chart.

	Now	In Two Years
Hector	x	$x + 2$
Matt	$x + 6$	$x + 8$

Now, use the problem to set up an equation:

In two years Matt will be twice as old as Hector.
$$\underbrace{x+8}_{} \quad \underbrace{=}_{} \quad \underbrace{2}_{} \quad \underbrace{\text{times}}_{} \quad \underbrace{(x+2)}_{}$$

$$x + 8 = 2x + 4$$
$$x + 8 - x = 2x + 4 - x$$
$$8 = x + 4$$
$$8 - 4 = x + 4 - 4$$
$$4 = x$$

Therefore, Hector now is 4 years old.

Geometry

Example:

If a rectangle's length is twice its width and its area is 200 square inches, find its length and width.

First, circle what you must find: *length and width.* Now let x denote the rectangle's width. Therefore, its length will be twice the width, or $2x$. Now, set up an equation.

$$\underbrace{\text{Width}}_{(x)} \text{ times } \underbrace{\text{length}}_{(2x)} \underbrace{\text{equals}}_{=} \underbrace{\text{area.}}_{200}$$

$$2x^2 = 200$$
$$\frac{2x^2}{2} = \frac{200}{2}$$
$$x^2 = 100$$

$$x = 10 \text{ and } 2x = 20$$

Therefore, the width is 10 inches and the length is 20 inches. (***Note:*** Drawing diagrams in geometry problems is often helpful.)

Practice: Geometry Problems

1. In a triangle, the smallest angle is 20° less than the largest angle. The third angle is 10° more than the smallest angle. What is the measure of each angle?

2. The length of a rectangle is 6 inches less than four times the width. If the perimeter of the rectangle is 28 inches, find its length and width.

3. Each of the equal sides of an isosceles triangle is 5 inches more than twice the third side. If the perimeter of the triangle is 45 inches, find the sides of the triangle.

4. One angle of a triangle is 44°. The second angle is 4° larger than the third angle. How many degrees are in the measure of the other two angles?

5. Find the measure of the sides of a rectangle if the length is 5 inches longer than the width and the perimeter is 50 inches.

Answers: Geometry Problems

1. In a triangle, the smallest angle is 20° less than the largest angle. The third angle is 10° more than the smallest angle. What is the measure of each angle?

First, circle what you must find: *the measure of each angle.* Now let the largest angle be known as x. Therefore, the smallest angle, because it is 20° less than the largest, will be $x - 20$. The third angle is 10° more than the smallest, or $x - 20 + 10$, which equals $x - 10$. Now, set up the equation:

$$\underbrace{\text{The sum of the degrees in each angle of a triangle}}_{x + (x - 20) + (x - 10)} \underbrace{\text{equals}}_{=} \underbrace{180°.}_{180}$$

$$3x - 30 = 180$$
$$3x - 30 + 30 = 180 + 30$$
$$3x = 210$$
$$\frac{3x}{3} = \frac{210}{3}$$
$$x = 70$$

The largest angle is 70°; the smallest angle is $70 - 20 = 50°$; the third angle is $70 - 10 = 60°$.

2. The length of a rectangle is 6 inches less than four times the width. If the perimeter of the rectangle is 28 inches, find its length and width.

First, circle what you must find: *length and width.* Now, let x denote the width of the rectangle. Therefore, its length will be $4x - 6$ (6 less than four times the width). Now, set up the equation:

The perimeter of the rectangle equals 28 inches.

or

$$\underbrace{\text{2 widths}}_{2x} \underbrace{\text{plus}}_{+} \underbrace{\text{2 lengths}}_{2(4x - 6)} \underbrace{\text{equal}}_{=} \underbrace{\text{28}}_{28} \text{ inches}$$

$$2x + 8x - 12 = 28$$
$$10x - 12 = 28$$
$$10x - 12 + 12 = 28 + 12$$
$$10x = 40$$
$$\frac{10x}{10} = \frac{40}{10}$$
$$x = 4$$

Therefore, the width of the rectangle is 4; the length of the rectangle, $4x - 6$, is $(4 \times 4) - 6 = 10$.

3. Each of the equal sides of an isosceles triangle is 5 inches more than twice the third side. If the perimeter of the triangle is 45 inches, find the sides of the triangle.

First, circle what you must find: *sides of the triangle*. Therefore, each of the equal sides will be $2x + 5$. Now, set up the equation:

$$\underbrace{\text{The sum of the sides of a triangle}}\ \underbrace{\text{equals}}\ \underbrace{\text{the perimeter.}}$$
$$x+(2x+5)+(2x+5) \qquad = \qquad 45$$

$$5x + 10 = 45$$

$$5x + 10 - 10 = 45 - 10$$

$$5x = 35$$

$$\frac{5x}{5} = \frac{35}{5}$$

$$x = 7$$

Therefore, one side is 7 and the other two sides are $2x + 5$ each, or $(2 \times 7) + 5 = 19$ for each of the other two sides.

4. One angle of a triangle is 44°. The second angle is 4° larger than the third angle. How many degrees are in the measure of the other two angles?

First, circle what you must find: *the other two angles*. Now, let the third angle be denoted as x. Then the second angle will be $x + 4$. Now, set up an equation:

$$\underbrace{\text{The sum of the angles in a triangle}}\ \underbrace{\text{equals}}\ \underbrace{180°.}$$
$$44+x+(x+4) \qquad = \qquad 180$$

$$2x + 48 = 180$$

$$2x + 48 - 48 = 180 - 48$$

$$2x = 132$$

$$\frac{2x}{2} = \frac{132}{2}$$

$$x = 66$$

$$x + 4 = 70$$

Therefore, the other two angles of the triangle are 66° and 70°.

5. Find the measure of the sides of a rectangle if the length is 5 inches longer than the width and the perimeter is 50 inches.

First, circle what you must find in the problem: *the measure of the sides.* Now, let the width be denoted as x. Therefore, the length will be $x + 5$. Now, set up the equation:

$$\underbrace{\text{2 widths}}_{2x} \underbrace{\text{plus}}_{+} \underbrace{\text{2 lengths}}_{2(x+5)} \underbrace{\text{equal}}_{=} \underbrace{\text{the perimeter.}}_{50}$$

$$2x + 2x + 10 = 50$$

$$4x + 10 = 50$$

$$4x + 10 - 10 = 50 - 10$$

$$4x = 40$$

$$\frac{4x}{4} = \frac{40}{4}$$

$$x = 10$$

Therefore, the width is 10 and the length is $x + 5 = 15$.

Work

Example:

Ernie can plow a field alone in four hours. It takes Sid five hours to plow the same field alone. If they work together (and each has a plow), how long should it take to plow the field?

First, circle what you must find: *how long . . . together.* Work problems of this nature may be solved by using the following equation:

$$\frac{1}{\text{first person's rate}} + \frac{1}{\text{second person's rate}} + \frac{1}{\text{third person's rate}} + \ldots = \frac{1}{\text{rate together}}$$

Therefore,

$$\frac{1}{\text{Ernie's rate}} + \frac{1}{\text{Sid's rate}} = \frac{1}{\text{rate together}}$$

$$\frac{1}{4} + \frac{1}{5} = \frac{1}{t}$$

Find a common denominator:

$$\frac{5}{20} + \frac{4}{20} = \frac{1}{t}$$

$$\frac{9}{20} = \frac{1}{t}$$

Cross-multiply:

$$9t = 20$$

$$\frac{9t}{9} = \frac{20}{9} = 2\frac{2}{9} \text{ hours}$$

Therefore, it will take them $2\frac{2}{9}$ hours working together.

Practice: Work Problems

1. Tom can mow Harry's lawn in exactly three hours. Bill can mow Harry's lawn in exactly six hours. If Harry hires Bill and Tom to work together using two lawn mowers, how long should it take to mow the lawn working together?

2. Tom can paint a house in eight hours. Dick can paint the house in six hours. Harry can also paint the house in six hours. How long should it take to paint the house if they all work together?

3. Working alone, Bill can do a job in 4 hours. With Fred's help, it takes only $2\frac{2}{9}$ hours. How long should it take Fred working alone to do the job?

4. A tank is being filled at a rate of 10 gallons per hour. However, a hole in the tank allows water to run off at a rate of 2 gallons per hour. How long should it take to fill an empty 50-gallon tank?

5. Sue, Maria, and Lucy decide to type Lucy's term paper. Sue can type three chapters per hour, Lucy can type five chapters per hour, and Maria can type six chapters per hour. If Lucy's paper consists of 30 chapters, how long should it take them working together to type the entire paper?

Answers: Work Problems

1. Tom can mow Harry's lawn in exactly three hours. Bill can mow Harry's lawn in exactly six hours. If Harry hires Bill and Tom to work together using two lawn mowers, how lng should it take to mow the lawn working together?

   First, circle what you must find: *how working together . . . together.* Now, using the information given in the problem, plug into the equation:

   $$\frac{1}{A} + \frac{1}{B} = \frac{1}{T}$$

   $$\frac{1}{3} + \frac{1}{6} = \frac{1}{T}$$

$$\frac{2}{6} + \frac{1}{6} = \frac{1}{T}$$

$$\frac{3}{6} = \frac{1}{T}$$

$$\frac{1}{2} = \frac{1}{T}$$

Cross-multiply:

$$T = 2$$

It should take 2 hours working together.

2. Tom can paint a house in eight hours. Dick can paint the house in six hours. Harry can also paint the house in six hours. How long should it take to paint the house if they all work together?

   First, circle what you must find: *how long . . . together.* Now, using the information given in the problem, plug into the equation:

   $$\frac{1}{A} + \frac{1}{B} + \frac{1}{C} = \frac{1}{T}$$

   $$\frac{1}{8} + \frac{1}{6} + \frac{1}{6} = \frac{1}{T}$$

   $$\frac{3}{24} + \frac{4}{24} + \frac{4}{24} = \frac{1}{T}$$

   $$\frac{11}{24} = \frac{1}{T}$$

   Cross-multiply:

   $$11T = 24$$

   $$\frac{11T}{11} = \frac{24}{11}$$

   $$T = 2\frac{2}{11} \text{ hours}$$

   Therefore, it should take $2\frac{2}{11}$ hours working together.

3. Working alone, Bill can do a job in 4 hours. With Fred's help, it takes only $2\frac{2}{9}$ hours. How long should it take Fred working alone to do the job?

   First, circle what you must find: *how long . . . Fred . . . alone.* Now, using the information given in the problem, plug into the equation:

$$\frac{1}{A} + \frac{1}{B} = \frac{1}{T}$$

$$\frac{1}{x} + \frac{1}{4} = \frac{1}{2\frac{2}{9}}$$

$$\frac{1}{x} + \frac{1}{4} = \frac{1}{\frac{20}{9}}$$

$$\frac{1}{x} + \frac{1}{4} = \frac{9}{20}$$

$$\frac{1}{x} = \frac{9}{20} - \frac{1}{4}$$

$$\frac{1}{x} = \frac{9}{20} - \frac{5}{20}$$

$$\frac{1}{x} = \frac{4}{20}$$

Cross-multiply:

$$4x = 20$$

$$x = 5 \text{ hours}$$

Therefore, it should take Fred 5 hours working alone.

4. A tank is being filled at a rate of 10 gallons per hour. However, a hole in the tank allows water to run off at a rate of 2 gallons per hour. How long should it take to fill an empty 50-gallon tank?

First, circle what you must find in the problem: *how long . . . to fill an empty 50-gallon tank.* Note that, because the hole allows water to leave at 2 gallons per hour, the tank is being filled at only $10 - 2 = 8$ gallons per hour. Therefore, a 50-gallon tank will take $\frac{50}{8} = 6.25$ hours to fill.

5. Sue, Maria, and Lucy decide to type Lucy's term paper. Sue can type three chapters per hour, Lucy can type five chapters per hour, and Maria can type six chapters per hour. If Lucy's paper consists of 30 chapters, how long should it take them, working together, to type the entire paper?

First, circle what you must find in the problem: *how long . . . working together.* In this type of problem, their combined rate may be found by *adding* their chapters typed each hour:

$3 + 5 + 6 = 14$ chapters typed each hour

Now, simply divide 30 by 14 and you get $2\frac{2}{14}$ or $2\frac{1}{7}$ hours.

Therefore, together it should take them $2\frac{1}{7}$ hours.

Mixture

Example:

Coffee worth $1.05 per pound is mixed with coffee worth 85¢ per pound to obtain 20 pounds of a mixture worth 90¢ per pound. How many pounds of each type are used?

First, circle what you're trying to find: *how many pounds of each type.* Now, let the number of pounds of $1.05 coffee be denoted as x. Therefore, the number of pounds of 85¢-per-pound coffee must be the difference between the 20 pounds and the x pounds, or $20 - x$. Make a chart for the cost of each type and the total cost:

	Cost per Pound	Amount in Pounds	Total Cost of Each
$1.05 coffee	$1.05	x	$1.05x
85¢ coffee	$0.85	$20 - x$	$0.85(20 - x)$
Mixture	$0.90	20	$0.90(20)$

Now set up the equation:

$$\underbrace{\$1.05x}_{\text{Total cost of one type}} \underbrace{+}_{\text{plus}} \underbrace{0.85(20-x)}_{\text{total cost of other type}} \underbrace{=}_{\text{equal}} \underbrace{0.90(20)}_{\text{total cost of mixture.}}$$

$$1.05x + 17.00 - 0.85x = 18.00$$

$$17.00 + 0.20x = 18.00$$

$$-17.00 + 17.00 + 0.20x = 18.00 - 17.00$$

$$0.20x = 1.00$$

$$\frac{0.20x}{0.20} = \frac{1.00}{0.20}$$

$$x = 5$$

Therefore, 5 pounds of coffee worth $1.05 are used. And $20 - x = 20 - 5 = 15$ pounds of 85¢-per-pound coffee are used.

Practice: Mixture Problems

1. Tea worth 75¢ per pound is mixed with tea worth 90¢ per pound to produce 10 pounds of a mixture worth 85¢ per pound. How much of each type is used?

2. One solution is 75% saltwater and another solution is 50% saltwater. How many gallons of each should be used to make 10 gallons of a solution that is 60% saltwater?

3. Ms. Gomez invests $1,000, part of it in a bank paying 8% interest and the remainder in a bank paying 10% interest annually. If her total income for one year was $94, how much has she invested at each rate?

4. Ellen has collected nickels and dimes worth a total of $6.30. If she has collected 70 coins in all and each is worth face value, how many of each kind does she have?

5. At a game, adult tickets sold for $2.50 and children's tickets sold for $1.50. If 400 tickets were sold and the income was $900, how many of each type were sold?

Answers: Mixture Problems

1. Tea worth 75¢ per pound is mixed with tea worth 90¢ per pound to produce 10 pounds of a mixture worth 85¢ per pound. How much of each type is used?

   First, circle what you're trying to find: *how much of each type.* Now let the number of pounds of 75¢ tea be denoted by x. Then the number of pounds of 90¢ tea is what's left of the total, or $10 - x$. Now make a chart.

	Cost per Pound	Amount in Pounds	Total Cost of Each
75¢ tea	$0.75	x	0.75x
90¢ tea	$0.90	$(10 - x)$	0.90(10 − x)
Mixture	$0.85	10	10(0.85)

   Now set up the equation:

   $$\underbrace{\text{Total cost of one type}}_{0.75x} \underbrace{\text{plus}}_{+} \underbrace{\text{total cost of other type}}_{0.90(10-x)} \underbrace{\text{equal}}_{=} \underbrace{\text{total cost of mixture.}}_{10(0.85)}$$

   $$0.75x + 9 - 0.90x = 8.5$$
   $$-0.15x + 9 - 9 = 8.5 - 9$$
   $$-0.15x = -0.5$$

$$\frac{-0.15x}{-0.15} = \frac{-0.5}{-0.15}$$

$$x = 3\frac{1}{3}$$

Therefore, $3\frac{1}{3}$ pounds of 75¢ tea was used. And the amount of the 90¢ tea is $10 - x = 10 - 3\frac{1}{3} = 6\frac{2}{3}$ pounds.

2. One solution is 75% saltwater and another solution is 50% saltwater. How many gallons of each should be used to make 10 gallons of a solution that is 60% saltwater?

First, circle what you're trying to find: *how many gallons of each.* Now, let the number of gallons of 75% saltwater be x. Then the remainder of the amount of the 50% solution will be what's left from the total of 10 gallons, or $10 - x$. Now set up a chart:

	Rate	Amount of Solution	Amount of Salt
75% solution	0.75	x	0.75x
50% solution	0.50	$(10 - x)$	0.50(10 − x)
Mixture	0.60	10	0.60(10)

Now set up the equation.

$$\underbrace{\text{Salt in one solution}}_{0.75x} \underbrace{\text{plus}}_{+} \underbrace{\text{salt in other solution}}_{0.50(10-x)} \underbrace{\text{equal}}_{=} \underbrace{\text{salt in mixture.}}_{0.60(10)}$$

$$0.75x + 5 - 0.50x = 6$$

$$0.25x + 5 = 6$$

$$0.25x + 5 - 5 = 6 - 0.5$$

$$0.25x = 1$$

$$\frac{0.25x}{0.25} = \frac{1}{0.25}$$

$$x = 4$$

Therefore, 4 gallons of 75% solution are used and $10 - 4 = 6$ gallons of 50% solution are used.

3. Ms. Gomez invests $1,000, part of it in a bank paying 8% interest and the remainder in a bank paying 10% interest annually. If her total income for one year was $94, how much has she invested at each rate?

First, circle what you're trying to find: *how much . . . invested at each rate*. Now, let the amount invested at 8% be denoted as x. Therefore, the remainder invested at 10% will be $1,000 - x$. Now set up a chart:

Amount Invested	Interest Rate	Interest Income
x	0.08	$0.08x$
$(1,000 - x)$	0.10	$0.10(1,000 - x)$

Now set up the equation.

Interest income from 8% plus interest income from 10% equal total income.

$$0.08x \quad + \quad 0.10(1,000 - x) \quad = \quad 94$$

$$0.08x + 100 - 0.10x = 94$$

$$-0.02x + 100 = 94$$

$$-0.02x + 100 - 100 = 94 - 100$$

$$-0.02x = -6$$

$$\frac{-0.02x}{-0.02} = \frac{-6}{-0.02}$$

$$x = 300$$

Therefore, the amount invested at 8% was $300, and the remainder of the $1,000, or $700, was invested at 10%.

4. Ellen has collected nickels and dimes worth a total of $6.30. If she has collected 70 coins in all and each is worth face value, how many of each kind does she have?

First, circle what you must find: *how many of each kind*. Now, let x denote the number of nickels. Therefore, the remainder of the coins $(70 - x)$ will be the number of dimes. Now set up a chart:

Type of Coin	Number of Coins	Value of Each Coin	Total Value
Nickels	x	0.05	$0.05x$
Dimes	$(70 - x)$	0.10	$0.10(70 - x)$

Now set up the equation:

$$\underbrace{\text{Total value of nickels}}_{0.05x} \underbrace{\text{plus}}_{+} \underbrace{\text{total value of dimes}}_{0.10(70-x)} \underbrace{\text{equal}}_{=} \underbrace{\text{total worth.}}_{6.30}$$

$$0.05x + 7 - 0.10x = 6.30$$

$$-0.05x + 7 = 6.30$$

$$-0.05x + 7 - 7 = 6.30 - 7$$

$$-0.05x = -0.70$$

$$\frac{-0.05x}{-0.05} = \frac{-0.70}{-0.05}$$

$$x = 14$$

Therefore, Ellen has 14 nickels and $70 - 14 = 56$ dimes.

5. At a game, adult tickets sold for $2.50 and children's tickets sold for $1.50. If 400 tickets were sold and the income was $900, how many of each type were sold?

First, circle what you must find: *how many of each type.* Now, let x denote the number of adult tickets sold. Therefore, the remainder $(400 - x)$ will denote the number of children's tickets sold. Set up a chart:

Type of Ticket	Number of Tickets	Cost Per Ticket	Income
Adults	x	2.50	$2.50x$
Children	$(400 - x)$	1.50	$1.50(400 - x)$

Now set up the equation:

$$\underbrace{\text{Income from adult tickets}}_{2.50x} \underbrace{\text{plus}}_{+} \underbrace{\text{income from children's tickets}}_{1.50(400-x)} \underbrace{\text{equal}}_{=} \underbrace{\text{total income.}}_{900}$$

$$2.50x + 600 - 1.50x = 900$$

$$x + 600 = 900$$

$$x + 600 - 600 = 900 - 600$$

$$x = 300$$

Therefore, 300 adult tickets were sold and 100 children's tickets were sold.

Word Problems Review Test

Questions

1. What is the simple interest on a loan of $5,000 for eight years at an annual interest rate of 14%?

2. If a woman earns $2,000 simple interest over four years on an investment of $5,000, what is the annual interest rate she receives?

3. Mr. Lincoln deposits $4,000 in a savings account that pays 12% annually, but interest is compounded quarterly. What is the total in his account after one year? (**Remember:** 3% interest will be paid each quarter.)

4. If Jim can bake 27 pies in 12 days, how many pies can he bake in 20 days?

5. If p pencils cost k cents, at the same price how much will q pencils cost?

6. How long will it take a train traveling at an average speed of 80 miles per hour to travel a distance of 5,600 miles?

7. Two automobiles, A and B, leave at the same time and travel the same route. Automobile A goes at a rate of 55 miles per hour. Automobile B travels at a rate of 40 miles per hour. How many hours after they begin their trip will automobile A be 60 miles ahead of automobile B?

8. Mrs. Baum won $5,600 on a television quiz show. If she has to pay 20% of her winnings to the Internal Revenue Service, how much of her winnings will she have left?

9. A prized Amazon yellow nape parrot is placed on sale at a bird show for $900. It doesn't sell immediately, so its owner discounts the bird 30%. When the parrot still does not interest any buyers, the owner offers another 20% discount off the new price. What is the final price of the bird?

10. Last year's Los Angeles Dodgers attendance was 2,800,000. This year's attendance was 3,200,000. What was the Dodgers' percent increase in attendance?

11. If Arnold's 2010 salary reflects a percent drop of 15% from the previous year, what was his 2010 salary if in 2009 he earned $60,000?

12. Three consecutive odd integers add up to total 33. What is the smallest of the three integers?

13. A green flag costs ten times the price of a blue flag. A red flag costs half the price of a green flag. An orange flag costs $10 less than a red flag. If the four different color flags cost a total of $200, what is the price of an orange flag?

14. Judith is exactly 18 years older than Brad. If today the sum of their ages is 52, how old will Brad be in one year?

15. Carole is 7 years older than Lenn. Ann is twice as old as Lenn, and her mother is 65. If the total age of all four persons is 116, how old was Lenn 5 years ago?

16. One angle of a triangle is twice as big as the smallest angle, and the third angle is three times as big as the smallest angle. What are the three angles of the triangle?

17. If in quadrilateral *ABCD*, side *AB* is twice side *BC*, side *BC* is twice side *CD*, and side *CD* is twice side *DA*, what is the length of side *DA* if the perimeter of *ABCD* is 75 inches?

18. Bob can cut a lawn in four hours. Bette can cut the same lawn in three hours. If they both use lawn mowers and work together, how long should it take them to cut the lawn?

19. Gina can build a house in 12 months alone. Bart can build a house in six months alone. How long should it take them to build a house if they work together?

20. A chemistry teacher has two quarts of 25% acid solution and one quart of 40% acid solution. If she mixes these, what will be the concentration of acid in the final mixture?

21. Programs sell at a baseball game for $2 each, and scorecards sell for 75¢ each. If a total of 200 items was sold (programs *and* scorecards) for a cash income of $250, how many of each were sold?

Answers

Page numbers following each answer refer to the review section applicable to this problem type.

1. $5,600 (p. 320)

2. 10% (p. 320)

3. $4,502.04 (p. 323)

4. 45 pies (p. 326)

5. $\dfrac{qk}{p}$ or $\dfrac{kq}{p}$ (p. 326)

6. 70 hours (p. 329)

7. 4 hours (p. 329)

8. $4,480 (p. 329)

9. $504 (p. 323)

10. approximately 14.3% (p. 336)

11. $51,000 (p. 336)

12. 9 (p. 339)

13. $40 (p. 339)

14. 18 years old (p. 343)

15. 6 years old (p. 343)

16. 30°, 60°, 90° (p. 347)

17. 5 inches (p. 347)

18. $1\dfrac{5}{7}$ hours (p. 351)

19. 4 months (p. 351)

20. 30% acid concentration (p. 355)

21. 80 programs, 120 scorecards (p. 355)

Word Problems Glossary of Terms

annual: Once per year.

balance: Beginning balance is the principal in interest problems. Ending balance is the principal plus interest acquired.

biannual: Twice per year, or every six months.

compounded: In interest problems, the interest is to be added to the principal at specific intervals and used in the computation of the next interest amount.

consecutive: What comes immediately after. For example, consecutive numbers are 1, 2, 3, 4, and so on. Consecutive odd numbers are 1, 3, 5, 7, 9, and so on.

difference: The result obtained by subtracting.

dividend: In interest problems, the amount of interest paid.

equation: A number sentence with a balance relationship between numbers or symbols.

evaluate: To determine the value or numerical amount.

exceeds: Is more than.

inequality: A number sentence in which the relationships between numbers or symbols are not equal.

integer: A whole number or the opposite of a whole number. For example, 6, 109, 0, –52.

percentage change: Expressed also as percent rise, percent difference, percent increase, percent decrease, percent drop, and so on. Found by dividing the actual amount of change by the numerical starting point and then converting to a percent.

principal: The amount of money invested or loaned upon which interest is paid.

product: The result obtained by multiplying.

quarterly: Four times per year, or every three months.

quotient: The result obtained by dividing.

rate: How fast an object moves (speed).

ratio: A comparison between items. For example, the ratio of 2 to 3 may be written as 2:3 or $\frac{2}{3}$.

semiannual: Twice per year, or every six months.

simple interest: Interest calculated by multiplying the principal with the interest rate with the length of time of the investment, $I = prt$.

simplify: To combine several terms into fewer terms.

speed: The rate at which an object moves.

sum: The result obtained by adding.

value: The numerical amount.

velocity: The speed, or rate, at which an object moves.

PART II

STRATEGIES AND PRACTICE

This section is designed to introduce you to important test-taking strategies and to some typical problem types encountered on many standardized exams. Although some of these question types do not appear on all standardized tests, you'll find it valuable to practice them, as such practice will increase your understanding and strengthen your mastery of concepts.

Your most effective plan of attack to best prepare for the test you must take is to first ensure that you have a firm grasp of the basics, which will enable you to answer the easy or average-in-difficulty problems correctly. Only then should you move on to the more difficult problems.

Because standardized tests vary greatly in difficulty and because the purpose of this guide is to be instructional for as wide a range of test takers as possible, some extremely easy and extremely difficult problem types are not given. The practice problems on the following pages encompass many problem types and are meant to give a sampling of a variety of questions.

Answer Key pages are cross-referenced to the appropriate review section. If you want to review the concepts again after working the practice problems, turn to the page indicated after that question number.

It's a good idea to accustom yourself to answering questions on a scoring sheet, because that's what you must do when taking the standardized tests. When you practice, be sure to blacken the space completely, and if you change an answer, erase thoroughly.

For these practice sections, the arithmetic and data analysis, algebra, geometry, and word-problem questions have been separated to help you strengthen your skills and pinpoint your problem areas. *Be aware that standardized tests do not separate arithmetic, algebra, and geometry sections in this way.* Rather, all these areas are combined under one question type (such as data sufficiency).

Answer Sheet for Practice Sections

(Remove This Sheet and Use It to Mark Your Answers)

Mathematical Ability

Arithmetic	Algebra	Geometry	Procedure Problems

Arithmetic

1 Ⓐ Ⓑ Ⓒ Ⓓ Ⓔ
2 Ⓐ Ⓑ Ⓒ Ⓓ Ⓔ
3 Ⓐ Ⓑ Ⓒ Ⓓ Ⓔ
4 Ⓐ Ⓑ Ⓒ Ⓓ Ⓔ
5 Ⓐ Ⓑ Ⓒ Ⓓ Ⓔ
6 Ⓐ Ⓑ Ⓒ Ⓓ Ⓔ
7 Ⓐ Ⓑ Ⓒ Ⓓ Ⓔ
8 Ⓐ Ⓑ Ⓒ Ⓓ Ⓔ
9 Ⓐ Ⓑ Ⓒ Ⓓ Ⓔ
10 Ⓐ Ⓑ Ⓒ Ⓓ Ⓔ
11 Ⓐ Ⓑ Ⓒ Ⓓ Ⓔ
12 Ⓐ Ⓑ Ⓒ Ⓓ Ⓔ
13 Ⓐ Ⓑ Ⓒ Ⓓ Ⓔ
14 Ⓐ Ⓑ Ⓒ Ⓓ Ⓔ
15 Ⓐ Ⓑ Ⓒ Ⓓ Ⓔ
16 Ⓐ Ⓑ Ⓒ Ⓓ Ⓔ
17 Ⓐ Ⓑ Ⓒ Ⓓ Ⓔ
18 Ⓐ Ⓑ Ⓒ Ⓓ Ⓔ
19 Ⓐ Ⓑ Ⓒ Ⓓ Ⓔ
20 Ⓐ Ⓑ Ⓒ Ⓓ Ⓔ
21 Ⓐ Ⓑ Ⓒ Ⓓ Ⓔ
22 Ⓐ Ⓑ Ⓒ Ⓓ Ⓔ
23 Ⓐ Ⓑ Ⓒ Ⓓ Ⓔ
24 Ⓐ Ⓑ Ⓒ Ⓓ Ⓔ
25 Ⓐ Ⓑ Ⓒ Ⓓ Ⓔ
26 Ⓐ Ⓑ Ⓒ Ⓓ Ⓔ
27 Ⓐ Ⓑ Ⓒ Ⓓ Ⓔ
28 Ⓐ Ⓑ Ⓒ Ⓓ Ⓔ
29 Ⓐ Ⓑ Ⓒ Ⓓ Ⓔ
30 Ⓐ Ⓑ Ⓒ Ⓓ Ⓔ

Algebra

1 Ⓐ Ⓑ Ⓒ Ⓓ Ⓔ
2 Ⓐ Ⓑ Ⓒ Ⓓ Ⓔ
3 Ⓐ Ⓑ Ⓒ Ⓓ Ⓔ
4 Ⓐ Ⓑ Ⓒ Ⓓ Ⓔ
5 Ⓐ Ⓑ Ⓒ Ⓓ Ⓔ
6 Ⓐ Ⓑ Ⓒ Ⓓ Ⓔ
7 Ⓐ Ⓑ Ⓒ Ⓓ Ⓔ
8 Ⓐ Ⓑ Ⓒ Ⓓ Ⓔ
9 Ⓐ Ⓑ Ⓒ Ⓓ Ⓔ
10 Ⓐ Ⓑ Ⓒ Ⓓ Ⓔ
11 Ⓐ Ⓑ Ⓒ Ⓓ Ⓔ
12 Ⓐ Ⓑ Ⓒ Ⓓ Ⓔ
13 Ⓐ Ⓑ Ⓒ Ⓓ Ⓔ
14 Ⓐ Ⓑ Ⓒ Ⓓ Ⓔ
15 Ⓐ Ⓑ Ⓒ Ⓓ Ⓔ
16 Ⓐ Ⓑ Ⓒ Ⓓ Ⓔ
17 Ⓐ Ⓑ Ⓒ Ⓓ Ⓔ
18 Ⓐ Ⓑ Ⓒ Ⓓ Ⓔ
19 Ⓐ Ⓑ Ⓒ Ⓓ Ⓔ
20 Ⓐ Ⓑ Ⓒ Ⓓ Ⓔ
21 Ⓐ Ⓑ Ⓒ Ⓓ Ⓔ
22 Ⓐ Ⓑ Ⓒ Ⓓ Ⓔ
23 Ⓐ Ⓑ Ⓒ Ⓓ Ⓔ
24 Ⓐ Ⓑ Ⓒ Ⓓ Ⓔ
25 Ⓐ Ⓑ Ⓒ Ⓓ Ⓔ

Geometry

1 Ⓐ Ⓑ Ⓒ Ⓓ Ⓔ
2 Ⓐ Ⓑ Ⓒ Ⓓ Ⓔ
3 Ⓐ Ⓑ Ⓒ Ⓓ Ⓔ
4 Ⓐ Ⓑ Ⓒ Ⓓ Ⓔ
5 Ⓐ Ⓑ Ⓒ Ⓓ Ⓔ
6 Ⓐ Ⓑ Ⓒ Ⓓ Ⓔ
7 Ⓐ Ⓑ Ⓒ Ⓓ Ⓔ
8 Ⓐ Ⓑ Ⓒ Ⓓ Ⓔ
9 Ⓐ Ⓑ Ⓒ Ⓓ Ⓔ
10 Ⓐ Ⓑ Ⓒ Ⓓ Ⓔ
11 Ⓐ Ⓑ Ⓒ Ⓓ Ⓔ
12 Ⓐ Ⓑ Ⓒ Ⓓ Ⓔ
13 Ⓐ Ⓑ Ⓒ Ⓓ Ⓔ
14 Ⓐ Ⓑ Ⓒ Ⓓ Ⓔ
15 Ⓐ Ⓑ Ⓒ Ⓓ Ⓔ
16 Ⓐ Ⓑ Ⓒ Ⓓ Ⓔ
17 Ⓐ Ⓑ Ⓒ Ⓓ Ⓔ
18 Ⓐ Ⓑ Ⓒ Ⓓ Ⓔ
19 Ⓐ Ⓑ Ⓒ Ⓓ Ⓔ
20 Ⓐ Ⓑ Ⓒ Ⓓ Ⓔ
21 Ⓐ Ⓑ Ⓒ Ⓓ Ⓔ
22 Ⓐ Ⓑ Ⓒ Ⓓ Ⓔ
23 Ⓐ Ⓑ Ⓒ Ⓓ Ⓔ
24 Ⓐ Ⓑ Ⓒ Ⓓ Ⓔ
25 Ⓐ Ⓑ Ⓒ Ⓓ Ⓔ

Procedure Problems

1 Ⓐ Ⓑ Ⓒ Ⓓ Ⓔ
2 Ⓐ Ⓑ Ⓒ Ⓓ Ⓔ
3 Ⓐ Ⓑ Ⓒ Ⓓ Ⓔ
4 Ⓐ Ⓑ Ⓒ Ⓓ Ⓔ
5 Ⓐ Ⓑ Ⓒ Ⓓ Ⓔ
6 Ⓐ Ⓑ Ⓒ Ⓓ Ⓔ
7 Ⓐ Ⓑ Ⓒ Ⓓ Ⓔ
8 Ⓐ Ⓑ Ⓒ Ⓓ Ⓔ
9 Ⓐ Ⓑ Ⓒ Ⓓ Ⓔ
10 Ⓐ Ⓑ Ⓒ Ⓓ Ⓔ

Quantitative Comparison

Arithmetic	Algebra	Geometry

Arithmetic						Algebra						Geometry					
1	Ⓐ	Ⓑ	Ⓒ	Ⓓ	Ⓔ	1	Ⓐ	Ⓑ	Ⓒ	Ⓓ	Ⓔ	1	Ⓐ	Ⓑ	Ⓒ	Ⓓ	Ⓔ
2	Ⓐ	Ⓑ	Ⓒ	Ⓓ	Ⓔ	2	Ⓐ	Ⓑ	Ⓒ	Ⓓ	Ⓔ	2	Ⓐ	Ⓑ	Ⓒ	Ⓓ	Ⓔ
3	Ⓐ	Ⓑ	Ⓒ	Ⓓ	Ⓔ	3	Ⓐ	Ⓑ	Ⓒ	Ⓓ	Ⓔ	3	Ⓐ	Ⓑ	Ⓒ	Ⓓ	Ⓔ
4	Ⓐ	Ⓑ	Ⓒ	Ⓓ	Ⓔ	4	Ⓐ	Ⓑ	Ⓒ	Ⓓ	Ⓔ	4	Ⓐ	Ⓑ	Ⓒ	Ⓓ	Ⓔ
5	Ⓐ	Ⓑ	Ⓒ	Ⓓ	Ⓔ	5	Ⓐ	Ⓑ	Ⓒ	Ⓓ	Ⓔ	5	Ⓐ	Ⓑ	Ⓒ	Ⓓ	Ⓔ
6	Ⓐ	Ⓑ	Ⓒ	Ⓓ	Ⓔ	6	Ⓐ	Ⓑ	Ⓒ	Ⓓ	Ⓔ	6	Ⓐ	Ⓑ	Ⓒ	Ⓓ	Ⓔ
7	Ⓐ	Ⓑ	Ⓒ	Ⓓ	Ⓔ	7	Ⓐ	Ⓑ	Ⓒ	Ⓓ	Ⓔ	7	Ⓐ	Ⓑ	Ⓒ	Ⓓ	Ⓔ
8	Ⓐ	Ⓑ	Ⓒ	Ⓓ	Ⓔ	8	Ⓐ	Ⓑ	Ⓒ	Ⓓ	Ⓔ	8	Ⓐ	Ⓑ	Ⓒ	Ⓓ	Ⓔ
9	Ⓐ	Ⓑ	Ⓒ	Ⓓ	Ⓔ	9	Ⓐ	Ⓑ	Ⓒ	Ⓓ	Ⓔ	9	Ⓐ	Ⓑ	Ⓒ	Ⓓ	Ⓔ
10	Ⓐ	Ⓑ	Ⓒ	Ⓓ	Ⓔ	10	Ⓐ	Ⓑ	Ⓒ	Ⓓ	Ⓔ	10	Ⓐ	Ⓑ	Ⓒ	Ⓓ	Ⓔ
11	Ⓐ	Ⓑ	Ⓒ	Ⓓ	Ⓔ	11	Ⓐ	Ⓑ	Ⓒ	Ⓓ	Ⓔ	11	Ⓐ	Ⓑ	Ⓒ	Ⓓ	Ⓔ
12	Ⓐ	Ⓑ	Ⓒ	Ⓓ	Ⓔ	12	Ⓐ	Ⓑ	Ⓒ	Ⓓ	Ⓔ	12	Ⓐ	Ⓑ	Ⓒ	Ⓓ	Ⓔ
13	Ⓐ	Ⓑ	Ⓒ	Ⓓ	Ⓔ	13	Ⓐ	Ⓑ	Ⓒ	Ⓓ	Ⓔ	13	Ⓐ	Ⓑ	Ⓒ	Ⓓ	Ⓔ
14	Ⓐ	Ⓑ	Ⓒ	Ⓓ	Ⓔ	14	Ⓐ	Ⓑ	Ⓒ	Ⓓ	Ⓔ	14	Ⓐ	Ⓑ	Ⓒ	Ⓓ	Ⓔ
15	Ⓐ	Ⓑ	Ⓒ	Ⓓ	Ⓔ	15	Ⓐ	Ⓑ	Ⓒ	Ⓓ	Ⓔ	15	Ⓐ	Ⓑ	Ⓒ	Ⓓ	Ⓔ

Data Sufficiency

Arithmetic	Algebra	Geometry

Arithmetic						Algebra						Geometry					
1	Ⓐ	Ⓑ	Ⓒ	Ⓓ	Ⓔ	1	Ⓐ	Ⓑ	Ⓒ	Ⓓ	Ⓔ	1	Ⓐ	Ⓑ	Ⓒ	Ⓓ	Ⓔ
2	Ⓐ	Ⓑ	Ⓒ	Ⓓ	Ⓔ	2	Ⓐ	Ⓑ	Ⓒ	Ⓓ	Ⓔ	2	Ⓐ	Ⓑ	Ⓒ	Ⓓ	Ⓔ
3	Ⓐ	Ⓑ	Ⓒ	Ⓓ	Ⓔ	3	Ⓐ	Ⓑ	Ⓒ	Ⓓ	Ⓔ	3	Ⓐ	Ⓑ	Ⓒ	Ⓓ	Ⓔ
4	Ⓐ	Ⓑ	Ⓒ	Ⓓ	Ⓔ	4	Ⓐ	Ⓑ	Ⓒ	Ⓓ	Ⓔ	4	Ⓐ	Ⓑ	Ⓒ	Ⓓ	Ⓔ
5	Ⓐ	Ⓑ	Ⓒ	Ⓓ	Ⓔ	5	Ⓐ	Ⓑ	Ⓒ	Ⓓ	Ⓔ	5	Ⓐ	Ⓑ	Ⓒ	Ⓓ	Ⓔ
6	Ⓐ	Ⓑ	Ⓒ	Ⓓ	Ⓔ	6	Ⓐ	Ⓑ	Ⓒ	Ⓓ	Ⓔ	6	Ⓐ	Ⓑ	Ⓒ	Ⓓ	Ⓔ
7	Ⓐ	Ⓑ	Ⓒ	Ⓓ	Ⓔ	7	Ⓐ	Ⓑ	Ⓒ	Ⓓ	Ⓔ	7	Ⓐ	Ⓑ	Ⓒ	Ⓓ	Ⓔ
8	Ⓐ	Ⓑ	Ⓒ	Ⓓ	Ⓔ	8	Ⓐ	Ⓑ	Ⓒ	Ⓓ	Ⓔ	8	Ⓐ	Ⓑ	Ⓒ	Ⓓ	Ⓔ
9	Ⓐ	Ⓑ	Ⓒ	Ⓓ	Ⓔ	9	Ⓐ	Ⓑ	Ⓒ	Ⓓ	Ⓔ	9	Ⓐ	Ⓑ	Ⓒ	Ⓓ	Ⓔ
10	Ⓐ	Ⓑ	Ⓒ	Ⓓ	Ⓔ	10	Ⓐ	Ⓑ	Ⓒ	Ⓓ	Ⓔ	10	Ⓐ	Ⓑ	Ⓒ	Ⓓ	Ⓔ
11	Ⓐ	Ⓑ	Ⓒ	Ⓓ	Ⓔ	11	Ⓐ	Ⓑ	Ⓒ	Ⓓ	Ⓔ	11	Ⓐ	Ⓑ	Ⓒ	Ⓓ	Ⓔ
12	Ⓐ	Ⓑ	Ⓒ	Ⓓ	Ⓔ	12	Ⓐ	Ⓑ	Ⓒ	Ⓓ	Ⓔ	12	Ⓐ	Ⓑ	Ⓒ	Ⓓ	Ⓔ
13	Ⓐ	Ⓑ	Ⓒ	Ⓓ	Ⓔ	13	Ⓐ	Ⓑ	Ⓒ	Ⓓ	Ⓔ	13	Ⓐ	Ⓑ	Ⓒ	Ⓓ	Ⓔ
14	Ⓐ	Ⓑ	Ⓒ	Ⓓ	Ⓔ	14	Ⓐ	Ⓑ	Ⓒ	Ⓓ	Ⓔ	14	Ⓐ	Ⓑ	Ⓒ	Ⓓ	Ⓔ
15	Ⓐ	Ⓑ	Ⓒ	Ⓓ	Ⓔ	15	Ⓐ	Ⓑ	Ⓒ	Ⓓ	Ⓔ	15	Ⓐ	Ⓑ	Ⓒ	Ⓓ	Ⓔ

Mathematical Ability Strategies

Mathematical ability problems are a standard question type appearing on many different examinations. Typically, you must answer a question or solve an equation using the information given in the problem and your knowledge of mathematics. Complex computation is usually not required. Five answer choices are commonly given and you must choose the correct answer from the five. Some exams will have problems that will require you to derive information from graphs and charts.

Information Provided in the Test Booklet

On many standardized exams (SAT, PSAT, and CBEST), some basic mathematical formulas and information may be provided. Although this information may appear at the beginning of the test, you should already have a working knowledge of these facts even if you haven't completely committed them to memory.

Data That May Be Used as Reference for the Test

The area formula for a circle of radius r is: $A = \pi r^2$.
The circumference formula is: $C = 2\pi r$.
A circle is composed of 360°.
A straight angle measures 180°.

Triangle: The sum of the angles of a triangle is 180°.
If $\angle ADB$ is a right angle, then

- The area of triangle ABC is $\dfrac{AC \times BD}{2}$
- $AD^2 + BD^2 = AB^2$

Symbol References

$=$ is equal to	$\leq$ is less than or equal to
$\neq$ is not equal to	$\parallel$ is parallel to
$>$ is greater than	$\perp$ is perpendicular to
$<$ is less than	$\approx$ is approximately equal to
$\geq$ is greater than or equal to	

Suggested Approach with Examples

Here are a number of approaches that can be helpful in attacking many types of mathematics problems. Of course, these strategies will not work on *all* problems, but if you become familiar with them, you'll find they'll be helpful in answering quite a few questions.

Mark Key Words

Circling and/or underlining key words in each question is an effective test-taking technique. Many times, you may be misled because you may overlook a key word in a problem. By circling or underlining these key words, you'll help yourself focus on what you're being asked to find. ***Remember:*** You are allowed to mark and write on your testing booklet. Take advantage of this opportunity.

Examples:

1. In the following number, which digit is in the ten-thousandths place?

   56,874.12398

   (A) 5
   (B) 7
   (C) 2
   (D) 3
   (E) 9

The key word here is *ten-thousandths.* By circling it, you'll be paying closer attention to it. This is the kind of question which, under time pressure and testing pressure, may be easily misread as *ten-thousands* place. Your circling the important words will minimize the possibility of misreading it. Your completed question may look like this after you mark the important words or terms:

1. Which (digit) is in the (ten-thousandths) place?

   56,874.123(9)8

   (A) 5
   (B) 7
   (C) 2
   (D) 3
   (E) 9

2. If 6 yards of ribbon cost $3.96, what is the price per foot?

   (A) $0.22
   (B) $0.66
   (C) $1.32
   (D) $1.96
   (E) $3.96

The key word here is *foot*. Dividing $3.96 by 6 will tell you only the price per *yard*. Notice that $0.66 is one of the choices, B. *You* must still divide by 3 (since there are 3 feet per yard) to find the cost per foot: $0.66 ÷ 3 = $0.22, which is Choice A. Therefore, it would be very helpful to circle the words *price per foot* in the problem.

3. If $3x + 1 = 16$, what is the value of $x - 4$?

   (A) −1
   (B) 1
   (C) 5
   (D) 16
   (E) 19

The key here is to find the value of $x - 4$. Therefore, circle $x - 4$. Note that solving the original equation will tell only the value of x:

$$3x + 1 = 16$$
$$3x = 15$$
$$x = 5$$

Here again, notice that 5 is one of the choices, C. But the question asks for the value of $x - 4$, not just x. To continue, replace x with 5 and solve:

$$x - 4 =$$
$$5 - 4 = 1$$

The correct answer choice is B.

4. Together, a hat and coat cost $125. The coat costs $25 more than the hat. What is the cost of the coat?

   (A) $25
   (B) $50
   (C) $75
   (D) $100
   (E) $125

The key words here are *cost of the coat,* so circle those words. If you solve this algebraically:

> x = the cost of the hat

> $x + 25$ = the cost of the coat (costs $25 more than the hat)

Together they cost $125.

$$(x + 25) + x = 125$$
$$2x + 25 = 125$$
$$2x = 100$$
$$x = 50$$

But this is the cost of the *hat.* Notice that $50 is one of the answer choices, B. Because $x = 50$, $x + 25 = 75$. Therefore, the coat costs $75, which is Choice C. *Always answer the question that is being asked.* Circling the key word or words will help you do that.

Pull Out Information

Pulling information out of the wording of a word problem can make the problem more workable for you. Pull out the given facts and identify which of those facts will help you to work the problem. Not all facts will always be needed to work out the problem.

Examples:

1. Bill is ten years older than his sister. If Bill was 25 years old in 1983, in what year could he have been born?

   (A) 1948
   (B) 1953
   (C) 1958
   (D) 1963
   (E) 1968

The key words here are *in what year* and *could he have been born.* Thus the solution is simple: 1983 − 25 = 1958, which is Choice C. Notice that you pulled out the information *25 years old* and *in 1983.* The fact about Bill's age in comparison to his sister's age was not needed and was not pulled out.

2. Bob is 20 years old. He works for his father for $\frac{3}{4}$ of the year, and he works for his brother for the rest of the year. What is the ratio of the time Bob spends working for his brother to the time he spends working for his father per year?

(A) $\frac{1}{4}$

(B) $\frac{1}{3}$

(C) $\frac{3}{4}$

(D) $\frac{4}{3}$

(E) $\frac{4}{1}$

The key word *rest* points to the answer:

$$1 - \frac{3}{4} = \frac{4}{4} - \frac{3}{4} = \frac{1}{4} \text{ (the part of the year Bob works for his brother)}$$

Also, a key is the way in which the ratio is to be written. The problem becomes that of finding the ratio of $\frac{1}{4}$ to $\frac{3}{4}$:

$$\frac{\frac{1}{4}}{\frac{3}{4}} = \frac{1}{4} \div \frac{3}{4} = \frac{1}{\cancel{4}} \times \frac{\cancel{4}}{3} = \frac{1}{3}$$

Therefore the answer is Choice B. Note that here Bob's age is not needed to solve the problem.

Sometimes you may not have sufficient information to solve the problem. *For example:*

3. The average rainfall for the first few months of 2005 was 4 inches. The next month's average rainfall was 5 inches. What was the average rainfall per month for all those months?

(A) 4 inches

(B) $4\frac{1}{4}$ inches

(C) $4\frac{1}{2}$ inches

(D) $4\frac{3}{4}$ inches

(E) not enough information

To calculate an average, you must have the total amount and then divide by the number of items. The difficulty here, however, is that *first few months* does not specify exactly *how many* months averaged 4 inches. Does *few* mean two? Or does it mean three? *Few* is not a precise mathematical term. Therefore, there is not enough information to pull out to calculate an average. The answer is Choice E.

4. If gasohol is $\frac{2}{9}$ alcohol by volume and $\frac{7}{9}$ gasoline by volume, what is the ratio of the volume of gasoline to the volume of alcohol?

   (A) $\frac{2}{9}$

   (B) $\frac{2}{7}$

   (C) $\frac{7}{9}$

   (D) $\frac{7}{2}$

   (E) $\frac{9}{2}$

The first bit of information that you should pull out should be what you are looking for, *ratio of the volume of gasoline to the volume of alcohol.* Rewrite it as $G{:}A$ and then into its mathematical working form $\frac{G}{A}$. Next, you should pull out the volumes of each: $G = \frac{7}{9}$ and $A = \frac{2}{9}$. Now the answer can be easily figured by inspection or substitution. Using $\dfrac{\frac{7}{9}}{\frac{2}{9}} = ?$, which is the same as $\frac{7}{9} \div \frac{2}{9} = ?$, invert the second fraction and multiply to get $\frac{7}{9} \times \frac{9}{2} = ?$ The answer is $\frac{7}{2}$ (the ratio of gasoline to alcohol), so the correct answer is D. When pulling out information, actually write out the numbers and/or letters to the side of the problem, putting them into some form and eliminating some of the wording.

Plug in Numbers

When a problem involving *variables* (unknowns or letters) seems difficult and confusing, simply *replace those variables with numbers.* Simple numbers will make the arithmetic easier for you to do. Usually, problems using numbers are easier to understand. Be sure to make logical substitutions. Use a positive number, a negative number, or zero when applicable to get the full picture.

Examples:

1. If x is a positive integer in the equation $12x = q$, then q must be

    (A) a positive even integer
    (B) a negative even integer
    (C) zero
    (D) a positive odd integer
    (E) a negative odd integer

At first glance, this problem appears quite complex. But plug in some numbers and see what happens. For instance, first plug in 1 (the simplest positive integer) for x:

$$12x = q$$
$$12(1) = q$$
$$12 = q$$

Now try 2:

$$12x = q$$
$$12(2) = q$$
$$24 = q$$

Try it again. No matter what positive integer is plugged in for x, q will always be positive and even. Therefore, the answer is A.

2. If a, b, and c are all positive integers greater than 1 such that $a < b < c$, which of the following is the largest quantity?

    (A) $a(b + c)$
    (B) $ab + c$
    (C) $ac + b$
    (D) they are all equal
    (E) cannot be determined

Substitute 2, 3, and 4 for a, b, and c, respectively:

$$a(b+c) = \qquad ab + c = \qquad ac + b =$$
$$2(3+4) = \qquad 2(3)+4 = \qquad 2(4)+3 =$$
$$2(7) = 14 \qquad 6+4 = 10 \qquad 8+3 = 11$$

Since 2, 3, and 4 meet the conditions stated in the problem and Choice A produces the largest numerical value, it will consistently be the largest quantity. Therefore, Choice A, $a(b + c)$, is the correct answer. Remember to substitute simple numbers, since *you* have to do the work.

3. If $x > 1$, which of the following decreases as x decreases?

I. $x + x^2$

II. $2x^2 - x$

III. $\dfrac{1}{x+1}$

(A) I

(B) II

(C) III

(D) I and II

(E) II and III

This problem is most easily solved by substituting simple numbers for x and observing the changes in the values of the different expressions. Recall that you were told that $x > 1$ and it decreases in value.

x	I. $x + x^2$	II. $2x^2 - x$	III. $\dfrac{1}{x+1}$
4	$4 + (4)^2 = 20$	$2(4)^2 - 4 = 28$	$\dfrac{1}{4+1} = \dfrac{1}{5}$
3	$3 + (3)^2 = 12$	$2(3)^2 - 3 = 15$	$\dfrac{1}{3+1} = \dfrac{1}{4}$
2	$2 + (2)^2 = 6$	$2(2)^2 - 2 = 6$	$\dfrac{1}{2+1} = \dfrac{1}{3}$

From the table above, you can observe that, as x decreases, the values for I also decrease, which implies that the final answer must include I. This eliminates choices B, C, and E. As x decreases, the values for II also decrease, which implies that the final answer must include II. Only Choice D includes both I and II. Notice that as x decreased, the values for III increased $(\frac{1}{5} < \frac{1}{4} < \frac{1}{3})$, which implies the final answer *cannot* have III, which would have eliminated choices C and E.

Work from the Answers

Sometimes the solution to a problem will be obvious to you. At other times, it may be helpful to work *from the answers.* This technique is even more efficient when some of the answer choices are easily eliminated.

Examples:

1. Approximate $\sqrt{1,596}$.

    (A) 10
    (B) 20
    (C) 30
    (D) 40
    (E) 50

Without the answer choices, this would be a very difficult problem, requiring knowledge of a special procedure to calculate square roots. With the answer choices, however, the problem is easily solvable. How? By working up from the answer choices. Since $\sqrt{1,596}$ means *what number times itself equals 1,596,* you can take any answer choice and multiply it by itself. As soon as you find the answer choice that, when multiplied by itself, approximates 1,596, you've got the correct answer.

But here's another strategy: Start to work up from the *middle answer choice.* Why? Watch.

1. Approximate $\sqrt{1,596}$.

    (A) 10
    (B) 20
    (C) 30
    (D) 40
    (E) 50

Start with Choice C, 30. Multiplying it by itself, you get $30 \times 30 = 900$. Since 900 is too small (you're looking for approximately 1,596), you may eliminate Choice C. But notice that you may *also eliminate choices A and B,* because they are also too small.

Working up from the middle choice will often allow you to eliminate more than one answer choice, because the answers are usually in increasing order. This should save you valuable time.

Here's another solution:

$$\sqrt{1,596} \approx \sqrt{1,600}$$
$$= \sqrt{16}\sqrt{100}$$
$$= 4 \cdot 10$$
$$= 40$$

2. If $\left(\frac{x}{4}\right) + 2 = 22$, find x.

  (A) 40

  (B) 80

  (C) 100

  (D) 120

  (E) 160

If you cannot solve this algebraically, you may use the *work up from your choices* strategy. But start with Choice C, 100. What if $x = 100$?

$$\left(\frac{x}{4}\right) + 2 = 22$$

$$\left(\frac{100}{4}\right) + 2 \overset{?}{=} 22$$

$$25 + 2 \overset{?}{=}$$

$$27 \neq 22$$

Note that since 27 is too large, choices D and E will also be too large. Therefore, try Choice A. If Choice A is too small, then you know the answer is Choice B. If Choice A works, the answer is Choice A.

$$\left(\frac{x}{4}\right) + 2 = 22$$

$$\left(\frac{40}{4}\right) + 2 \overset{?}{=} 22$$

$$10 + 2 \overset{?}{=} 22$$

$$12 \neq 22$$

Because Choice A is too small, the answer must be Choice B.

3. If Barney can mow the lawn in five hours and Fred can mow the lawn in four hours, how long will it take them to mow the lawn together?

  (A) 1 hour

  (B) $2\frac{2}{9}$ hours

  (C) 4 hours

  (D) $4\frac{1}{2}$ hours

  (E) 5 hours

Suppose that you aren't familiar with the type of equation for this problem. Try the "reasonable" method. Because Fred can mow the lawn in four hours by himself, you know he'll take less than four hours if Barney helps him. Therefore choices C, D, and E are ridiculous. Taking this method a little further, suppose that Barney could also mow the lawn in four hours. Then together it would take Barney and Fred two hours. But, because Barney is a little slower than Fred, the total time should be a little more than two hours. The correct answer is Choice B, $2\frac{2}{9}$ hours. Using the equation for this problem would give the following calculations:

$$\frac{1}{\text{person A's rate}} + \frac{1}{\text{person B's rate}} = \frac{1}{\text{rate together}}$$

$$\frac{1}{4} + \frac{1}{5} = \frac{1}{x}$$

In 1 hour, Barney could do $\frac{1}{5}$ of the job and in 1 hour Fred could do $\frac{1}{4}$ of the job; unknown $\left(\frac{1}{x}\right)$ is that part of the job they could do together in one hour. Now solving, you calculate as follows:

$$\frac{4}{20} + \frac{5}{20} = \frac{1}{x}$$

$$\frac{9}{20} = \frac{1}{x}$$

Cross-multiplying gives $9x = 20$. Therefore, $x = \frac{20}{9}$, or $2\frac{2}{9}$.

4. Find the counting number between 11 and 30 that, when divided by 3, has a remainder of 1 but, when divided by 4, has a remainder of 2.

(A) 12
(B) 13
(C) 16
(D) 21
(E) 22

By working from the answers, you can eliminate wrong answer choices. For instance, choices A and C can be immediately eliminated because they are divisible by 4, leaving no remainder. Choices B and D can also be eliminated because they leave a remainder of 1 when divided by 4. Therefore, the correct answer is Choice E: 22 leaves a remainder of 1 when divided by 3 and a remainder of 2 when divided by 4.

Approximate

If a problem involves calculations with numbers that seem tedious and time consuming, scan your answer choices to see if you can *round off or approximate* those numbers. If so, replace those numbers with numbers that are easier to work with. Find the answer choice closest to your approximated answer.

Examples:

1. The value for $\dfrac{(0.889 \times 55)}{9.97}$ to the nearest tenth is

   (A) 0.5
   (B) 4.63
   (C) 4.9
   (D) 17.7
   (E) 49.1

Before starting any computations, take a glance at the answers to see how far apart they are. Notice that the only close answers are choices B and C, but Choice B is not a possible choice, because it is to the nearest hundredth, not the nearest tenth. Now, making some quick approximations, $0.889 \approx 1$ and $9.97 \approx 10$, leaving the problem in this form:

$$\frac{1 \times 55}{10} = \frac{55}{10} = 5.5$$

The closest answer is Choice C; therefore, it is the correct answer. Notice that choices A and E are not reasonable.

2. The value of $\sqrt{\dfrac{9,986}{194}}$ is approximately

   (A) 7
   (B) 18
   (C) 35
   (D) 40
   (E) 50

Round off both numbers to the hundreds place. The problem then becomes $\sqrt{\dfrac{10,000}{200}}$. This is much easier to work. By dividing, the problem now becomes $\sqrt{50}$ = slightly more than 7. The closest answer choice is Choice A.

Make Comparisons

At times, questions will require you to *compare* the sizes of several decimals, or of several fractions. If decimals are being compared, make sure that the numbers being compared have the same number of digits. (***Remember:*** Zeros to the far right of a decimal point can be inserted or eliminated without changing the value of the number.)

Examples:

1. Put these in order from smallest to largest: $0.6, 0.16, 0.66\frac{2}{3}, 0.58$.

   (A) $0.6, 0.16, 0.66\frac{2}{3}, 0.58$

   (B) $0.58, 0.16, 0.6, 0.66\frac{2}{3}$

   (C) $0.16, 0.58, 0.6, 0.66\frac{2}{3}$

   (D) $0.66\frac{2}{3}, 0.6, 0.58, 0.16$

   (E) $0.58, 0.6, 0.66\frac{2}{3}, 0.16$

Rewrite 0.6 as 0.60 so that all the decimals now have the same number of digits: $0.60, 0.16, 0.66\frac{2}{3}, 0.58$. Treating these as though the decimal point were not there (this can be done only when all the numbers have the same number of digits to the right of the decimal), the order is as follows: $0.16, 0.58, 0.60, 0.66\frac{2}{3}$. The correct answer is C. Remember to circle *smallest to largest* in the question.

2. Put these in order from smallest to largest: $75\%, \frac{2}{3}, \frac{5}{8}$.

   (A) $\frac{2}{3}, 75\%, \frac{5}{8}$

   (B) $\frac{2}{3}, \frac{5}{8}, 75\%$

   (C) $\frac{5}{8}, \frac{2}{3}, 75\%$

   (D) $75\%, \frac{5}{8}, \frac{2}{3}$

   (E) $75\%, \frac{2}{3}, \frac{5}{8}$

Using common denominators, you find

$$\frac{2}{3} = \frac{16}{24}$$

$$\frac{5}{8} = \frac{15}{24}$$

$$75\% = \frac{3}{4} = \frac{18}{24}$$

Therefore, the order becomes $\frac{5}{8}$, $\frac{2}{3}$, 75%. Using decimal equivalents:

$$\frac{5}{8} = 0.625$$

$$\frac{2}{3} = 0.666\frac{2}{3}$$

$$75\% = 0.750$$

The order again is $\frac{5}{8}$, $\frac{2}{3}$, 75%. The answer is C.

Mark Diagrams

When a figure is included with the problem, *mark the given facts on the diagram.* This will help you visualize all the facts that have been given.

Examples:

1. If each square in the figure has a side of length 3, what is the perimeter?

   (A) 12
   (B) 14
   (C) 21
   (D) 30
   (E) 36

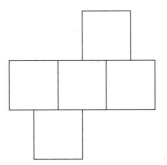

Mark the known facts.

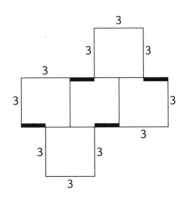

You now have a calculation for the perimeter: 30 *plus* the darkened parts. Now look carefully at the top two darkened parts. They will add up to 3. (Notice how the top square may slide over to illustrate that fact.)

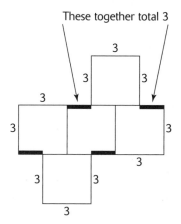

These together total 3

The same is true for the bottom darkened parts. They will add to 3.

Thus, the total perimeter is 30 + 6 = 36, or Choice E.

Here's another way to look at things. Since all the squares are identical in size, move the upper square to the left and the lower square to the right to form the figure below:

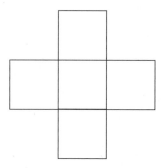

Because each side of each square has a length of 3, the perimeter becomes 12 groups of 3, or 36.

2. What is the maximum number of pieces of birthday cake of size 4" × 4" that can be cut from the cake to the right?

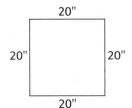

(A) 5
(B) 10
(C) 16
(D) 20
(E) 25

Marking in as follows makes this a fairly simple problem.

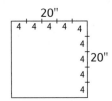

Notice that five pieces of cake will fit along each side; therefore 5 × 5 = 25. The correct answer is E. Finding the total area of the cake and dividing it by the area of one of the 4 × 4 pieces would have also given you the correct answer, but beware of this method because it may not work if the pieces do not fit evenly into the original area.

3. The perimeter of the isosceles triangle is 44 inches. The two equal sides are each five times as long as the third side. What are the lengths of each side?

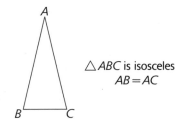

△ABC is isosceles
AB = AC

(A) 21, 21, 21
(B) 6, 6, 18
(C) 18, 21, 3
(D) 20, 20, 4
(E) 4, 4, 36

Mark the equal sides on the diagram.

AB and *AC* are each five times as long as *BC*.

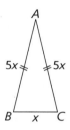

The equation for perimeter is

$$5x + 5x + x = 44$$
$$11x = 44$$
$$x = 4$$

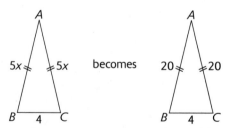

The answer is D. *Note:* This problem also could have been solved by working from the answers given.

4. In the following triangle, $\overline{CD}$ is an angle bisector, $\angle ACD$ is 30°, and $\angle ABC$ is a right angle. What is the measurement of angle x in degrees?

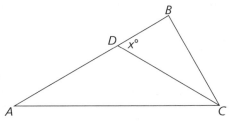

(A) 30°
(B) 45°
(C) 60°
(D) 75°
(E) 180°

You should have read the problem and marked as follows:

In the following triangle, $\overline{CD}$ is an angle bisector *(Stop and mark in the drawing)*, $\angle ACD$ is 30° *(Stop and mark in the drawing)*, and $\angle ABC$ is a right angle *(Stop and mark in the drawing)*. What is the measurement of angle x in degrees? *(Stop and mark or circle what you are looking for in the drawing.)*

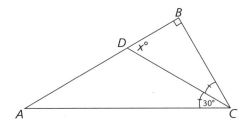

Now with the drawing marked in, it is evident that, given that $\angle ACD$ is 30°, $\angle BCD$ is also 30° because they are formed by an angle bisector (which divides an angle into two equal parts). Given that $\angle ABC$ is 90° (right angle) and $\angle BCD$ is 30°, angle x is 60° because there are 180° in a triangle: 180° − (90 + 30) = 60. The correct answer is C. *Always mark in diagrams as you read descriptions and information about them. This includes what you are looking for.*

Draw Diagrams

Drawing diagrams to meet the conditions set by the word problem can often make the problem easier for you to work. Being able to "see" the facts is more helpful than just reading the words.

Examples:

1. If all sides of a square are halved, the area of that square

   (A) is halved
   (B) is divided by 3
   (C) is divided by 4
   (D) remains the same
   (E) not enough information to tell

One way to solve this problem is to draw a square and then halve all its sides. Then compare the two areas.

Your first diagram:

Halving every side:

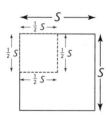

Notice that the total area of the new square will now be one-fourth the original square. The correct answer is C.

2. A hiking team begins at camp and hikes 5 miles north, then 8 miles west, then 6 miles south, then 9 miles east. In what direction must they now travel in order to return to camp?

   (A) north
   (B) northeast
   (C) northwest
   (D) west
   (E) They already are at camp.

For this question, your diagram would look something like this:

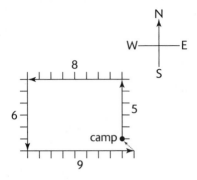

Thus, they must travel northwest (Choice C) to return to camp. Note that, in this case, you must draw your diagram very accurately.

Procedure Problems

Some problems (commonly on the PPST and CBEST) may not ask you to solve and find a correct numerical answer. Rather, you may be asked *how to work* the problem.

Examples:

1. To find the area of the following figure, a student would use which formula?

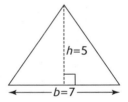

  I.   area = base times height

  II. area = $\frac{1}{2}$ times base times height

  III. area = one side squared

(A) I
(B) II
(C) III
(D) I and II
(E) I and III

Notice that it is not necessary to use any of the numerical values given in the diagram. You are to simply answer how the problem is to be worked. In such cases, don't bother working the problem; it's a waste of time. The correct answer is Choice B, II.

2. $108 \div 4$ could be quickly mentally calculated by

    (A) $100 \div 4 + 8$
    (B) $27 + 27 + 27 + 27$
    (C) $(100 \div 4) + (8 \div 4)$
    (D) $(54 \div 4) \times 2$
    (E) 4 into 108

Answer (C) is correct. The quickest method of calculating $108 \div 4$ is to first break down 108 into $100 + 8$. Then divide each value by 4 and, finally, add them together. Choices D and E will give the correct answer but are not the best ways to *quickly* calculate the answer. And choices A and B are simply incorrect.

Sometimes, however, actually working the problem can be helpful, as follows.

3. The fastest method to solve $\frac{9}{48} \times \frac{8}{9}$ would be to

    (A) invert the second fraction and then multiply
    (B) multiply each column across and then reduce to lowest terms
    (C) find the common denominator and then multiply across
    (D) divide 9 into the numerator and denominator, divide 8 into the numerator and denominator, and then multiply across
    (E) reduce the first fraction to lowest terms and then multiply across

In this problem, the way to determine the fastest procedure may be to actually work the problem as you would if you were working toward an answer. Then see if that procedure is listed among the choices. You should then compare it to the other methods listed. Is one of the other *correct* methods faster than the one you used? If so, select the fastest.

These types of problems are not constructed to test your knowledge of *obscure* tricks in solving mathematical equations. Rather, they test your knowledge of common procedures used in standard mathematical equations. Thus, the fastest way to solve this problem would be to first divide 9 into the numerator and denominator.

$$\frac{\overset{1}{\cancel{9}}}{48} \times \frac{8}{\underset{1}{\cancel{9}}} =$$

389

Then divide 8 into the numerator and denominator.

$$\frac{\overset{1}{\cancel{9}}}{\underset{6}{\cancel{48}}} \times \frac{\overset{1}{\cancel{8}}}{\underset{1}{\cancel{9}}} =$$

Then multiply across.

$$\frac{\overset{1}{\cancel{9}}}{\underset{6}{\cancel{48}}} \times \frac{\overset{1}{\cancel{8}}}{\underset{1}{\cancel{9}}} = \frac{1}{6}$$

The correct answer is (D).

Holiday bouquets cost the Key Club $2.00 each. The Key Club sells them for $4.75 each.

---

4. Based on the above information, how could Clark determine how many bouquets must be sold (Q) to make a profit of $82.50?

(A) $Q = \$82.50 \div \$2.00$
(B) $Q = \$82.50 - \$2.00$
(C) $Q = \$4.75 - \$2.00$
(D) $Q = \$82.50 \div \$4.75 - \$2.00$
(E) $Q = \$82.50 \div \$2.75$

The correct answer is E. Notice that, because the bouquets are bought for $2.00 each but sold at $4.75 each, the profit on each bouquet is $2.75. Therefore, to determine how many bouquets equal a profit of $82.50, you need only divide $82.50 by $2.75.

Multiple-Multiple-Choice

Some mathematical ability questions use a *multiple-multiple-choice* format. At first glance, these appear more confusing and more difficult than normal five-choice (A, B, C, D, E) multiple-choice problems. Actually, when you understand multiple-multiple-choice problem types and technique, they're often easier than a comparable standard multiple-choice question.

Example:

If x is a positive integer, then which of the following *must* be true?

I. $x > 0$

II. $x = 0$

III. $x < 1$

(A) I only
(B) II only
(C) III only
(D) I and II
(E) I and III

Since x is a positive integer, it must be a counting number. Note that possible values of x could be 1, or 2, or 3, or 4, and so on. Therefore, statement I, $x > 0$, is always true. So next to I on your question booklet place a T for *true.*

Now realize that the correct final answer choice (A, B, C, D, or E) *must* contain *true statement I.* This eliminates choices B and C as possible correct answer choices, because they do *not* contain true statement I. You should cross out choices B and C on your question booklet.

Statement II is *incorrect.* If x is positive, x cannot equal zero. Thus, next to II, you should place an *F* for false.

Knowing that statement II is false allows you to eliminate any answer choices that contain *false statement II.* Therefore, you should cross out Choice D, because it contains a false statement II. Only choices A and E are left as possible correct answers. Finally, you realize that statement III is also false, because x must be 1 or greater. So you place an F next to statement III, thus eliminating Choice E and leaving Choice A, I only.

This technique often saves some precious time and allows you to take a better educated guess should you not be able to complete all parts (I, II, III, IV, and so on) of a multiple-multiple-choice question.

A Patterned Plan of Attack

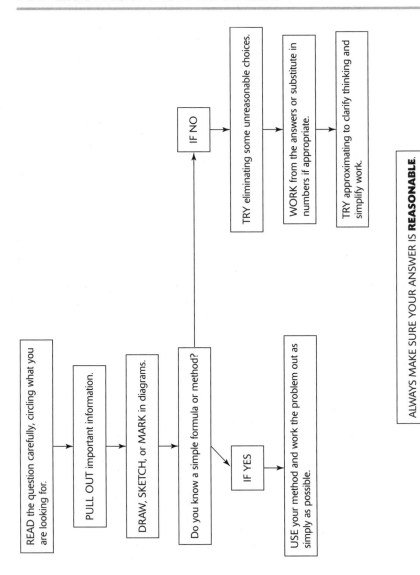

READ the question carefully, circling what you are looking for.

PULL OUT important information.

DRAW, SKETCH, or MARK in diagrams.

Do you know a simple formula or method?

IF YES

USE your method and work the problem out as simply as possible.

IF NO

TRY eliminating some unreasonable choices.

WORK from the answers or substitute in numbers if appropriate.

TRY approximating to clarify thinking and simplify work.

ALWAYS MAKE SURE YOUR ANSWER IS **REASONABLE**.

Mathematical Ability Practice

Arithmetic

Questions

1. Which of the following pairs are *not* equal?

   (A) $\frac{2}{5}$, 0.4

   (B) $\frac{1}{3}$, $\frac{11}{33}$

   (C) $\frac{5}{4}$, $1\frac{1}{4}$

   (D) $\frac{13}{4}$, $3\frac{1}{4}$

   (E) $\frac{7}{11}$, $\frac{72}{112}$

2. The number 103,233,124 is divisible by

   (A) 3
   (B) 4
   (C) 5
   (D) 6
   (E) 8

3. The product of 1.5 and 0.4 expressed as a fraction is

   (A) $\frac{2}{5}$

   (B) $\frac{1}{2}$

   (C) $\frac{3}{5}$

   (D) $\frac{2}{3}$

   (E) $\frac{4}{5}$

4. The greatest common factor of 32, 48, and 64 is

   (A) 4
   (B) 6
   (C) 8
   (D) 16
   (E) 32

5. Dividing a number by $\frac{8}{2}$ is the same as multiplying by

   (A) 4
   (B) 2
   (C) $\frac{1}{4}$
   (D) $\frac{1}{6}$
   (E) $\frac{1}{8}$

6. What is 0.25 percent of 2,000?

   (A) 500
   (B) 50
   (C) 5
   (D) 0.5
   (E) 0.05

7. $(9.3 \times 10^7) - (2.1 \times 10^2) =$

   (A) 92,000,790
   (B) 92,999,790
   (C) 93,000,210
   (D) 93,000,790
   (E) 93,999,790

8. A national birth rate of 72,000 newborn babies each day is equal to how many births per minute?

   (A) 5
   (B) 10
   (C) 50
   (D) 120
   (E) 500

9. If the average of 30 numbers is 50, what is the sum of the numbers?

   (A) 300
   (B) 600
   (C) 1,500
   (D) 3,050
   (E) 5,030

10. The number 24 is 20 percent of what number?

   (A) 12
   (B) 28
   (C) 100
   (D) 120
   (E) 480

11. If the ratio of males to females at a party is 4 to 5 and the ratio of adults to children at the party is 3 to 2, which of the following could be the number of people at the party?

   (A) 18
   (B) 25
   (C) 35
   (D) 45
   (E) 60

12. A television regularly selling for $850 is discounted 20%. What is the new selling price of the television?

   (A) $650
   (B) $670
   (C) $680
   (D) $700
   (E) $750

13. In the table below, the greatest percent increase was between which years?

DOW JONES AVERAGE	
2004	830.0
2005	870.0
2006	910.0
2007	950.0
2008	990.0
2009	1030.0

(A) 2004 and 2005
(B) 2005 and 2006
(C) 2006 and 2007
(D) 2007 and 2008
(E) 2008 and 2009

14. Find the sum of $\frac{1}{3}$, $\frac{1}{8}$, and $\frac{5}{6}$.

(A) $\frac{13}{24}$

(B) $\frac{15}{24}$

(C) $\frac{31}{24}$

(D) $\frac{33}{24}$

(E) $\frac{35}{24}$

15. Approximate the value for $0.26 \times 0.67 \times 0.5 \times 0.9$.

(A) 0.08
(B) 0.13
(C) 0.8
(D) 0.32
(E) 0.04

16. A teacher gave a test to a class and all the boys averaged 82% while all the girls averaged 85%. If there were 20 boys and 10 girls in the class, what was the average for the entire class?

    (A) $82\frac{1}{2}\%$
    (B) 83%
    (C) $83\frac{1}{2}\%$
    (D) 84%
    (E) 85%

17. If the average (arithmetic mean) of 10, 14, 16, and q is 14, then $q =$

    (A) 10
    (B) 12
    (C) 14
    (D) 16
    (E) 18

18. If the price of apples is decreased from two dozen for $5 to three dozen for $6, how many more apples can be purchased for $30 now than could be purchased before?

    (A) 36
    (B) 48
    (C) 72
    (D) 144
    (E) 180

19. If 28 millimeters is equivalent to 2.8 centimeters, how many millimeters are in 50 centimeters?

    (A) 0.5
    (B) 5
    (C) 50
    (D) 500
    (E) 5,000

20. Which of the following is (are) equal to $\frac{3}{8}$?

    I. 0.375

    II. $37\frac{1}{2}\%$

    III. $\dfrac{37\frac{1}{2}}{100}$

    IV. $\dfrac{375}{100}$

    (A) I and II
    (B) I, II, and III
    (C) I, II, and IV
    (D) II and III
    (E) IV

21. What is the arithmetic mean of six Tigers each averaging 0.280 and four Padres averaging 0.250 each?

    (A) 0.268
    (B) 0.270
    (C) 0.272
    (D) 0.274
    (E) 0.276

22. Find the simple interest on $3,000 if it is left in an account for four months paying a 2% quarterly rate of interest.

    (A) $8
    (B) $60
    (C) $80
    (D) $120
    (E) $600

23. How many paintings were displayed at the County Museum of Art if 30% of them were by Monet and Monet was represented by 24 paintings?

    (A) 48
    (B) 50
    (C) 60
    (D) 76
    (E) 80

24. A motorist travels 120 miles to his destination at the average speed of 60 miles per hour and returns to the starting point at the average speed of 40 miles per hour. His average speed for the entire trip is

    (A) 40 mph
    (B) 45 mph
    (C) 48 mph
    (D) 50 mph
    (E) 53 mph

25. A special race is held in which runners may stop to rest. However, if a runner stops, he may then run only half as far as his previous distance between stops, at which point he must stop to rest again. If a runner finishes running when stopping for the fifth time, what's the farthest distance Albert can run if he takes his first rest stop after 0.8 kilometers?

    (A) 1.5 km
    (B) 1.55 km
    (C) 1.75 km
    (D) 1.80 km
    (E) 2.0 km

26. A used bicycle pump, for sale originally at $7.00, is discounted 20%. Because it doesn't sell, it is discounted an additional 10%. What is its new selling price?

    (A) $4.90
    (B) $5.00
    (C) $5.04
    (D) $5.21
    (E) $5.60

27. A student scored 80% on each of two tests. What does he have to score on the third test in order to raise his overall average to 85%?

    (A) 90%
    (B) 93%
    (C) 95%
    (D) 98%
    (E) 100%

28. Successive discounts of 40% and 20% are equal to a single discount of

    (A) 20%
    (B) 30%
    (C) 52%
    (D) 60%
    (E) 80%

29. A solution must contain at least 30% orange juice but not more than 20% ginger ale in addition to its other ingredients. If the punch bowl is to hold 400 cups of this solution, which of the following are allowable amounts of orange juice and ginger ale?

    (A) 120 cups of orange juice, 130 cups of ginger ale
    (B) 130 cups of orange juice, 140 cups of ginger ale
    (C) 150 cups of orange juice, 70 cups of ginger ale
    (D) 20 cups of orange juice, 80 cups of ginger ale
    (E) 14 cups of orange juice, 100 cups of ginger ale

30. $\frac{1}{2^3}$ is approximately what percent of 2^3?

    (A) 0.016%
    (B) 0.16%
    (C) 1.6%
    (D) 16%
    (E) 160%

Algebra

Questions

1. If $x = -3$ and $y = (x + 5)(x - 5)$, then the value of y is

    (A) 64
    (B) 16
    (C) 9
    (D) −9
    (E) −16

2. If $9x + 4 = -32$, then what is $x + 1$?

(A) −5
(B) −4
(C) −3
(D) 4
(E) 5

3. If $(4)(4)(4)(4) = \dfrac{(8)(8)}{p}$, then p must equal

(A) $\dfrac{1}{4}$

(B) $\dfrac{1}{2}$

(C) 1
(D) 2
(E) 4

4. Find the value of a^{bc} if $a = 2$, $b = 3$, and $c = 2$.

(A) 8
(B) 16
(C) 32
(D) 64
(E) 128

5. $\sqrt{(9-x)^2} = 9 - x$

In the real number system, which of the following cannot be a value for x in the statement above?

(A) −10
(B) −9
(C) 0
(D) 9
(E) 10

6. If $\frac{1}{t} + \frac{1}{p} = \frac{1}{2}$, then $t + p =$

    (A) 8
    (B) 2
    (C) 1
    (D) $\frac{1}{2}$
    (E) cannot be determined

7. If a and b are positive integers and $a^2 - b^2 = 11$, then $2a + 2b$ must equal

    (A) 11
    (B) 12
    (C) 22
    (D) 26
    (E) 36

8. If $x + 2 = y$, what is the value of $x - 2$ in terms of y?

    (A) $y - 4$
    (B) $y - 2$
    (C) $y + 2$
    (D) $y + 4$
    (E) $y + 6$

9. If $ab = -5$ and $(a + b)^2 = 16$, then $a^2 + b^2 =$

    (A) 11
    (B) 15
    (C) 21
    (D) 25
    (E) 26

10. If x is an even integer, which of the following must also be an even integer?

    (A) $9x + 1$
    (B) $9x - 1$
    (C) $\frac{x}{2} + 1$
    (D) $\frac{x}{2}$
    (E) $4x + 6$

11. For all m, $m^2 + 11m + 30 = (m + y)(m + z)$. What is the value of yz?

(A) 5

(B) 6

(C) 11

(D) 30

(E) cannot be determined

12. If $2x + 5y = 32$, then $4x + 10y =$

(A) 16

(B) 34

(C) 64

(D) 128

(E) cannot be determined

13. If $25q^2p^2 = 8x$, then $\dfrac{q^2p^2}{4} =$

(A) $16x$

(B) $4x$

(C) $2x$

(D) $\dfrac{2x}{25}$

(E) $\dfrac{x}{25}$

14. If n is a positive integer, then which of the following must be true about (n) and $(n + 1)$?

(A) n is odd and $(n + 1)$ is even.

(B) n is even and $(n + 1)$ is odd.

(C) The product of the two terms is odd.

(D) The sum of the two terms is even.

(E) The product of the two terms is even.

15. On the coordinate grid below, for which point must the product of its x and y coordinates be positive?

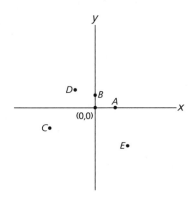

(A) A
(B) B
(C) C
(D) D
(E) E

16. If x, y, and z are all positive integers and $x < y < z$, then which of the following must be true?

(A) $(x + y) > z$
(B) $xy > z$
(C) $(z - y) > x$
(D) $(z - 2) = x$
(E) $z > \dfrac{y}{x}$

17. If $0.002 \leq a \leq 0.05$ and $0.01 \leq b \leq 0.50$, then what is the greatest possible value of $\left(\dfrac{a}{b}\right)^2$?

(A) 0.25
(B) 0.5
(C) 1
(D) 5
(E) 25

18. If $\dfrac{x^2yz + xyz^2}{xyz} = x + z$, then a necessary condition for this to be true is

   I. $x + z < y$

   II. $x^2 > z$

  III. $xyz \neq 0$

  (A) I

  (B) I and II

  (C) I and III

  (D) III

  (E) II and III

19. If $\dfrac{1}{5} + \dfrac{1}{2} + \dfrac{1}{x} = 7$, then $x =$

  (A) $\dfrac{10}{63}$

  (B) $\dfrac{60}{7}$

  (C) $\dfrac{63}{10}$

  (D) $\dfrac{3}{19}$

  (E) $\dfrac{7}{60}$

20. A fruit drink made from orange juice and water is diluted with more water so that the final solution is $\dfrac{1}{4}$ water. If the original solution was 90% orange juice and 2 liters of water were added, how many liters are in the final solution of fruit drink?

  (A) 6

  (B) 8

  (C) 10

  (D) 12

  (E) 14

21. Ernie purchased some apples from a grocer for $5.00 and later learned that if he had purchased 20% more apples, he would have been given a 20% discount in price per apple. What would the difference have been in total cost if he had purchased 20% more apples?

    (A) 20¢ less
    (B) 10¢ less
    (C) the same cost
    (D) 20¢ more
    (E) cannot be determined

22. A college student invests $2,000, part at 7% in a savings account and some at 12% in a special money market account. The annual income from this investment is $200. How much was invested in the money market account?

    (A) $400
    (B) $600
    (C) $1,000
    (D) $1,200
    (E) $1,350

23. If p pencils cost c cents, n pencils at the same price will cost

    (A) $\dfrac{pc}{n}$ cents

    (B) $\dfrac{cn}{p}$ cents

    (C) npc cents

    (D) $\dfrac{np}{c}$ cents

    (E) $\dfrac{pc}{np}$ cents

24. A woman bought a set of porch furniture at a 40% reduction sale held late in the summer. The furniture cost her $165. What was the original price of the furniture?

    (A) $66
    (B) $231
    (C) $275
    (D) $412.50
    (E) $510

25. The midpoint of line segment *AB* is

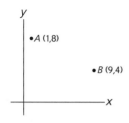

(A) (8,4)
(B) (3,6)
(C) (6,5)
(D) (5,6)
(E) (4,8)

Geometry

Questions

Note: Figures used in the following problems are not necessarily drawn to scale.

1. If, in the figure, l_1 is parallel to l, then $x + y$ must equal

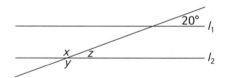

(A) 40°
(B) 120°
(C) 160°
(D) 180°
(E) 320°

2. In the figure, find the degree measure of ∠y.

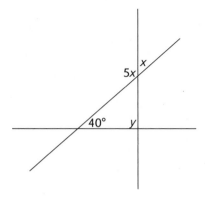

(A) 40
(B) 50
(C) 80
(D) 90
(E) 110

3. In the figure, what is the value of p?

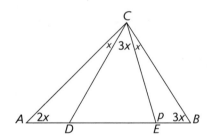

(A) 18
(B) 36
(C) 72
(D) 108
(E) 135

4. In circle O, arc $AD = 80°$. Find the measure of inscribed angle MDA.

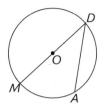

   (A) 40°
   (B) 50°
   (C) 60°
   (D) 80°
   (E) 100°

5. In $\triangle ABC$, $AB = BC$. Therefore, angles r and p each equal

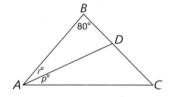

   (A) 50°
   (B) 25°
   (C) 20°
   (D) 10°
   (E) cannot be determined

6. In the figure, $x =$

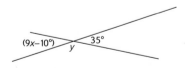

   (A) 15
   (B) 10
   (C) 9
   (D) 5
   (E) 4

7. What is the maximum number of cubes 3 inches on an edge that can be packed into a carton with dimensions as shown?

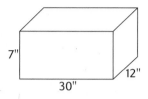

7" 30" 12"

(A) 70
(B) 74
(C) 80
(D) 84
(E) 88

8. Find the volume of a cube in cubic inches if the area of one of its faces is 49 square inches.

(A) 49
(B) 64
(C) 125
(D) 144
(E) 343

9. Square *ABCD* is inscribed in circle *O* with a radius of $\sqrt{2}$, as shown. Find the area of square *ABCD*.

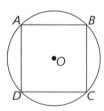

(A) 1
(B) 2
(C) 4
(D) 8
(E) 16

10. If the five angles of a pentagon are in the ratio 2:3:4:5:6, what is the degree measure of the largest angle?

    (A) 27
    (B) 54
    (C) 108
    (D) 162
    (E) 180

11. Circle O intersects circle Q only at point K. $PQ = 13$, and the radius of circle O is 5. What is the area of circle Q?

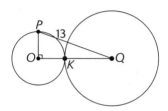

    (A) 144π
    (B) 100π
    (C) 81π
    (D) 64π
    (E) 49π

12. In the diagram, circle O inscribed in square $ABCD$ has an area of 36π square inches. Find the perimeter of square $ABCD$.

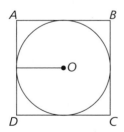

    (A) 24
    (B) 48
    (C) 60
    (D) 144
    (E) 200

13. A regular cylindrical tank is to be $\frac{2}{3}$ filled with water. If its height is 9 feet and its diameter is 12 feet, how many cubic feet of water will be needed?

    (A) 144π
    (B) 216π
    (C) 256π
    (D) 324π
    (E) 720π

14. In the figure, what is the area of the shaded region?

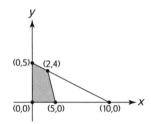

    (A) 15
    (B) 18
    (C) 20
    (D) 21
    (E) 25

15. Using the figure to determine the values of q and p, the product qp must equal

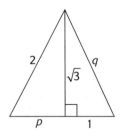

    (A) $\frac{1}{2}$
    (B) 1
    (C) 2
    (D) $2\sqrt{3}$
    (E) $3\sqrt{2}$

16. If a square has the same perimeter as a rectangle with sides 2 and 16, what is the area of the square?

    (A) 4
    (B) 9
    (C) 16
    (D) 36
    (E) 81

17. In the diagram, if one side of the regular hexagon *ABCDEF* is 10, find the area of the entire hexagon.

    (A) 75
    (B) $75\sqrt{3}$
    (C) 150
    (D) $150\sqrt{2}$
    (E) $150\sqrt{3}$

18. If, at point *P*, l_2 bisects the angle formed by l_1 and l_3, what is the degree measure of *x* if *z* equals 100°?

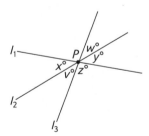

    (A) 30
    (B) 40
    (C) 45
    (D) 80
    (E) 90

19. In circle *O*, if chord *SP* = 6 and the radius of circle *O* = 5, find the length of chord *RS*.

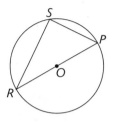

(A) 3
(B) $\sqrt{11}$
(C) 6
(D) 8
(E) cannot be determined

20. In the figure, side *AB* = 6 and side *BC* = 8. Find the area of △*ADC*.

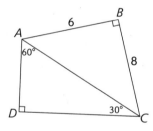

(A) $25\sqrt{3}$
(B) 24
(C) $\dfrac{25\sqrt{3}}{2}$
(D) 20
(E) $20\sqrt{2}$

21. On the coordinate grid, what is the length of segment AB if the coordinates at point A are (7,9) and the coordinates at point B are (13,17)?

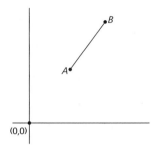

(A) $7\frac{1}{2}$ units

(B) $8\frac{1}{2}$ units

(C) 9 units

(D) 10 units

(E) $12\frac{1}{2}$ units

22. The figure shown represents the end of a garage. Find, in feet, the length of one of the equal rafters $\overline{AB}$ or $\overline{CB}$ if each extends 12 inches beyond the eaves.

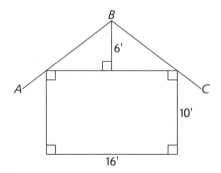

(A) 10

(B) 11

(C) 13

(D) 22

(E) 33

23. The figure represents a rectangle, whose dimensions are *l* and *w*, surmounted by a semicircle, whose radius is *r*. Express the area of this figure in terms of *l*, *w*, *r*, and π.

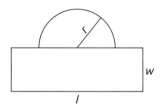

   (A) $lw + \frac{\pi r^2}{2}$

   (B) $lw + \pi r$

   (C) $lw + \pi r^2$

   (D) $\frac{\pi}{2} - r^2 lw$

   (E) lwr^2

24. The width of the ring (the shaded portion of the figure) is exactly equal to the radius of the inner circle. What percent of the entire area is the area of the shaded portion?

   (A) 25

   (B) 50

   (C) $66\frac{2}{3}$

   (D) 75

   (E) 90

25. By what number is the area of a circle multiplied if its radius is doubled?

   (A) $2\pi r$

   (B) 2

   (C) 3.1416

   (D) 4

   (E) 6

Procedure Problems

1. Jose purchased three items for his new car—a steering-wheel grip,
    a floor mat, and a seat cushion. The steering-wheel grip cost three
    times the seat cushion. The floor mat cost exactly $5.75 with tax.
    Which of the following can be derived from the above information?

    I.   the cost of all three items
    II.   the cost of the seat cushion
    III. the cost of the steering-wheel grip
    IV.   the cost of the floor mat without the tax

    (A) I only
    (B) II only
    (C) III only
    (D) IV only
    (E) none of these

John's car is one year older than Sue's car. Maria's truck is one
year newer than John's car. Sue's car, a 2009 model, is newer
than Maria's truck.

---

2. Fred is given the information above in a problem in his math class.
    With just the information given, Fred should be able to determine
    the approximate age(s) of

    (A) Sue's car
    (B) Sue's car and Maria's truck
    (C) Sue's car and John's car
    (D) Sue's car, Maria's truck, and John's car
    (E) Maria's truck

3. Harold is given the following information about the class treasury.

   I. The current balance is $5 less than last year's final balance, which was $10.

   II. This year's balance of $10 is $5 more than last year's balance.

   III. Ten percent is half of this year's goal, which is $100.

   Which of these statements can be calculated by subtracting 5 from 10?

   (A) I
   (B) II
   (C) III
   (D) I and II
   (E) I, II, and III

Arnold's Scores on Four Tests

Test 1: 83%

Test 2: 85%

Test 3: 100%

Test 4: ?

---

4. If Arnold's score on Test 4 was weighted double that of each of the previous three tests, and if his overall average was 90%, how could Arnold determine his score on Test 4?

   (A) $(83 + 85 + 100 + x) = 90$

   (B) $(83 + 85 + 100 + x + x) = 90$

   (C) $\dfrac{(83+85+100+x)}{4} = 90$

   (D) $\dfrac{(83+85+100+x+x)}{4} = 90$

   (E) $\dfrac{(83+85+100+x+x)}{5} = 90$

27,456 may be represented as *P*.

845 may be represented as *Q*.

5. Based on the above information, 27,456 times 846 may be expressed as

   (A) $PQ + 1$
   (B) $(P + 1)(Q)$
   (C) $P(Q + 1)$
   (D) $(P + 1)(Q + 1)$
   (E) $(P)(Q + 845)$

6. When Francisco multiplies $(x + 1)(x + 2)$ he gets $x^2 + 3x + 2$ as an answer. One way to check this answer would be to

   (A) divide $(x + 1)$ by $(x + 2)$
   (B) divide $(x + 2)$ by $(x + 1)$
   (C) plug in a positive integer for x
   (D) square $(x + 1)$
   (E) use reciprocals

The sum of two numbers equals one of the numbers.

7. If the above statement is true, which of the following best represents the relationship?

   (A) $x + y = y + x$
   (B) $(x)(y) = 1$
   (C) $x + y = 1$
   (D) $x + y = y$
   (E) $x + y = x + 1$

8. Last year, Jorge was three years less than twice Teresa's age now. If Jorge is 10 years old now, which equation will enable Jorge to correctly find Teresa's present age, *T*?

   (A) $10 + 1 = 2T - 3$
   (B) $9 - 3 = 2T$
   (C) $9 = 2T - 3$
   (D) $11 = 2T - 3$
   (E) $10 = -3 + 2T$

9. If a tie costs T dollars and a suit jacket costs four times the price of the tie, which of the following best expresses the cost of two ties and three suit jackets?

(A) $4T$
(B) $T + 4(T)$
(C) $2(T) + 3(T)$
(D) $T + 3(4T)$
(E) $2(T) + 3(4T)$

Rosanna knows that a geometric figure is a rectangle and that it has sides of 18 and 22.

---

10. How can Rosanna compute the area of a square that has the same perimeter as the rectangle above?

(A) Add 18 and 22, double this sum, divide by 4, then multiply by 2.
(B) Add 18 and 22, double this sum, divide by 4, then multiply by 4.
(C) Add 18 and 22, double this sum, divide by 4, then square the quotient.
(D) Add 18 and 22, double this sum, then multiply by 4.
(E) Add twice 18 to twice 22, divide by 2, then square the quotient.

Answer Key for Mathematical Ability Practice

The boldface page number in parentheses following each answer will direct you to the complete explanation for that specific problem. *Read this explanation first.* The other page numbers in parentheses refer to the suggested basic review section.

Arithmetic

1. E (p. **423**, 29, 53)
2. B (p. **423**, 24)
3. C (p. **423**, 50, 52)
4. D (p. **423**, 33)
5. C (p. **423**, 46)
6. C (p. **423**, 58)

7. B (p. **423**, 66)
8. C (p. **423**, 94)
9. C (p. **423**, 83)
10. D (p. **424**, 58)
11. D (p. **424**, 34)
12. C (p. **424**, 58)

13. A (p. **424,** 63)
14. C (p. **424,** 35)
15. A (p. **424,** 18, 52)
16. B (p. **425,** 83)
17. D (p. **425,** 83)
18. A (p. **425,** 94)
19. D (p. **425,** 94)
20. B (p. **425,** 58)
21. A (p. **426,** 83)

22. C (p. **426,** 320)
23. E (p. **426,** 60)
24. C (p. **427,** 329)
25. B (p. **427,** 51)
26. C (p. **427,** 58, 332)
27. C (p. **427,** 84)
28. C (p. **428,** 58)
29. C (p. **428,** 58)
30. C (p. **428,** 60, 64)

Algebra

1. E (p. **429,** 122)
2. C (p. **429,** 125)
3. A (p. **429,** 125, 134)
4. D (p. **429,** 122)
5. E (p. **430,** 200)
6. E (p. **430,** 136, 374)
7. C (p. **430,** 374)
8. A (p. **430,** 125)
9. E (p. **430,** 122)
10. E (p. **430,** 122, 374)
11. D (p. **430,** 158)
12. C (p. **431,** 125)
13. D (p. **431,** 125, 169)

14. E (p. **431,** 374)
15. C (p. **431,** 180)
16. E (p. **431,** 374)
17. E (p. **431,** 122)
18. D (p. **431,** 169)
19. A (p. **432,** 125)
20. D (p. **432,** 125, 355)
21. A (p. **432,** 326)
22. D (p. **433,** 125, 355)
23. B (p. **433,** 125, 326)
24. C (p. **433,** 125, 332)
25. D (p. **433,** 182)

Geometry

1. E (p. **434,** 247)
2. E (p. **434,** 239, 251)
3. D (p. **434,** 251)
4. B (p. **435,** 287)
5. E (p. **435,** 251, 252)
6. D (p. **435,** 241)
7. C (p. **435,** 290)
8. E (p. **435,** 290)
9. C (p. **435,** 281)
10. D (p. **435,** 276)
11. E (p. **436,** 262, 284)
12. B (p. **436,** 277, 284)
13. B (p. **436,** 290)
14. A (p. **437,** 182, 277)
15. C (p. **437,** 267)
16. E (p. **437,** 277)
17. E (p. **437,** 251, 267)
18. B (p. **438,** 241)
19. D (p. **438,** 262, 281)
20. C (p. **438,** 262, 267)
21. D (p. **438,** 182, 262)
22. B (p. **439,** 262)
23. A (p. **439,** 277, 284)
24. D (p. **439,** 284)
25. D (p. **439,** 284)

Procedure Problems

1. E (p. **440,** 339)
2. D (p. **440,** 343)
3. D (p. **440,** 120)
4. E (p. **440,** 84)
5. C (p. **440,** 120)
6. C (p. **441,** 374)
7. D (p. **441,** 120)
8. C (p. **441,** 343)
9. E (p. **441,** 120)
10. C (p. **441,** 277)

Mathematical Ability Answers and Explanations

Arithmetic

1. **E** Dividing 7 by 11 gives 0.63+. Dividing 72 by 112 gives 0.64+.

2. **B** Since the last two digits are divisible by 4, the number is divisible by 4. Note that since the last *three* digits are not divisible by 8, the number is not divisible by 8. The sum of the digits is 19, so the number is not divisible by 3 or 6. Because the number does not end in a 0 or 5, it is not divisible by 5.

3. **C** Change the terms into fractions and then multiply:
$$\frac{3}{2} \times \frac{2}{5} = \frac{6}{10} = \frac{3}{5}$$

4. **D** The greatest common factor is the largest factor, which divides into all the numbers. Of the choices, 16 is the largest number that can divide evenly into 32, 48, and 64.

5. **C** To divide by a fraction, you may invert the divisor and then multiply. Thus, 5 divided by $\frac{8}{2}$ is

$$5 \div \frac{8}{2} =$$

$$5 \times \frac{2}{8} =$$

$$5 \times \frac{1}{4} =$$

which is the same as multiplying by $\frac{1}{4}$.

6. **C** 0.25 percent is 0.0025. Therefore, 0.25 percent of 2,000 equals $0.0025 \times 2,000 = 5$.

7. **B** $(9.3 \times 10^7) - (2.1 \times 10^2) = 93,000,000 - 210 = 92,999,790$.

8. **C** Divide 72,000 births by 24 (hours per day) to find the number every hour (3,000). Divide this by 60 (minutes per hour) to find the number of births per minute (50).

9. **C** Since the average equals the sum divided by the number of items,
$$\text{average} = \frac{\text{sum}}{\text{number of items}}$$
to find the sum, simply multiply the average times the number of items:
$$\frac{\text{average}}{1} = \frac{\text{sum}}{\text{number of items}}$$

Cross-multiplying:

(average) (number of items) = 1(sum)

$$50 \times 30 = \text{sum}$$

$$1{,}500 = \text{sum}$$

10. **D** To find any part of a simple percentage problem, use

$\dfrac{\text{is}}{\text{of}} = \%$

Plugging in the givens,

$\dfrac{24}{?} = 20\%$

$\dfrac{24}{x} = \dfrac{20}{100}$

Cross-multiplying:

$20x = 2{,}400$

$x = 120$

11. **D** Since the ratio of males to females is 4 to 5, the males must be a multiple of 4 and the females must be a multiple of 5. Therefore, the total number of people at the party must have been 4 + 5 = 9, or a multiple of 9. Similarly, adding adults and children means that 3 + 2 = 5. The number of partygoers must also be a multiple of 5. The only choice that is both a multiple of 5 and a multiple of 9 is Choice D, 45.

12. **C** Twenty percent off the original price of $850 is a discount of (0.20)($850), or $170. Therefore, the new selling price is $850 – $170 = $680.

13. **A** Notice that each change was an increase of 40 points. Therefore, the largest percent increase will have the smallest starting point (denominator). Thus, 830.0 will be the smallest denominator or starting point:

$\text{percent increase} = \dfrac{\text{change}}{\text{starting point}} = \dfrac{40}{830.0}$

14. **C** Use a common denominator of 24:

$\dfrac{1}{3} + \dfrac{1}{8} + \dfrac{5}{6} = \dfrac{8}{24} + \dfrac{3}{24} + \dfrac{20}{24} = \dfrac{31}{24}$

15. **A** Changing the decimals to the nearest fraction gives

$0.26 \times 0.67 \times 0.5 \times 0.9 = \dfrac{1}{4} \times \dfrac{2}{3} \times \dfrac{1}{2} \times \dfrac{9}{10}$

Canceling leaves $\dfrac{1}{4} \times \dfrac{3}{10} = \dfrac{3}{40} = 0.075$ or 0.08.

16. **B** One method to solve this problem is to compute total percentage points. For the boys, 20×82 percentage points each = 1,640. For the girls, 10×85 percentage points each = 850. Adding gives 2,490 total percentage points. 2,490 total percentage points divided by 30 students gives an average of 83% per student.

Another method is to realize that, for every two boys averaging 82%, there is one girl averaging 85%. So the problem is simply, what is the average of 82, 82, and 85? Again, the answer is 83%.

17. **D** If the average of four numbers is 14, then their sum must be 4(14), or 56. Since three of the numbers (10, 14, and 16) sum to 40, the fourth number must be $56 - 40$, or 16.

18. **A** Thirty dollars previously would purchase six times two dozen apples, or $6 \times 2 \times 12 = 144$. Now, $30 will buy five times three dozen apples, or $5 \times 3 \times 12 = 180$. Therefore, $180 - 144 = 36$ more apples can be purchased now.

19. **D** Setting up a proportion using ratios is one way to solve this problem:

$$\frac{mm}{cm} = \frac{mm}{cm}$$

$$\frac{28}{2.8} = \frac{x}{50}$$

Cross-multiplying:

$$1,400 = 2.8(x)$$

Dividing each side by 2.8:

$$\frac{1,400}{2.8} = x$$

$$500 = x$$

Another way to solve this problem is to realize that the number of millimeters is ten times the number of centimeters. Thus, 10 times 50 centimeters equals 500 millimeters.

20. **B** To determine an equivalent for $\frac{3}{8}$, simply divide 3 by 8.

$$8\overline{)3.000} \quad 0.375$$

Therefore, $\frac{3}{8}$ is equal to 0.375, which may also be expressed as $\frac{37\frac{1}{2}}{100}$ or $37\frac{1}{2}\%$.

425

21. **A** To determine the arithmetic mean (composite averages) of the items in question, simply determine total points for all players, and then divide by the total number of players. For example,

6 Tigers each averaging 0.280 = 1.680 total points

4 Padres each averaging 0.250 = 1.000 total points

All together = 2.680 total points

Now, divide the final total of 2.680 points by the total number of players (10):

$\frac{2.680}{10} = 0.268$ average for all ten players

22. **C** To determine simple interest, use the following equation:

$I = prt$

Interest = (principal)(annual rate)(time in years)

2% quarterly = 8% annually

4 months = $\frac{1}{3}$ year

Now plug in the given values:

$I = (\$3,000)(0.08)\left(\frac{1}{3} \cdot \text{year}\right)$

$I = (\$1,000)(0.08)$

$I = \$80$

23. **E** To find the total number of paintings, use the following equation:

$\frac{\text{is}}{\text{of}} = \%$

and simply plug in the given values. The question is essentially, 24 is 30% of how many? Therefore, 24 is the "is," 30 is the percent, and "how many" (the unknown) is the "of." Plugging into the equation, you get

$\frac{24}{x} = \frac{30}{100}$

Note that the fractional percent is used to simplify the math.

Cross-multiplying:

$30x = 2,400$

Dividing both sides by 30:

$$\frac{30}{x} = \frac{2,400}{30}$$

$$x = 80$$

24. **C** Use $\qquad d = rt$

Going: $\qquad$ 120 miles = (60 mph)(t_1)

$\qquad\qquad$ 2 hours = t_1

Returning: $\quad$ 120 miles = (40 mph)(t_2)

$\qquad\qquad$ 3 hours = t_2

Entire trip: $\quad$ 240 miles = (r)(5 hours)

$\qquad\qquad$ 48 mph = r

25. **B** Since Albert stops after 0.8 km, he may then run half that distance, 0.4 km, before stopping again, after which he may run 0.2, then 0.1, then 0.05 km. After his 0.05 km distance, he will make his fifth stop and must stop running. Adding the distances: 0.8 + 0.4 + 0.2 + 0.1 + 0.05 = 1.55 km.

26. **C** The original price, $7.00, is first discounted 20%:

$7.00 – 0.20(7.00) =

$7.00 – $1.40 = $5.60

Then the price is discounted an additional 10%:

$5.60 – 0.10($5.60) =

$5.60 – $0.56 = $5.04

27. **C** To find the average percentage for the three tests, you would find the sum of the three percentage scores and divide this by 3. In order for this average to be 85%, the sum of the percentages must be $3 \times 85\%$, or 255%. Because the student scored 80% on each of two tests, he has accumulated 160% and, thus, needs 95% more to get the total of 285%.

28. **C** Suppose you begin with a list price of $100.

$100   List price
$\times\ 0.40$
$40.00   First discount

$60   First selling price
$\times\ 0.20$
$12   Second discount

$60
$-$12$
$48   Second selling price

$100   List price
$-$48$ Selling price
$52   Total discount

$$\frac{\$52}{\$100} = 52\%$$

29. **C** In this problem, the words *at least* and *not more than* play an important role. Note that *at least 30% of* the total means *30% or more*. And *not more than 20%* means *20% or less*. Requirement for orange juice = 30% of 400 cups = (0.30) (400) = 120 cups of orange juice. Note, however, that this is only the minimum. The punch bowl may contain 120 *or more* cups of orange juice. Ginger ale may be 80 cups or less.

30. **C**

$$\frac{\text{is}}{\text{of}} = \%$$

"is" becomes $\dfrac{1}{2^3} = \dfrac{1}{8}$

"of" becomes $2^3 = 8$

$$\frac{\text{is}}{\text{of}} = \frac{\frac{1}{8}}{8} = \frac{1}{8} \div \frac{8}{1} = \frac{1}{8} \cdot \frac{1}{8} = \frac{1}{64} = 0.016 \approx 1.6\%$$

Algebra

1. **E** Substituting $x = -3$ leaves

$$y = (-3 + 5)(-3 - 5)$$
$$y = (2)(-8)$$
$$y = -16$$

2. **C** First, circle $x + 1$, because that's what the ultimate question is. Solving the given equation, subtract 4 from both sides:

$$9x + 4 = -32$$
$$\underline{-4 \quad -4}$$
$$9x = -36$$

Divide both sides by 9:

$$\frac{9x}{9} = \frac{-36}{9}$$
$$x = -4$$

Therefore, plugging in the value –4 for x gives $x + 1 = -4 + 1 = -3$.

3. **A** Notice that $(4)(4)(4) = 64$ and $(8)(8) = 64$. Therefore,

$$(4)(4)(4)(4) = \frac{(8)(8)}{p}$$
$$(64)(4) = \frac{64}{p}$$

Canceling 64 on each side:

$$4 = \frac{1}{p}$$

Cross-multiplying:

$$4p = 1$$
$$p = \frac{1}{4}$$

4. **D** Plugging in the given values for a, b, and c:

$$a^{bc} =$$
$$2^{(3)(2)} =$$
$$2^6 = 64$$

5. **E** The square root of a number is always assumed to be a positive answer unless the square root symbol has a negative sign preceding it. Only Choice E, when replaced for x, produces a negative answer for the square root, thus cannot be the value for x in the given statement.

6. **E** If t and p both equal 4, then $\frac{1}{4} + \frac{1}{4} = \frac{1}{2}$. In this case, $t + p$ would equal 8. But t could equal 1 and p could equal -2, which would also make

$$\frac{1}{t} + \frac{1}{p} = \frac{1}{2}$$

$$\frac{1}{1} + \frac{1}{-2} = \frac{1}{2}$$

In this case, $t + p$ would equal -1. No definitive sum of $t + p$ can be determined.

7. **C** Since a and b are positive integers, they must be 6 and 5, respectively, because they are the only integers whose difference of their squares will equal 11 ($36 - 25 = 11$). Therefore, twice 6 plus twice 5 is $12 + 10$, or 22.

8. **A** $x - 2$ is exactly four less than $x + 2$. Because $x + 2$ equals y, you know that $x - 2$ will be four less, or $y - 4$.

9. **E** $(a + b)^2 = a^2 + 2ab + b^2$. If $ab = -5$, then $2ab = -10$. Plugging this in for $2ab$:

$$(a + b)^2 = a^2 - 10 + b^2$$

Plugging in the given $(a + b)^2 = 16$:

$$16 = a^2 - 10 + b^2$$

$$26 = a^2 + b^2$$

10. **E** The key phrase in this problem is *must also be an even integer*. A multiple of an even integer will result in an even number. Thus, adding or subtracting 1 from any even multiple will result in an odd number, eliminating choices A and B. In Choice C, if you were to select x as 2, $\frac{x}{2} + 1$ would produce an even answer. But if you were to select x as 4, $\frac{x}{2} + 1$ would produce an odd answer, thus Choice C is eliminated. In a similar manner, Choice D can be eliminated. Therefore, only Choice E will *always* produce an even integer.

11. **D** Factoring the quadratic expression $m^2 + 11m + 30$ gives $(m + 5)(m + 6)$. Noting that the 5 and 6 represent y and z (or z and y), $yz = 5(6)$, or 30.

12. **C** Notice that $4x + 10y$ is exactly twice $2x + 5y$. Therefore, the answer is twice 32, or 64.

13. **D** Start with $25q^2p^2 = 8x$. Since you want an expression for $\dfrac{q^2p^2}{4}$, begin by dividing each side of $25q^2p^2 = 8x$ by 25. Then multiply each side of that result by $\dfrac{1}{4}$.

$$25q^2p^2 = 8x$$
$$\frac{25q^2p^2}{25} = \frac{8x}{25}$$
$$q^2p^2 = \frac{8x}{25}$$
$$\frac{1}{4}(q^2p^2) = \frac{1}{4}\left(\frac{8x}{25}\right)$$
$$\frac{q^2p^2}{4} = \frac{8x}{100} = \frac{2x}{25}$$

14. **E** Either n or $(n + 1)$ may be even and the other odd. Since you're looking for what "must be true," this eliminates choices A and B. Since n and $(n + 1)$ are consecutive integers, they may be 1 and 2, or 2 and 3, or 3 and 4, or 4 and 5, and so on. Notice that their product will always be an even integer.

15. **C** The coordinates of point C are both negative. Thus, the product of two negative numbers will be positive. All the other points will either have a negative or a zero product.

16. **E** First, try using 1, 2, and 3 as the three integers, because these integers usually illustrate the exception to the rule. Using these three integers reveals that choices A, B, and C are incorrect, because they will not be true with 1, 2, and 3. Choice D will be true with 1, 2, and 3, but it may not be true with many other integers (say, 5, 10, and 15). Notice that no matter what positive integers are inserted in Choice E, the largest of the integers will always be greater than the middle integer divided by the smallest.

17. **E** To find the greatest possible value of $\left(\dfrac{a}{b}\right)^2$, use the largest possible value for a (as the numerator) and the *smallest* possible value for b as the denominator). Thus, $\dfrac{a}{b}$ would equal $\dfrac{0.05}{0.01}$, which equals 5. Therefore, $\left(\dfrac{a}{b}\right)^2$ will be 5^2, or 25.

18. **D** The necessary condition refers to the denominator not equaling 0, because you cannot divide by 0. Therefore, $xyz \neq 0$.

19. **A** Multiplying each side of the equation $\frac{1}{5} + \frac{1}{2} + \frac{1}{x} = 7$ by the common denominator $10x$ gives $\frac{10x}{5} + \frac{10x}{2} + \frac{10x}{x} = 7(10x)$.

Reducing:

$$2x + 5x + 10 = 70x$$
$$7x + 10 = 70x$$

Subtracting $7x$ from both sides:

$$\begin{array}{r} 7x + 10 = 70x \\ -7x \qquad -7x \\ \hline 10 = 63x \end{array}$$

Dividing by 63:

$$\frac{10}{63} = x$$

20. **D** Set up an equation:

Let x be the unknown amount of original solution. Solutions will be expressed in terms of concentration of water: 90% orange juice implies 10% water and $\frac{1}{4}$ water implies 25% water.

$$(\text{water at the beginning}) + (\text{water added}) = (\text{water at the end})$$
$$0.10(x) + 2 = 0.25(x + 2)$$
$$0.10x + 2 = 0.25x + 0.50$$
$$1.5 = 0.15x$$
$$10 = x$$

x is the number of liters in the original solution. Because the final solution is 2 additional liters of water, the final solution will contain 12 liters.

21. **A** Ernie first purchased a certain number of apples (x) for a certain price per apple (y). Therefore, he paid xy, which equals $5. He later learned that by purchasing 20% more apples ($1.2x$), he would have been given 20% off the per item price ($0.8y$). Therefore, he would have paid $(1.2x)(0.8y) = 0.96xy$. Since $xy = 5, Ernie would have paid a new total of $0.96($5) = 4.80, which equals 20¢ less than the original total.

22. **D** Setting up an equation, let x be the amount at 12%. Then ($2,000 – x$) is the amount at 7%.

$$0.12x + 0.07(2,000 - x) = 200$$
$$0.12x + 140 - 0.07x = 200$$
$$0.05x + 140 = 200$$
$$0.05x = 60$$
$$\frac{0.05x}{0.05} = \frac{60}{0.05}$$
$$x = \$1,200$$

23. **B** Formula:

$$\frac{\text{number}}{\text{cost}} = \frac{\text{number}}{\text{cost}}$$

If x represents the cost of n pencils, we have, by substitution,

$$\frac{p}{c} = \frac{n}{x}$$
$$px = cn$$
$$x = \frac{cn}{p} \text{ cents}$$

24. **C** Formula:

selling price = original price – discount

If x = the original price, we substitute

$$165 = x - 0.40x$$
$$\frac{165}{0.60} = \frac{0.60x}{0.60}$$
$$275 = x$$

25. **D** Adding the x values together and y values together of points A and B

$$(1,8)$$
$$+ \ (9,4)$$
$$\overline{(10,12)}$$

Dividing each by 2 to find the midpoint leaves (5,6).

Geometry

1. **E** If l_1 and l_2 are parallel, then $z = 20°$. Therefore, supplementary angle x equals 160°, as does vertical angle y.

   Therefore, $160° + 160° = 320°$.

2. **E** Since angle x and angle $5x$ are supplementary (their sum is a straight line, or 180°), then $5x + x = 180°$, and therefore, $x = 30°$. So the third angle of the triangle within the intersecting lines is the vertical angle of x, or 30°. The three angles of the triangle are thus 30°, 40°, and y. Therefore, $30 + 40 + y = 180$. So $y = 110°$.

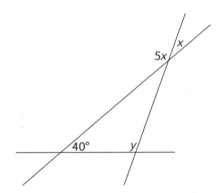

3. **D** Totaling the sum of the three angles in large $\triangle ABC$,

   $2x + 3x + (x + 3x + x) = 10x$

   Since there are 180° in a triangle, $10x = 180°$. Then $x = 18°$.

   Thus, in small $\triangle CEB$,

   $x + 3x + p = 180°$

   $\quad 4x + p = 180°$

   Since x is 18°,

   $\quad 4(18) + p = 180°$

   $\quad\quad 72 + p = 180°$

   $\quad\quad\quad\quad p = 108°$

4. **B** Chord *MOD* is a diameter cutting the circle in half. Therefore, arc *MAD* is 180°. Since arc *AD* is 80°, that leaves 100° in arc *MA*. ∠*MDA* is an inscribed angle intercepting arc *MA*, 100°. Since an inscribed angle equals half its intercepted arc, ∠*MDA* is 50°.

5. **E** △*ABC* is an isosceles triangle, so the base angles are equal, but nothing in the information given in the problem allows you to draw any conclusions about the relationship of *r* to *p*. $\overline{AD}$ is not necessarily an angle bisector.

6. **D** Since vertical angles are equal,

$$9x - 10 = 35$$
$$9x = 45$$
$$x = 5$$

7. **C** Ten cubes can be fitted across. Four cubes can be fitted along the depth. Only two cubes can be stacked along the height. Thus, $10 \times 4 \times 2 = 80$ cubes.

8. **E** Since the area of one face of a cube is 49, its edges must each be 7 (as each face is a perfect square). Knowing each edge is 7, you may now figure its volume using $V =$ length times width times height, or $7 \times 7 \times 7 = 343$.

9. **C** Since the radius of circle *O* is $\sqrt{2}$, its diameter is $2\sqrt{2}$, which is also the diagonal of the square. The side of a square and its diagonal are always in a 1 to $1\sqrt{2}$ ratio. Therefore, if the diagonal is $2\sqrt{2}$, a side of the square must be 2. Hence, its area is 2 times 2, or 4.

10. **D** First, find the total interior degrees in a pentagon:

$$\text{total interior degrees} = (\text{number of sides} - 2)(180)$$
$$= (5 - 2)(180)$$
$$= 3(180)$$
$$= 540$$

Now, let the angles equal $2x$, $3x$, $4x$, $5x$, and 6x. Their sum is $20x$. Therefore,

$$20x = 540$$
$$x = 27$$

Therefore, the largest angle, $6x$, is $6(27) = 162°$.

11. **E** Since $\angle POQ$ is marked a right angle, $\triangle POQ$ is a right triangle with hypotenuse 13 and one leg 5 (the radius of circle O). Therefore, the other leg, OQ, must be 12 (a 5-12-13 right triangle). Because line segment OK is a radius of circle O, that equals 5, leaving a distance of 7 for KQ, the radius of circle Q.

Thus, the area of circle Q is

$A = \pi r^2$

$A = \pi(7)^2$

$A = 49\pi$

12. **B** Since you know the area of circle O, you can find its radius.

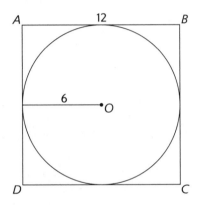

$A = \pi r^2$

$36\pi = \pi r^2$

$36\cancel{\pi} = \cancel{\pi} r^2$

$6 = r$

Now that you know the radius of the circle is 6, you can see that each side will be twice 6, or 12. Thus, its perimeter is 4(12), or 48.

13. **B** The volume of the cylindrical tank is

$V = \pi r^2 h$

$V = \pi(6)^2(9)$

$V = \pi 36(9)$

$V = 324\pi$

However, the tank must be filled only $\frac{2}{3}$ full. Therefore,
$\frac{2}{3}(324\pi) = 216\pi$

14. **A** To find the area of the shaded region, first find the area of the larger triangle. Then subtract the area of the smaller, unshaded triangle. The area of the large triangle is $\frac{1}{2}bh$, or $\frac{1}{2}(10)5 = 25$. Now find the area of the small, unshaded triangle.

$A = \frac{1}{2}bh$

$A = \frac{1}{2}(5)(4)$

$A = 10$

Subtracting, $25 - 10 = 15$, the area of the shaded region.

15. **C** The larger triangle is actually two 30-60-90 degree triangles, whose sides are in the ratio $1 : \sqrt{3} : 2$. Therefore, $p = 1$, and $q = 2$. Their product is $(1)(2) = 2$.

16. **E** Since the rectangle's sides are 2 and 16, its perimeter is $2 + 2 + 16 + 16 = 36$. Therefore, a square with the same perimeter, 36, has sides of 9 each. Therefore, the area of the square is $9 \times 9 = 81$.

17. **E** The hexagon is composed of six individual equilateral triangles, each having a base of 10. If a height is constructed within one of these triangles, then the height divides the triangle into equal 30-60-90 degree triangles. Thus, the height may be quickly calculated, using the relationship of the sides of any 30-60-90 degree triangle: $1, \sqrt{3}, 2$. The area of one triangle is therefore $\frac{1}{2}bh$, or $\frac{1}{2}(10)(5\sqrt{3}) = 25\sqrt{3}$. The area of the hexagon is 6 times this, or $150\sqrt{3}$.

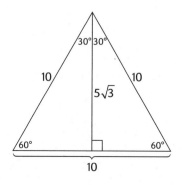

18. **B** If z equals 100°, $x + v = 80°$, since x, v, and z together equal 180° (a straight angle). Since l_2 bisects the angle composed of x and v, each must equal 40°.

19. **D** Since $\overline{RP}$ passes through center O, chord ROP is a diameter. Thus, inscribed angle RSP intercepts 180° of arc. Therefore, $\angle RSP$ measures 90°. $\triangle RSP$ is, therefore, a right triangle with hypotenuse of 10 (its diameter) and one leg 6 and is a 3-4-5 right triangle. The other side must be 8.

20. **C** $\triangle ABC$ is a 3-4-5 right triangle. Because $AB = 6$ and $BC = 8$, you know that $AC = 10$. Notice that $\triangle ADC$ is a 30-60-90 triangle. Its sides are always in the ratio of $1 : \sqrt{3} : 2$. Therefore, since the "2 side" is here 10, each side is actually multiplied by 5. Hence the other two sides are 5 and $5\sqrt{3}$. Now the area of $\triangle ADC$ may be computed.

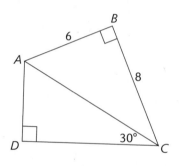

$$A = \frac{1}{2}bh$$

$$A = \frac{1}{2}\left(5\sqrt{3}\right)(5)$$

$$A = \frac{25\sqrt{3}}{2}$$

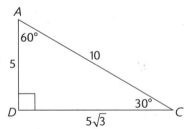

21. **D** Using the coordinates of the points given, a right triangle may be constructed as shown. Notice that the horizontal length of the triangle is 6; its vertical leg is 8. Therefore, it is a 3-4-5 right triangle. Its hypotenuse (side AB) must be 10.

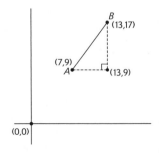

22. **B** Since $FG = 16$ feet, $EH = 16$ feet. (Opposite sides of a parallelogram are equal.) Since $\overline{BD}$ is an altitude, $ED = DH = 8$ feet. (The altitude of an isosceles triangle is also the median.)

$(EB)^2 = (BD)^2 + (ED)^2$ (right triangle)

$(EB)^2 = 6^2 + 8^2 = 100$

$EB = 10$ feet

$AB = BE + EA$ (given: $EA = 1$ foot)

Therefore, $AB = 11$ feet.

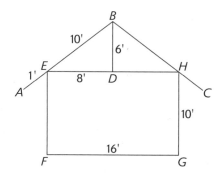

23. **A** This figure represents both a rectangle and a semicircle. Use the following formulas:

area of a rectangle $= lw$

area of a semicircle $= \dfrac{\pi r^2}{2}$

area of this figure $= lw + \dfrac{\pi r^2}{2}$

24. **D** Given that $r =$ width of the ring (shaded portion) and $r =$ radius of the inner circle, $2r =$ radius of the entire circle. The area of a circle $= \pi r^2$. The area of the entire circle minus the area of the inner circle equals the area of the shaded portion. By substitution, then,

$\pi(2r)^2$ or $4\pi r^2$ minus $\pi(r)^2$ or $\pi r^2 = 3\pi r^2$ (area of shaded portion)

$\dfrac{\text{area of the shaded portion}}{\text{area of the entire circle}} = \dfrac{3\pi r^2}{4\pi r^2} = \dfrac{3}{4} = 75\%$

25. **D** The area of a circle $= \pi r^2$. If $x =$ radius of the original circle, then $2x =$ radius of the new circle. The area of the original circle $= \pi x^2$. The area of the new circle $= \pi(2x)^2 = 4\pi x^2$. Therefore, the area of the original circle has been multiplied by 4.

Procedure Problems

1. **E** Since the steering wheel grip cost three times the seat cushion, call the seat cushion x, and the steering wheel grip will then be $3x$. Now notice that you do not have any other information except the price of the floor mat with tax. You have no way of determining in terms of dollars any of the statements, I, II, III, or IV. Deriving an answer in terms of an unknown (for example, $3x$) is not determining a value.

2. **D** The only concrete piece of information from which you can begin is that Sue's car is a 2009 model. Therefore, you can first determine the approximate age of Sue's car (by subtracting 2003 from the year it is now). When you know the age of Sue's car, you can find the age of John's car, because statement I says that his car is a year older than Sue's car. You can then find the age of Maria's truck, since statement II says it is one year newer than John's car. So you can determine the approximate age of Sue's car, Maria's truck, and John's car.

3. **D** Statements I and II are equations finding a balance by subtracting 5 from 10. In statement I, since the current balance is $5 less than last year's balance, $10, the current balance equals $10 − $5. In statement II, the same equation will also work to calculate last year's balance. Statement III cannot be calculated by 10 − 5, because 10 *percent* equals 0.10.

4. **E** To find the average of a number of items, you must find the sum of the items and then divide by the number of items. Note that since Test 4 is weighted double, it will actually count as *two* scores (hence, as tests 4 and 5). So, setting up the equation:

$$\frac{\text{sum of the scores}}{\text{number of scores}} = \text{average}$$

$$\frac{83 + 85 + 100 + x + x}{5} = 90$$

Note that since Test 4 is weighted double, the number of scores is 5, not 4.

5. **C** Since 845 equals Q, then 846 equals $Q + 1$. Therefore, 27,456 times 846 may be expressed as $(P)(Q + 1)$.

6. **C** To check $(x + 1)(x + 2) = x^2 + 3x + 2$, Francisco merely has to plug in any positive value for x. If the equation balances, it is correct. For example, using 1 for x

$$(x + 1)(x + 2) = x^2 + 3x + 2$$
$$(1 + 1)(1 + 2) = 1^2 + 3(1) + 2$$
$$(2)(3) = 1 + 3 + 2$$
$$6 = 6$$

The equation balances. Plugging in 1 enables Francisco to check his answer.

7. **D** The word *sum* indicates addition. The sum of two numbers is therefore $x + y$. If this sum equals one of the numbers, then the equation will be either $x + y = x$ or $x + y = y$.

8. **C** If Jorge is 10 years old now, then last year he was $10 - 1$. The question states that Jorge's age last year (9) is three years less than twice Teresa's age now. Therefore, letting T equal Teresa's age now, three years less than twice T can be represented as $2T - 3$. Thus,

$$10 - 1 = 2T - 3$$
$$9 = 2T - 3$$

9. **E** If a tie costs T dollars, then each tie $= T$. If a suit jacket costs four times the price of a tie, then each suit jacket $= 4T$. Hence, the cost of two ties and three suit jackets is $2(T) + 3(4T)$.

10. **C** To determine the area of a square that has the same perimeter as a rectangle 18 by 22, Rosanna must:

    a. First find the perimeter of the rectangle by adding 18 and 22 and then doubling that sum.

    b. Divide the result by 4 to find the side of a square of the same perimeter.

    c. Square that to find the area.

Quantitative Comparison Strategies

This unique problem type appears on the SAT, the PSAT, and the GRE, among other exams. It tests your ability to compare two given quantities using your knowledge of mathematics.

Complex computation is not required. In fact, mathematical insight allows you to solve this type of problem more quickly than you can solve the more common math ability type of problem (see Chapter 5).

Directions

In this section, you will be given two quantities—one in column A and one in column B. You are to determine a relationship between the two quantities and mark

A if the quantity in Column A is greater than the quantity in Column B

B if the quantity in Column B is greater than the quantity in Column A

C if the two quantities are equal

D if the comparison cannot be determined from the information given

Analysis

The purpose here is to make a comparison; therefore, exact answers are not always necessary. (***Remember:*** In many cases, you can tell whether you're taller than someone without knowing that person's height. Comparisons such as this can be made with only partial information—just enough to compare.) Choice D is not a possible answer if there are *values* in each column, because you can always compare values.

If you get different relationships, depending on the values you choose for variables, then the answer is always Choice D. Notice that there are only four possible choices here. *Never* mark Choice E on your answer sheet for quantitative comparison questions.

Suggested Approach with Examples

Quantitative comparison questions emphasize shortcuts, insight, and quick techniques. Long and/or involved mathematical computations are unnecessary and are contrary to the purpose of this section.

Cancel Out Equal Amounts

Note that you can add, subtract, multiply, and divide both columns by the same value, and the relationship between them will not change. ***Exception:*** You should *not* multiply or divide each column by negative numbers, because then the relationship reverses. Squaring both columns is permissible, as long as each side is positive.

Column A	**Column B**
$21 \times 43 \times 56$	$44 \times 21 \times 57$

Canceling (or dividing) 21 from each side leaves you with:

43×56	44×57

You should do the rest of this problem by inspection—Column B is obviously greater than Column A without doing any multiplication. Each number in Column B is larger than the corresponding number in Column A. You could've reached the correct answer by actually multiplying out each column, but you save valuable time if you don't. The correct answer is Choice B.

Make Partial Comparisons

Partial comparisons can be valuable in giving you insight into finding a comparison. If you can't simply make a complete comparison, look at each column part by part. For example:

Column A	**Column B**
$\dfrac{1}{3} - \dfrac{1}{65}$	$\dfrac{1}{58} - \dfrac{1}{63}$

Because finding a common denominator would be too time-consuming, you should first compare the first fraction in each column (a partial comparison). Notice that $\frac{1}{3}$ is greater than $\frac{1}{58}$. Now compare the second fractions and notice that $\frac{1}{65}$ is less than $\frac{1}{63}$. Using some common sense and insight, if you start with a larger number and subtract a smaller number, it must be greater than starting with a smaller number and subtracting a larger number, as illustrated here:

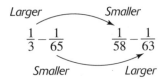

The correct answer is Choice A.

Keep Perspective

Always keep the column in perspective before starting any calculations. Take a good look at the value in each column before starting to work on one column. For example:

Column A	Column B
7^2	2^8

After looking at each column—note that the answer cannot be Choice D because there are values in each column—compute the value on the left: $7^2 = 49$. There is no need to take 2 out to the 8th power. Just do as little as necessary: $2^2 = 4$, $2^3 = 8$, $2^4 = 16$, $2^5 = 32$. Stop. You can tell now that 2^8 is much greater than 49. The correct answer is Choice B. Approximating can also be valuable while remembering to keep the columns in perspective.

Plug In 0, 1, −1

If a problem involves variables (without an equation), substitute in the numbers 0, 1, and −1. Then try $\frac{1}{2}$, and 2 if necessary. Using 0, 1, and −1 will often tip off the answer. For example:

Column A	Column B
$a + b$	ab

Substituting 0 for *a* and 0 for *b* gives

$$0 + 0 \qquad\qquad 0(0)$$

Therefore,

$$0 \qquad = \qquad 0$$

Using these values for *a* and *b* gives the answer: Choice C. But anytime you multiply two numbers, it isn't the same as when you add them, so try some other values.

Substituting 1 for *a* and –1 for *b* gives

$$1 + (-1) \qquad\qquad 1(-1)$$

Therefore,

$$0 \qquad > \qquad -1$$

and the answer is now Choice A.

Anytime you get more than one comparison (different relationships), depending on the values chosen, the correct answer must be Choice D (the relationship cannot be determined). Notice that if you had substituted the values $a = 4$ and $b = 5$, or $a = 6$ and $b = 7$, or $a = 7$ and $b = 9$, and so on, you would repeatedly have gotten Choice B and might have chosen the incorrect answer.

Simplify

Often, simplifying one or both columns can make an answer evident. For example:

Column A	**Column B**

a, b, c, all greater than 0

$a(b + c)$	$ab + ac$

Using the distributive property on Column A to simplify, gives *ab* and *ac*; therefore, the columns are equal.

Look for a Simple Way

Sometimes you can solve for a column in one step, without solving and substituting. If you have to solve an equation or equations to give the columns values, take a second and see if there is a very simple way to get an answer before going through all the steps. For example:

Column A	Column B

$$4x + 2 = 10$$

$2x + 1$	4

Hopefully, you would spot that the easiest way to solve for $2x + 1$ is directly by dividing $4x + 2 = 10$ by 2, leaving $2x + 1 = 5$.

Therefore,

5	>	4

Solving for x first in the equation, and then substituting, would also have worked, but it would have been more time-consuming. The correct answer is Choice A.

Mark Diagrams

Marking diagrams can be very helpful for giving insight into a problem. Remember that figures and diagrams are meant for positional information only. Just because something *looks* larger isn't enough reason to choose an answer. For example:

Column A	Column B

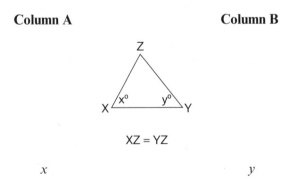

XZ = YZ

x	y

Even though *x* appears larger, this isn't enough. Mark in the diagrams as shown.

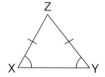

Notice that you should mark things of equal measure with the same markings, and because angles opposite equal sides in a triangle are equal, *x* = *y*. The correct answer is Choice C.

Use Easier Numbers

If you're given information that's unfamiliar to you and difficult to work with, change the number slightly (but remember what you've changed) to something easier to work with. For example:

Column A   **Column B**

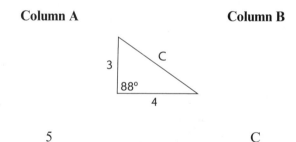

5   C

Since the 88° shown in the figure is unfamiliar to work with, change it to 90° for now, so that you may use the Pythagorean theorem to solve for *c*.

Solving for *c*:

$$a^2 + b^2 = c^2$$
$$3^2 + 4^2 = c^2$$
$$9 + 16 = c^2$$
$$25 = c^2$$
$$5 = c$$

But because you used 90° instead of 88°, you should realize that the side opposite the 88° will be slightly smaller or less than 5. The correct answer is then Choice A, 5 > *c*. (You may have noticed the 3-4-5 triangle relationship and not needed the Pythagorean theorem.)

A Patterned Plan of Attack

Quantitative Comparison

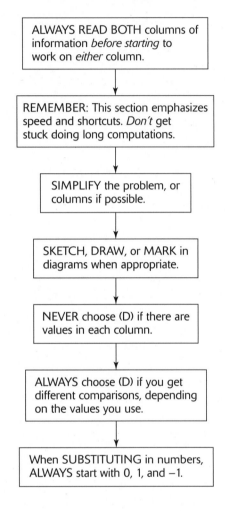

ALWAYS READ BOTH columns of information *before starting* to work on *either* column.

REMEMBER: This section emphasizes speed and shortcuts. *Don't* get stuck doing long computations.

SIMPLIFY the problem, or columns if possible.

SKETCH, DRAW, or MARK in diagrams when appropriate.

NEVER choose (D) if there are values in each column.

ALWAYS choose (D) if you get different comparisons, depending on the values you use.

When SUBSTITUTING in numbers, ALWAYS start with 0, 1, and −1.

When in DOUBT, plug in numbers.

Quantitative Comparison Practice

Directions

In this section, you will be given two quantities—one in Column A and one in Column B. You are to determine a relationship between the two quantities and mark

A if the quantity in Column A is greater than the quantity in Column B

B if the quantity in Column B is greater than the quantity in Column A

C if the quantities are equal

D if the comparison cannot be determined from the information given

Common information:

Information centered above both columns refers to one or both columns.

All numbers used are real numbers.

Figures are intended to provide useful positional information, but they are not necessarily drawn to scale and should not be used to estimate sizes by measurement.

Lines that appear straight can be assumed to be straight.

Arithmetic and Data Analysis

Questions

	Column A	Column B
1.	$\frac{2}{5} \times \frac{1}{9} \times \frac{3}{8}$	$\frac{2}{11} \times \frac{2}{5} \times \frac{3}{8}$
2.	$\frac{1}{8} \times \frac{1}{4} \times \frac{1}{9}$	$0.125 \times 0.25 \times 0.1$
3.	The average of 12, 14, 16, 18, 20, and 22	The average of 11, 13, 15, 17, 19, and 21
4.	The average speed (in miles per hour) of a car that travels 8 miles in 15 minutes	30

	Column A	**Column B**
5.	0.004	0.04%

6.
$$\frac{1}{79} - \frac{1}{81}$$
$$\frac{1}{71} - \frac{1}{80}$$

7. The percentage increase from
$400 to $500

20%

8. The price of 2 pounds of candy
at 42¢ per pound

The price of 3 pounds of candy
at 32¢ per pound

9. 4% interest on $2,000 for 1 year

8% interest on $1,000 for 2 years

10.
$$9^5 - 9^4$$
$$9^4$$

11.
$$7\sqrt{3}$$
$$3\sqrt{7}$$

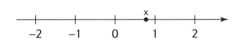

12. 1
$$\frac{1}{x}$$

13.
$$9^2 + 8 \times 10^4 - 6^{10}$$
$$9^2 + 8 \times 10^4 + 6^{10}$$

14.
$$\frac{8 \times 10^4}{2 \times 10^2}$$
400

A hat contains 3 blue pegs, 2 red pegs, and 1 white peg.

15. The probability of randomly
picking a blue peg

The probability of randomly
picking something other than a
blue peg

Algebra

Questions

	Column A	Column B

$$x > 2$$

1.　　$3x + 2$　　　　　　$2x + 3$

$$\frac{2x}{7} = 8$$

$$3y = 87$$

2.　　x　　　　　　y

$$\frac{s}{r} > \frac{3}{5}$$

3.　　s　　　　　　r

x is a negative fraction

4.　　$\dfrac{1}{x}$　　　　　　$-x$

5.　　$-(r - s)$　　　　　　$-r + s$

6.　　$(a^4 + b^3)^2$　　　　　　$(a^3b^6)^3$

	Column A	**Column B**

$$x < 4 < 0$$

7. $\qquad x + 4 \qquad\qquad\qquad\qquad y - 4$

$$x \neq 0$$
$$y \neq 0$$

8. $\qquad 1 + \dfrac{x}{y} \qquad\qquad\qquad\qquad \dfrac{x + y}{y}$

$$y > 0$$

9. The average of $3y$, $5y$, 3, and 5 $\qquad$ The average of $2y$, $6y$, 4, and 10

$$0 < y < x$$

10. $\qquad (x + 2)(y + 3) \qquad\qquad\qquad (x + 3)(y + 2)$

15 is 30% of x

12 is 25% of y

11. $\qquad\qquad x \qquad\qquad\qquad\qquad\qquad y$

Column A	Column B

$$m > 0$$

12. m^3 $2m^2$

$$\frac{r}{3} = \frac{s}{5}$$

13. $5r$ $3s$

$$x > 0$$
$$y > 0$$

14. $\sqrt{x + y}$ $\sqrt{x} + \sqrt{y}$

$$x + 3y = 7$$
$$4x + 12y = 28$$

15. x y

Geometry

Questions

Questions 1 and 2 refer to the following diagram.

Column A	Column B

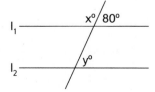

l_1 and l_2 are parallel lines

453

	Column A	**Column B**
1.	x	y
2.	The circumference of a semicircle with radius 4 inches	The perimeter of a pentagon with each side 4 inches long

Questions 3, 4, and 5 refer to the following diagram.

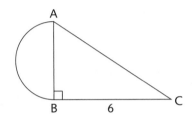

$\overline{AB}$ is a diameter of the semicircle.

$\triangle ABC$ is an isosceles right triangle.

	Column A	**Column B**
3.	Area of a semicircle	Area of a triangle
4.	$\overparen{AB}$	AC
5.	$\angle A$	$45°$

Questions 6 through 9 refer to the following diagram.

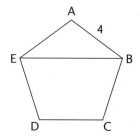

ABCDE is a regular pentagon.

Column A	**Column B**

6.   *AB*   *EB*

7.   Sum of interior angles of   360°
     pentagon *ABCDE*

8. $\angle AEB$ $\angle ABE$

9. $\angle D + \angle C$ 180°

Questions 10, 11, and 12 refer to the following diagram.

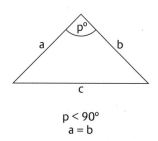

$p < 90°$
$a = b$

	Column A	**Column B**
10.	$b + c$	a
11.	c^2	$a^2 + b^2$
12.	a	$c - b$

Questions 13, 14, and 15 refer to the following diagram.

Vertices of square ABCD lie on the circle.

	Column A	**Column B**
13.	$\angle DAC$	$\angle BCA$
14.	Radius of circle	$\dfrac{\sqrt{2}}{2}$
15.	$2 \times$ area square $ABCD$	Area of circle

Answer Key for Quantitative Comparison Practice

The boldface page number in parentheses following each answer will direct you to the complete explanation for that specific problem. *Read this explanation first.* The other page numbers in parentheses refer to the suggested basic review section.

Arithmetic and Data Analysis

1. B (p. **458,** 43)
2. A (p. **458,** 43, 50)
3. A (p. **458,** 83)
4. A (p. **458,** 329)
5. A (p. **458,** 55)
6. B (p. **458,** 35)
7. A (p. **459,** 63)
8. B (p. **459**)
9. B (p. **459,** 320)
10. A (p. **459,** 64)
11. A (p. **459,** 75)
12. B (p. **459,** 19)
13. B (p. **459,** 16)
14. C (p. **460,** 69)
15. C (p. **460,** 77)

Algebra

1. A (p. **460,** 122)
2. B (p. **460,** 125)
3. D (p. **460,** 130, 176)
4. B (p. **461,** 122)
5. C (p. **461,** 21)
6. D (p. **461,** 122, 144)
7. D (p. **461,** 122)
8. C (p. **461,** 172)
9. B (p. **461,** 143, 144)
10. A (p. **462,** 122, 145)
11. A (p. **462,** 58)
12. D (p. **462,** 122)
13. C (p. **462,** 134)
14. B (p. **463,** 202)
15. D (p. **463,** 136)

Geometry

1. A (p. **463,** 246)
2. B (p. **463,** 250, 284)
3. B (p. **463,** 265, 284)
4. A (p. **464,** 265, 283)
5. C (p. **464,** 265)
6. B (p. **464,** 258, 276)
7. A (p. **464,** 276)
8. C (p. **465,** 258)
9. A (p. **465,** 276)
10. A (p. **465,** 258)
11. B (p. **465,** 262)
12. A (p. **465,** 258)
13. C (p. **465,** 287)
14. C (p. **465,** 265, 287)
15. A (p. **466,** 277, 284)

Quantitative Comparison Answers and Explanations

Arithmetic and Data Analysis

1. **B** Dividing out equal fractions from both sides ($\frac{2}{5}$ and $\frac{3}{8}$), leaves Column A with $\frac{1}{9}$ and Column B with $\frac{2}{11}$. Cross-multiply up:

   $$\overset{\textstyle\textcircled{11}}{\underset{\textstyle\frac{1}{9}}{}}\diagdown\hspace{-1.2em}\diagup\overset{\textstyle\textcircled{18}}{\underset{\textstyle\frac{2}{11}}{}}$$

   Since the larger product is always over the larger fraction, Column B is greater.

2. **A** Change the decimals in Column B to fractions:

   $$\frac{125}{1,000}\times\frac{25}{100}\times\frac{1}{10}$$

   and reduce to the simplest form, and you get this comparison:

   $$\frac{1}{8}\times\frac{1}{4}\times\frac{1}{9} \qquad \frac{1}{8}\times\frac{1}{4}\times\frac{1}{10}$$

   Canceling out the $\frac{1}{8}$ and $\frac{1}{4}$ from each side leaves

   $$\frac{1}{9}>\frac{1}{10}$$

3. **A** The fastest way to determine which average is greater is to notice that each of the numbers in Column A is one larger than its corresponding number in Column B. Therefore, Column A's average must be greater than Column B's average.

4. **A** To find the average speed of the car in miles per hour, multiply 8 miles by 4, since 15 minutes is $\frac{1}{4}$ of an hour:

   $$8 \times 4 = 32$$

   32 miles per hour is the average speed and 32 > 30.

5. **A** Expressed as a percent, Column A equals 0.4%, which is greater than Column B.

6. **B** This problem is best solved by inspection. Notice that the values in Column A are very close together; therefore, their difference would be very small. Column B's values are farther apart, having a greater difference.

7. **A** To find percent increase, use the following formula:

   $$\text{percent change} = \frac{\text{change}}{\text{starting point}}, \text{ then convert to a percent}$$

   So,

   $$\frac{500-400}{400} = \frac{100}{400} = \frac{1}{4} = 25\% \text{ and } 25\% > 20\%$$

8. **B** Column A equals two times 42¢, or 84¢. Column B equals three times 32¢, or 96¢. Therefore, Column B is greater.

9. **B** The interest in Column A equals $2,000 times 0.04 times 1 year, or $80. The interest in Column B equals $1,000 times 0.08 times 2 years, or $160. Therefore, Column B is greater.

10. **A** 9^5 is 9×9^4, so if 9^4 is subtracted from 9^5, the remainder is obviously much greater than 9^4. Here is an alternate method:

$$\underbrace{9^5}_{\underbrace{(9 \times 9 \times 9 \times 9 \times 9)}_{59,049}} - \underbrace{9^4}_{\underbrace{(9 \times 9 \times 9 \times 9)}_{6,561}} = 52,488$$

$$52,488 > 6,561$$

11. **A** The fastest and most accurate way to compare two terms, each of which contains a square root, is to change each term to a single term under a radical. For example,

   $$7\sqrt{3} = \sqrt{3 \times 49} = \sqrt{147} \qquad 3\sqrt{7} = \sqrt{7 \times 9} = \sqrt{63}$$

   Since $\sqrt{147}$ is greater than $\sqrt{63}$, Column A is greater.

12. **B** On the number line, x is between 0 and 1. Therefore, x is a positive fraction less than 1. Plugging in a simple value for x (use $\frac{1}{2}$, an easy-to-work-with fraction less than 1), we find Column B equals $\frac{1}{\frac{1}{2}}$, which equals 2.

   Every other fraction less than 1 will also make Column B greater than 1. Therefore, Column B is greater than Column A.

13. **B** Note that the only difference in the two columns is the signs of the last values, 6^{10}. Since Column B is positive $(+6^{10})$ and Column A is negative (-6^{10}), Column B is greater than Column A. Actually calculating the numerical values is a waste of time and not necessary.

459

14. **C** Canceling in Column A gives

$\dfrac{8\times10^{4}}{2\times10^{2}}$	400
4×10^{2}	400
4×100	400
400	400

The columns are equal.

15. **C** In Column A, the probability of randomly selecting a blue peg is 3 out of a total of 6, or $\frac{3}{6}$ or $\frac{1}{2}$. In Column B, the probability of randomly selecting a color other than blue is 2 + 1 out of 6, or, again, $\frac{3}{6}$, or $\frac{1}{2}$. The columns are equal.

Algebra

1. **A** First, subtracting 2 from both sides gives $3x$ in Column A and $2x + 1$ in Column B. Since $x > 2$, start by plugging in values greater than 2 for x. Trying 2.1, then 3, then, say, 10, you'll find that Column A will always be larger.

2. **B** Solve each equation:

$$\frac{2x}{7}=8 \qquad\qquad 3y=87$$
$$\frac{7}{2}\times\frac{2x}{7}=\frac{8}{1}\times\frac{7}{2} \qquad\qquad \frac{3y}{3}=\frac{87}{3}$$
$$x=28 \qquad\qquad y=29$$

$$28 < 29$$

3. **D** Trying some values in the equation gives different outcomes. For example, when $s = 4$ and $r = 5$,

$$\frac{4}{5}>\frac{3}{5}$$
$$s < r$$

When $s = -4$ and $r = -5$,

$$\frac{-4}{-5}>\frac{3}{5}$$
$$s > r$$

No determination is possible.

4. **B** Substituting a value for x and considering the given condition (x is a negative fraction) makes it evident that Column B will always be positive and Column A will always be negative. Let $x = -\frac{1}{2}$:

$$\frac{1}{-\frac{1}{2}} \qquad -\left(\frac{-1}{2}\right)$$

$$-2 < +\frac{1}{2}$$

5. **C** This is really an example of the distributive property and can be solved by inspection. Or using an alternate method, let $r = 3$ and $s = 2$. Then

$$-(3 - 2) \qquad\qquad -3 + 2$$

$$-1 \qquad = \qquad -1$$

6. **D** Let $a = 0$ and $b = 0$. Then both columns are obviously equal. If $a = 1$ and $b = 0$, then Column A is greater than Column B. Therefore, the answer cannot be determined.

7. **D** Because x must be less than 4, Column A ($x + 4$) can equal any value less than 8. Because y must be more than 4, Column B ($y - 4$) can be any value more than 0. Therefore, between the range of 0 and 8, Column A and Column B could be equal or one column could be greater than the other. Therefore, no relationship can be determined.

8. **C** By changing the value of 1 in Column A to equal $\frac{y}{y}$, Column A can also equal $\frac{y}{y} + \frac{x}{y}$, which, combined into one fraction, equals $\frac{y+x}{y}$. Therefore, the two columns are equal. Likewise, Column B could've been broken into two fractions: $\frac{x}{y} + \frac{y}{y}$, which is the same as $\frac{x}{y} + 1$ and, thus, equal to Column A.

9. **B** Find the averages and simplify:

$$\frac{3y + 5y + 3 + 5}{4} \qquad\qquad \frac{2y + 6y + 4 + 10}{4}$$

$$\frac{8y + 8}{4} \qquad\qquad\qquad \frac{8y + 14}{4}$$

$$\frac{8y}{4} + \frac{8}{4} \qquad\qquad\qquad \frac{8y}{4} + \frac{14}{4}$$

$$2y + 2 \qquad\qquad\qquad 2y + \frac{14}{4}$$

Subtracting $2y$ from both:

$$2 < \frac{14}{4}$$

10. **A** Simplifying each column leaves

    $xy + 3x + 2y + 6$ $\qquad\qquad$ $xy + 2x + 3y + 6$

    Subtracting xy, $2x$, $2y$, and 6 from both sides leaves

    $$x > y$$

    from the condition given, $0 < y < x$.

11. **A** Solving each problem, first for x: 15 is 30% of x.

    $\dfrac{30}{100} = \dfrac{15}{x}$

    $\dfrac{3}{10} = \dfrac{15}{x}$

    Cross-multiply:

    $3x = 150$

    $x = 50$

    Solving for y: 12 is 25% of y.

    $\dfrac{25}{100} = \dfrac{12}{y}$

    $\dfrac{1}{4} = \dfrac{12}{y}$

    Cross-multiply:

    $y = 48$

    $50 > 48$

12. **D** Trying the value $m = 1$ gives

    $(1)^3$ $\qquad\qquad$ $2(1)^2$

    $1 < 2$

    Now, letting $m = 2$ gives

    $(2)^3$ $\qquad\qquad$ $2(2)^2$

    $8 = 8$

    No solution can be determined because different values give different answers.

13. **C** Cross-multiply the given equation:

    $\dfrac{r}{3} = \dfrac{s}{5}$

    leaves $5r = 3s$.

14. **B** Substituting $x = 1$ and $y = 1$ gives

   $\sqrt{1+1}$ $\qquad\qquad$ $\sqrt{1} + \sqrt{1}$

   $\sqrt{2}$ $\qquad\qquad\quad$ $1 + 1$

   1.4 $\qquad\qquad\quad$ 2

   $1.4 < 2$

   Trying other values gives the same result.

15. **D** By inspection, the two given equations are the same: $x + 3y = 7$ is the same as $4x + 12y = 28$ if the second equation is simplified by dividing by 4. Because the two equations are equivalent, no definite values for x and y can be determined.

Geometry

1. **A** That $y = 80°$ is evident by the diagram and the rules of a transversal through parallel lines. You know that $x = 100°$ because $x + 80$ must equal a straight line of $180°$, or $180 - 80 = 100$. Therefore, $100 > 80$.

2. **B** Because the circumference of a circle equals $2\pi r$, the circumference of the semicircle in Column A equals $\frac{1}{2}(2\pi r) = 4\pi$. Because π equals about 3, Column A equals approximately 12 inches. In Column B, if each side of a pentagon equals 4 inches, its perimeter equals 5 times $4 = 20$ inches. Therefore, Column B is greater.

3. **B** $AB = 6$ because $\triangle ABC$ is isosceles. The radius of the semicircle is $\frac{1}{2} AB$, or 3. Using the area formula for the circle:

   $A = \pi r^2$

   $A = \pi(3)^2$

   $A = \pi(9)$

   $A \approx 28$

   Taking $\frac{1}{2}$ of this leaves the area of the semicircle as approximately 14.

   Now, using the area formula for the triangle:

   $A = \frac{1}{2} bh$

   $A = \frac{1}{2}(6)(6)$

   $A = \frac{1}{2}(36)$

   $A = 18$

   $14 < 18$

4. **A** Using the circumference formula for a circle of diameter 6:

$C = \pi d$

$C = \pi(6)$

$C \approx 18$

Taking $\frac{1}{2}$ of this leaves 9 as the length of $\overset{\frown}{AB}$. Now, using the Pythagorean theorem to find AC:

$(AB)^2 + (BC)^2 = (AC)^2$

$(6)^2 + (6)^2 = (AC)^2$

$36 + 36 = (AC)^2$

$72 = (AC)^2$

$\sqrt{72} = AC$

Since $\sqrt{72}$ is approximately 8.5, $9 > \sqrt{72}$.

5. **C** Since $\triangle ABC$ is an isosceles right triangle, $\angle A = \angle C$ and $\angle B = 90°$. This leaves 90° to be divided evenly between $\angle A$ and $\angle C$. Therefore, $\angle A$ is 45°.

6. **B** Any diagonal of a regular pentagon is greater than any of the sides. Using an alternate method, use the formula for finding the interior degrees of a polygon—$180(N - 2)$ using 5 for N (number of sides of a pentagon):

$180(N - 2)$

$180(5 - 2)$

$180(3)$

540

There are 540° in the interior of the pentagon. Dividing this by 5 for the number of equal angles, leaves 108° in each angle. $\angle A$ is 108° in $\triangle ABE$ and, therefore, is the greatest angle in the triangle. The longest side of a triangle is across from the largest angle, so $AB < EB$.

7. **A** As you know from the previous problem, the sum of the interior angles of pentagon $ABCDE$ is 540° and 540° > 360°. Using an alternate method, the sum of the interior degrees of a pentagon can be derived by dividing the pentagon into triangles as shown:

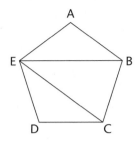

Because there are three triangles and 180° in a triangle, there are $3 \times 180° = 540°$ in the pentagon.

8. **C** Because the pentagon is equilateral, $AB = AE$, and, therefore, $\angle AEB = \angle ABE$, because angles opposite equal sides in a triangle are equal.

9. **A** As shown in the previous problems, each angle of the pentagon is 108°. Therefore, $108° + 108° = 216°$, and $216° > 180°$.

10. **A** The sum of any two sides of a triangle is greater than the third side.

11. **B** If $p = 90°$, then $c^2 = a^2 + b^2$, but since $p < 90°$, the opposite side, C, gets smaller. Therefore, $c^2 < a^2 + b^2$.

12. **A** The sum of any two sides of a triangle is greater than the third side. Therefore, the difference of any two sides of a triangle is less than the third side. Solving algebraically, $a + b > c$. Subtracting b from both sides leaves $a > c - b$.

13. **C** Since all sides of a square are equal and each corner of a square is 90°, $\triangle ADC$ and $\triangle ABC$ would each become isosceles right triangles. The acute angles in an isosceles right triangle each have measures of 45°. Therefore, $\angle DAC = \angle BCA$.

14. **C** Using the Pythagorean theorem to find the length of diameter AC gives

$$(AB)^2 + (BC)^2 = (AC)^2$$

$$(1)^2 + (1)^2 = (AC)^2$$

$$1 + 1 = (AC)^2$$

$$2 = (AC)^2$$

$$\sqrt{2} = AC$$

Since the radius is $\frac{1}{2}$ of the diameter, $\frac{1}{2}$ of $\sqrt{2}$ is $\frac{\sqrt{2}}{2}$ and $\frac{\sqrt{2}}{2} = \frac{\sqrt{2}}{2}$.

465

15. **A** Using the proper formulas:

$A = s \times s$ (area of a square)

$A = \pi r^2$ (area of a circle)

and substituting $s = 1$ and $r = \frac{\sqrt{2}}{2}$ from the previous problem,

$2 \times$ area of square ABCD	Area of circle
$2 \times (1 \times 1)$	$\pi \left(\dfrac{\sqrt{2}}{2} \right)^2$
	$\pi \times \dfrac{2}{4}$
	$\approx 3.14 \times \dfrac{1}{2}$
	≈ 1.57
$2 \;>$	1.57

Data Sufficiency Strategies

Data sufficiency is a unique problem type that appears on the GMAT. Data sufficiency problems test your ability to determine whether enough information is present in order to solve given questions. These problems usually require no complex calculations.

Directions

Each of the problems below consists of a question and two statements, labeled (1) and (2), in which certain data are given. You must decide whether the data given in the statements are *sufficient* to answer the question. Using the data given in the statements *plus* your knowledge of mathematics and everyday facts (such as the number of days in July or the meaning of *counterclockwise*), you are to mark

A if statement (1) *alone* is sufficient, but statement (2) alone is not sufficient to answer the question asked.

B if statement (2) *alone* is sufficient, but statement (1) alone is not sufficient to answer the question asked.

C if *both* statements (1) and (2) *together* are sufficient to answer the question asked, but *neither* statement *alone* is sufficient.

D if *each* statement *alone* is sufficient to answer the question asked.

E if statements (1) and (2) *neither alone nor together* are sufficient to answer the question asked, and additional data specific to the problem is needed.

Analysis

The purpose here is to determine whether information given is *sufficient* to answer the question; therefore, *do not solve the problem* unless it is absolutely necessary.

The memory aid 12TEN will simplify the directions, making them easier to memorize and/or refer to. 12TEN stands for:

1: *First* statement *alone* is sufficient, not the second. Choose A.

2: *Second* statement *alone* is sufficient, not the first. Choose B.

T: *Together* is the only way they are sufficient. Choose C.

E: *Either* statement *alone* is sufficient. Choose D.

N: *Neither* statement, *together* or *alone,* is sufficient. Choose E.

Remember: 1, 2, together, either, neither, or 12TEN. (Note: *Either* means choose D *not* E.)

Because of the structure of this type of question, you should always be able to eliminate some of the choices. If statement (1) *alone* is sufficient to answer the question, then the answer *must* be choice A or D.

If statement (1) *alone* is *not* sufficient to answer the question, then the answer *must* be choice B, C, or E. If statements (1) or (2) *alone* are *not* sufficient, then the answer *must* be choice C or E.

If statements (1) or (2) *alone* are sufficient, then you *never* try them *together.*

Sometimes geometric figures are included. Use them only for positional value; don't measure them, because they aren't necessarily drawn to scale.

Suggested Approach with Examples

Determine Necessary Information

Quickly decide what is the necessary basic information to answer the question. Then see if the data supplies that information. *For example:*

What is the area of circle *O*?

(1) The circumference is 12π.

(2) The diameter is 12.

To find the area of a circle, it is necessary to have the radius. Statement (1) gives enough information to find the radius by substituting into the circumference formula, $C = 2\pi r$, and getting $12\pi = 2\pi r$. Then simply solve for r, which is 6. Thus this area is 36π. None of this solving was necessary, though—all you need to know is that you needed the radius and could find it from the information given. Statement (2) also gives enough information to find the radius; therefore, the answer is Choice D: either will be sufficient.

Don't Solve Unless Necessary

Don't solve unless it is absolutely necessary. *For example:*

What is the value of *x*?

(1) $83x + 12 = 360$

(2) $25x + 3y = 16$

This problem is most easily solved by inspecting the first bit of data and quickly noticing that statement (1) is enough to answer the question (one variable, one equation, solvable), and statement (2) does not answer the question, which you can also determine by inspection (two variables, one equation, not solvable for a single value). The correct answer is Choice A, yet no actual solving had to be done.

Use a Simple Marking System

Use a simple marking system to assist you in making your decision. *For example:*

What is the average height of Tom, Bob, and Luke?

(1) Bob is 4 inches shorter than Luke, and Tom is 4 inches taller than Luke.

(2) Luke is 5 feet 6 inches tall.

Statement (1) is not sufficient, because no actual height is given; therefore, mark a slash through (1). Note that the answer is immediately narrowed to choice B, C, or E. Statement (2) by itself is also not sufficient, because the other two, Tom and Bob, aren't mentioned; therefore, a slash should be made through statement (2). Notice that the answer is now narrowed to choice C or E. Your markings should look as follows:

What is the average height of Tom, Bob, and Luke?

(1) Bob is 4 inches shorter than Luke, and Tom is 4 inches taller than Luke.

(2) Luke is 5 feet 6 inches tall.

Now trying them together, they are sufficient. The answer is Choice C. In marking the data, if you're not sure whether it's sufficient, put a question mark by the data and try the next bit of data. Don't waste time trying one bit of data for more than about 30 seconds.

Use Only Common Knowledge

Don't read in specialized knowledge. Use only the information given and general, or common, knowledge.

What is the runner's average speed in running around the track?

(1) One lap took 49 seconds.

(2) He ran 5 seconds faster than his previous best time.

Someone familiar with track and field might quickly assume that one lap is the standard 440 yards and would then *incorrectly* answer Choice A. This sort of assumption cannot be made, because it is from specialized knowledge in the area and, therefore, is not general knowledge. The correct answer is Choice E, because the distance around the track is not given in either bit of data.

Mark Diagrams

If a geometric figure is involved in the question, mark the figure with the information and circle what you are looking for. *For example:*

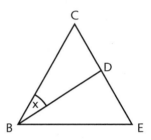

In the equilateral triangle above, what is the measure of angle x?

(1) $\overline{BD}$ is a median.

(2) $\angle BDE$ is 90°.

Notice the markings from the information given:

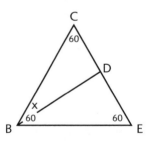

Mark in information given in statement (1) as you read it, *but remember to erase that information before you try statement (2)*. In statement (1), if $\overline{BD}$ is a median in an equilateral triangle, then it's also an angle bisector, making angle x equal to 30°. (Once again, the answer is not necessary, just the knowledge that it could be found.) Statement (2) also gives enough information because if $\angle BDE$ is 90°, then $\angle BDC$ is 90°, and $\angle x$ is 30°, as there are 180° in a triangle. Marking the diagram makes the problem easier to solve.

Draw Diagrams

If a geometric diagram is discussed but no figure is given, draw a simple diagram. *For example:*

If the legs of a trapezoid are equal, what is the area?

(1)　The smaller base is 8 inches and the legs are 6 inches.

(2)　The height is 5 inches.

Drawing the diagram helps give important insight into what is needed to answer the question.

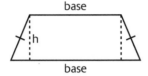

base

base

The formula for the area of a trapezoid is $A = \frac{1}{2}h(b_1 + b_2)$ or $A = \frac{h(b_1 + b_2)}{2}$.

Statement (1) does not give sufficient information to find the larger base or the height. Statement (2), by itself, does not give enough information to find the bases. Statements (1) and (2) together give enough information to find the bases and the height. The answer is Choice C. The Pythagorean theorem would be necessary to find the length of the difference between the smaller and larger bases. Adding this difference to the length of the shorter base would give the longer base. You now have the necessary information. Notice the markings on the diagram below, to assist you in deciding what you have to work with.

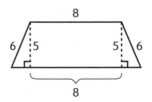

8

6　5　　　　　5　6

8

A Patterned Plan of Attack

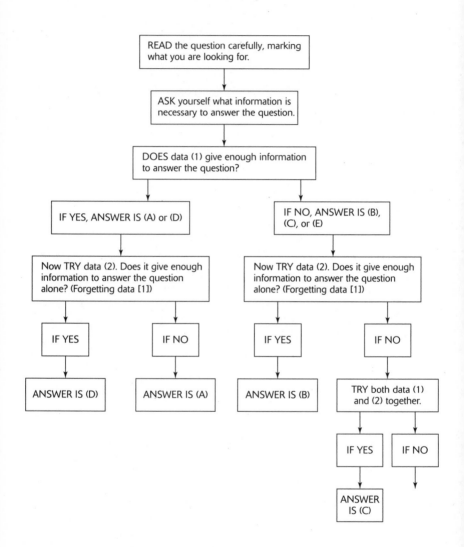

Data Sufficiency

READ the question carefully, marking what you are looking for.

ASK yourself what information is necessary to answer the question.

DOES data (1) give enough information to answer the question?

IF YES, ANSWER IS (A) or (D)

IF NO, ANSWER IS (B), (C), or (E)

Now TRY data (2). Does it give enough information to answer the question alone? (Forgetting data [1])

Now TRY data (2). Does it give enough information to answer the question alone? (Forgetting data [1])

IF YES

IF NO

IF YES

IF NO

ANSWER IS (D)

ANSWER IS (A)

ANSWER IS (B)

TRY both data (1) and (2) together.

IF YES

IF NO

ANSWER IS (C)

KEEP THE FOLLOWING TIPS IN MIND.
1. Don't solve unless it is absolutely necessary.
2. Use a simple marking system (slashes, question marks, etc.).
3. Don't read in specialized knowledge. Use only common information.
4. Mark in or draw geometric figures when appropriate.

Data Sufficiency Practice

Directions

Each of the problems below consists of a question and two statements, labeled (1) and (2), in which certain data are given. You must decide whether the data given in the statements are *sufficient* to answer the question. Using the data given in the statements *plus* your knowledge of mathematics and everyday facts (such as the number of days in July or the meaning of *counterclockwise*), you are to mark

A if statement (1) *alone* is sufficient, but statement (2) alone is not sufficient to answer the question asked.

B if statement (2) *alone* is sufficient, but statement (1) alone is not sufficient to answer the question asked.

C if *both* statements (1) and (2) *together* are sufficient to answer the question asked, but *neither* statement *alone* is sufficient.

D if *each* statement *alone* is sufficient to answer the question asked.

E if statements (1) and (2) *neither alone nor together* are sufficient to answer the question asked, and additional data specific to the problem is needed.

Arithmetic

Questions

1. The product of two integers is 6. What are the integers?

    (1) Both integers are positive.
    (2) One integer is 2.

2. How far did the airplane travel?

    (1) It flew from east to west for 9 hours.
    (2) It flew at a rate of 300 miles per hour for the first 8 hours.

3. The average of two numbers is 5. What are the numbers?

    (1) 7 is one of the numbers.
    (2) 3 is one of the numbers.

4. What must Maria's salary increase be in order to meet a 6% cost of living increase?

   (1) Maria's current salary is $15,000.
   (2) Maria's new salary will be $15,900 if her raise meets the increase in the cost of living.

5. John can jump half his height. How tall is he?

   (1) John is shorter than his brother.
   (2) John's brother can jump 5 feet.

6. What two fractions add to one?

   (1) The fractions are equal.
   (2) The reciprocal of the first fraction is 2.

7. How many people at the party are men?

   (1) There are twice as many men at the party as women.
   (2) There are 9 women at the party.

8. How many ounces does a full water bottle hold if 12 ounces of water remain?

   (1) The full bottle holds an even number of ounces.
   (2) 25% of the bottle has been used.

9. Bob can read 25 pages an hour. How long will it take him to finish the book?

   (1) Bob has read half the book by midnight.
   (2) Bob reads consistently from 8 p.m. until he finishes the book.

10. How much taller is Alice than her brother?

    (1) Her brother is 5 feet, 4 inches tall.
    (2) Alice is 180 centimeters tall. (1 inch = 2.54 cm)

11. How many miles per gallon did Bruce get on his 300 mile trip?

    (1) He used $\frac{3}{4}$ of a tank of gas.
    (2) The tank holds 12 gallons.

12. Two integers are in the proportion 1 to 5. What is the larger number?

    (1) The smaller integer is one digit and prime.
    (2) The larger integer is greater than 30.

13. What is Hal's average weekly salary?

    (1) Hal's monthly salary is over $800.
    (2) Hal's average daily salary is $40.

14. What is the annual rate of simple interest in Arlene's bank?

    (1) Arlene receives $36 interest for two years on savings of $120.
    (2) If Arlene were to open an account of $50, after one year she would receive $7.50 interest.

15. If the volume of a mixture doubles every 20 minutes, at what time was its volume 1 cubic meter?

    (1) At 8 p.m., its volume was 64 cubic meters.
    (2) Twenty minutes ago, its volume was 16 cubic meters.

Algebra

Questions

1. What is the value of a if $3a - 2b = 4$?

    (1) $a = 2b$
    (2) a and b are integers.

2. John is twice as old as his brother, who is older than his sister. How old is John?

    (1) John's brother is two years older than their sister.
    (2) Their sister is 3 years old.

3. What is the value of x?

    (1) The square of x is three more than twice x.
    (2) x is negative

4. If $a^n a^m = a^{15}$, what is the value of n?

    (1) n is even and m is 3.
    (2) n is four times as large as m.

5. What is the value of p?

   (1) $p + 3h = 10$
   (2) $9 + h = 15 - h$

6. If $\sqrt{ab} = 4$ and $a > 0$, what is the value of a?

   (1) $ab = 16$ and b is even.
   (2) $a = b$

7. John's first long jump was 1 foot short of the school record. His second jump exceeded the school's record by a foot. What was the old record that John broke by 1 foot?

   (1) The average of John's two jumps was 18 feet.
   (2) The sum of John's two jumps was 36 feet.

8. John has x dollars and Mary has y dollars. Together, they can buy a $45 ticket. How much money does John have?

   (1) After the purchase, they have a total of $3 left.
   (2) John started with less money than Mary.

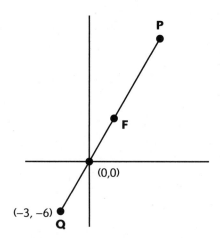

9. In the figure above, what are the coordinates of point P?

   (1) The midpoint of segment QP is at point F (2,4).
   (2) Line QP passes through origin (0,0).

10. For all integers a and b, the operation $\odot$ is defined by $a \odot b = \dfrac{a}{b}$ where $b \neq 0$. If x and y are integers, is $x \odot y$ an integer?

    (1) $x^2 = y^2$
    (2) $x = 0$

11. What is the average of a, b, and c if $a + c = 20$?

    (1) $a - c = 12$ and $a + b = 18$
    (2) $b = 2$

12. How tall is Larry?

    (1) Three years ago, Larry was 4 inches shorter than his brother, Bill.
    (2) Larry has grown 3 inches in the last three years. Bill has grown only 2 inches.

13. Is $y > \dfrac{1}{y}$?

    (1) $y > 0$
    (2) $y > 1$

14. If x is an integer multiple of 7, what is the value of x?

    (1) $x = 5y$, where y is an integer
    (2) $27 < x < 43$

15. What is the value of $xy - 8$?

    (1) $x + y = 5$
    (2) $xy - 10 = 22$

Geometry

Questions

1. In parallelogram $ABCD$, what is the length of $\overline{AE}$?

    (1) $AB = 10$ and $\angle AEB = 90°$
    (2) $AC = 12$

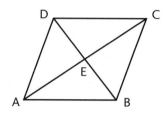

2. Are lines l_1 and l_2 parallel?

    (1) $\angle 1 = \angle 2$
    (2) $\angle 1 + \angle 3 = 180°$

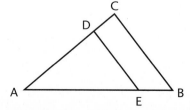

3. Is $\triangle AED$ similar to $\triangle ABC$?

    (1) $\angle ACB = 90°$
    (2) $DE = \frac{2}{3}CB$

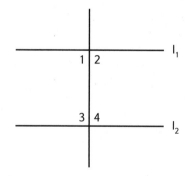

4. Is $\triangle ABC$ an isosceles triangle?

    (1) $\overline{CD}$ is perpendicular to $\overline{AB}$.

    (2) $\angle ACB$ is bisected by $\overline{CD}$.

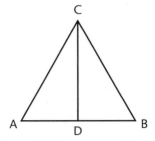

5. What is the measure of $\angle ACB$ in the circle with center O?

    (1) $CA = CB$

    (2)   The arc AB is $\frac{1}{5}$ the circumference of the circle.

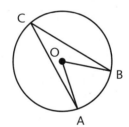

6. What is the area of $\triangle ABC$?

    (1) $AC = 6$

    (2) $BD = 10$

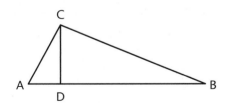

7. What is the measure of $\angle x$?

    (1) $\angle y$ is twice $\angle x$.
    (2) $\angle x = \angle z$

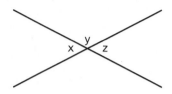

8. What is the measure of $\angle DBC$?

    (1) $\angle ADB = 100°$
    (2) $AD = DB$

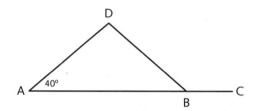

9. The small circle with center B is tangent to the large circle with center D. What is the area of the small circle?

    (1)   The large circle has area 9π and $CD = 1$.
    (2) $BD = 2$

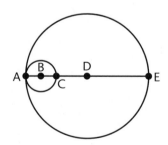

10. What is the area of the shaded portion?

    (1) $ABCD$ is a square and $\overarc{DB}$ is an arc of a circle with center A.
    (2) $AD = 2$

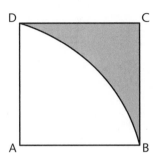

11. The volume of a box is 216 cubic inches. What are the dimensions of the box?

    (1) Length, width, and height are equal.
    (2) The length and width are each 6".

12. What is the length of the hypotenuse of a 45°-45°-90° triangle?

    (1) The area is 8.
    (2) The perimeter equals $8 + 4\sqrt{2}$.

13. What is the volume of the right circular cylinder?

    (1) The height is 4.
    (2) The radius is an integer that is less than the height.

14. The circle centered at O has $\overline{AD}$ passing through O. What is the radius of the circle?

    (1) $AB = 1$
    (2) $BD = 2$

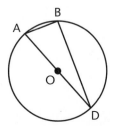

15. Does $AB = CD$?

    (1) C is the midpoint of $\overline{AE}$.

    (2) $BC = CD$

Answer Key for Data Sufficiency Practice

The boldface page number in parentheses following each answer will
direct you to the complete explanation for that specific problem. *Read this
explanation first.* The other page numbers in parentheses refer to the suggested basic review section.

Arithmetic

1. B (p. **483**, 10)

2. E (p. **483**, 329)

3. D (p. **483**, 83)

4. D (p. **483**, 58)

5. E (p. **483**)

6. D (p. **484**, 35)

7. C (p. **484**)

8. B (p. **484**, 58)

9. C (p. **484**, 326)

10. C (p. **484**, 94)

11. C (p. **484**, 43)

12. C (p. **484**, 10)

13. E (p. **485**, 83)

14. D (p. **485**, 320)

15. A (p. **485**)

Algebra

1. A (p. **485**, 136)

2. C (p. **485**, 339)

3. C (p. **485**, 122)

4. D (p. **485**, 64, 122)

5. C (p. **486**, 136)

6. B (p. **486**, 200)

7. D (p. **486**, 120, 125)

8. E (p. **486**)

9. A (p. **486**, 182)

10. D (p. **486**, 206)

11. D (p. **486**, 136)

12. E (p. **487**)

13. B (p. **487**, 122)

14. C (p. **487**, 32)

15. B (p. **487**, 125)

Geometry

1. B (p. **488**, 262, 270)
2. B (p. **488**, 246)
3. E (p. **488**, 289)
4. C (p. **488**, 252)
5. B (p. **488**, 283, 287)
6. E (p. **488**, 277)
7. A (p. **488**, 241)
8. D (p. **488**, 258)

9. A (p. **489**, 284)
10. C (p. **489**, 277, 284)
11. D (p. **489**, 289, 290)
12. D (p. **489**, 265)
13. E (p. **489**, 290)
14. C (p. **489**, 262, 281)
15. E (p. **490**, 245)

Data Sufficiency Answers and Explanations

Arithmetic

1. **B** 6 can be shown as the product of two integers in the following manner: (1)(6), (–1)(–6), (2)(3), or (–2)(–3). Statement (1) says that both integers are positive, but that still leaves two choices. Statement (2) says that one of the integers is 2. Therefore, the other must be 3. Statement (2) suffices.

2. **E** Without your knowing the rate at which the airplane flew, statement (1) does not suffice. Statement (2) provides more information but does not say how long the total travel time was or the speed after eight hours. The statements together do not provide sufficient data to answer the question, because you don't know the speed for the final hour.

3. **D** Knowing that the two numbers average 5, you can use either statement alone to determine both numbers. For example, using statement (1), which says that 7 is one of the numbers, you can determine that the other number must be 3, because the average of the two numbers is 5. The same process works for statement (2) alone.

4. **D** Statement (1) is sufficient to determine an answer. Just multiply $15,000 by 0.06. Statement (2) is also sufficient to determine an answer. Just divide $15,900 by 1.06.

5. **E** John's being shorter than his brother has nothing to do with John's jump; so statement (1) alone does not solve the problem.

483

Because no information is given about how John's jump compares to his brother's jump, statement (2) is not useful either.

6. **D** Statement (1) implies that the fractions are both $\frac{1}{2}$. Statement (2) implies that the first fraction is $\frac{1}{2}$; therefore, the second is $\frac{1}{2}$. Each statement is separately sufficient.

7. **C** Statement (1) gives the ratio of men to women, but because no numbers are given, it is insufficient to determine the number of men. Statement (2) alone is insufficient to determine the number of men. If you take them together, however, you know that the number of men is twice the number of women, 9. Therefore, there are 18 men at the party.

8. **B** Statement (1) tells you nothing of value for this problem. Statement (2) suffices. Since 75% of the total is 12 ounces, then $0.75T = 12$, or $T = \frac{12}{0.75}$.

9. **C** Statement (1) tells you that Bob has read half the book by midnight. But because you don't know when he started or how long he has been reading, you can't calculate when he'll finish. Statement (2) alone is also insufficient but together with statement (1), it allows you to calculate that it takes Bob four hours to read half the book; therefore, he will finish in four more hours. The answer is (C). Note that your knowledge of Bob's reading speed is useless, because you don't know the page length of the book.

10. **C** Statement (1) gives the brother's height in feet and inches. Statement (2) gives Alice's height in centimeters. Neither statement alone will suffice. Converting centimeters to feet and inches and subtracting the height in statement (1) from that in statement (2) shows the answer is (C).

11. **C** To answer the question, you need to know how much gas was used. Statement (1) says how much of the tank was used but not how much gas. Statement (2) says how much gas is in a full tank. Neither alone is enough, but taking the statements together, you find that Bruce used 9 gallons. You can then divide 300 miles by 9 gallons of gas.

12. **C** From statement (1), you know that the smaller integer must be 2, 3, 5, or 7, because those are the only one-digit prime numbers. This statement alone is insufficient. From statement (2), you know that 5 times the smaller integer will give the second integer, greater than 30. Statement (2) alone is insufficient. Together, however, the statements provide the information that only 7 could be the smaller integer, because $5 \times 7 > 30$.

13. **E** Because you know only that Hal's salary is *over* $800 per month, no precise average weekly salary may be determined from statement (1). Statement (2) is also insufficient, because you don't know how many days each week Hal works.

14. **D** By using the simple interest formula ($I = prt$), either statement alone will suffice to determine rate of interest (15% in this case).

15. **A** Statement (1) alone allows you to extrapolate back 20 minutes at a time to determine when volume was 1 cubic meter. (Each previous 20 minutes the mixture is halved.) Statement (2) is insufficient because you aren't given any information regarding what the *present* time is.

Algebra

1. **A** The problem states that $3a - 2b = 4$. Statement (1) gives $a = 2b$, resulting in two equations in two unknowns, which leads to a unique solution. Statement (2) does not lead to a unique solution, however, because many pairs of integers a and b will satisfy $3a - 2b = 4$.

2. **C** Let x = John's brother's age, and $2x$ = John's age. Statement (1) tells you that John's brother is two years older than their sister. Hence, $x - 2$ = the sister's age. But you have no value for x. Thus, statement (1) alone is insufficient. Statement (2) tells you the sister's age, 3 years old, but you have no exact relationship between the sister and either of her brothers. So statement (2) alone is insufficient. Taking the statements together you have

    x = John's brother

    $2x$ = John

    $x - 2 = 3$ = sister

    Thus, you can solve for x (5 years) and find John's age, 10.

3. **C** Statement (1) says that $x^2 = 3 + 2x$; so $x^2 - 2x - 3 = 0$, which factors to give $(x - 3)(x + 1) = 0$. This has two answers, $x = 3$ or $x = -1$, which in data sufficiency problems does not constitute a solution. Statement (2) says that the answer is negative, which alone does not suffice. However, taken together, the data are sufficient to determine a unique solution, $x = -1$.

4. **D** Because $a^n a^m = a^{15}$ and you know that $a^n a^m = a^{n+m}$, you have $n + m = 15$. Statement (1) says that n is even and m is 3, which results in $n + 3 = 15$, or $n = 12$, a solution. Statement (2) says $n = 4m$. This together with $n + m = 15$ gives two equations in two unknowns, which lead to a solution also.

5. **C** Statement (1) alone is not sufficient because it is an equation with two unknowns. Statement (2) allows you to solve for the unknown, h, which you may then plug into statement (1) to determine the value of p. Both statements taken together will answer the question.

6. **B** The fact that $\sqrt{ab} = 4$ implies that $ab = 16$. Statement (1) says $ab = 16$ and b is even. This does not allow you to find a, because several choices are possible : (2)(8), (4)(4), and so on. If statement (2) is used, you have $a^2 = 16$, and there is only one positive integer solution, 4.

7. **D** If you let x represent the original school record, then John's first jump was $x - 1$ feet and his second jump was $x + 1$ feet. Statement (1) says that the average of the two jumps was 18 feet. This means that

$$\frac{(x-1)+(x+1)}{2} = 18$$

$$\frac{2x}{2} = 18$$

$$x = 18$$

18 feet was the old record. Statement (1) will suffice. Statement (2) says that $(x - 1) + (x + 1) = 36$. Solving this for x gives 18 feet. So this, too, gives a solution.

8. **E** The question implies that $x + y$ must be 45 or larger. Statement (1) implies that $(x + y) - 45 = 3$. So $x + y = 48$, which does not allow you to find x. Statement (2) implies that $x < y$, but neither this nor the previous piece of information allows you to determine x.

9. **A** Statement (1) alone is sufficient to determine the coordinates of point P. Because the coordinates are given for endpoint Q $(-3,-6)$, using the midpoint, you can derive coordinates for the other endpoint, P. (The midpoint coordinates are the averages of the endpoint coordinates. Thus, coordinates of point P are (7,14). Statement (2) tells you nothing of value.

10. **D** Either statement (1) or (2) alone is sufficient to answer the question conclusively. Statement (1) tells you that $x = y$ or $x = -y$. In either case, $x \odot y$ (or $\frac{x}{y}$) will be an integer, as it will equal either 1 or -1. Statement (2) tells you that $x = 0$. Therefore, $x \odot y = \frac{0}{y} = 0$, which is also an integer.

11. **D** The average of a, b, and c is

$$\frac{a+b+c}{3}$$

Statement (1) and the information in the question give you three equations:

$a + c = 20$

$a - c = 12$

$a + b = 18$

If you add the first two equations, you get $2a = 32$, so $a = 16$. This allows you to find b and c. So statement (1) is sufficient. Statement (2) says $b = 2$. So this together with $a + c = 20$ allows you to find $a + b + c = 12 + 20 = 32$. Thus, statement (2) will suffice.

12. **E** If you let x represent Larry's height three years ago and y represent Bill's height three years ago, statement (1) says $x = y - 4$. This does not allow you to find x or Larry's present height. Statement (2) gives no relationship between the heights. Putting both statements together allows you to write the second condition as

$(x + 3) =$ Larry's height now

$(y + z) =$ Bill's height now

Since Larry was 4 inches shorter, he is now only 3 inches shorter than Bill, so

$(x + 3) = (y + z) - 3$

$\qquad x = y - 4$

Thus, no new information is gained and the problem cannot be solved.

13. **B** Statement (1) alone is insufficient. Substituting 1 and 2 as values of y will result in a "no" then a "yes" answer for the original question. Statement (2), however, is alone sufficient. Any value of y greater than 1 will yield a consistent answer ("yes") to the question.

14. **C** Statement (1) allows you to know that x is a multiple of both 5 and 7. Thus, x may be 35, 70, 105, and so on. Since statement (2) alone tells you that x may be 28, 35, or 42 (all multiples of 7), it, too, is insufficient. Both statements taken together, however, will suffice to determine that x is 35.

15. **B** Statement (1) is insufficient, because it contains two unknowns. Statement (2) is sufficient alone. Although it contains two unknowns, notice that $xy - 10$ is simply two less than $xy - 8$. Therefore, if $xy - 10$ equals 22, $xy - 8$ equals 24.

Geometry

1. **B** The key here is that the diagonals of a parallelogram bisect each other. Statement (1) does not provide enough information to compute the length of $\overline{AE}$. However, the fact that $\triangle AEB$ is a right triangle with hypotenuse 10 does not determine the lengths of $\overline{AE}$ or $\overline{EB}$. Statement (2) allows you to determine $\overline{AE}$ at once.

2. **B** Although statement (1) allows you to conclude that both $\angle 1$ and $\angle 2$ are right angles, this does not suffice to conclude that l_1 and l_2 are parallel. You can conclude from statement (2), however, that l_1 and l_2 are parallel because $\angle 1$ and $\angle 2$ are supplementary angles.

3. **E** In order to conclude that the triangles are similar, you would need to know that $\overline{DE}$ and $\overline{CB}$ are parallel. Neither statement (1) nor statement (2) gives enough information to allow this conclusion.

4. **C** An isosceles triangle has two sides of equal length. To conclude this, the information provided in statement (1) does not suffice because no conclusions about the sides AC and BC can be drawn. Similarly, statement (2) alone is insufficient. The information combined, however, leads to the conclusion that $\triangle ACD$ and $\triangle BCD$ are congruent (angle-side-angle). Hence $AC = BC$.

5. **B** $\angle ACB$ is an inscribed angle. Hence, its measure is equal to one-half of $\angle AOB$. Statement (1) gives no information about the number of degrees in $\angle ACB$. Statement (2), however, tells you that $\angle AOB$ is $\frac{1}{5}$ of 360°. This, together with the initial observation, is sufficient to answer the question.

6. **E** The area of a triangle is equal to one-half the product of a base and an altitude. Neither statement (1) nor statement (2) allows you to determine the altitude of the triangle.

7. **A** The key here is that $\angle x$ and $\angle y$ are supplementary angles. Thus, statement (1) implies that $\angle x$ is 60° and $\angle y$ is 120°. Statement (2) is always true (because vertical angles are equal).

8. **D** $\angle DBC$ is an exterior angle of $\triangle ABD$ and, hence, it is equal to the sum of the angles BAD and ADB. Since $\angle BAD$ is given as 40° and statement (1) tells you that $\angle ADB$ is 100°, you can determine $\angle DBC$. Statement (2) tells you that $\triangle ABD$ has two equal sides. Therefore, it is isosceles. Thus, $\angle BAD = \angle ABD$, and because $\angle ABD$ and $\angle DBC$ are supplementary, you can determine $\angle DBC$ based on statement (2) alone.

9. **A** You would need either the radius or the diameter of the small circle to find its area. Statement (1) tells you that the radius of the large circle (AD or DE) is 3 (because the area is π times the square of the radius). Because AE must, therefore, be 6 and $CE = CD + DE = 1 + 3 = 4$, you know that $AC = 2$, and you can find the area of the small circle. Statement (2) does not give you any information about the relationship between BD and the other parts of the circle.

10. **C** Statement (1) tells you that if you knew the radius of the circle (or equivalently the length of the side of the square), you could find the area of the shaded portion by subtracting the area of one-quarter of the circle from that of the square. However, statement (1) does not alone suffice. Statement (2) alone is of little use, because you know nothing of the nature of the geometric figures. You need both statements to solve the problem.

11. **D** Statement (1) tells you that your box is a cube. From the known volume, the length of its edge can be found. So statement (1) is sufficient. Statement (2) tells you that $(6)(6)(h) = 216$. Thus, you can find the third dimension, height.

12. **D** The right triangle is isosceles and, thus, its sides are in the proportion of $1:1:\sqrt{2}$. Statement (1) tells you that if you multiply one-half the length of a base times the altitude, you get 8. Because the legs in this case give you a base and an altitude, you can solve for the length of a leg and, hence, find the hypotenuse.

$$\frac{1}{2}(s)(s) = 8$$
$$s^2 = 16$$
$$s = 4$$

hypotenuse $= 4\sqrt{2}$

Using statement (2), you know that $s + s + s\sqrt{2} = 8 + 4\sqrt{2}$.

Thus, $s = 4$ and, again, hypotenuse $= 4\sqrt{2}$.

13. **E** The volume of a right circular cylinder is $\pi r^2 h$, where r is the radius of the base and h is the height. Hence, statement (1) does not give sufficient information to compute the volume. Statement (2) does not specify the radius.

14. **C** Because $\overline{AD}$ is a diameter, $\triangle ABD$ is inscribed in a semicircle and is, therefore, a right triangle, because $\angle ABD = 90°$. You can find the

radius OA if you can determine $\overline{AD}$ (the diameter). Statement (1) gives you one leg of the right triangle. Statement (2) gives you the second leg. The Pythagorean theorem allows you to find AD and, hence, the radius.

15. **E** Although statement (1) shows you that $AC = CE$, even taken with statement (2), no relationship may be derived between AB and CD. Note that with both pieces of data, a diagram may be drawn as follows.

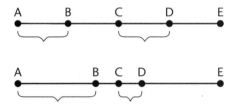

Final Suggestions

Now that you have completed this guide you should

1. Obtain the *CliffsNotes* preparation guide for your specific test. This guide will key in on your specific math problem types, offer more practice problems, and prepare you for the nonmathematical questions on your exam.

2. Practice working problems under time pressure. Now that you've reviewed the basic skills, the next hurdle is being comfortable using them under timed test pressure.

3. Use this guide as a reference should problems arise.